Social Avalanche

CW01426311

Individuality and collectivity are at the heart of sociological inquiry. Through a tour de force of cultural history, social theory, urban sociology and economic sociology, Christian Borch offers an innovative rethinking of these terms and their interconnections via the concept of the social avalanche. Drawing on classical sociology, he argues that while individuality embodies a tension between collective mimetic forces and anti-mimetic autonomy, certain situations, such as crowds and moments of collective behaviour, can subsume the individual entirely within the collective. These events, or social avalanches, produce an experience of being swept away suddenly and losing one's sense of self. Cities are often on the verge of social avalanches, their urban inhabitants torn between de-individualising external pressure and autonomous self presentation, and Borch explores the role of tensional individuality and social avalanches within them. Similarly, present-day financial markets, dominated by computerised trading, abound with social avalanches and the tensional interplay of mimesis and autonomous decision-making – although it is not humans but fully automated algorithms that avalanche there.

CHRISTIAN BORCH is Professor of Economic Sociology and Social Theory at the Copenhagen Business School. He is author of several books, including the award-winning *The Politics of Crowds: An Alternative History of Sociology*.

Social Avalanche

Crowds, Cities and Financial Markets

Christian Borch

Copenhagen Business School

CAMBRIDGE
UNIVERSITY PRESS

CAMBRIDGE
UNIVERSITY PRESS

University Printing House, Cambridge CB2 8BS, United Kingdom

One Liberty Plaza, 20th Floor, New York, NY 10006, USA

477 Williamstown Road, Port Melbourne, VIC 3207, Australia

314–321, 3rd Floor, Plot 3, Splendor Forum, Jasola District Centre,
New Delhi – 110025, India

79 Anson Road, #06–04/06, Singapore 079906

Cambridge University Press is part of the University of Cambridge.

It furthers the University's mission by disseminating knowledge in the pursuit of
education, learning, and research at the highest international levels of excellence.

www.cambridge.org
Information on this title: www.cambridge.org/9781108489218
DOI: 10.1017/9781108774239

© Christian Borch 2020

First published 2020

Printed in the United Kingdom by TJ International Ltd. Padstow Cornwall

A catalogue record for this publication is available from the British Library.

ISBN 978-1-108-48921-8 Hardback
ISBN 978-1-108-73363-2 Paperback

For Albert and Martha

Contents

Figures

Acknowledgements

The seeds of motivation for writing this book were planted in a previous research project that culminated with my book *The Politics of Crowds: An Alternative History of Sociology* (2012b). In it, I analysed how crowd theory and notions of crowd behaviour were relegated to the periphery of sociological attention despite occupying a central place in sociological work at the end of the nineteenth century, when the discipline of sociology was born. That project was driven by an interest in the historical sociology of knowledge and the development of sociological theorising, unearthing theoretical developments without committing to their content. Along the way, I nonetheless developed a certain sympathy for particular types of late nineteenth-century social theory, which, to my mind, were often too quickly dismissed as irrelevant by twentieth-century sociologists. The present book is an attempt to revivify this *fin-de-siècle* crowd theory tradition. Certainly, my aim is not to resuscitate this tradition *en bloc*. It was not entirely without reason that subsequent sociologists turned away from it. Still, I believe that the classical crowd theory tradition has been underappreciated and that much can be learned from it that remains useful to present-day theorisation. I hope to be able to convince the reader about this claim. The book is also an attempt to bring together my research interests in crowd theory, urban sociology/architecture and economic sociology, especially the sociology of financial markets. While these domains are often treated separately, there is in fact much that unites them. Demonstrating this, and hopefully opening further research into such interconnections, is one of the main ambitions of the book.

I have been fortunate to have had the opportunity to present ideas from the book at several seminars and conferences over the past few years. I thank my colleagues and audiences at the Catholic University of Portugal, Lisbon; Copenhagen Business School; New School for Social Research; New York University; Lund University; University of Copenhagen; University of Konstanz and the University of Tampere for helpful comments.

Several people have read and commented on parts of the book, and I am particularly grateful for their constructive feedback. Anker Brink Lund, Justine Pors and Daniel Souleles each read one or more chapters, and their insightful comments helped me rethink the framing and presentation of the overall argument. Bjørn Schiermer Andersen, Kristian Bondo Hansen and Bo Hee Min deserve special gratitude for taking the exceptional effort to read an earlier version of the entire manuscript. Their expert advice on the book's discussion of classical sociology, crowd theory and financial markets was immensely important and helped me add new layers to the argument as well as sharpen the analysis. Thanks also go to Thomas Presskorn-Thygesen and Marius Gudmand-Høyer, with whom I have had productive conversations about several topics addressed in the book.

The book has been written in the context of two research projects I have had the pleasure to lead over the past few years. The first project was titled 'Crowd Dynamics in Financial Markets' (2013–17) and was funded by the Danish Council for Independent Research. The second project is titled 'Algorithmic Finance: Inquiring into the Reshaping of Financial Markets' (2017–21). This project has received funding from the European Research Council (ERC) under the European Union's Horizon 2020 research and innovation programme (grant agreement No 725706). I am immensely grateful to the two funding bodies for their support of and belief in the ideas we have been pursuing on these topics. In particular, the ERC grant has opened opportunities of research that are truly exciting. I gesture towards some of these in the book.

I have benefitted a lot from daily conversations with former and present colleagues from these two research projects – Zach David, Kristian Bondo Hansen, Pankaj Kumar, Ann-Christina Lange, Bo Hee Min, Nicholas Skar-Gislinge and Daniel Souleles. These conversations have contributed to shaping the ideas put forth in the book. Several student assistants have provided valuable research support for various parts of the book. Special thanks go to Sophia van Bon, Tobias Brask, Thomas Lauronen, Maria Lucchi, Benjamin Schwarz and Caitlin Welch.

I am also grateful to Kenneth Wee for his vigilant language editing. Warm thanks as well to Kirse Junge-Stevnsborg, who has curated the artistic footprint of the book. Each in their way, Kenneth and Kirse have made the book a more pleasant read. Thanks as well to John Haslam, my editor at Cambridge University Press, for supporting this new book, and to the two anonymous reviewers for their positive and helpful comments. Though I have benefitted tremendously from the comments and suggestions from all these intellectual resources, I am of course responsible for this book's final version.

Finally, and most important, my greatest thanks go to my wife, Susanne, and our kids, Albert and Martha, for continuous love, support and inspiration. This book is dedicated to Albert and Martha – my own wonderful avalanches.

★★★

Chapters 2 and 5 expand on ideas I have previously published in two journal articles: 'Tensional individuality: a reassessment of Gabriel Tarde's sociology', *Distinktion: Journal of Social Theory* 18(2), 2017: 153–72; and 'High-frequency trading, algorithmic finance and the Flash Crash: reflections on eventalization', *Economy and Society* 45(3–4), 2016: 350–78. Content from these articles are reprinted by permission of the publisher (Taylor & Francis Ltd, www.tandfonline.com).

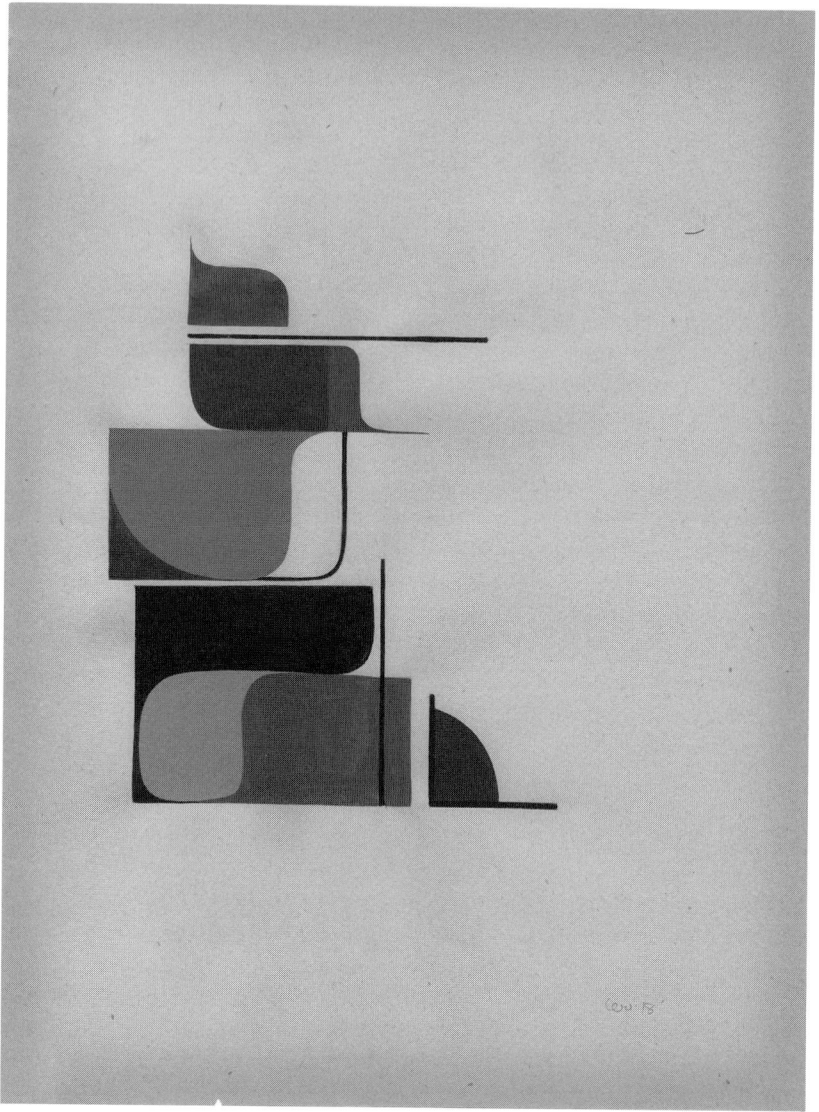

Clare E. Rojas, *Untitled*, 2017. Gouache on paper, 8 × 10 in.
Source: Courtesy Kavi Gupta gallery and Clare E. Rojas.

Introduction: Reimagining Collective Life

The world is going astray. Pillars long taken for granted are rapidly crumbling, and ideas that once constituted fixed points in life are being widely attacked. A sense of stability, predictability and progress is being replaced by a loss of orientation. These tropes, reflected in such gloomy book titles as *The Retreat of Western Liberalism* (Luce, 2017) and *The Strange Death of Europe* (Murray, 2017), populate the ways in which many observers portray the world of today. Rising inequality; the 2008 financial crisis and the recession it unleashed; comprehensive migration flows, including the one that shook Europe in 2015; the Brexit referendum in 2016; the election later that year of Donald Trump to the presidency of the United States; and the ebb of populism (including the commitment to 'illiberal democracy') in many parts of the world form the common backdrop to these accounts. Each of these factors stands as a catalyst or symptom, or both, of the familiar order breaking down.

While the analytical lenses various observers deploy to diagnose these developments may differ, most agree that the kind of optimism announced by Francis Fukuyama in his seminal 1989 article, further developed in his bestseller *The End of History and the Last Man* (1992), has taken a severe blow. Fukuyama famously suggested that the close of the Cold War marked 'the end point of mankind's ideological evolution and the universalization of Western liberal democracy as the final form of human government' (1989: 4). Revisiting his thesis two decades after the book's publication and discussing 'whether any other form of govern-ance' that would challenge his original proposition 'has emerged in the last 20 years', Fukuyama's answer was a resounding 'no' (2013: 31). Yet much has happened since Fukuyama's twentieth-anniversary defence of his widely discussed analysis. Addressing recent developments like those listed above, observers such as the philosopher Slavoj Žižek (2015) suggest that capitalism and liberal democracy are divorcing – the former's need for the latter is simply evaporating – and configurations of authoritarian capitalism are gaining traction instead, thereby ousting liberal democracy as the leading political model.

My aim with this book is neither to reach any conclusion on this debate nor to provide a thorough analysis of, say, the current wave of populism or the fate of democracy (for interesting discussions of these topics, see Müller, 2016; Runciman, 2018; Sánchez, 2016). Rather, what interests me here is that discussions about our present political predicament resonate with a current of sociological analysis that portrays the twenty-first century as an age of flux and radical transformation, whether social, political, demographic, technological or financial. In such a diagnosis, change seems to take on an ever-more crucial role in the machinery of social life.

An illustrative example of this type of analysis is Zygmunt Bauman's *Liquid Modernity*, which puts forth an account of present-day modernity that assumes an increasingly fluid, constantly changing character (2000). Bauman argues that while it may always have been a crucial feature of modernity, change permeates life so deeply today that modernity has effectively entered a new, entirely liquid phase. Bauman's thesis goes beyond classical sociological conceptions. Notably, when Karl Marx and Friedrich Engels suggest that modernity melts the rigid social and institutional structures of the past, they assign change a pivotal role in their understanding of modern society. For Bauman, such diagnoses by early modern observers often remained tied to an imagery of transformation as clearing 'the site for *new and improved solids*', i.e. for a new, stable social order (2000: 3, orginal emphasis). It is this replacement of solids with other solids that, in his view, has become irrelevant today, giving way to a wholly fluid state of affairs: institutions and individuality are constantly exposed to change, and neither stable reference points nor clear ends exist anymore.

Bauman suggests that this present-day liquid modernity has led to a reconfiguration of temporal patterns. When change allegedly pervades all aspects of contemporary life, speed, instantaneity and acceleration become increasingly dominant features of the liquid social order (e.g. 2000: 123–9). Other observers concur that our current time is one of acceleration, with ever-faster temporal structures colonising still more spheres of life, in part due to the rise of new technologies (Crary, 2013; Rosa, Dörre and Lessenich, 2017). A tremendous increase in speed can certainly be identified in financial markets in the wake of algorithmic and high-frequency trading's rise, as I discuss later in this book. Yet, paradoxically, sweeping assertions about the increasing acceleration of society often work best when history itself, the sedimentation of time, is ignored. Indeed, the analytical desire amongst many sociologists to identify epochal ruptures – in which the present is portrayed as radically different from the past, including former phases of modernity – often ignores the changes and transformations that characterise former periods.

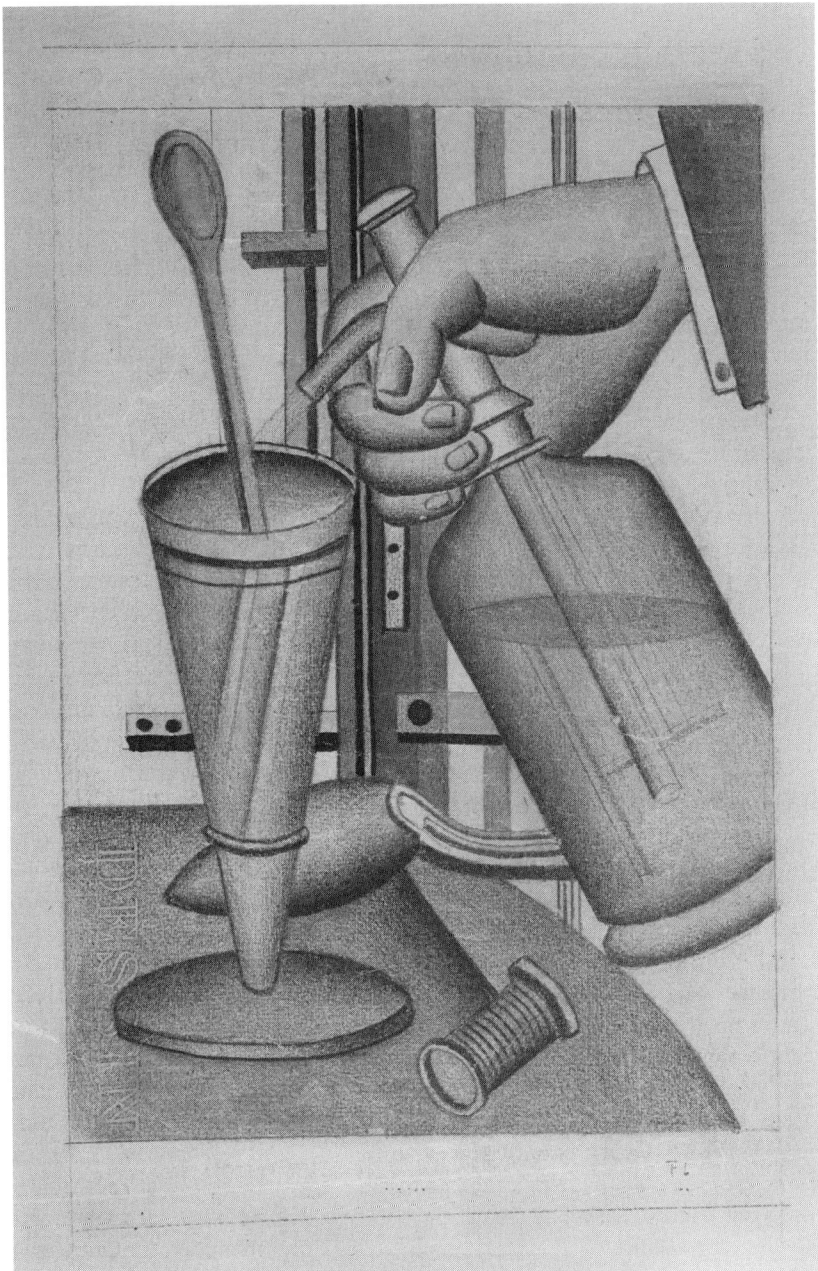

Figure I.1 Liquid modernity.
Note: Fernand Leger (1881–1955), *The Siphon; Le Siphon*, 1924. Christie's Images Limited. Pencil, pen and india ink and watercolour on paper, 26.4 × 18 cm.
Source: © 2019. Christie's Images, London/Scala, Florence. © Fernand Leger/VISDA

This book takes as its starting point one of these earlier phases of modernity: the late nineteenth and early twentieth centuries, during which sociology, like many other disciplines, gained its footing and developed into a set of more-or-less coherent ways of conceiving the world. The *fin-de-siècle* era and its early twentieth-century aftermath are central to my argument; they were periods during which Western societies underwent profound transformations at a scale arguably more radical and penetrating than what we see today. Indeed, I argue, the late nineteenth and early twentieth centuries were like a riptide in which social sea changes suddenly carried people past their moorings, stranding them in unknown waters. In other words, keeping with the terminology I develop later in the book, it was a period of social avalanches.

This experience of a comprehensive reformatting of the world, of people losing firm ground, is one reflected in much social theory at the time. This is hardly surprising: just as present-day sociologists seek to understand the contemporary world, so too did the burgeoning discipline of sociology back then develop analytical templates with which to understand its situation. That said, it seems to me that the analytical horizon that took shape in the late nineteenth century has not been fully appreciated by subsequent scholars. I argue that it is possible, through fresh exegetic digging, to identify several analytical ideas and concerns from this time period which responded to a generalised experience of radical societal transformation and which are not sufficiently understood in usual portrayals of the sociological 'classics'. What such portrayals tend to lack – especially those that seek to carve out a set of distinct traditions (whether Marxist, Durkheimian or Weberian) or conceive of sociology in strict opposition to its adjacent disciplines – is the common ground that existed between *fin-de-siècle* ideas and concerns across sociological theories, even across disciplines.

In late nineteenth and early-twentieth-century reflections on deep social change, the idea that people may be carried away by collective mimesis in ways that lead to a (temporary) loss of self once they become part of collective formations such as crowds, cities and financial markets gained traction. I describe the collective dynamism in which heterogeneity amongst actors is momentarily eliminated and replaced by imitative homogeneity via the notion of *social avalanches*, a term I develop by drawing from theories of crowd psychology that became popular in the 1890s, the shadows of which stretch well into the twentieth century. Though harking back to this tradition might seem a surprising ambition, not least considering the beating it suffered through long stretches of the twentieth century,[1] I find the same tradition often too readily dismissed and its analytical potential underestimated in scholarship spanning the past 50 years. I substantiate this point in this book, demonstrating the ways in which sociological work on crowds, collective behaviour and social movements from the late 1960s onwards has painted a picture of *fin-de-siècle* crowd theory that is lacking in nuance.

Notably, a major point that many late-twentieth-century scholars held against classical crowd theory revolved around its supposed subscription to the 'transformation hypothesis': the assertion 'that crowds transform individuals, diminishing or eliminating their ability to control their behavior rationally' (McPhail, 1991: 1). Central to the transformation hypothesis – in crude form, at least – is the view that crowd members are entirely mouldable creatures, always ready to submit to the crowd leader's whims. Against this notion, sociologists from the 1960s onwards have placed much stronger analytical emphasis on individual crowd members' autonomy and correspondingly less stress on the power of collective forces. I demonstrate that several *fin-de-siècle* scholars in fact advanced a much more complex conception of individuality. Rather than seeing individuality as mouldable from the outside (implied by the transformation thesis) or depicting individuality in terms of autonomy and independence (a popular approach amongst late-twentieth-century sociologists), many late-nineteenth and early twentieth-century social theorists in effect argued for a more dialectical conception of individuality, or what I call a *tensional individuality*. The concept's core idea is that individuality is given in a tensional relationship between mimetic features and anti-mimetic ones. In my reading, scholars who promoted a tensional notion of individuality conceived of individuality as neither fully mimetically malleable nor entirely sovereign. Instead, they believed individuality oscillates between these two poles, demonstrating both mimetic and anti-mimetic features. People retain independence in some contexts and submit to collective mimesis in others. In some cases mimetic submission is a wilful act, presupposing the independence it annuls; in other cases, being carried away is a condition of possibility for autonomy and independence. Only in rare cases, however, is individuality exclusively a matter of one or the other.

This book distils the notions of social avalanches and tensional individuality from the vast corpus of late-nineteenth and early-twentieth-century social theory to demonstrate that these notions arose out of specific experiences with abrupt social and technological change.

---

[1] I have traced the destiny of crowd thinking, including its gradual marginalisation within the discipline of sociology, in Borch (2012b).

Though primarily derived from theoretical reflections on crowd behaviour, the analytical commitments of social avalanches and tensional individuality manifest in many other contexts as well, especially in cities and financial markets. In the early twentieth century, both urban sociology and urban planning were deeply concerned with social avalanches and portrayed modern metropolitan life in ways that dovetail with tensional individuality. Similarly, late-nineteenth and early twentieth-century reflections on financial markets put a premium on the idea that markets can quickly avalanche and that measures are required to ensure that individual investors are not carried away in the frenzy – essentially casting the individual in a tensional relationship between mimesis and anti-mimesis. Close connections indeed exist between cities and financial markets, and attending to crowd thinking is an effective means of capturing these links and their transformations. Concerns about the dynamics of financial markets thus echo debates about the avalanching properties of modern cities, and American economist Edward D. Jones's *Economic Crises* (1900) offers just one example of how such interconnections have been conceived. Jones, then an assistant professor at the University of Wisconsin, argued that dangerous forms of crowd-like imitation and mental contagion do not just greatly intensify in (and characterise) cities but also manifest in places such as 'stock and produce exchanges', giving rise to 'intense emotion' that 'paralyze[s] thought' and propels market instability (1900: 205–6). Following observers such as Jones, one recognises how cities and markets are united not least by their common foundation in crowd dynamics.

The idea of drawing connections between crowds and cities might seem straightforward. After all, there is a long tradition of academic work that sees cities as hotbeds of crowd behaviour. With masses of people pulled together by the centripetal forces of metropolises, favourable conditions for crowding are in place. Some argue, however, that there are theoretical reasons for treating crowds and financial markets as different domains. Alex Preda, citing the Canadian philosopher Charles Taylor, captures this concisely:

Marketplace transactions are ultimately individualistic and different from forms of action which aim at attaining a common goal. [...] The actions of market participants can be similar or based on imitation; nevertheless, their irreducible feature is individuality. Markets are 'the negation of collective action'. (Preda, 2009b: 7)

Although this suggests that classical crowd behaviour is fundamentally at odds with processes in financial markets – the former characterised by a collective gist, the latter an individualistic core – there is enough evidence to suggest that Preda's take on imitation in the quote above can be taken further. As the wide array of financial bubbles and crashes suggests, cascades of crowd-like behaviour are not uncommon in financial markets. And even if market participants are concerned about their individual gains and losses, their pursuit of profit often takes them down collective routes, leading them to follow the paths of others in such intense situations of being carried away that the boundaries between markets and collective action become rather more blurred than Taylor claims.[2]

The discussion of financial markets that follows has both historical and contemporary components. In relation to the latter, I argue that the current configuration of financial markets, in which fully automated algorithms have in effect supplanted human beings when it comes to placing orders in markets, is also characterised by social avalanches and tensional individuality – albeit now materialised in a purely algorithmic, emphatically non-human domain. In this way, and in spite of the particular non-human incarnations they assume today, social avalanches and tensional individuality remain visible and important in our present era. This, I assert, testifies to a broader insight: social avalanches and tensional individuality may in fact constitute central features of collective life. Rather than belonging to a bygone era, they capture an experience that is also ours: we continue to be carried away in collective formations, and this may take place in ways that bear witness to a tensional constitution of individuality.

A Modern Affair? Or Getting at the Roots of the Social?

It is tempting to interpret the notions of social avalanches and tensional individuality as belonging to a distinctly modern register, a set of ideas that rose to prominence in modernity and still resonates in our current,

---

[2] Further to this point, it may be remarked that, contra Taylor's assertion, several empirical studies have established that collective action need not be antithetical to financial markets. One example is Donald MacKenzie and Yuval Millo's analysis of the ways in which the establishment of the Chicago Board Options Exchange in 1973 arose out of the joint efforts of a number of Chicago Board of Trade members whose collective action defied narrow self-interests. Essentially invalidating Taylor's claim, MacKenzie and Millo note that this particular case illustrates 'a delightful paradox: the very markets in which *homo œconomicus* appears to thrive cannot be created (if they require the solution of collective action problems, as in Chicago) by *homines œconomici*,' (2003: 116, original emphasis). Along slightly different lines, collective action in markets has also been addressed by Melissa S. Fisher in her important study *Wall Street Women* (2012). In it, Fisher details the role played by collective action – through platforms such as the Financial Women's Association – in bringing particular feminist ideas (about the right to work) to bear on Wall Street in the 1970s.

twenty-first-century instantiation of modernity. Such a reading suggests that the kinds of flux and fluidity Bauman takes as emblematic of a recent transition within modernity are in fact modernity's general features regardless of modernity's specific manifestations. Nonetheless, I am ambivalent about phrasing my argument only in terms of modernity or as a kind of rethinking of modernity, as there are reasons for speculating that social avalanches and tensional individuality have wider purchase. As mentioned above, they may well point to aspects that are characteristic to collective life independent of its societal context.

To see what this book has in common with analyses of modernity, it is helpful to compare my approach to that of Marshall Berman. Berman deployed that famous refrain from the *Communist Manifesto*, 'All that is solid melts into air', to capture the experience of modernity in his seminal 1982 book titled after this exact dictum. He meticulously scrutinised writings on various phases of modernity: from the sixteenth century, when people had their first glimpses of it; to the nineteenth century, when modernity developed full scale but against a background memory of non-modern forms of life; to the twentieth century, when any recollection of a non-modern configuration was finally lost, and modernity appeared to permeate every aspect of life as second nature. Berman took pains to stress that the phrase has a twofold, dialectical, nature. On the one hand, it referred to the loss of orientation that modernity introduces as a new factor in life: the evaporation of stable institutions and firm anchors as well as the whirlwind of impressions, innovations and transformations that swelled in their stead. On the other hand, it pointed to new possibilities and the hope that when old institutions dissolve, a new sense of freedom may emerge. One of Berman's central achievements is his contention that for nineteenth-century observers such as Karl Marx and Friedrich Nietzsche, this dialectical dimension was core to modernity. In fact, he argued, it is foundational to modern society and hence has a stickiness and permanence that cannot easily be eliminated, if at all. Consequently, Berman was highly critical of those types of mid- to late-twentieth-century social theory – he had in mind, rightly or not, thinkers such as Herbert Marcuse and Michel Foucault (Berman, 2010: 28–35) – whom he believed partisan and unduly focused on modernity's negative dimensions, such as its ability to crush particular forms of life. He felt that these types of analysis could but lead to an impoverished conception of modernity. To use Marcuse's (1991) phrase against himself, these accounts could not escape being overly one-dimensional.

Aside from obvious differences in style, tone and empirical corpus, there is a certain underlying congeniality between the central arguments I develop in this book and what Berman puts forth in *All That Is Solid Melts into Air*.

Like Berman, I venture into historical terrain to distil a concept and experience of modernity that, while expressed more than a hundred years ago and largely forgotten since, may yet capture central dimensions of present-day modernity. Akin to Berman's basic point, I insist that the notion of individuality that rose to prominence in the late nineteenth and early twentieth centuries is one that has a tensional constitution, thereby shunning any one-dimensional conception of it. Similarly, my proposed concept of social avalanche has no a priori normative connotations. True, *fin-de-siècle* crowd thinkers have often been charged with conceiving crowd behaviour in pejorative terms, attributing to crowds all sorts of attributes (barbarianism, irrationality, femininity) that served to highlight their allegedly suspicious and dangerous character. Much more rarely noted, however, is that many of these crowd theorists in fact kept open the possibility that crowds may not simply negate the social but equally be one of its chief manifestations. This book takes as a central point the demonstration of this dialectical, or perhaps paradoxical, nature of social avalanches.

All that is solid melts into air. The metaphor of melting is perhaps an unfortunate choice: the term Marx and Engels use is *verdampft*, meaning evaporation. Also, though everyday experience might suggest that melting is a gradual process, it is in fact, as physics makes clear, an abrupt phase transition, a sudden qualitative change from solid to liquid – or, in the case of evaporation, a sudden phase change from liquid to gas. I propose social avalanche as a way to better stress the sense of rupture and abrupt change crucial to the late-nineteenth and early twentieth-century experiences I excavate in this book. However, it is worth noting that even Marx and Engels had such a sense of rupture in mind when they penned their famous phrase about the evaporation of existing structures: 'All fixed, fast-frozen relations, with their train of ancient and venerable prejudices and opinions, are swept away, all new-formed ones become antiquated before they can ossify. All that is solid melts into air [*Alles Ständische und Stehende verdampft*]' (Marx and Engels, 2012: 77). It is precisely this sudden sweeping away of existing institutions and ways of life that constitutes a central experiential element in the writings of the *fin-de-siècle* theorists I discuss here. Importantly, however, only a few of these theorists subscribed to Marxist ideas. This non-Marxist legacy does not refute the present book's congeniality with Berman's analysis; it merely suggests that the experience of modernity Berman identified in his corpus of thinkers echoes, too, in the body of literature I analyse. For this reason, the present book lends credence to some of Berman's basic ideas. In fact, it might even be argued that attending to *fin-de-siècle* crowd theorists better brings home some of his principal insights. Take, for example, his definition of what it means to be modern:

Figure I.2 Modernity's maelstrom.
Note: 'The boat appeared to be hanging, as if by magic, … upon the interior surface of a funnel vast in circumference'. Illustration for Edgar Allan Poe's story, *A Descent into the Maelstrom: Tales of Mystery and Imagination*, first published 1841. Illustrated by Harry Clarke. London: G. G. Harrap. London: British Library.
Source: © 2019. The British Library Board/ Scala, Florence

To be modern [...] is to experience personal and social life as a maelstrom, to find one's world and oneself in perpetual disintegration and renewal, trouble and anguish, ambiguity and contradiction: to be part of a universe in which all that is solid melts into air. (2010: 345)

I contend that the sense of being in a maelstrom (one of Berman's favourite expressions) is nowhere as vividly portrayed as in late-nineteenth-century discussions of crowds and collective formations. It is not least in such crowds that people experience the frenzy of being carried away.

At the same time, however, this book differs considerably from both Berman's analysis and other histories of modernity. By paying special heed to crowd theory and the ways in which collective formations and their participants may be captured by – or struggle with – mimetic forces, I conjure themes that need not be confined to modernity (although they may well acquire a particular relevance and prominence within it). Illustratively, Emile Durkheim wrote on these matters based on anthropological observations of pre-modern societies. Although I argue in Chapter 3 that Durkheim's interpretation of pre-modern crowd rituals was framed by a horizon of modern concerns, this anthropological backdrop is nonetheless both telling and consequential. If anthropologists can identify patterns of social avalanche as well as tensions between mimesis and anti-mimesis in multiple types of societies – modern or otherwise – it seems overly restrictive to conceive of these patterns purely as manifestations of the specific form of Western modernity that has preoccupied (Western) sociologists for so long.

My point is not that this broader appreciation of social avalanches should lead to a quest for, say, some kind of basic mimetic desire 'hidden since the foundation of the world', to borrow from René Girard, a famous theorist of mimesis (1977; 1987). Yet, important work by anthropologists such as Michael Taussig (1993) and William Mazzarella (2017) has demonstrated that collective energy and mimetic forces are phenomena that seem to knit together modern and premodern societies. I take this as an invitation to, at the very least, keep open the possibility that social avalanches and tensional individuality may in fact point to core aspects of the social itself and the ways in which collectivity and individuality are interconnected.

Reassessing Crowd Theory

Reviving ideas from the tradition of classical crowd thinking and arguing for their analytical relevance today is an unusual undertaking, especially given the critique this tradition faced throughout the twentieth century.

In order to understand what is at stake here, an introductory framing of why classical crowd theory fell into disrespect and why it might deserve reassessment is necessary. Consider the following: could it be that when people crowd in the same physical locality some collective joy, excitement or anger builds up, unleashing and capturing them if only for a moment? Might this generate a feeling of being carried away in and by the collective formation, in which external influences temporarily suspend individuality? Is this experience a defining trait of collective formations? And could this type of experience in fact extend beyond body-to-body crowding, i.e. to situations in which people need not be physically co-present?

It is unlikely that the type of sociological research on crowd and collective behaviour that gained traction in the United States in the late 1960s through the 1990s would answer these questions in the affirmative (though this might have been different in anthropology). The thrust of this branch of research was to dismantle the notion that crowd and collective behaviour amount to some sort of mimetic, de-individualising phenomenon. Instead, many scholars devoted to social movement studies and collective behaviour theory then argued that collective formations are more adequately understood as means through which individuals pursue what they perceive as reasonable, just and rational goals, in which their sense of individuality and goal-orientation is never lost in the amassing.

What came to the fore in this conceptualisation of crowd and collective behaviour was the manifestation of an essentially rationalist-individualist perspective, in which agglomeration is rendered reducible to the actions of rational individuals. The adoptions of this approach are legion, but my aim here is neither to provide a comprehensive inventory of such illustrations nor to study them in detail.[3] Here, American sociologist Richard A. Berk's game-theory model of crowd behaviour offers an illustrative example. Rejecting the idea that crowds are mimetic forces of de-individualisation, Berk argued for the exact opposite view: 'crowd participants (1) exercise a substantial degree of rational decision-making and (2) are not defined a priori as less rational than in other [non-crowded] contexts' (1974: 356). A similar gesture is found in the work of another American sociologist, Clark McPhail, whose book *The Myth of the Madding Crowd* (1991) is particularly illuminating. In it, McPhail picks apart as a simple myth the idea of irrational, de-individualising crowds, replacing it with what he considers a sounder sociological understanding that emphasises the role of rationality and individuality in collective gatherings.

---

[3] I examine a range of these rationalist-individualist approaches elsewhere. See Borch (2012b: 251–68), in which the two below illustrations are studied in greater depth.

While Berk and McPhail have different emphases – with Berk leaning more towards pure rational-choice assumptions and McPhail towards an unconventional mélange of symbolic interactionism and socio-cybernetics – the two are representative of a broader theoretical transition in American sociology. This transition, beginning in the late 1960s, privileged a rationalist-individualist notion of crowds and collective behaviour; it did so in critical response to older conceptions deemed analytically inadequate, even derided as downright unsophisticated 'arm-chair' speculations without any systematic evidence to support them (see e.g. McCarthy, 1991: xv–xvi). Admittedly, the critical impetus behind this theoretical reorientation was not entirely unjustified. The tradition typically associated with the image of de-individualising crowd behaviour – namely, the kind of crowd psychology that gained momentum in the 1890s, with Frenchmen such as Gustave Le Bon and Gabriel Tarde playing lead roles – was certainly marred by a host of problems. There is no doubt, for example, that against current standards the methodological repertoire of classical crowd theory was less than convincing; in fact, it often barely existed. Further, it is easy to identify particular political biases, especially in Le Bon's account of crowds, which associated purportedly dangerous, pathological, irrational crowds (that threatened to undermine society) explicitly with socialism (e.g. 1974: 225).

Le Bon's linking socialism discursively to foolish barbarian crowds was a faux pas he was never forgiven. When new winds blew in at the end of the 1960s and attempts to rethink crowd and collective behaviour arose, these were pushed forward in part by leftist scholar-activists who objected to having their protest activities viewed in an 'irrational' or abnormal register (McAdam, 2007). Related to this, the language of crowds from the late nineteenth century onwards had been deployed mainly as a template for observing and describing others (Jonsson, 2013). Its strong connotations to irrationality prevented its use in self-description as a vocabulary with which to account for one's own behaviour. It was partly in order to correct this bias and to offer a new analytical terminology better tailored to self-description that American sociologists began their quest for a redefinition of crowd and collective behaviour along rationalist-individualist lines. So strong was the urge to leave the old jargon and its troubling connotations behind that many scholars soon abandoned notions of 'crowd' and 'collective behaviour' theory altogether in favour of 'social movement studies', a term that, according to its champions, promised a fresh beginning.[4]

---

[4] Again, I trace this development in greater detail in Borch (2012b).

Unfortunately, this reorientation was in important respects a tad too fresh. It generated new problems that also manifested in those strands of sociological research that retained the vocabulary of crowds and collective behaviour but bestowed it with new meanings. Thus, while the work of Berk, McPhail and others who took part in the reformulation of crowd and collective behaviour theory in the 1960s and 1970s (including scholars such as Lewis M. Killian, Neil J. Smelser, Charles Tilly and Ralph M. Turner) clearly tackled some problems that were rightly identified in earlier accounts, the alternative framework introduced a new set of issues.

One such problem was that the new framework of collective behaviour in effect produced a negative mirroring of its earlier counterpart: it was as unduly rationalistic as classical crowd theory's supposedly irrationalist edge (Borch, 2012b: ch. 7). Similarly, and with no less irony, the same issues of political bias in classical crowd theory emerged in the rationalist framework, although these were rarely as openly articulated as in the case of Le Bon. In addition to the leftist leanings of some of the activist scholars mentioned above, American sociological discussions of crowd and collective behaviour had been wedded to certain liberal commitments ever since American scholars adopted French notions in the early twentieth century. Indeed, as soon as the French theoretical repertoire landed on American shores, it was clothed in liberal attire to evade scandalising liberal thought by claiming that the crowd's alleged de-individualising forces would undermine the notion of an autonomous self. In order to safeguard the liberal subject, American sociologists, with Robert E. Park an early advocate,[5] embarked on a mission of theorising crowds in ways that were compatible with an independent (strong rather than malleable) individual, a mission finally sealed with Berk's work. One interesting corollary of this is that even if McPhail (1991) was highly critical of Park, whose work he considered too closely aligned with the French tradition of crowd theory, there is in fact a continuity between the two when it comes to defending the analytical role and relevance of the liberal (autonomous) subject.

The central problem with the rationalist-individualist template is not so much these little-recognised political commitments, liberal or otherwise, but rather that it too hastily discarded any relevant facets of classical crowd theory, arguably due to an underestimation of the latter's analytical potency. In particular, Berk and others ended up dismissing the

---

[5] I am thinking in particular of Park's 1904 dissertation *Masse und Publikum*, which laid the foundation for Chicago-style ways of theorising collective behaviour in the early twentieth century (Park, 1972).

possibility, so dear to earlier thinking on the crowd, that crowd and collective behaviour might be characterised by self-organising dynamics, i.e. that something emergent may take place in the crowd or collective setting which is specific to that setting and irreducible to the individual level. For Berk and likeminded sociologists, by contrast, there is no true surplus in the collective formation: the latter merely amounts to an aggregation of individuals and their interests, a lumping together that does not (perhaps even *cannot*) produce anything qualitatively extra. Similarly, the notion that people may be carried away in and by the collective formations they partake in is beyond the analytical radar of the rationalist-individualist framework. Any reference to the potentially mimetic, de-individualising effects of crowding is antithetical to the framework's strong emphasis on the singularity and decision-making autonomy of the individuals who participate in crowds and in collective behaviour. Indeed, in the rationalist-individualist tradition, crowd members are conceptualised as *taking* active part rather than being passively de-subjectified in the collective formation.

Of course, this brief sketch collapses some complexities and nuances. There are all sorts of differences across theories about crowds, collective behaviour and social movements. Especially in recent decades, there have been many attempts to correct the lack of attention to the role of (collective) emotions in more rationalist-individualist approaches to collective behaviour. Scholars such as James M. Jasper have played an instrumental role in bringing this topic back on the agenda of social movement studies (e.g. 1998),[6] passing the baton carried by John Lofland (1982), who made related calls in the early 1980s but without gaining much resonance then. Similarly, in some of his more recent work, McPhail assigns importance to the Le Bonian emphasis on collective irrationality, alongside more rational factors, when analysing specific episodes of collective behaviour, thereby offering a more balanced estimation of the potential analytical contribution of various otherwise opposing traditions (McPhail et al., 2015). Nevertheless, it is still widely assumed in the sociological community that late-nineteenth-century crowd thinking is of historical interest at best and of no analytical value at present.

There is no doubt that the *fin-de-siècle* tradition of crowd theory is of vast historical importance. When sociology took shape as an independent

---

[6] Interestingly, and testifying to the stronghold of the rationalist-individualist framework and its critique of classical crowd theory, Jasper (1998) takes pains to stress that attending to the emotional dimensions of collective behaviour need not entail that individuals be seen as irrational. The fear of returning to the pool of seemingly dark *fin-de-siècle* ideas is patent here.

discipline in the late nineteenth and early twentieth centuries, the *fin-de-siècle* tradition occupied a most central role in conceptions of collectivity (Borch, 2012b). Missing out on the crowd theory tradition would mean overlooking a fundamental building block in the edifice of early sociology. However, as I argue in this book, it would be wrong to reduce this tradition to a concern with crowd behaviour in a narrow sense. It is more accurate to say that this tradition dealt with broader concerns about change, mimesis and forms of being-carried-away, concerns that found manifestations beyond situations of urban crowding. For this reason, classical crowd theory deserves attention beyond specialist circles of scholars interested in (the history of) crowd and collective behaviour or social movement studies. This tradition should be taken seriously as an attempt to come to terms with the experience of concrete forms of *fin-de-siècle* life and their transformations – an experience that, I conjecture, is similar to ours in the twenty-first century.

I uncork the *fin-de-siècle* tradition of crowd theory in order to provide a sense of this experience and to demonstrate that this tradition contains analytical layers that have so far generally gone unnoticed. In so far as current scholars of collective behaviour attend explicitly to the late-nineteenth-century tradition, they do so in an ad hoc fashion that does not seem to recognise – let alone tease out in a deeper and more systematic manner – its broader analytical promise. In fact, it might be said that a different myth of the madding crowd is at play than McPhail's – that late-nineteenth-century scholars of the crowd viewed collective behaviour in strictly negative terms. In response to this, I argue that it is possible to reconstruct from readings of classical late-nineteenth and early twentieth-century sources a theoretically productive framework of the relationship between individuality and collectivity, one which evades some of the biases usually associated with this literature (e.g. regarding unjustified negative political valorisations of crowd and collective formations) and proposes a new conception of how crowding, individuality and the social relate. The crux of this discussion centres on how to conceive of individuality, crowd behaviour and their interconnections – as well as how to mobilise insights into these links in analyses of cities, financial markets and *their* own unique ties.

Outline of the Book

Discussing the ways in which social avalanche and tensional individuality can be deployed in examinations of cities and financial markets, I pursue three interests. The first establishes that social avalanches and tensional individuality indeed capture a vast array of ways in which cities and markets have been conceived. The second traces the various incarnations that these notions have had in discussions of cities and financial markets. This historical variability is important and precisely one of the reasons why it is possible to suggest that a common thread connects late nineteenth-century debates about radical social and technological transformations to a profound reformatting of metropolitan life as well as to present-day discussions about the interactions of fully automated algorithms in financial markets. Finally, returning to the proposition that social avalanches and tensional individuality may address core features of sociality and how the collective and individual are intertwined, I gesture towards the possibility that current algorithmically dominated financial markets might be characterised by a type of sociality which, despite playing out among algorithms rather than humans, still has avalanching as a recognizable feature.

In Chapter 1, I provide a sense of the rupture characterising the late nineteenth and early twentieth centuries by focusing on a series of political, technological and scholarly developments which contributed to creating a widespread atmosphere and experience of fundamental social change. Crucially, much late-nineteenth-century commentary on these deep and rapid transformations coalesced in discussions of crowd behaviour, with crowds seen as particular embodiments of broader social transformations. Urbanisation and industrialisation pulled masses of people to the cities, and in these exploding metropolises mass consumption, mass protests and technological advances produced a sense of people losing stable ground. Relatedly, crowd behaviour seemed to unleash particular forms of being-carried-away by collective forces, an unsettling of individuality that corresponded to the effects of broader social changes.

This is the backdrop to the emergence of crowd psychology and sociological theories of crowd behaviour that rose to prominence in the 1890s. By trying to understand the dynamics of crowds, scholars effectively responded to a broader experience of de-familiarisation and de-individualisation at the time. I discuss the proposition of using the crowd as a window into broader social transformations with reference to Le Bon's work, briefly relating some of his main views on crowds and demonstrating his analytical indebtedness to late-nineteenth-century debates about hypnotic suggestion as these played out within psychotherapy. Importantly, the theory that people can be subjected to hypnotic suggestion – in which they seemingly lose their sense of self – quickly spread from clinical circles to become a central conceptual source inspiring many strands of theorisation, including crowd psychology. This did not happen uncontested; hypnotic suggestion soon attracted considerable criticism that would continue well into the twentieth century. In fact, McPhail's dismissal of

Le Bonian classical crowd theory is tied to a critique of the idea that crowd members are hypnotised and that this hypnotic feature produces the alleged de-individualisation in crowds. Against the grain of this type of critique, I argue that *fin-de-siècle* discussions of hypnotic suggestion did not simply propose that individuals are completely plastic creatures, always malleable in the hands of a powerful hypnotist. Rather, at the heart of the psychotherapy discussions at this time was the proposition that suggestion need not entail de-individualisation: the mimesis generated through suggestion may well depend on anti-mimetic individuals who must voluntarily let go of themselves in order for the mimetic suggestion to work. It is from this idea that the notion of tensional individuality springs.

In Chapter 2, I trace the late-nineteenth-century sociological equivalent to the idea of tensional individuality, demonstrating that this notion formed part of early foundational reflections in the discipline. I do this by carefully reconstructing the considerations of individuality of French criminologist, crowd theorist and sociologist Gabriel Tarde. On the one hand, Tarde promoted an image of the so-called 'somnambulistic myself', the notion that the individual is multiplicitous and that every person is constituted through the mimetic influences of others. A person's thoughts and desires are in fact inherited from others, resulting in a rather shallow conception of individuality. On the other, Tarde maintained that this somnambulistic constitution of the individual co-exists with an anti-mimetic core: elements that persist despite external mimetic influence. What transpires out of this is, I posit, a conception of tensional individuality – one that, in contrast to the psychotherapy discussions detailed in Chapter 1, is then placed at the centre of early sociological thinking. Chapter 2 identifies its relevance in a broader theoretical landscape stretching from *fin-de-siècle* philosophy to twentieth-century psychology.

While Tarde's contributions to *fin-de-siècle* criminology and crowd theory are widely recognised, his status as a key sociologist is more contested. This has not least to do with the disputes he entertained with younger fellow sociologist Emile Durkheim about the role and nature of sociology, an encounter that has often been perceived as a conflict between two opposing camps. I argue here that the supposed antagonism between Durkheim and Tarde is overblown and that the two found common ground on several important issues. This is not to suggest that all differences between them can be ironed out; but there are certainly crucial commonalities between them that should not be disregarded, including their emphasis on and analyses of crowd behaviour.

I highlight these unities to create a platform for reviving ideas often associated with Tarde, stressing that despite, and *contra*, the critique his work has often suffered, his sociological programme is, like Durkheim's, a valuable resource for twenty-first-century social theory. In Chapter 3, I further show that it is possible to identify across a range of thinkers often seen as representing disparate traditions (such as Durkheim and Tarde, but also Georg Simmel) a shared analytical investment in collective behaviour that allows one to distil the notion of social avalanches or social avalanching.[7] Again, the fundamental claim I make is that Durkheim, Simmel, Tarde and many others sought to respond to an experience that gained particular prominence in the late nineteenth and early twentieth centuries: various forms of social change increasingly produced situations in which individuals felt the ground disappearing beneath them, carrying them away in a collective turbulence, which, once set in motion, acquired its own self-organising properties. In addition to developing the notion of social avalanching from late-nineteenth-century social theory, Chapter 3 explores the *prosocial* character of avalanches. Instead of seeing crowd and collective behaviour as a kind of aberration or exceptionality, standing in opposition to the social, I analyse how collective dynamics can reflect positive social content through the lens of social avalanches: they make manifest particular social bonds and therefore should not be dismissed a priori from a moral point of view. Elaborating on the concept of social avalanching, I examine the extent to which a metaphor such as 'avalanche' merits inclusion in the realm of proper sociological concepts and connect it to discussions within physics about self-organised criticality. Finally, I discuss the notion of social avalanche in relation to social action as conceived in the sociology of Max Weber.

With the notions of tensional individuality and social avalanching in place (Chapters 2 and 3, respectively), and having explored the social transformations that led to the formulation of the set of ideas I seek to capture with these notions (Chapter 1), I then embark on two more empirical analyses. In Chapter 4, the focus is on cities. This empirical setting constitutes a kind of home turf for the discussion of social avalanching and tensional individuality, as the rise of the conceptual horizon behind these notions was not least developed in response to late-nineteenth-century urbanisation processes. Chapter 4 discusses this connection in detail by examining the ways in which contemporary sociologists and other commentators on nineteenth-century urbanisation associated it with concerns about contagion, whether the contagion of various diseases or mental contagion, the uncontrolled spread of unhealthy

---

[7] I use the noun (avalanche) and verb (avalanching) forms interchangeably in this work.

ideas. Regardless of its transmitted content, contagion dynamics laid bare a mimetic logic that several observers found deeply disturbing, especially the idea that modern cities seemed to constitute the optimal habitat for the emergence and rapid diffusion of ideas. Several argued that in the metropolis one's immunity against corrupt ideas is constantly weakened, paving the way for contagion dynamics that could escalate into social avalanches carrying urban inhabitants away in collective frenzy. I demonstrate that scholars such as American sociologist Edward A. Ross feared that such dynamics would not only affect the lives of modern cities but eventually spill over into politics and threaten the foundation of democracy. While Ross put forth a highly negative appraisal of *fin-de-siècle* cities, others were more ambivalent. Referring to classical texts in urban sociology such as those by Simmel and Park, I show how both sociologists examined, albeit with different accents, metropolitan life as wedded to a notion of tensional individuality: in the city, the individual is at once exposed to a bombardment of external mimetic forces which threaten to undermine individuality *and* characterised by an anti-mimetic core which works to counteract such external influences.

Chapter 4 also goes beyond foundational sociological texts to argue that many of the concerns that sociologists expressed concerning late-nineteenth and early twentieth-century cities were shared by architects and urban planners at the time, such as Le Corbusier, Ebenezer Howard and Frank Lloyd Wright. Their contemplations led to a series of design proposals: suggestions for urban planning believed to eliminate the problem of social avalanching in cities and minimise the mimetic component of urban individuality. Architecture and urban planning place objects and materiality centre stage. Taking this as my cue, I end the chapter by examining the relation between objects and avalanching, specifically the idea that paying careful attention to objects can dampen the propensity of social avalanches. I discuss this by examining the work of the Austrian architect Adolf Loos, whose reflections on architecture exerted a strong influence on the kind of twentieth-century modernist architecture that planners such as Le Corbusier helped make popular.

In Chapter 5, the empirical setting shifts from cities to financial markets in a recognition of their historically close, if presently changing and loosening, ties. The intimate links between cities and financial markets were already identified by Park in his seminal essay 'The City' (1915). According to Park, the avalanching forces characterising urban crowds find an even more intense equivalent in the stock exchanges of financial markets. I argue that this view, shared by late-nineteenth and early twentieth-century market professionals, led to at least two interesting developments. The first was the architectural redesign of the trading floors of stock and commodity exchanges, where trading pits became a conduit for exchanges hoped to create an orderly market environment not marred by the turmoil of older market settings, which seemed to mimic the turbulence of collective urban life in disturbing ways. The second dealt with ideas and suggestions for how to avoid being carried away by the mimetic pull of the market. Drawing upon insights from crowd psychology, contrarian investment theory developed a set of techniques of the self that individual investors could adopt to retain their independent decision-making capabilities when faced with avalanching markets. I demonstrate that this contrarian position ultimately subscribes to a tensional notion of individuality.

Though trading pits were invented in the nineteenth century, and contrarianism gained footing in the early twentieth century, this chapter moves closer to the present via a discussion of the increasing computer-isation of financial markets during recent decades. I focus on the rise of algorithmic finance, in which fully automated computer algorithms are behind the majority of activity in financial markets. Such algorithms increasingly place orders in markets, doing so without human interven-tion. Algorithmic finance is especially fascinating because it is a field in which humans are progressively being moved to the background. Of course, human beings programme the algorithms, but once these are set to operate in markets, they do so independently and sometimes in unanticipated ways. While this increasingly de-humanised organisation of financial markets might suggest a decoupling from classical socio-logical ideas, since inter-human activity is no longer centre stage, the ways in which these algorithms operate are strikingly akin to social avalanching. I demonstrate this through a discussion of the Flash Crash that took place in US markets in May 2010, caused in part, according to some accounts, by inter-algorithmic activity. The central and controver-sial assumption underpinning the analysis of the ways in which fully automated algorithms may engage in social avalanching is that sociality can indeed be ascribed to non-human algorithms. Chapter 5 discusses the sociality of algorithms in detail and provides arguments for why it is not far-fetched to conceive of inter-algorithmic activity as an extension of inter-human sociality.

One of the intermediary steps towards the development of present-day algorithmic finance was the transition from open-outcry trading on the trading floors of exchanges – where traders were physically co-present, trading face to face with one another – to electronic screen trading, in which traders engage the market via their computer screens. The latter type of market configuration has been the object of various sociological and anthropological analyses. Most important for present purposes, Karin Knorr Cetina and Urs Bruegger's examination of screen trading argues for the relevance of a new conception of sociality, the 'postsocial' (Knorr Cetina and Bruegger, 2002), describing situations in which sociality no longer refers to inter-human relationships. Rather than other human beings, non-human objects of various sorts increasingly come to constitute entities with whom humans develop social bonds. This is precisely what happens with screen traders, according to Knorr Cetina. Whereas traders on traditional trading floors established social bonds with their human peers, screen traders are so attached to their screens that for them, the screen becomes an object with which they forge social ties. Such human–screen relationships are postsocial

in that they step into the place of more traditional human bonds, which become a sort of legacy environment for postsocial relations. One distinctive feature of contemporary life might be that perhaps for the first time in recent history it appears unclear whether, for individuals, other persons are indeed the most fascinating part of their environment – the part they are most responsive to and devote most attention to. (Knorr Cetina and Bruegger, 2002: 163)

Knorr Cetina's analysis is of great importance. It persuasively makes the point that when financial markets transformed from open-outcry trading to electronic screen trading, the sociality of markets also changed from an inter-human to a postsocial (human–object) form. In Chapter 5, I take this suggestion one step further: open-outcry trading has virtually ceased to be of any significance in today's financial markets, and human screen traders are increasingly being replaced by fully automated algorithms which place orders in markets at speeds that vastly outcompete what any human screen trader could accomplish. It might be speculated that this reconfiguration of markets, no less radical than the shift from open outcry to screen trading, has given rise to new forms of sociality. Arguing along similar lines, sociologists of finance such as Donald MacKenzie (2019) suggest that a particular Goffman-like 'interaction order' characterised by the interaction of fully automated algorithms can be identified in algorithmically dominated markets. Following that line, I suggest that to the extent that present-day algorithmic markets are postsocial, they are so in a more radical way than that proposed by Knorr Cetina: humans have been practically relegated today, and the postsociality of algorithmic finance is one of purely inter-algorithmic relationships. Consequently, I argue that Knorr Cetina's proposition needs rephrasing: the central question becomes whether, for *algorithms*, human *persons* are indeed the most fascinating part of their environment – the part they are most responsive and devote most attention to.

I conclude by summarising key findings and delineating routes for further research that could continue in the footsteps of, and further flesh out, the ideas developed in the book.

A Montage Approach

As the chapter outline above makes plain, this book plunges into and integrates several different fields and traditions. Parts of the book are historical, delineating actual transformations, events and experiences, with a particular focus on the late nineteenth and early twentieth centuries. Other parts are exegetic, delving into close readings of scholars, especially Tarde, in whose work is buried the notions of social avalanching and tensional individuality. Still other parts analyse broader discursive currents, examining various observers' reflections on cities and financial markets, the dangers and challenges associated with these two settings, and materials spanning texts by sociologists, architects, financial-market observers and so forth. Much of this discussion centres on academic texts, or what Niklas Luhmann refers to as 'cultivated' (*gepflegte*) or 'serious' (*ernste*) semantics (Luhmann, 1980). This includes canonised works as well as lesser-known resources that have nonetheless helped nurture these ways of conceiving crowds, cities and financial markets. That said, in the final chapter on financial markets my argument is informed by interviews and fieldwork as well.

A key argument in my book is that the *fin-de-siècle* body of literature I reinvigorate should be seen as responding to a particular experience with societies undergoing deep transformations. It is therefore important to ground some of the scholarly texts in broader accounts, and I supplement their cultivated semantics with examples from 'popular' semantics (Stäheli, 1997): a vocabulary located closer to a quotidian level. I use literary sources for that purpose, following an existing, if somewhat small, branch of sociology that has demonstrated the analytical value of examining the rich sociological imaginations of the novel and other literary genres (e.g. Harrington, 2002; Isenberg, 2018; Jonsson, 2000; Nisbet, 2017). While popular semantics plays second fiddle to academic literature in my argument, it nonetheless serves an important function: it operates simultaneously as a barometer of widely held beliefs, as an echo chamber reinforcing such beliefs and as a baton that defines the rhythm, inculcation and dissemination of novel ideas.

Besides this diversity of materials, the chapters are also characterised by different analytical modalities: some seek to develop new concepts while others mobilise these for analytical purposes. This duality reflects the book's aim to be at once analytical and interpretative, or rather, reinterpretative. What emerges from this is a deliberate montage-like strategy which assembles elements from seemingly different fields (crowd behaviour, cities and financial markets) and noticeably different time periods (from late-nineteenth-century discussions about therapeutic suggestion techniques to twenty-first-century developments in finance). While this runs the risk of producing an inchoate picture, my hope is that with the different materials – and their varying textures and colours – a fresh and illuminating portrayal of the basic dynamics of collective life will materialise.

Although the book clearly aims to develop a new conceptual apparatus with which to understand the important dimensions and interconnections of crowds, cities and financial markets, its analysis has obvious limitations. For starters, I draw upon sources and empirical contexts found within a European or US geography, though similar traits emerge in other contexts. Arguably more important, given my emphasis on the crowd theory tradition and its reinterpretation to shed new light on collective formations and the interrelations of individuality and the social, I focus on corners and categories of sociological theory to the exclusion of many that have occupied sociologists elsewhere – namely, more organised forms of collectivity that may be found between crowds and individuals, such as corporations, associations and groups.

1   *Fin-de-siècle* Landslides

'The present epoch is one of [those] critical moments in which the thought of mankind is undergoing a process of transformation. [...] the modern age represents a period of transition and anarchy'.

If not for the reference to mankind, which comes across as a bit dated today, it would be easy to mistake this quote for a comment on the changes taking place in the early twenty-first century. However, the author of these lines is not offering a sociology of liquid (post)modernity; nor is he commenting on waves of present-day populism or the demolishing – post-Donald Trump – of a well-known world order of international politics, and the attendant rise of a more anarchic regime. The lines appear instead in the opening pages of French crowd theorist Gustave Le Bon's *The Crowd* (2002: ix–x). Besides being a cornerstone of the crowd psychology debates that flourished in France and elsewhere at the end of the nineteenth century, Le Bon's treatise deserves attention as an illustration of the pitfalls of presentism. While his remarks about the social world undergoing profound change may themselves reflect a certain presentism, they should at least vaccinate one from falling prey to the similar snare of portraying the twenty-first century as fundamentally different from the past or undergoing unprecedented changes. Subduing an inclination to presentism allows for the observation that many present-day accelerations of society seem rather miniscule compared to the European situation in the late nineteenth and early twentieth centuries. Not only was that era extremely liquid and accelerated, to use contemporary sociological vocabulary, but also understated and inadequately characterised by a twenty-first-century sociological idiom of transformation. That age is more accurately described as an overheated, heavily boiling pot on the verge of – or actually – overflowing, with minor and major changes piling up in ways that elicited a widespread sense of disruption, as Le Bon's book lays bare.

In this chapter I focus on this epoch – the time span from the 1870s and eighties to the 1920s and thirties, in which sociology and other social sciences gradually evolved into distinct disciplines – to provide a glimpse of the virtual landslides in which the late-nineteenth and early-twentieth-century world was caught. Under these conditions, familiar ways of life and structures of meaning entered a deep-seated instability and indeterminacy, if not outright collapse. Much has already been written about transformations in social and economic life, in art and culture, as well as in technology between the *fin de siècle* and the fall of the Weimar Republic. I shall therefore be somewhat selective in what follows. My account will not only be Eurocentric but also focus mainly, though not exclusively, on developments in France, Germany and Austro-Hungary, since this is where the sense of change and collapse I wish to portray were most pronounced and vividly expressed (for a discussion of British experiences with this era, see Marshall, 2007).

Admittedly, the biases informing the discussion below are not merely geographical; arguably more important are the kinds of developments selected for discussion as well as their interpretation. For example, when zeroing in on some of the significant changes in social life in the late nineteenth and early twentieth centuries, I intentionally set aside the many continuities that exist alongside the transformations I excavate. In that sense, I forward something of a counter-narrative to the one advanced by historian Arno Mayer in his analysis of the overall persistence of premodern elements in the social and political constitution of this time period. In his *The Persistence of the Old Regime*, Mayer argued that certain 'forces of inertia and resistance' had often been overlooked by historians of the early twentieth century, forces that were firmly rooted in 'preindustrial economic interests, prebourgeois elites, predemocratic authority systems, premodernist artistic idioms, and "archaic" mentalities', all of which cast long-lasting shadows over European social and political life and played no small role in triggering the First World War (Mayer, 1981: 4, 5). Mayer's central point is that these forces of inertia and resistance did much to curtail the effects of all the melting of solids that surely did take place, he admits, in the late nineteenth century.

While I recognise the merits of Mayer's analysis, I nonetheless wish to cast my net elsewhere in the sea of historical developments to demonstrate a point not easily grasped from Mayer's Marxist perspective. Not only did stability and tranquillity come under immense pressure in the late nineteenth century – as a result of a mushrooming of technological advances, industrialisation, urbanisation, and other factors (developments that were sometimes intimately connected, sometimes not) – but also, and more crucial, this sense of change prompted new discussions and conceptions of collectivity and individuality. Indeed, as Le Bon's work demonstrates, the experience of radical change permeated reflections on *fin-de-siècle* and early twentieth-century society, with particular configurations of collectivity and individuality arising as responses to and corollaries of this experience. Most important, I argue, this ensuing form of individuality was neither one of immanent flux and fluidity nor one of staunch autonomy. Rather, the notion of individuality that surfaced saw the individual as torn between collectively generated fluidity and, in a nod to Mayer, what may be referred to as *singular inertia*.

The patchwork of analyses that follows weaves together existing scholarly investigations and literary sources, the latter as a handy means of accessing experiences from a bygone era. While I do not assume here that the historical analyses offered in novels should be treated on par with scholarly examinations, I suggest that some novels may not only enrich our sociological imagination but also be sensitive to experiences that are historically, factually correct, although the historical details they describe are rendered in a literary or journalistic form. Reflecting this point, the few literary sources I evoke are written by historical eyewitnesses who took approaches both evaluative and factually descriptive. Although their writings do not conform to standard sociological methods, these authors provide a window into their historical situation and widespread everyday experiences of it, making them valuable sources for a historical sociology.

I thus begin with a set of literary accounts discussing the sense of change that swept across great parts of European social life in the late nineteenth and early twentieth centuries. Combining these literary sources with historical analyses of this time, I demonstrate how particular meaning structures and ways of life were undermined by political, technological, scientific and cultural developments as well as how a sense of de-individualised subjectivity gained traction in the wake of these transformations. I suggest that while the landslide events experienced at this time were multifaceted, several of their features overlapped and found expression in late-nineteenth and early-twentieth-century social and political discourse. Thus, for several observers throughout Europe (and beyond), many of the profound changes that took place in society seemed to coalesce in the manifestation of a new collective subject: the crowd. In particular, these observers, led by Le Bon, concurred that crowds laid bare one of the significant experiences that emerged in the late nineteenth century: that of being swept away collectively (by crowds, themselves unleashed by and entangled with the many changes occurring in this time period). I further demonstrate that this concern with crowds was closely related to discussions of de-individualising hypnosis and suggestibility integral to the sense of *fin-de-siècle* change; these discussions portrayed individuality as moulded from the outside rather than as an expression of autonomy and independence.

Finally, I zero in on the conception of hypnosis underpinning much late-nineteenth-century crowd theory. While notions of hypnosis and suggestion are often believed to imply a passive, externally mimetic conception of individuality, late-nineteenth-century debates were more ambivalent on this point. Indeed, they characterised the individual as being cast between external mimesis and an anti-mimetic sense of autonomous individuality. My central claim is that this individuality was predicated on and conditioned by the wider social changes described throughout the chapter.

From Slow Past to Fast Past

The sense of society undergoing profound changes in the late nineteenth century was widespread, and it manifested in both scholarly and literary accounts. I focus on two eminent Austrian novelists, Joseph Roth and Stefan Zweig, who have vividly portrayed a sense of the radical social, cultural and mental transformations that swept across Europe in a mere few decades of the late nineteenth and early twentieth centuries. That Austrian writers would be particularly attentive to such changes is hardly surprising, given the collapse of the Austro-Hungarian Empire after the First World War. In particular, Roth's best-known novel, *The Radetzky March* (Roth, 2002), offers a meditation on the downfall of the Empire. With the death of Franz Joseph I in 1916 and the Empire's defeat in the First World War, the Empire and its structures of meaning vanished. Much of the narrative in *The Radetzky March*, set at a slow pedestrian pace, chronicles the quotidian incidents experienced by three generations of a fictive family, the Trottas, whose destiny is intimately linked to that of Franz Joseph I. The novel focuses on the years between 1890 and 1914 under the Austro-Hungarian Empire; its historical value arises from the fact that at the time of its writing in the early 1930s, the decelerated and predictable life depicted in the book had become scenes from a distant past. This sense of rupture was not a sudden insight to Roth. His comprehensive journalistic reportage from Berlin in the 1920s vividly detailed that Europe then was an entirely different animal from the world in which he grew up (Roth was born in Galicia, a north-eastern part of the Austro-Hungarian Empire, in 1894). The city of Berlin, suffering from the effects of Germany's defeat in the First World War, is portrayed in Roth's writings as filled with homeless people, immigrants and extreme poverty – a chaos greatly amplified by hyperinflation (Roth, 2003).

What Roth reported from Berlin echoed a wider modernist rupture. As Stefan Jonsson aptly puts it:

It is well known that modernist culture, and Weimar modernism in particular, articulates radically new ideas about the human subject. In early-twentieth-century art, we witness a decomposition and asymmetric reconstruction of the human face and body. In architecture, the idea of the interior as the padded case of the individual's essence gives way to the utopian living spaces of Walter Gropius or Ludwig Mies van der Rohe, in which the person became a variable function of his or her environment. Numerous novels chronicle how the space of individuality, materialised in the *intérieur* and set apart from public life, is invaded by external forces, to the extent that the self appears as a random mass of impersonal elements. (2013: 143, original emphasis)

It is this severance of the individual from recognizable structures that Roth wanted to bring into relief in *The Radetzky March* by recalling how the sense of acceleration and dramatic change during the Weimar period, including its manifold pressures on stable forms of subjectivity, starkly contrasted the ways in which life had been lived only a few decades earlier. And so, while a certain nostalgia flows from Roth's pen, Michael Hofmann, the authoritative Roth translator, is right to note that the novel 'is actually a far bleaker, more unconsoling book than it is [often] taken for, by no means the revanchist or reinstating celebration of a gone order, more the anatomy of a dismantlement' or 'an account of a formidable collapse, a deadly loss of scale and illusion' (Hofmann, 2002: xv).[1] Bluntly put, the dismantlement Roth portrayed was that of individuals being catapulted out of their protecting milieus, losing their social, cultural and political reference points in the sudden landslide of once-familiar patterns.

An early reviewer of *The Radetzky March* cogently characterised it as a 'sociological novel', hinting at its ability to bring factual events and experiences into fictional shape (Chamberlain, 1933). If Roth captured a notion of devastating rupture in both his fiction and journalistic writings, Stefan Zweig's *The World of Yesterday* shares elements from both these genres (Zweig, 2009). Born in Vienna in 1881, Zweig carried the adolescent's experience of the Austro-Hungarian Empire as seen from its centre, more so than Roth did. Completing his memoirs in 1942, shortly before he and his wife committed suicide, Zweig provided a rich account of a sixty-year-period during which the old world, the world of his youth, figuratively and literally came to ashes. Not surprisingly, a significant portion of his memoirs is devoted to the Hitler

---

[1] This assessment gains support from the ambivalence radiating from some of Roth's retrospective essays on the Austro-Hungarian Empire. In one of these, for example, he noted that while he had been opposed to the rule of Franz Joseph I, he also mourned the death of the Emperor as it entailed 'the passing of a fatherland. [...] The chilly sun of the Habsburgs was being extinguished, but it had at least been a sun' (Roth, 2015: 92).

experience, which forced Zweig, like so many others, to flee his native Austria in 1934. Yet, similar to *The Radetzky March* – and in no way underestimating the singularity and radical consequences of Hitler's reign[2] – the most striking passages of *The World of Yesterday* are those in which Zweig detailed a way of life in the Austro-Hungarian Empire at the turn of the nineteenth century which, from the perspective of the late 1930s and early 1940s, appeared almost unfathomable.

Naturally, continuities between these two time periods can be identified in Zweig's writing. For one, Zweig drew attention to the antisemitism that persisted in the political life of Vienna in the 1880s and nineties by the likes of Georg Schönerer and Karl Lueger. But he also noted that their antisemitic policies had no immediate impact on his daily life as a Jew (2009: 46). Thus, despite antisemitism's permanence, an inescapable nostalgia lingers over Zweig's memoirs, a longing for a world in which tranquillity dominated and life was safeguarded against external turmoil as if wrapped up in cotton wool. Zweig, in his account of what he fittingly called 'the world of security' in the late nineteenth and early twentieth centuries, affirmed the same peacefulness of life in the Austro-Hungarian Empire reflected in *The Radetzky March*:

Time and age were judged by different criteria [back then]. People lived a more leisurely life, and when I try to picture the figures of the adults who played a large part in my childhood it strikes me how many of them grew stout before their time. [...] Even in my earliest childhood, when my father was not yet forty, I cannot remember ever seeing him run up or down a staircase, or indeed do anything in visible haste. Haste was not only regarded as bad form, it was in fact superfluous, since in that stable bourgeois world with its countless little safeguards nothing sudden ever happened. Those disasters that did take place on the periphery of our world did not penetrate the well-lined walls of our secure life. The Boer War, the Russo-Japanese War, even the Balkan Wars did not make any deep impression on my parents' lives. They skimmed all the war reporting in the paper as indifferently as they looked at the sports headlines. [...] When an old newspaper from those days happens to fall into my hands, and I read the excitable reports of some small local council election, when I try to remember the plays at the Burgtheater with their tiny problems, or think of the disproportionate agitation of our youthful debates on fundamentally unimportant matters, I cannot help smiling. How Lilliputian all those anxieties were, how serene that time! (Zweig, 2009: 46–7)

Zweig admitted that such recollections from his youth may well depict an artificial world, a time pocket, the historical oddity of which would be evident to any *entre-deux-guerres* observer or post-war reader of his great book. This peculiarity aside, it is important to note that while the old

---

[2] The most dreadful acts of Hitler's destructive regime were not known to Zweig when he wrote the book.

Austro-Hungarian era seemed devoid of them, rupture and suddenness would soon manifest themselves with great force – with tangible consequences for an individuality increasingly regarded as being subsumed under external collective forces. Indeed, outside of the well-protected bubble of the Austro-Hungarian Empire at the time, change was already boiling, and the tectonic plates of the European societies would soon be set in motion with such dramatic effect that the life forms and experiential qualities of the Empire relayed by Zweig could only appear strangely archaic. I trace of some these transformations, loosely organising the following discussion around politics, science and technology, moving from an international level seemingly detached from people's everyday lives to developments around more quotidian experiences.

International Politics and Law

In his 1950 book *The* Nomos *of the Earth*, the legal and political theorist Carl Schmitt details how the so-called *jus publicum Europaeum* – the public law that governed the relations between the European states – collapsed as a result of a seemingly minor event in international affairs in the mid-1880s (Schmitt, 2003). During the colonisation surge of European states at the end of the nineteenth century, a discussion ensued about how to legally regulate the colonisation of African territory to avoid conflicts between different European powers over the same land. While much of this discussion had previously taken place as an intra-European debate dominated by European concerns and interests, the 1884–5 Berlin Conference (or Congo Conference) on international land appropriation would change that dramatically, with the United States undermining the existing balance:

the United States assumed a decisive position when, on April 22, 1884, it recognized the flag of the International Congo Society, which was not a state. This opened the door to the confusion, whereby an international colony was treated as an independent state. The core concept of the traditional interstate European international law was thus thrown into disorder. (2003: 217)

Schmitt argues that even if this American move was 'perceived to be a peripheral matter' at first, its ramifications are difficult to overestimate. From around 1890, international law, formerly synonymous with European international law, now had to reckon with the United States, meaning that the regime of 'a self-conscious, Eurocentric international law' had been demolished (2003: 227). In other words, from seeing the world in its own image, Europe had to reconcile itself with a stronger external influence. 'The relativization of Europe' that Schmitt (2003:

217) associates with the Congo Conference resembles the relativisation of the individual that I excavate from the *fin-de-siècle* discourses below, according to which the individual is neither independent nor entirely subjected to external control.

Schmitt also registered changes more internal to the state in his 1932 book *The Concept of the Political,* which argues for a change of hierarchy in the conceptual lexicon with which to understand states. Instead of taking as his starting point the conception of the state and deriving the political from it, he foregrounded the notion of the political and asserted in his opening observation that 'The concept of the state presupposes the concept of the political' (1996: 19). This is tied to Schmitt's famous understanding of the political as based on the difference between friend and enemy. The Schmitt expert Ernst-Wolfgang Böckenförde observes that although this reshuffling of the relationship between the state and the political was immediately contested in the academic community, it was in fact also anchored in actual contemporaneous developments. Most notably, Schmitt's de-centering of the state as a guarantor of internal peace was made all too plain by both the Russian and German Revolutions (Böckenförde, 2002: 8–9). One might say that Schmitt's achievement here was to formularise a situation and development that had already taken place and only awaited conceptual framing.

For other observers, the European decline Schmitt described in the realm of international law and statehood was in fact a minor manifestation of a deeper collapse: the veritable breakdown of the cultural pillars of Europe. This sentiment crystallised especially in the German philosopher Oswald Spengler's grand epos *The Decline of the West,* a book originally published in two volumes in 1918 and 1922, respectively. Given the book's appearance after the First World War, it is easy to interpret its analysis of the cultural self-exhaustion of the West as a comment on that tragic war. Yet the book was more than that: as Spengler notes in the introduction to the 1918 edition, its title has remained unchanged since 1912, when he conceived of the book's main ideas (Spengler, 1980a: xv). Consequently, for Spengler, the war merely epitomised a decline already well under way. Equally important for present purposes, while Spengler traced this far-reaching deterioration through a comprehensive historical analysis spanning several millennia, the book was not just an illustration of Hegel's dictum that 'the owl of Minerva begins its flight only with the onset of dusk' – that philosophical insight comes staggering up *after* the fact (Hegel, 1991: 23). It is more correct to say that Spengler's analysis had a highly contemporaneous affinity: it was conceived in and sought to capture a historical situation of Spengler's own. In other words, it is unlikely that Spengler could have authored his book independently of the sense of profound change that permeated the late nineteenth and early twentieth centuries.

The fact that Spengler laid the building blocks of his thesis prior to the First World War should not lead to a disregard of the war's devastating consequences on stability. Indeed, as the political theorist Jan-Werner Müller rightly argues, the First World War effectively ended the old world of security Zweig portrayed: the Great War 'put into question every single institutional arrangement and every single political idea (or even just moral intuition) on which the Age of Security had rested' (Müller, 2011: 16). Still, the Spengler case testifies to the importance of casting the net wider: the First World War's undeniable significance notwithstanding, transformation was in the air many years ahead of 1914. This is easily seen if the perspective is shifted to more local political developments, developments that had more immediate influence on the quality of everyday experience. France at the end of the nineteenth century provides a strong sense of some of the changes that can be registered at this level, suggesting a situation that differed considerably from the world of security relayed by Zweig. Susanna Barrows nicely summarises some of the simmering turmoil:

Between 1889 and 1898 France would witness the inauguration of the May Day demonstrations, a wave of terrorist 'propaganda of the deed,' a marked increase in the number of strikes and violent demonstrations, the Panama scandal, the assassination of President Sadi Carnot, and the opening chapters of the Dreyfus Affair. (Barrows, 1981: 2)

Barrows carefully examines the ways in which French political havoc in the late nineteenth century arose out of rising industrialisation, urbanisation, unionisation, socialism and democratisation. Yet the factors upending the social order and instating a widespread experience of flux, acceleration and profound alteration went far beyond the openly political articulations found in strikes, demonstrations and the like. Barrows notes that, in anticipation of how Weimar Germany's fragile social and political structure was followed by a veritable cultural blossoming, the delicate French *fin-de-siècle* situation enjoyed a countermovement that inspired a range of *scientific advances*. Paradoxically, while these were in large part attempts to better understand the rupture that seemed to threaten the country – as well as to suggest possible remedies towards the re-stabilisation of society – they further augmented the sense of change at the time.

Scientific Advances

In the social sciences, a range of newly established disciplines such as criminology, crowd psychology, and sociology (and to some extent psychotherapy), were united in championing a notion of de-individualisation as well as comprehending and responding to the rupture in its various manifestations. More specifically, these disciplines concurred that individual actions were in large part attributable to extra-individual dynamics and that in order to achieve the desired re-stabilisation of society, measures were needed to address this supra-individual maelstrom before it swept people away.

In criminology this surfaced in critiques of the Italian criminologist Cesare Lombroso's promotion of a highly individualised biological conception of crime. The founding father of the so-called criminal-anthropological school, Lombroso saw crime as tied to supposedly crime-prone individuals: some people were believed to be biologically predisposed to commit crimes, but fortunately, Lombroso and his followers argued, these individuals could be identified via biological markers (e.g. the shape of their head). Society could then single them out and introduce proper measures to curb their antisocial behaviour (Lombroso, 2006). Lombroso's criminal-anthropological school was critiqued most notably by Gabriel Tarde, who offered an important alternative analytical programme which portrayed crime as detached from biological predispositions. In Tarde's view, criminal activity should be conceived in relation to how it imitates other criminal acts, i.e. as a distinctively social – and in that sense, de-individualised – phenomenon (Tarde, 1968).[3] In other words, rather than focusing on particular individuals and their biological constitutions, Tarde analysed crime from a much more mimetic-relational approach, according to which singular criminal acts were understood in connection to other criminal acts they sought to imitate. Tarde's de-individualised analysis not only entailed that a person's biological set-up was no longer a driver of criminal activity but also suggested a democratisation of criminal life: in principle all persons could fall prey to crime-inducing imitative currents regardless of their biological constitution. Put differently, Tarde lent scholarly shape to the thought that every person, high or low in social position, could become overwhelmed by external mimetic forces.

Along similar lines, Durkheim's sociological programme – which received powerful political backing in its attempt to reinvigorate the

---

[3] For a discussion of Lombroso, Tarde and other early criminologists, see Borch (2015: ch. 1).

French educational system (Borch, 2012b: 68–9; Lepenies, 1988: ch. 2) – was centred on understanding society and the social in de-individualised, *sui generis* terms. Here too the central point was to see social dynamics not as reducible to individual authorship but, as it were, characterised by supra-individual forces supposedly inculcated into the behaviours of individuals. Let me briefly note here, as a final mention of how prominently de-individualisation was gaining traction at the end of the nineteenth century, that the concept was particularly taken up in the scholarly discourse on crowd psychology that emerged in the 1890s (as well as in the psychotherapy discussions which inspired it). This discourse suggested that crowd dynamics were becoming increasingly prevalent in modern society, to the extent that the late nineteenth century became synonymous with an era of the crowd; in this view, crowds effected a de-individualising change in their members, who suddenly succumbed to their leaders' impulses. Taken together, these points suggest that de-individualisation was becoming the new normal. I return to the basic analytical ideas of crowd psychology and psychotherapy below and to a deeper examination of Tarde and Durkheim in the following chapter.

Another reconceptualisation of the individual followed from changes in the area of perception. As Jonathan Crary argues in his cross-examination of late-nineteenth-century advances in art and modern culture vis-à-vis a host of scholarly contributions to philosophy, psychology and sociology, a 'generalized crisis in perception [took place] in the 1880s and 1890s' (Crary, 1999: 2). Questions of perception increasingly revolved around the problem of *attention*, in large part due to industrialisation and urbanisation. 'Inattention, especially within the context of new forms of large-scale industrialized production, began to be treated as a danger and a serious problem, even though it was often the very modernised arrangements of labor that produced inattention' (Crary, 1999: 13). Crary stresses that while the heterogeneous late-nineteenth-century debates on what constitutes attention and how it may be managed did not coalesce into a uniform understanding of attention, they did much to recast contemporary understandings of individuality and its connections to perception. The problem of attention engendered a tensional notion of individuality, in which the individual was seen as both capable of paying attention to something (say, a task in the factory) and being guided externally (by stimuli beyond the person's control).

The issue of perception also drew on scholarly developments taking place beyond the social sciences. In November 1895, the German physicist Wilhelm Roentgen discovered the X-ray and its ability to disclose bone structures, sparking a sea change in the connections between perception and individuality. The X-ray, itself indiscernible by human perception, 'was capable of penetrating [people's] clothes and flesh to reveal their most intimate organs' (Friedman and Friedland, 1998: 124). By providing a penetrating view of the individual, the X-ray preempted psychoanalysis's claim to fame – the alleged ability to shed light on the innermost aspects of an individual – albeit via entirely different techniques.

Interestingly, the scientific debate on perception ventured far beyond the terrain of intra-human exploration. Beginning in the 1890s, the discipline of physics gradually asserted that the same psychical 'fact' could be variously represented, making perception pivotal to understanding a reality that could no longer be considered objective in the term's traditional sense (Crary, 1999: 162–3; Crary here builds on the discussion in Hacking, 1983: 143). Reflecting upon the broader cultural implications of this shift away from a Newtonian worldview, Wilfrid Mellers and Rupert Hildyard write that the work of modern physicists such as Albert Einstein, James Clerk Maxwell and others produced 'the obscure feeling that "objective reality" no longer existed in quite the same way and could no longer be depended upon to underpin "commonsense" attitudes to life' (1989: 36) – an idea later radicalised by the likes of Niels Bohr and Werner Heisenberg. In this way, even the hard sciences contributed to shaking the solid ground of familiar experience.

A final implication of the sedimentation of modern science that took place at the end of the nineteenth century is its contribution to the increasing *secularisation* of society. Durkheim attended to this development and associated it with a growing differentiation, or division, of labour in society where originally, 'everything social was religious [...] gradually political, economic and scientific functions broke free from the religious function' (2013: 132). As a result, God, 'from being at first present in every human relationship, has progressively withdrawn' – 'The individual thus feels himself [*sic*], and he is in reality, much less *acted upon* [by God]; he becomes more a source of spontaneous activity' (2013: 132, original emphasis). Given the supra-individual forces noted above, what transpired here was a more general *problematique* that Durkheim and other sociologists grappled with at this time: modern society gives rise to autonomous individuality (the 'cult of the individual', as Durkheim called it, see 2013: 317) yet creates new dependencies that practically annul this autonomy in certain respects (2013: 7). Durkheim's argument reveals this two-sidedness: 'it is possible, without contradiction, to be an individualist while asserting that the individual is a product of society, rather than its cause' (Durkheim in Lukes, 1969: 28, n. 21). In other words, individualism and individual autonomy need

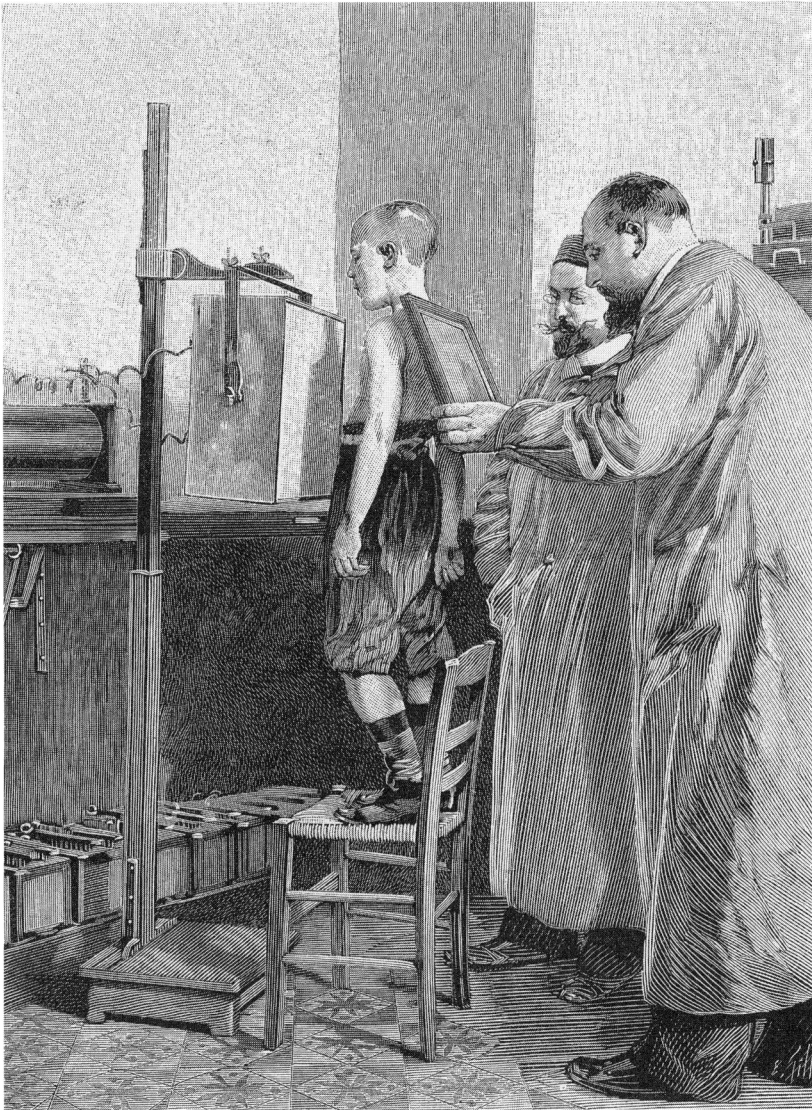

Figure 1.1 Roentgen's X-rays.
Note: A child taking X-rays in a clinic of the hospital of Villiers, France.
Source: Illustration from the magazine *L'Illustration*, vol. 56, no. 2886, 18 June 1898. Milan, Biblioteca Ambrosiana. © 2019. Veneranda Biblioteca. Ambrosiana/DeAgostini Picture Library/Scala, Florence

not be opposed to collectivism but may indeed be artefacts of society – a point crystallised in the concept of tensional individuality.

Technological Innovations

The experiential landslides did not end there. Alongside sweeping political developments and scientific discoveries that challenged inherited conceptions, a deluge of technological innovations characterised the late nineteenth century. Some of these contributed to the rise of consumer culture, as Rosalind Williams cogently documents:

> After 1850 many notable inventions were consumer products themselves – the bicycle, the automobile, chemical dyes, the telephone, electric lighting, photography, the phonograph. Never before or since has there been such a concentration of technological change affecting the ordinary consumer. What he [*sic*] ate, what he ate with, where he lived, what he wore, how he moved around – all these daily activities and more were being altered simultaneously. (Williams, 1982: 10)

The advent of mass consumption was closely linked to the reconfiguration of cities, in which new forms of advertisement posters and window arrangements became common (e.g. Gleber, 1999: 35–6). Furthermore, as Carolyn Marvin demonstrates, the invention of the telephone generated new forms of distanced intimacy; just as electricity, a replacement for gas fuel, was seen as a facilitator of cleaner homes and eventually as a mechaniser of domestic tasks, thereby freeing (some) women from their stereotypical household duties (1988: 67–85). The rise of consumer culture and its many material manifestations brought about a change in everyday perception by reshuffling the organisation and experience of quotidian life.

That the late nineteenth century was the hotbed of technological innovations, several with huge socio-cultural ramifications despite their pedestrian character, is well-corroborated by scholars. As Lisa Tickner summarises:

> A single generation experienced the impact of the typewriter (1874), the telephone (1876), the gramophone (1877), electric lighting (1880), the internal combustion engine (1885), the underground tube-train (1890), wireless telegraphy (1895), the cinema (1895), the cheap, mass-circulation daily newspaper (1896), the motor-bus (1897) and powered flight (1903). (2000: 190)[4]

---

[4] Referencing some of these as well as other inventions, James R. Beniger similarly notes that 'even the word *revolution* seems barely adequate to describe the development, within the span of a single lifetime, of virtually all of the basic communication technologies still in use a century later' (1986: 7, original emphasis).

Media theorist Friedrich A. Kittler analysed these innovations in detail in his work on media technologies, demonstrating how individuality also became newly co-constituted by technological developments. Starting from the premise that 'media determine our situation' (Kittler, 1999: xxxix), in that media co-constitute the ways in which people act and think of themselves and others, Kittler explored a range of technological transformations in media that took shape at a time when the peacefulness of Zweig's youthful years was about to collapse. More precisely, these inventions contributed to shaking the scaffold of tranquillity Zweig depicts.

Focusing on the gramophone, the typewriter and film, Kittler claimed that each of these technological innovations had drastic effects on many facets of everyday life, including the ways in which individuality was seen and problematised. For example, the typewriting machine prompted a consequential retailoring of the shape and meaning of writing and its relation to individuality. Quoting Nietzsche's pronouncement that 'Our writing tools are also working on our thoughts' (Kittler, 1999: 200), Kittler recounts how handwriting was seen in Goethe's time as a means of self-formation: by cultivating a continuous handwriting style (as opposed to block letters), writers give visual expression to and manifest their individuality. In Kittler's words, 'To develop handwriting formed as out of one mold means to produce individuals' (1990: 84). A century after Goethe's birth, the invention of the typewriter challenged this intimate relationship between writing and individuality. The continuous flow of handwriting and its reference to the identity and singularity of the writer was now replaced with rows of anonymous block letters, rescinding the immediacy of recognizable self-expression on the part of the writer.[5]

Reflecting the era of mass consumption, technologies such as the typewriting machine soon gained immense popularity. Testifying to this success, Kittler (1999: 183–4) reports that in the US, the word 'typewriter' soon acquired a dual meaning, referring both to the machine itself and to female typists – since between 1870 and 1930 the number of women employed as typewriters grew massively and far outstripped the number of men in the occupation. Although Kittler and others may therefore be right that 'the typewriter, the tape machine and the telephone restructured (and regendered) the modern office' (Tickner, 2000:

---

[5] Or partly so, at least. People such as the German philosopher and psychologist Ludwig Klages would retain a belief in the ability to read personality characteristics out of handwriting and develop a whole graphological programme to that end in the early twentieth century (Ash, 2013: 47).

Figure 1.2 The Odell typewriter.
Note: The Odell typewriter, invented in 1887, gained popularity in the late nineteenth century. Perry & Co's Odell Typewriter, 1893. London, History of Advertising Trust.
Source: © 2019. Photo Scala Florence/Heritage Images

190), Kittler arguably ended up exaggerating their socio-cultural implications in his wish to take media technology seriously. Indeed, parts of his analyses have an idiosyncratic twist, such as his penchant for analysing media technologies in a war-inflected jargon.[6] This is not to deny that connections existed between war and technologies such as film and typewriting machines: indeed, there is a rich tradition of establishing such links,[7] and war experiences were clearly crucial to Europeans in the time period from the Franco-Prussian War in 1870 to the First World

---

[6] One illustration of this is his claim that 'the typewriter became a discursive machine-gun. A technology whose basic action not coincidentally consists of strikes and triggers proceeds in automated and discrete steps [contrary, again, to the ideal of continuous handwriting], as does ammunitions transport in a revolver and a machine-gun, or celluloid transport in a film projector' (1999: 191).

[7] For example, as Walter Benjamin famously pointed out, links between aesthetic and technological dimensions and war were prevalent in Filippo Tommaso Marinetti's futuristic movement, which accorded war aesthetic qualities (Benjamin, 2008: 41–2).

War. Rather, my point is that warfare may not permeate these technologies quite as deeply as Kittler suggested, and his attempts to link them together therefore seem forced at times.[8] Yet his analysis does hint that one might find in private space (including office space) an equivalent to the kind of de-individualisation that crowd psychologists associated with crowd behaviour in public space. In other words, despite the many differences in their subject matter, observations of crowd behaviour and typewriting highlighted de-individualisation as a problem of their time.

The invention of film contributed considerably to this shaking up of individuality. Kittler details how the entertainment potential of film was readily recognised when it came into being in the 1890s. Still, film did more than prepare the way for a cinematic experience featuring, and sometimes blending, entertainment and propaganda. According to Kittler, the technology's early stages played a pivotal role in the development of late-nineteenth-century French psychotherapy. Much of the discussion within French psychotherapy at this time concerned the therapeutic potential of hypnosis and suggestion, the latter defined by the Nancy doctor Hippolyte Bernheim as 'an idea conceived by the operator, seized by the subject, and accepted by his [sic] mind' (Bernheim quoted in Chertok and Stengers, 1992: 27). Together with hypnosis, suggestion questioned the idea of the autonomous individual. One of the key characters in this discussion, the neurologist Jean-Martin Charcot, would be among the first to establish a connection between filming and therapeutic practice. Consequently, states Kittler, in 1883 Charcot 'ordered his chief technician [...] to start filming' his treatment of hysterics with serial cameras (1999: 141). These efforts did not amount to filming the patients in any modern sense, but they did document Charcot's work through still images which, when put in sequence, demonstrated the phases patients went through, for better understanding and scrutiny.

Charcot's initial steps would set the direction for a genuine mélange of film and psychotherapy. Kittler (1999: 145) notes that when it became possible decades later to project serial photographs as films, the opportunity was quickly seized by psychiatrists. Hans Hennes, a Bonn-based psychiatrist, celebrated in 1909 the possibility of converting 'a rapid succession of movements into a slow one through cinematographic

---

[8] One characteristic example of his associations running wild is this: 'If the joysticks of Atari video games make children illiterate, President Reagan welcomed them for just that reason: as a training ground for future bomber pilots. Every culture has its zones of preparation that fuse lust and power, optically, acoustically, and so on. Our discos are preparing our youth for a retaliatory strike' (Kittler, 1999: 140).

reproduction', making it 'possible to see things "whose precise observation is, in real life, hardly or not at all possible"' (Hennes quoted in Kittler, 1999: 145). In other words, the medium of film constituted a dramatic experiential innovation through which individuality could be decomposed into a decelerated sequence of events that escape ordinary perception. Lived temporality could thus be studied at different paces, rendering possible the careful inspection of dynamics and experiences that would otherwise go unnoticed. While this bears some resemblance to how typewriting chopped up continuous writing and the subject formation associated with the latter, post-Charcotean psychotherapy triangulated the technological medium, experiential effects and the psychotherapeutic.

Walter Benjamin's classic analysis of the artwork in the age of its technological reproducibility further argued that the reproducibility of film as an artistic medium bid farewell to the aura of preceding art forms such as paintings, an aura procured through their non-reproducible singularity (Benjamin, 2008). According to Benjamin:

> On the one hand, film furthers insight into the necessities governing our lives by its use of close-ups, by its accentuation of hidden details in familiar objects, and by its exploration of commonplace milieux through the ingenious guidance of the camera; on the other hand, it manages to assure us of a vast and unsuspected field of action. [...] It is through the camera that we first discover the optical unconscious, just as we discover the instinctual unconscious through psychoanalysis. (2008: 37)

Yet for Benjamin, the film medium did not merely contribute to effecting a decomposition of subjects and objects, in the sense that these could now be scrutinised in unprecedented ways that might unearth layers of individuality beyond the control of the subject (as psychoanalysis proclaimed). Equally important, Benjamin argued, the technological reproducibility of art that the medium of film supposedly incarnated '*changes the relation of the masses to art*' (2008: 36, original emphasis). In contrast to how, in Zweig's childhood, artworks such as paintings were approached by onlookers individually or in small groups, films (including, of course, entertainment movies) are typically viewed in larger collective cinematic settings. The central corollary of this, Benjamin posited, was that onlookers no longer form individual opinions about the artwork. Rather, 'nowhere more than in the cinema are the reactions of individuals, which together make up the massive reaction of the audience, determined by the imminent concentration of reactions into a mass' (2008: 36). In other words, individual judgment is replaced by mass judgment; verdicts are de-individualised and shaped by collective forces.

Benjamin's essay was written around 1935–6, then existing in two versions (a third version was written between 1936 and 1939). The text thus antedates by more than a decade the American sociologist David Riesman's famous mid-century analysis of other-directed behaviour (Riesman, 1950), an analysis that left a bigger imprint on sociological discussions than Benjamin's account did, although the latter better appreciated the ways in which other-directedness may be spurred by technological innovations. Thus, Benjamin's analysis articulates a broader experience at the end of the nineteenth and early twentieth centuries – the dramatic consequences for conceptions of individuality brought about by technological innovations such as film. In fact, in the era in which the film medium was invented, notions of autonomous individuality came under attack both from beneath and above, as it were. The mergers and homologies between film and psychoanalysis undermined autonomous individuality from beneath in that they pointed to deeper, now suddenly analysable levels of individuality that had previously escaped attention. By contrast, disciplines such as psychotherapy, crowd psychology, sociology and criminology, as well as the types of collectively formed (mass) experiences pointedly identified in Benjamin's film analysis, challenged notions of individual autonomy from above, stressing that individuality was intrinsically tied to supra-individual forces and dynamics. These developments touted the message that individuality is not self-bound in any way but rather enmeshed in otherness.

Although Benjamin's analysis dates to the second half of the 1930s, it captures an important experiential layer from the late nineteenth and early twentieth centuries, as Stefan Andriopoulos's examination of intersections between film and psychotherapy in this era shows (Andriopoulos, 2008). Andriopoulos's analysis echoes aspects of Kittler's examination, albeit with somewhat different emphases. Let me address only two points here which relate to what Andriopoulos characterises as the 'mutually constitutive interrelation that links hypnotism and cinema's emergence and cultural appropriation' (2008: 110). In a discussion of movies such as Robert Wiene's *The Cabinet of Dr. Caligari* (1919–20) and Fritz Lang's *Dr. Mabuse, the Gambler* (1922), Andriopoulos details how late-nineteenth-century discussions of hypnosis and suggestion became important cinematic themes in the early twentieth century. The plots of these movies were deeply inspired by scholarly discussions about the seemingly overwhelming capacities of hypnosis – including the inciting question of whether it is possible to hypnotise someone to commit crimes without his or her consent and conscious knowledge (a question that received considerable attention in criminological and psychotherapeutic circles in the 1890s). But more than that, the *reception* of such movies

Figure 1.3 Somnambulist in action.
Note: Scene from *The Cabinet of Dr. Caligari*, 1920. German Expressionist silent film with a story of murder and intrigue. Director: Robert Wiene. Still showing Cesare the somnambulist (Conrad Veidt) making off with Jane (Lil Dagover).
Source: Artist: Robert Wiene. London: Ann Ronan Picture Library. © 2019. Photo Ann Ronan/Heritage Images/Scala, Florence

also evoked tropes from academic debates on hypnotic suggestion: observers claimed that the film medium was endowed with hypnotic powers.

This latter possibility might be said to underlie Benjamin's assertion that film changes the audience's reaction, rendering each individual's response a function of the collective sentiment. While such a collective response might also be said to pertain to older art forms such as theatre plays, early twentieth-century observers asserted that films hold considerably stronger suggestive powers, so much so that they were attributed the ability of 'addressing and interpellating the human mind' in an immediate fashion (Andriopoulos, 2008: 119). In other words, film was accorded the ability to accelerate de-individualising hypnotism, a

Figure 1.4 Charcot practising hypnotic suggestion.
Note: Jean Martin Charcot demonstrating hypnosis, 1879.
Source: Oxford, Science Archive. © 2019. Photo Scala Florence/Heritage Images

perspective widely accepted in the early twentieth century. For example, Michael Tratner reports that the Hollywood film industry formulated a Movie Production Code in 1930, the so-called Hays Code, which advised that care should be taken in regards to the effects films might have on audiences. As the Code states, the problem was that 'Psychologically, the larger the audience the lower the moral mass resistance to suggestion' (cited from Tratner, 2008: 15).[9] But in fact, this imminent potential (or threat) had been recognised much earlier. Andriopoulos relates that 'Before 1918, during the Wilhelmine Empire, the anxiety about this affinity between cinema and hypnotism had even led to repeated censorship of films showing, or inducing, hypnosis' (2008: 121; see also Benjamin, 2008: 37–8).

---

[9] This perspective even made it to the political domain. A notorious example from the German context is the way in which it surfaced in Hitler's *Mein Kampf*, which argued that bringing people together in mass settings is crucial for propaganda to be effective. While resistance to propaganda might otherwise be too strong, Hitler claimed that the mass setting ensures that the individual will '[succumb] to the magic influence of what we might designate as "mass suggestion"' (Hitler, 1992: 435). I discuss this further in Borch (2013).

The second important point from Andriopoulos's analysis addresses the flip side of the 'mutually constitutive interrelation' between cinema and hypnotism: the ways in which cinematic conceptions inflected discussions of hypnotism. Parallel to Charcot's experimentations with serial cameras in the early 1880s, Bernheim, his chief rival in French psychotherapeutic discussions on the role of hypnotic suggestion, almost simultaneously 'experimented with the hypnotic production of visual, film-like hallucinations' (Andriopoulos, 2008: 113). Andriopoulos goes so far as to suggest that in 1886 Bernheim 'offered a film theory *avant la lettre*', as evinced by his use of 'the curious notion of a "nervous light", in order to elucidate the mental processes of suggestion' – one which, according to Andriopoulos, 'seems derived from the cultural knowledge about the projection of images that nine years later allowed the brothers Lumière to present the cinematograph to an astounded audience' (2008: 111, original emphasis). Andriopoulos's analysis thus suggests film and psychotherapy are even more closely entangled than Kittler argues they are, and that the ways in which each reinforces the other did much to reshuffle conceptions of individuality in the late nineteenth and early twentieth centuries.

I recognise that this summary account of political, scholarly and technological landslides has only provided selected historical snapshots and that many more elements can be added to this list. For example, I have paid little attention to the rise of modernist art and how modernism can be seen as 'a heterogeneous response to a shared experience of seismic upheaval' in the modern order of the late nineteenth and early twentieth centuries (Tickner, 2000: 184). While further historical illustrations of the sense of transformation permeating this era follow in Chapters 4 and 5, I stress that my core concern here has not been to offer a systematic historical treatment of late-nineteenth-century developments. More modestly, I aimed to contour the ways in which a range of profound changes took place in the late nineteenth and early twentieth centuries, causing a widespread sense of seemingly stable patterns to give way, with established conceptions and experiential modalities being replaced by a sense of collectively induced de-individualisation. This all added up to a particular modern experience – that is, the experience of a particular phase and situation in modern society. I now delve further into a range of scholarly responses to this modern experience, examining theoretically informed attempts to understand how individuality and collectivity were changing and entering new configurations at the end of the nineteenth century. My subsequent analysis of contributions to crowd psychology, psychotherapy, sociology and other fields is based on the central assertion that the theorists singled out here were all committed to understanding this modern experience and its implications.

Before getting to that, however, it is useful to note that this account of ways in which late-nineteenth-century developments in politics, academia and technology produced a notion and experience of de-individualisation is at odds with how classical sociological findings are often portrayed. For example, in his historical-semantic analysis of individuality, Luhmann (1989: 150) highlights Durkheim's plus-sum conception of collectivity and individuality as examined in *The Division of Labour in Society*: more collectivity does not lead to a decrease but rather an increase in individuality (Durkheim, 2013: 313–16). A similar point is made in Luhmann's own analysis of modern individuality, which takes as its point of departure not a division-of-labour perspective but a functional differentiation (on this difference, see Luhmann, 1982). According to Luhmann, modern society is characterised by its differentiation into a range of operationally autonomous function systems (law, politics, science, economy, religion, etc.). An important corollary of this is that individuals are only partially connected to, or included in, each function system. No individual is solely and fully part of, say, the political system or the scientific system; most people are included in many systems at different occasions. This stands in contrast to pre-modern societies in which no strong differentiation exists, meaning that individuals tend to belong to one undifferentiated system. Importantly, Luhmann (1989: 158–60) argues, the merely partial inclusion in function systems is precisely what guarantees modern individuality: a high degree of functional differentiation permits individuals to define their individuality *independently* of particular systems or, put differently, in those gaps that existing systems do not cover. Again, the discourse on and experience of collectively induced de-individualisation is a counter-narrative to such accounts. Rather than seeing modern society as increasing individuality, I suggest that the experiential layer of late-nineteenth and early-twentieth-century developments placed severe pressure on individuality. This became especially clear in contemporaneous discussions of crowds.

Crowds Everywhere: Capturing the Experience of De-Individualisation

The late-nineteenth-century processes of urbanisation, industrialisation, technologisation and political unrest appeared to coalesce in the *crowd*, which foregrounded in an embodied fashion the sentiment that modern society was on the brink of something radically new. A wide range of observers concurred in describing how crowds of people swarmed urban streets, seemingly attracted to cities by the gravitational pull of industrialisation and urbanisation. While the emergence of urban crowds owed much to the technological advances that went hand in hand with industrialisation, the crowd itself did not epitomise new technological developments. In fact, the crowds of people inhabiting urban spaces in the late nineteenth and early twentieth centuries were often anything but technologically sophisticated. The journalist Jacob A. Riis's visual portrayal of the 'other half' living in misery in New York City forcefully makes this point (Buk-Swienty, 2008). While Riis's efforts were mainly focused on documenting urban poverty, others were more concerned with the phenomenon of urban amassing as well as its broader social, cultural and political consequences, which were often pictured as negative. In particular, the Spanish philosopher José Ortega y Gasset saw a direct connection between the upsurge of physical crowds, on the one hand, and social and cultural decline, on the other.[10] In his 1929 essay *The Revolt of the Masses*, Ortega argues that the experience of crowds of people was inescapable to any urban dweller:

> Towns are full of people, houses full of tenants, hotels full of guests, trains full of travellers, cafés full of customers, parks full of promenaders, consulting-rooms of famous doctors full of patients, theatres full of spectators, and beaches full of bathers. What previously was, in general, no problem, now begins to be an everyday one, namely, to find room. (1960: 11–12)

The claustrophobic image of the city as a veritable tsunami of people who render available space an increasingly scarce resource reflected, in Ortega's point of view, a recent development only a few decades old. But this transformation was not merely one of quantity. Ortega admits that in the early twentieth century, the number of urban inhabitants was not significantly different from in the late 1920s, when he wrote his essay. What had changed was that human agglomeration, as per Riis's documentation, was collapsing into a zone of indistinction, where it had once neatly separated society into mass venues (of poverty) and places reserved for the upper tiers. The human flood into the city had broken the dikes that formerly upheld the social order:

> The multitude has suddenly become visible, installing itself in the preferential positions in society. Before, if it existed, it passed unnoticed, occupying the background of the social stage; now it has advanced to the footlights and it's the principal character. There are no longer protagonists; there is only the chorus. (1960: 13)

Ortega's observations cannot simply be dismissed as the pampered remarks of a well-established citizen who, never having had to consider

---

[10] I discuss Ortega's work and its relation to other contemporaneous thinking in Borch (2012b: 166–70).

the lives of the excluded masses, now confronted them with an ill-concealed sense of annoyance and regret. Such an interpretation ignores the more important aspect of his analysis: a widespread impression and experience, concordant with observers in the late nineteenth century, that the *quantitative* influx of people, the massification of cities and society, had *qualitative* repercussions in that it changed individuals' relation to themselves as well as to culture and society more broadly. Indeed, the direst parts of Ortega's diagnosis concern what he saw as a veritable cultural degradation, embodied in the rise of a new subject: the mass person. Whereas Western societies had previously cultivated a specific subject, the select person who strove for goals and values beyond him- or herself (truth, morality, etc.), a new character type crystallised with the advent of mass individuals: people 'who demand nothing special of themselves, but for whom to live is to be every moment what they already are, without imposing on themselves any effort towards perfection; mere buoys that float on the waves' (1960: 15). For Ortega, though the mediocrity this entailed was vulgar, it also was politically suspect, as he believed mass individuals possess an ingrained preference for illiberal forms of politics such as fascism and syndicalism. According to his analysis, these political forms depart from deliberative democracy based on discussion, reason and arguments, a concept later championed by Jürgen Habermas:

the mass-man [*sic*] would feel himself lost if he accepted discussion, and instinctively repudiates the obligation of accepting that supreme authority lying outside himself. Hence the 'new thing' in Europe is 'to have done with discussions,' and detestation is expressed for all forms of intercommunion which imply acceptance of objective standards, ranging from conversation to parliament, and taking in science. (1960: 74)

A politics of violence took hold in their stead, one which, Ortega warned, returned the political to the 'fauna of a past age' (1960: 92). This observation of a purported retrogression of politics was widely echoed by other observers of crowd and mass behaviour at the time.

Similarly, Ortega's linking of the visual experience of crowds to a new type of mass subject was undergirded by a claim that found widespread resonance in the late nineteenth and early twentieth centuries: these phenomena were intimately tied to more profound transformations of society throughout the nineteenth century, such as those analysed earlier in this chapter. In a Marxist parlance, albeit one not espoused by Ortega himself, it might be said that what Ortega diagnosed in terms of new character types and their corresponding forms of political action was but the superstructure that attended more material developments. In particular, he argued, the rise of liberal democracy, the advances of science and rapidly spreading industrialisation all contributed to the betterment of the life conditions of people, but this was, paradoxically, precisely what effected the change in character type from select individuals to mass individuals (1960: e.g. 107–14). In other words, all the industrious activity – all the cultural and technological developments analysed earlier – essentially ended up producing passive subjects. Ortega's diagnosis therefore entailed that modern society was digging its own grave: its many advances produced the conditions of its own collapse. Modernity was giving rise to a mass situation that was for all practical purposes pre-modern (1960: 125).

Much of Ortega's diagnosis echoes ideas that Le Bon expressed some 30 years earlier, though from a different theoretical perspective. Whereas Ortega based his analysis on demographic changes and on his immediate visual experiences with crammed city life, the Frenchman took inspiration from explanatory models derived from psychotherapy. Indeed, it was Le Bon's central objective to develop a genuine psychology of crowds tasked with conceptualising the modern mass era. The fruits of his labours were pulled together in *The Crowd*, published the same year Roentgen discovered how X-rays can penetrate singular bodies. Like Roentgen, Le Bon sought to account for a new type of perception. In contrast, however, Le Bon's analysis was wedded to a collective level: he argued for conceiving of 'the crowd as a particular modality of perception, as a specific social arrangement that conditions the limits of perceptual experience' (Crary, 1999: 245). Further, in contrast to Ortega's work, the psychological anchoring of Le Bon's work renders the spatial dimension of agglomeration less important. According to Le Bon, crowds are defined by neither numbers nor spatial proximity. What matters instead is the mental transformation they enact by annulling any differentiation between individuals: while individuals usually can be considered self-contained and, in most instances, law-abiding and sensible, they undergo a transition once they become part of a crowd, with all their individual differences collapsing into one homogeneous entity characterised by '*mental unity*' (Le Bon, 2002: 2, original emphasis). Since ever more life spheres were allegedly being subjected to crowd rule in modern society, Le Bon argued that autonomous self-contained individuality was becoming increasingly rare.

Accordingly, Le Bon's ruminations in effect reduce the liberal self to a mere romantic fiction, a patinated vocabulary belonging to a superseded social order. Once the lens zeroes in on the emergence and societal importance of crowds in the late-nineteenth-century configuration of modernity, the individual subject can no longer serve as an analytical starting point. Instead, Le Bon's analysis suggested that intellectual efforts should be invested in understanding how and why the crowd vortex was able to eliminate individuality and carry individuals away in aggregate flux in ever more realms of life. 'The substitution of the unconscious action of crowds for the conscious activity of individuals is one of the principal characteristics of the present age', he states (2002: iii), identifying it as the central phenomenon in need of explanation. Consequently, the problem for Le Bon was not just one of a mere change in individuality or character type, such as Ortega would later bemoan. What was at stake was the loss of individuality altogether. On an even graver note, and extending beyond the problem of the crumbling liberal self, Le Bon touted the message that the wider institutional foundations of society were equally being demolished by the runaway train of 'the power of crowds':

On the ruins of so many ideas formerly considered beyond discussion, and to-day decayed or decaying, of so many sources of authority that successive revolutions have destroyed, this power [of crowds], which alone has arisen in their stead, seems soon destined to absorb the others. While all our ancient beliefs are tottering and disappearing, while the old pillars of society are giving way one by one, the power of the crowd is the only force that nothing menaces, and of which the prestige is continually on the increase. The age we are about to enter will in truth be the ERA OF CROWDS. (2002: x, original emphasis)

Le Bon's analysis is rich in descriptions of how this era of crowds allegedly undermined the civilisational advances of modern society and replaced them with barbarianism, '[i]ntolerance and fanaticism', 'stupidity', 'irritability', 'impulsiveness', lack of responsibility, as well as the 'atavistic residuum' of primitives (2002: xiii, 6, 13, 22, 39). The list of undesirable features Le Bon attributed to crowds went on. Several of its entries were later reemphasised by Ortega, who similarly associated the modern age of crowds and masses with societal regression. Akin to Ortega's argument, moreover, a central point of Le Bon's analysis was that the focus on crowds and their dynamics served as a fractal manifestation of a broader diagnosis and experience of modern society. By asserting that crowds assumed an increasingly hegemonic position in modern society, Le Bon argued that its characteristic features were also becoming societally dominant. The plasticity and fickleness he attributed to crowds could be, in his view, ascribed to society more generally. As a result, the catapulting of crowds into a prevailing societal role appeared to transform society into a shabby laboratory filled with unstable explosives. In Spengler's later, no less dramatic, phrasing, 'The mass is the end, the radical nullity' (1980b: 358).

Le Bon's analysis certainly does not reflect Marxist ideas. Indeed, as I noted earlier, Le Bon often treated crowds synonymously with

Figure 1.5 The era of crowds.
Note: In Spain, Riots break out in Barcelona, 1901.
Source: Illustration published in *Le Petit Journal* 26 May 1901. © 2019. Photo Art Media/Heritage Images/Scala, Florence

socialism: they represented the same evil to him (1974; 2001). Yet his writings suggest that Marx and Engels's famous proverb only needed updating for the new mass era: *All that is solid is crushed by the crowd*! This was the modern experience Le Bon tried to capture. However, his attempt to understand this experience *psychologically* was a far cry from perspectives in a Marxist register. Instead, it was heavily indebted to contemporaneous developments in French psychotherapy. Like most other crowd psychologists at the end of the nineteenth century, Le Bon was particularly preoccupied with debates about the role and analytical potential of *hypnotic suggestion*, debates which crystallised in the so-called Nancy–Salpêtrière controversy. At the Salpêtrière Hospital in Paris, Charcot had since the 1870s grown increasingly interested in hysteria; he later discovered hypnotic suggestion as a means with which to treat hysterics. Charcot defended a constricted notion of hypnotic suggestion in that he argued that only hysterics are susceptible to this form of treatment. In contrast, Bernheim, who practiced in Nancy, was convinced that no such restrictions apply: no one group of people is solely susceptible to suggestion, and every person is suggestible, albeit with different propensities.[11]

The Nancy (Bernheimian) position gradually became the hegemonic interpretation in French psychotherapy at the end of the nineteenth century. But more than that, as I touched upon earlier, its prominence extended far beyond specialist clinical circles. By conceiving of *all* individuals as potentially susceptible to hypnotic suggestion, Bernheim triggered a minor revolution in the humanities and social sciences at the time. His refutation of Charcot's bounded notion of suggestion elevated hypnotic suggestion to the level of a general concept for analysing individuals and their interrelations in all kinds of settings. The analytical potential of this move was immediately recognised and highly consequential. As the medical historian Henri Ellenberger observes in *The Discovery of the Unconscious*, 'We can hardly realize today to what extent hypnotism and suggestion were invoked in the 1880's to explain countless historical, anthropological, and sociological facts such as the

---

[11] The interest in suggestible phenomena in fact predates both Bernheim's and Charcot's work. The mesmeric movement of the late eighteenth century was one crucial forerunner to the debates on hypnotic suggestion that would play out a century later (for discussions of mesmerism, including its links to late-nineteenth-century discussions, see Borch, 2019; Chertok and Stengers, 1992; Darnton, 1968; Ellenberger, 1970). It is also worth noting that the differences between Charcot and Bernheim were many. For example, Charcot affirmed a more physiological approach, whereas Bernheim espoused a stricter psychological one. For discussions of the polemic between the schools they each headed, see Harrington (1987: ch. 6) and van Ginneken (1992: ch. 4).

Figure 1.6 Charcot in action.
Note: Jean Martin Charcot, French neurologist and pathologist, 1887.
Source: Oxford, Science Archive. © 2019. Photo Scala Florence/Heritage Images

genesis of religions, miracles, and wars' (1970: 164–5). Indeed, once unleashed as a general conceptual apparatus (not necessarily related to hysterics), hypnotic suggestion became widely and rapidly appropriated in sociological and other analyses, with Le Bon's analysis just one drop in a larger sea. This also applied to investigations that zeroed in on human–object encounters over those between humans. For example, in his 1889 essay *Time and Free Will*, the French philosopher Henri Bergson repeatedly and explicitly likens the experience of art to hypnosis, arguing among other things that

the object of art is to put to sleep the active or rather resistant powers of our personality, and thus to bring us into a state of perfect responsiveness, in which we realize the idea that is suggested to us and sympathize with the feeling that is expressed. (2001: 14; see also Crary, 1999: 239–40)

As the earlier discussion of the interrelations between hypnotic suggestion and cinema makes clear, Ellenberger might in fact understate the prominence hypnosis and suggestion enjoyed: their conceptual repertoire had an immense impact on both popular culture and scholarly debates in psychology, psychoanalysis, sociology and other fields *well into the twentieth century.* Indeed, it is possible to identify a host of attempts to deploy this vocabulary for practical purposes during that century. For example, Andriopoulos (2008: 92) mentions that the American psychologist Walter Dill Scott subscribed to notions of hypnosis and suggestion in the latter's 1908 book *The Psychology of Advertising.* In fact, Scott devoted an entire chapter of this book to suggestion, rehearsing a number of ideas from late-nineteenth-century suggestion and crowd theory, on the basis of which he developed recommendations for supposedly successful advertising techniques (Scott, 1908: 80–92). Similarly, as I return to in Chapter 5, theories of crowd suggestion featured strongly in financial investment advice literature, including contrarian speculation theory (see, e.g. Hansen, 2017; Stäheli, 2006).

Bernheimian hypnotic suggestion seemingly entailed a highly plastic conception of the self.[12] This was particularly evident in Bernheim's reflections on his clinical treatment of patients, in which he argued that the *suggestionné* (the patient) was turned into an 'automatism' in the hands of the *suggestionneur* (the doctor/hypnotiser):

> The human organism [the *suggestionné*] has become almost a machine, obedient to the operator's will. I say 'Rise,' and he rises. One subject gets up very quickly, another obeys slowly, the machine is lazy, the command must be repeated in an authoritative voice. [...] General sensibility and the special senses may be modified, increased, diminished, or perverted at will. (Bernheim, 1889: 29)

Hypnotic suggestion applied as a general analytical framework beyond the clinic thus formed the grounds for a conception of the mouldable subject-automaton. In other words, suggestion theory radically discarded the liberal, self-constituting individual for one that was malleable and profoundly relationally constituted in its relationship to the *suggestionneur.*[13]

It is reasonable to speculate that the widespread adoption of the suggestion framework across the scholarly landscape in the late nineteenth and early twentieth centuries was due to its capturing a pervasive

---

[12] 'Seemingly' because, as I return to below, Bernheim's analysis was in fact rather more nuanced, or ambivalent, than is often recognised.

[13] A crude hypnotist position, in which the *suggestionné* is reduced to an entirely mouldable entity, could rather easily morph into a behaviourist account of the individual as responding completely to externally given stimuli. This was realised by the Russian neurologist and psychologist Vladimir Bekhterev (a rival of the more famous Ivan Pavlov), who developed a comprehensive collective reflexology tasked with analysing collective phenomena on the basis of reflexes (Bekhterev, 2001). For a discussion of Bekhterev's work and its connection to crowd theory, see Borch (2012b: 84–5). It will become clear later on when I focus on Tarde that he avoided this behaviourist slide, retaining a notion of a distinctive self that could, more or less successfully, resist external suggestion.

modernist experience of the plasticity of individuality (or its showing higher degrees of plasticity than the concept of a liberal self accepted). In addition, it represented the constant flux of people's ideas, beliefs, and so on – more precisely, that they were externally induced to the extent that what one person believed were his or her singular thoughts was in fact merely inherited, through suggestion, from the outside. It was only a short step from this observation to the argument that the tumultuous features of modern society – industrialisation, urbanisation, technological advances, etc. – created the optimal conditions for such suggestive forces to flourish and further destabilise individuality, thereby also bringing down the pillars of society. A vicious circle emerged out of this: while suggestion itself might be a general phenomenon, its societal significance was buttressed by the instability of the late-nineteenth-century social order, an instability itself propelled by suggestible crowds. For this reason, a connection surfaced between the various strands of literature devoted to hypnotic suggestion. While the central hunch of the Nancy doctors was that individuals can be transformed into automatons and that the notion of the autonomous self is highly empirically questionable as a result, Le Bon was concerned with the overall transformations of society as effected by crowds and their suggestive power. Put differently, what Le Bon analysed in society at the macro scale had intimate ties to what Bernheim and his colleagues identified at a micro level in the clinic.

How, specifically, did Le Bon draw on Bernheim's work? Two interrelated influences can be detected. The first relates to the main explanation Le Bon offered of crowd behaviour, in which he referred approvingly to 'recent physiological discoveries':

We know to-day that by various processes an individual may be brought into such a condition that, having entirely lost his [*sic*] conscious personality, he obeys all the suggestions of the operator who has deprived him of it, and commits acts in utter contradiction with his character and habits. The most careful observations seem to prove that an individual immerged for some length of time in a crowd in action soon finds himself – either in consequence of the magnetic influence given out by the crowd, or from some other cause of which we are ignorant – in a special state, which much resembles the state of fascination in which the hypnotised individual finds himself in the hands of the hypnotiser. (2002: 7)

Although this echoed Tarde's general idea of somnambulist individuals (see Chapter 2), this hypnotist explanation of crowd behaviour attracted piles of critical commentary in subsequent twentieth-century literature from sociologists, psychologists, historians and social psychologists alike (Borch, 2012b). Granted, what Le Bon provided here is all conceived in a vague language (of 'various processes', 'resembles', etc.). Nonetheless he championed the relation between hypnotiser and hypnotised found in Bernheim's Nancy clinic as a relevant template for understanding why individuals undergo profound de-individualisation once they become part of a crowd: they simply transform into malleable entities that do whatever the hypnotiser – in Le Bon's framework, the leader – demands. Echoing Bernheim's account, Le Bon asserted that the crowd member is in effect 'no longer himself [*sic*], but has become an automaton who has ceased to be guided by his will' (2002: 8).

The second main influence from Bernheim is implicit in the first. The notion of hypnotic suggestion to which Le Bon subscribed followed the Nancy School of interpretation, according to which all individuals are susceptible to suggestion, although to varying degrees (the machine can be lazy at times, as Bernheim noted). It was this interpretation that allowed Le Bon to portray crowd behaviour as a truly dangerous feature of modern society: anyone could be caught in crowd hypnosis – even the upper tiers of society, its otherwise unwavering mainstays. No escape seemed possible, and 'The individualities in the crowd who might possess a personality sufficiently strong to resist the suggestion are too few in number to struggle against the current' (2002: 8).

Against the backdrop of such *fin-de-siècle* crowd ideas, one might find appealing McPhail's argument that scholars from this tradition subscribed to a transformation hypothesis. In trying to capture a modern experience of crowding and massification, these scholars turned to ideas predicated on a notion of individuals undergoing a profound transformation once they became part of a crowd (Le Bon) or when massification took societal hold (Ortega). Two distinctly different situations inform this conception: with no crowding or massification, the liberal self is retained since individual autonomy is unaffected by outside influence; alternatively, crowding and massification dominate, creating a fully dissolved individuality. Especially in Le Bon's case, this *transformation* of the individual, the taking of the liberal self to pieces, is due to the broader materialisation of the suggestive processes described by Bernheim. Although this might all seem to validate McPhail's observation that the transformation hypothesis was central to early crowd theory, I argue that interpreting turn-of-the-nineteenth-century theories of crowd and collective behaviour as advancing a transformation hypothesis does not do them justice. Much more was at stake in this theoretical landscape than the transformation hypothesis alone can acknowledge. I thus suggest that the more interesting and important issue these crowd scholars grappled with was how to conceive of the individual in ways that allowed for both (anti-mimetic) volition and (mimetic-hypnotic) submission. In other words, these scholars tried to square de-individualising dynamics with some form of an autonomous self.

Individuality as a Matter of Mimetic and Anti-Mimetic Inter-Relations

As we have seen, Le Bon portrayed the individual as if there were a fundamental gulf between people left to themselves and those enmeshed in a crowd or collective formation. Allegedly, the former has the capacity to make independent, rational decisions, while the latter is bereft of this ability and at the mercy of collective impulses emanating from the crowd and its leader. Undergirding this image is a strong separation between mimesis and anti-mimesis, with the crowd as the force that transforms the anti-mimetic individual into a mimetic creature. This notion is indebted to Bernheim's interpretation of suggestion and how the physician (crowd leader) can turn patients (crowd members) into automatons. However, a closer inspection of Bernheim's work renders the neat division between mimesis and anti-mimesis rather less clear-cut. Mikkel Borch-Jacobsen, an expert on the history of hypnosis, captures this in an important intervention entitled 'The Bernheim effect' (2009), in which he upends widely held views on the Nancy–Salpêtrière controversy. Borch-Jacobsen's discussion revolves around what he characterises as

the paradox of suggestion: how can you induce someone to become passive (suggestible) if this passivity requires his [*sic*] prior acceptance? If he accepts, it is because he was already willing. But if he was willing, can we say that he passively executed a suggestion? (2009: 109; see also Chertok and Stengers, 1992: 37)

This problem can be further specified: there is in fact no problem at all if the subject (the *suggestionné*) is '*already* regressed, *already* plunged into some hypnoid state', since in this case the subject's consciousness will not work to inhibit the suggestions of the *suggestionneur* (2009: 111, original emphasis). Yet the problem or paradox remains very real 'if the subject is awake, lucid, in full possession of her [*sic*] faculties of inhibition […] How is it possible to suggest to this person … not to resist suggestion?' (2009: 111).

Borch-Jacobsen notes that Bernheim did not always seem to be aware that suggestion entails this paradox. The latter often 'invoke[d] the operator's suggestion to explain the patient's suggestibility' (Borch-Jacobsen, 2009: 111), which wound up in a circular argumentative structure: suggestibility is provoked by hypnosis, which is itself activated by suggestion (see e.g. Bernheim, 1889: 15). This circularity fuelled a series of critiques against Bernheim's project voiced by, among others, psychologists such as Alfred Binet, Pierre Janet and later, Sigmund Freud. Freud's 1921 essay *Mass Psychology and the Analysis of the 'I'* marshals this critique – also quoted by Borch-Jacobsen – as an explicit rejoinder to Bernheim. Freud's critique had several dimensions: for one, he criticised what he saw as Bernheim's inability to fully account for how suggestion actually worked, effectively treating it as some 'magic word': 'My resistance subsequently took the form of a rebellion against allowing suggestion, which explained everything, to evade explanation itself' (Freud, 2004: 40).[14] In addition, Freud recalled how he had seen Bernheim in action at the height of the latter's career, an experience he regarded with mixed feelings: Bernheim's 'astonishing skills I witnessed personally in 1889. However, I remember a vague hostility to this tyranny of suggestion even then. If a patient who was not proving submissive was told forcefully: But what are you doing? *Vous vous contresuggestionnez!* I said to myself that this was a clear case of injustice and an act of violence' (Freud, 2004: 40, original emphasis). In response to this, Freud published *Mass Psychology and the Analysis of the 'I'* as an attempt to rethink crowd theory by replacing the tyranny he associated with suggestion with a more positive terminology – in Freud's case, the notion of libido.[15]

Pulling the rug from under Freud's critique of suggestion being a magic word, Borch-Jacobsen points to a crucial dimension of Bernheim's conception that has escaped attention and which dissolves (or displaces, perhaps) the paradox of suggestion. Thus, Borch-Jacobsen argues, Bernheim's writings testify to an understanding of suggestion that runs counter to the notion sketched above. Bernheim realised that suggestion does not simply play out between an active *suggestionneur* and a passive *suggestionné*. Rather than follow this top-down model, which – per Freud – can be understood as a manifestation of tyranny and power, Bernheim attributed a key role to the *suggestionné*'s active and voluntary contribution to the suggestion. Borch-Jacobsen summarises:

So it is not *le suggestionneur* who provokes the receptivity to suggestions; it is the *suggestionné* himself [*sic*] who disinhibits himself, who lets himself go, who makes himself passive. [...] Just as Zeno's reasoning will never prevent Achilles from

---

[14] Freud's remark about suggestion explaining everything refers to Bernheim's assertion that 'everything is in suggestion' (Bernheim quoted in Borch-Jacobsen, 2009: 111).

[15] In spite of its intentions to turn away from such a register of tyranny and violence, Freud's own mass psychology was imbued with no fewer repressive features in its account of the violent primal father. For a discussion of Freud's mass psychology in relation to alternative accounts, see Borch (2012b: 103–8) and McClelland (1989: ch. 8).

catching the tortoise, so Binet's, Janet's, and Freud's arguments will never prevent the subject from allowing himself to be 'suggestioned' *if he is willing*. The mystery of hypnotic induction disappears as soon as one understands that suggestibility is not an automatism and that submission to suggestion is in fact a very voluntary servitude, revokable at any moment. In the end, there is no hypnosis, only a self-hypnosis, or a consent to hypnosis. (2009: 112, original emphasis)

What are the implications of this position, which emphasises instead the active part played in suggestion by the *suggestionné*? For one, it completely reshuffles the relation between power and suggestion – suggestion is not a question of the *suggestionneur* holding almost unlimited power over the *suggestionné*. Instead Bernheim presented a model expressing what would later become Michel Foucault's dictum: 'Power is exercised only over free subjects, and only insofar as they are free' (Foucault, 1982: 221). The power manifested by suggestion is entirely dependent on the *suggestionné*'s free submission to and partaking of it. This might read as a micro-level anticipation of the Austrian psychoanalyst Wilhelm Reich's famous attempts to understand – through a mélange of Freudian and Marxist theorisation – how, under fascism, '*the masses of people themselves assented to their own subjugation and actively brought it about*' (Reich, 1971: 209, original emphasis; see also 1975). However, Bernheim's conception suggested a somewhat different model that effectively undoes the notion of hypnosis (as well as those of the 'unconscious' or 'subconscious') intimated in the quotation above. Supported by the Belgian physician Joseph Delbœuf, his colleague, Bernheim clearly identified a relation between the *suggestionneur* and the *suggestionné* but one not of a hypnotic nature. Instead, this relation is better theorised as a 'state of suggestion', in which the *suggestionné* actively partakes in the suggestion by willingly conforming to 'the suggestion out of complaisance' (Borch-Jacobsen, 2009: 115). In the words of Delbœuf, 'The somnambulists are excellent actors, and they quickly enter into the spirit of their role. Nevertheless, even in this regard, a certain education seems indispensable to me. It is sometimes necessary to guide them, to train them' (cited from Borch-Jacobsen, 2009: 115). Returning to the dissolution of the paradox of suggestion, the *suggestionné* need not be a passive subject who blindly and hypnotically follows the suggestions of the *suggestionneur*; on the contrary, *suggestionnés* are active subjects who willingly adopt what they believe the *suggestionneur* wants them to do or think. Borch-Jacobsen likens this to the later notion of the 'experimenter expectancy effect', which describes situations in which the experimental subject responds and 'conform[s] to the expectations unintentionally communicated by the experimenter' (2009: 119).

For present purposes, the more significant point is that viewing the willpower of the *suggestionné* as pivotal dealt a considerable blow to Le Bon's damning critique of crowds as motors of mimetic de-individualisation: it suggested that crowd members might actually openly enter their mimetic de-individualising state. If this were indeed the case, the basis for Le Bon's denigration of crowds would crumble, and it would seem fair to ask why crowds should be seen as morally and politically suspect if in fact their members' de-individualisation is just as much a result of the latter's positive decision to let go of their subjectivity.

It is important to note that while Le Bon's conception of crowds might end up shaken by Bernheim's proposal, the latter should not be read as vindicating Berk's analysis, *contra* Le Bon, with its strong emphasis on an independent, anti-mimetic individual. After all, while volition might initially be at play in hypnotic suggestion, suggestion itself operates in a mimetic register. Rather than placing Bernheim's proposition in either the mimetic or anti-mimetic camp, it is more correct to say that it presents an early attempt to account for the tensions and oscillations between the two. On the one hand, it suggests that individuality is stretched out between mimesis and anti-mimesis. Similar to how Crary portrays late-nineteenth-century discussions of attention as torn between the ability of subjects to focus attention individually and their attention's susceptibility to being moulded from the outside, so the individual, in the Bernheimean template, can oscillate between a mimetic and an anti-mimetic position. At times it might operate in a mimetic fashion, at other times anti-mimetically, and often it is likely located on a continuum between the two poles. On the other hand, and arguably more provocative, Bernheim's analysis suggests that the anti-mimetically placed individual may well desire to be carried away by de-individualising mimesis. It goes without saying that this option, the deliberate letting go of individuality, is entirely incomprehensible from Berk's rationalist-individualist point of view – indeed, an outright scandal from the liberal stance undergirding Berk's analysis. Bernheim's work opened precisely that analytical option.

★★★

I have deliberately pooled together an array of historical developments from France, Germany, and Austro-Hungary, glossing over the varying local backgrounds against which these transformations took place. While this runs the risk of paying too little attention to the role of local context, my aim has not been to provide a comprehensive chronological account of a string of historical details. Instead of prioritising such granularity,

I have demonstrated that considerable changes took place in the overall European social and conceptual landscape within the time span of only a few decades. Indeed, I have argued that the late nineteenth and early twentieth centuries were a hotbed of a wide range of significant changes in social life (including inventions in science, culture, and technology as well as factors such as industrialisation and urbanisation), transformations that resulted in an experiential landslide that dramatically shook familiar modes of life and perception. Despite any forces of inertia in the broader politico-economic energies identified in this time period, per Mayer, these changes were so profound that when observers reflected retrospectively upon them in the 1930s, they could hardly recognise the social order that was left behind. My central argument is that this sense of change, this sweeping away of established life forms and their corresponding experiential qualities, should not be underestimated. Quite the opposite, it is a kind of modernist experience which is important to retain, and not merely to evade a forgetfulness of the past or, relatedly, to avoid a presentism which claims that our current, twenty-first-century age is uniquely fluid and accelerated. Most crucial, keeping this historical situation in mind helps elucidate why particular notions of individuality and collectivity emerged at this point in time. As evidence of this, Nidesh Lawtoo convincingly argues that a broad range of *fin-de-siècle* observers agree that modern developments put the subject in an entirely new situation, in which its autonomy was profoundly challenged by external forces even to the extent 'that the experience of mimesis, in its polymorphous manifestations, informs the subject from the very beginning' (2013: 18). Or, as Stefan Jonsson puts it, the ideas that emerged in this time period in response to real-life experiences suggested 'a vanishing of the subject' (2013: 143).

What I have tried to demonstrate is essentially that events of historic magnitude prompted a resultant landslide in conceptions of collectivity and individuality: in these analyses of (de-individualised) subjectivity occurring in tandem with the modern experience of rapid instability, the individual was seen as increasingly subdued by external collective dynamics, in whole or in part. I suggest that Bernheim not only articulated an early account of this conception of individuality but also added important nuance to it through his analysis of suggestion, which proposed that the individual may show *both* mimetic *and* anti-mimetic dimensions. That said, this duality was by no means exclusively tied to Bernheim's work. In Chapter 2, I discuss Gabriel Tarde's adoption of it: although Tarde's thought often swung more toward the mimetic, his concept of the individual is more ambivalent than scholars (e.g. McPhail) have recognised, seeing as even Tarde conceded that the subject might volitionally enter mimetic forms.

2   Tensional Individuality

The landslide events of the *fin de siècle* and the effects they were believed to have on individuality were given careful attention within the discipline of sociology, which quickly developed from its pupal stage into a well-established and powerful discipline at the turn of the nineteenth century. This transition, particularly lucid in France, was marked symbolically by Gabriel Tarde's appointment to the chair in Modern Philosophy at the Collège de France in 1900 and Émile Durkheim's appointment to *chargé de cours* in Science of Education at the Sorbonne in 1902. Both signified the rise of sociology as the new 'key-science' in France (Lepenies, 1988: 54). This was especially so for Durkheim, who had grand ambitions for a reform of the French educational system and was instrumental in preparing the way for the discipline's growing institutional power, exercised via new curricula. Unsurprisingly, the increasing dominance of sociology was not welcomed unanimously by representatives of other disciplines (for interesting historical accounts, see Fournier, 2013: ch. 15; Lukes, 1985: ch. 18). In particular, Durkheim's eventually successful attempt to make one of his courses a mandatory building block in the philosophy track at the Sorbonne faced strong opposition. Yet Durkheim was relentless. In addition to fighting battles vis-à-vis other disciplines, he was equally tough on his home ground of sociology, where he worked hard to promote his vision for the field. This manifested in a fierce oppositional relationship between him and Tarde, among other things.

Their debate is well known in the annals of sociology: conventional accounts of the discipline's history often note that at the end of the nineteenth century, Tarde and Durkheim were embroiled in an intense conflict about the proper definition of sociology (e.g. Aron, 1967: 38). This was not simply a clash of scholarly ideas but also one of power, in that it concerned who could speak authoritatively about and on behalf of the burgeoning sociological discipline. Here, too, a minor landslide took place. Tarde had been the dominant name in French criminology and sociology in the 1880s and 1890s, when Durkheim was still 'a younger, less successful upstart teaching in the provinces', to borrow Bruno

Latour's phrase (2002: 117). However, using Tarde as his favourite foil, Durkheim gradually ascended to the top of the French sociological hierarchy. Tarde, despite his position as Chair at the prestigious Collège de France, would eventually be relegated to obsolescence or become a footnote in the canonised history of sociology – not necessarily a more attractive fate – mainly figuring as Durkheim's badly beaten adversary.

Though my aim here is not to provide an extensive review of the Tarde–Durkheim conflict (for such an account see, e.g. Clark, 1969; Fournier, 2013; Karsenti, 2010; Lukes, 1985: esp. 302–13; Schiermer, 2019), I foreground it in this chapter because of the questions about the nature of individuality at its core and because of its centrality to much of the twenty-first-century scholarship that has since returned to Tarde's ideas. Because I wish to revive ideas from Tarde's work, revisiting his debate with Durkheim, who cast him as defending an untenable theoretical programme, is warranted. A key issue at stake was the question of what psychology and sociology are – and especially whether the latter could mature only if clearly separated from the former and purified of its traces, as Durkheim posited. The concept of imitation was central to this discussion: while Tarde saw the social as constituted by imitation and drew inspiration from psychology to better understand imitation dynamics, Durkheim argued that given its anchoring in psychology, imitation *eo ipso* had to be excluded from the domain of sociology proper. Any sociological importance granted imitation, Durkheim stated, would be through an analysis of the ways in which social facts oblige imitation. I want to suggest that these fronts should not be as categorically drawn as the two combatants and their adherents have proposed. Rather, their open disagreements obscure a set of shared analytical sentiments which, I hope, will help render Tarde's work more palatable to present-day readers when brought to light.

In this chapter, I examine some of the conflicting interpretations of Tarde that have crystallised in recent years. These interpretations hark back in varying degrees to Tarde's encounters with Durkheim about the role and definition of sociology. I propose that interpreting Tarde by restaging his battle with Durkheim should be done with care, because this antagonistic starting point tends to gloss over central similarities between the two Frenchmen. I also use this chapter to zero in on Tarde's conception of the individual. Through a close reading of his reflections on the topic, I demonstrate that Tarde proposed a tensional account of the individual as one caught in a mimetic–anti-mimetic relationship, an interpretation that runs counter to existing analyses of his work.

Identifying this tensional notion of individuality serves several purposes. It demonstrates that although this dimension of early French sociology has been ignored in subsequent scholarship, tensional individuality was indeed part of the discipline's agenda in its foundational years. As Chapter 1 elucidates, the sociological interest in tensional individuality resonated with a broader analytical sentiment responding to the modernist experience of rupture at the end of the nineteenth century; the present chapter further expands on the prominence of this tensional notion within it. Specifically, a conception of tensional individuality was crucial to and echoed by a range of modernist observations beyond French sociology. Considering its widespread adoption, I argue that tensional individuality is not just a matter of historical relevance but also a sensible concept to reintroduce for analytical purposes today.

Returning to the Durkheim–Tarde Debate

I revisit the debate between Durkheim and Tarde via recent analyses that discuss the contemporary relevance of Tarde's work; these typically take two rival interpretations of Tarde, the negative and the affirmative. The negative camp draws on what George Simpson (2002: xiv) refers to as Durkheim's 'unrelenting warfare' against Tarde at the turn of the nineteenth century: its points echo the critiques Durkheim articulated in that battle. This camp, represented by scholars such as Laurent Mucchielli (2000) and Anthony King (2016), essentially consigns Tarde's work to the dustbin of long-superseded theory, arguing that while his theory merits historical attention for its central role in late-nineteenth-century French sociological thought, it is of no sociological value today. King, in particular, sides with Durkheim's critique of Tarde, suggesting that Tarde 'was ultimately a teleological individualist' – something that supposedly 'fatally damage[s] Tarde as a relevant social theorist' (2016: 57, 48).

King's uncompromising interpretation does not seem justified. Indeed, he conveniently disregards aspects of Tarde's work that do not support his thesis; for example, he claims that Tarde's alleged individualism prevented him from developing 'the concept of the collective adequately' (2016: 58). Of course, whether a concept is adequately developed is debatable, and there may well be different theoretical tastes at play. Nonetheleess, King's assertion that Tarde neglected collectivity is emphatically incorrect and needs to be fundamentally revised if, for example, Tarde's many writings on crowds, sects and publics are taken into account (e.g. Tarde, 1892; 1893; 1989). King references none of these, although they constitute a substantial part of Tarde's oeuvre and have been central to the reception of his work both in his own time and in the recent revival of his thought (e.g. Borch, 2005; 2012b; Borch and

Stäheli, 2009; Leys, 1993; Niezen, 2014; Stäheli, 2009; Van Ginneken, 1992). There are other flaws in King's reading of Tarde,[1] but rather than detailing them here, I find it more interesting to go straight to Durkheim, the source of the type of critique King invokes.

Durkheim uncharitably characterised Tarde's work as a 'very special mode of speculation, halfway between philosophy and literature, in which some very general, theoretical ideas are aired in connection with all kinds of problems' (Durkheim and Fauconnet, 1982: 189). According to Durkheim, the more specific problem was that if sociology were to mature as an independent discipline, Tarde would be found guilty of an unforgivable sin because his theoretical programme was based on and reducible to a psychologism. In other words, Tarde's endeavours conflicted with the rules Durkheim fought to establish for what he considered proper sociological work – accordingly, Tarde's work would have to be discarded. Durkheim's dismissal of Tarde took particular aim at his notion of imitation, which the former characterised as 'a purely psychological phenomenon' (Durkheim, 2006: 115).[2] Labelling

---

[1] For example, at the end of his critical examination of Tarde, King (2016: 58) argues that in response to globalisation, 'many prominent scholars have sought to define the distinctive character of globalizing solidarities and societies, developing new concepts to articulate these transformations'; King mentions as a positive case in point the German philosopher Peter Sloterdijk's notion of spheres. 'Yet', King continues, 'it is precisely here that Tarde falls short. The central omission of Tarde's social theory was his doctrinaire rejection of the collective as an explanatory resource' (2016: 58). Interestingly, King here ignores work that has argued for Tarde's pertinence for understanding globalisation (Thomassen and Szakolczai, 2011). Even more surprisingly, King fails to note that the most sociological volume in Sloterdijk's trilogy on spheres, the book on foams, is thoroughly and explicitly indebted to Tarde's notion of the social (Sloterdijk, 2004). Indeed, like Simmel, Tarde is one of the sociologists most cited in that volume, and he is key to Sloterdijk's analysis of foam sociality. King's ignorance of this might be due to the fact that he only references the first two, less sociological volumes of Sloterdijk's spherology, i.e. the only volumes that had appeared in English translation at the time he published his article. I have discussed the Tardean influence on Sloterdijk's spheres project elsewhere (e.g. Borch, 2008; 2013).

[2] Following Bjørn Schiermer's (2019) fascinating reconstruction of Durkheim's reflections on imitation, it is important to add a dash of nuance here. Schiermer demonstrates – although this is often disregarded even by competent commentators such as Bruno Karsenti (2010) – that the heavy critique of imitation identifiable in Durkheim's writings from the 1890s is counterbalanced by a much more affirmative understanding of imitation in his later work, especially in his (ethnographically based) sociology of religion. As I come back to shortly, in his early phase Durkheim recognised imitation as an epiphenomenon of social facts at best. Schiermer refers to this as a conception of 'imitation-through-norms', i.e. imitation working through coercive influence (2019: 58). By contrast, in his sociology of religion Durkheim granted imitation a much more central and positive role. There, it refers to the ways in which collective energies emerge around and are projected onto objects – or what Schiermer calls 'imitation-through-objects' – a conception which, similar to Tarde's ideas, is based on a notion of prestige (2019: 59–60). I mention this to stress that my discussion in this chapter centres on Durkheim's early

imitation psychological is damning from a Durkheimean point of view, as it entails that imitation has no properly sociological qualities. More specifically, due to its psychological nature imitation does not qualify as a 'social fact', which Durkheim famously conceived as the true object of sociological study and defined as '*any way of acting, whether fixed or not, capable of exerting over the individual an external constraint*' (1982: 59, original emphasis). It is the ostensible lack of attention to this supra-individual level that reverberates throughout King's critique of Tarde's work. The allegedly psychological rather than genuinely sociological nature of imitation is due, in Durkheim's view, to imitation being possible

among individuals who have no social connection between them. A man can imitate another without their being linked to one another or coming from a single group on which they are equally dependent, and the imitative propagation does not in itself have the power to link them. A sneeze, a rhythmical movement or a homicidal impulse can be transferred from one individual to another without there being anything except a chance, momentary association between them. They do not need to have any intellectual or moral communion, or to exchange services, or to speak the same language, and they are no more linked after this transfer than they were before. In short, the procedure by which we imitate our fellows is the same that allows us to reproduce natural sounds, shapes of things and movements of creatures. Since there is nothing social in the latter case, the same is true of the former. (2006: 115)

Here, I take issue with two assertions. The first is the suggestion that if imitation takes place between individuals related to one another only by 'a chance, momentary association', the fleeting, happenstance character of their encounter means that the ensuing imitation cannot count as being properly social. Certainly, such transient encounters and their imitative patterns need not produce long-lasting social bonds. But as urban sociologists since Simmel have never tired of explaining, one can easily imagine contexts in which Durkheim's point is negated – in the city, particular forms of sociality and social bonds can clearly emerge in, and on the basis of, fleeting imitative contact (e.g. Bech, 1998; Maffesoli, 1996; Simmel, 1950b). This also means that Durkheim's assertion that people are 'no more linked after [the imitation] than they were before' is questionable. At the very least, the act of imitation plants a seed that might grow and consolidate, or perhaps be further imitatively transferred to others.

---

writings, i.e. the work he published while Tarde was still alive (Tarde died in 1904). I discuss Durkheim's later work, more directly influenced by Tarde, in Chapter 3.

One might argue that this part of Durkheim's critique is founded on the conviction that imitation in a Tardean sense has a more transitive than genuinely reciprocal nature: it spreads in a diffuse fashion, like a wave, without creating the conditions for reciprocal imitation, as in effervescence.[3] In Durkheim's defence, such an interpretation finds some support in Tarde's writings. For example, while Tarde was inspired by Adam Smith's notion of sympathy, or *mutual* imitation, he nonetheless privileged a notion of *unilateral* imitation (Tarde, 1962: 79). However, as Tarde was careful to point out, this was merely a matter of analytical primacy rather than sociological importance: 'Sympathy is certainly the primary source of sociability and the hidden or overt soul of every kind of imitation [...]. Only, it is certain that sympathy itself begins by being one-sided instead of mutual' (1962: 79, n. 72).

On a related note, the second assertion in Durkheim's critique – in a way more fundamental yet equally contentious – is that imitation must count as psychological because it can take place between individuals who are not socially connected. This critique is at the crux of the Durkheim–Tarde debate in the sense that it concerns the core relationship between imitation and the social. Durkheim's point is that if imitation takes place among individuals who share no social bond, then this imitation is merely psychological (and therefore, as mentioned above, insufficient for creating lasting social bonds). If, by contrast, imitation takes place between socially connected individuals, then the sociologically interesting question for Durkheim is not what constitutes such imitation but rather how the fundamental social bond came into being as something that predates the imitative behaviour. From this perspective, imitation may be considered a matter of some interest but only as a secondary sociological phenomenon: an epiphenomenon of social facts. In Durkheim's own words, 'Doubtless every social fact is imitated and has [...] a tendency to become generalised, *but this is because it is social*, i.e. obligatory' (1982: 59, n. 53, emphasis added). Tarde (1962) approaches the issue from the opposite direction, arguing that the social bond is *constituted by imitation*. In other words, from this theoretical vantage point, it would be a mistake to assume the social (and well-established social connections between individuals) before analysing the role of imitation. For Tarde, society is produced and reproduced *in and through imitative behaviour*: society is the product of – rather than merely the basis for – imitation.

---

[3] I am grateful to Bjørn Schiermer for drawing my attention to this.

Durkheim's particular conception of social facts – the idea that external coercive influences shape the behaviour of individuals – underpinned his critique of Tarde. According to Durkheim:

there are ways of acting, thinking and feeling which possess the remarkable property of existing outside the consciousness of the individual. Not only are these types of behaviour and thinking external to the individual, but they are endued with a compelling and coercive power by virtue of which, whether he [*sic*] wishes it or not, they impose themselves upon him. (1982: 51)[4]

Durkheim suggested that since these influences are external and exist 'outside the consciousness of the individual', they should be deemed genuinely social. By contrast, he continued, Tarde's conception of imitation as something supposedly not produced by supra-individual external forces should be located therefore in the consciousness of the individual, i.e. as something psychological. Against this background, Durkheim insisted that Tarde's flirtation with psychology, his alleged inability to establish a sociological programme devoid of psychological leftovers, not only amounted to the elevation of 'indeterminateness [...] to a principle' but, more devastatingly, rendered his endeavours 'no longer scientific' (Durkheim and Fauconnet, 1982: 189).

Granted, Durkheim's critique that Tarde flirted with psychology is not entirely unjustified: Tarde did use the term 'inter-psychology' to describe his sociological programme (e.g., 1903). Also, Tarde certainly took an interest in how one mind can make an imprint on others though imitation, as is evident in his conception of imitation as 'the action at a distance of one mind upon another, and of action which consists of a quasi-photographic reproduction of a cerebral image upon the sensitive plate of another brain' (1962: xiv). Further confirming Durkheim's suspicion, Tarde continued along these media-psychological lines, stating, 'By imitation I mean every impression of an inter-psychical photography, so to speak, willed or not willed, passive or active' (1962: xiv). And seeking answers to the question of what imitation is, Tarde drew explicitly on the work of Bernheim and the Nancy School to suggest that 'the sociologist should yield to the psychologist' (1962: 74).

While Durkheim was therefore right to point to the psychological dimensions of Tarde's theorisation, he nonetheless misunderstood their meaning and implications, apparently conflating any psychological impulse with a non-sociological psychologism. This means, as I have

---

[4] Schiermer notes that Durkheim would, in his sociology of religion, tone down this coercive aspect and become more inclined to accept a more positive-affirmative conception of social facts. See Durkheim (1995: 210–11, n. 6, 214, n. 213) and Schiermer (2016: 148, n. 2).

argued elsewhere (Borch, 2014), that the problem with Durkheim's critique is not so much that it targeted the psychological layer of Tarde's thought but that it was based on the assumption that all traces of psychology must be eradicated from sociology. What surfaces here is a puritanism that guided Durkheim's dismissal of Tarde's key ideas and contributions; this would be partially echoed in Weber's delineation of sociology, as Chapter 3 elucidates.

Having discussed one recent type of critical interpretation of Tarde's work and its Durkheimean roots, I now turn to the more affirmative camp in the current Tarde scholarship. Admittedly, describing it as a camp overstates the homogeneity of the scholars concerned. They come from different traditions and pursue different theoretico-analytical agendas, yet all consider the Durkheimean critique of Tarde's alleged psychologism a misfire. Some go a step further to argue that the most ostensibly psychological feature of Tarde's work – his interest in hypnotic suggestion – should be read affirmatively as a timely argument for conceiving of individuality as a matter of plasticity, i.e. as something that can be moulded from the outside.

A prominent example of an interpretation of Tarde that directly confronts Durkheim's critique is that of Latour, who claims that 'no sociology was ever further from psychology than Tarde's' (2002: 127). Similarly, Gilles Deleuze asserted that 'It is completely wrong to reduce Tarde's sociology to a psychologism or even an interpsychology' (1994: 314, n. 3). Instead, Deleuze suggested, '*What Tarde inaugurates is a microsociology*, which is not necessarily concerned with what happens between individuals but with what happens within a single individual', such as when an individual is caught in a moment of hesitation between conflicting rays of imitation (1994: 314, n. 3, original emphasis). In the light of Tarde's manifest commitments to psychological (and interpsychological) thought, these statements by Latour and Deleuze are rather odd and difficult to square with Tarde's explicit writings. More to the point, Latour's claim that Tarde's sociological project is non-psychological is flatly incorrect. To be sure, Tarde's work is not *reducible* to a psychologism (Deleuze is right about that), but the former certainly conceived of it in interpsychological terms: *contra* Latour's assertion, Tarde was profoundly indebted to contemporaneous psychological work when crafting his sociological programme. To ignore this psychological dimension is to considerably flatten Tarde's sociological project (for a similar assessment, see Blackman, 2007).

Another group of scholars acknowledges Tarde's psychological investments, including his interest in hypnotic suggestion, and seeks to develop a notion of individuality on that basis. Coming from partly overlapping, partly divergent traditions of critical psychology, poststructuralism, non-representational theory and Deleuze-inflected theorisation, this group includes Lisa Blackman (2007; 2012), Stefan Moebius (2004), Tony Sampson (2012) and Nigel Thrift (2008a; 2008b).[5] These scholars argue that one of Tarde's key achievements – and a main reason for his current sociological relevance – is that he put forth a *plastic notion of the individual*: instead of seeing the individual as pre-given or in essentialist terms, Tarde theorised the individual as profoundly socially entangled. In this view, the individual is deeply constituted by external suggestions – so much so that differences between individuals can be difficult to sustain. Advocating this reading, Thrift argues that contemporary capitalism is being reformatted in ways that make a Tardean notion of plastic individuality increasingly salient. Specifically, Thrift asserts, present-day capitalism increasingly seeks to mould consumer subjects through an 'engineering of propensity' (2008b: 92), which can be fruitfully analysed using Tarde's theorisation of the ability to influence imitative patterns through hypnotic suggestion (see also Thrift, 2008a: ch. 10). Similarly, Sampson argues that a central theoretical gain from Tarde's sociology lies in its 'radical questioning of what constitutes social subjectivity' and its 'concept of an agentless, half-awake subjectivity, nudged along by the force of relational encounter with contaminating events' (2012: 12, 13).

---

[5] Deleuze has profoundly influenced much of the Tarde revival that has taken place since the early 2000s, although his explicit reflections on Tarde are few and scattered. It has even been argued that Tarde may be characterised as a '*Deleuzean avant la lettre*' (Alliez, 2004: 50, original emphasis). Latour's interpretation has also been important to the recent return to Tarde, but less so when it comes to understanding the role of the individual in Tarde's work, since Latour takes hardly any interest in that topic. This lack of interest in Tardean individuality appears to be a corollary of Latour's hesitation to recognise and take seriously the psychological layer of Tarde's writings. Likewise, Luhmann's adaptation of Tarde does not emphasise the latter's notion of individuality. Instead, he highlights Tarde's alignment with Luhmann's ambitions to theorise on the basis of difference rather than identity or unity. This turn away from notions usually associated with a Hegelian tradition is represented, *inter alia*, by Luhmann's sociological systems theory (which, contrary to remarkably persistent beliefs in many sociological quarters – especially in the United States – has little to do with that of Talcott Parsons, precisely because Luhmann's theory is committed to a number of poststructuralist ideas). Luhmann built his entire theoretical edifice on the idea that sociological theory should start from a notion of difference, notably that between system and environment. He often quoted mathematician George Spencer-Brown's injunction to 'draw a distinction' (1969: 3). Luhmann saw Tarde as inaugurating this difference-oriented sociological tradition, arguing that the Frenchman 'conceived of a theory of imitation, a theory of the spread and consolidation of sociality by means of imitation that also did not begin with unity but with difference. If one imitates somebody else, this somebody else must exist in the first place' (2013: 45). Just as Luhmann's systems theory is based on a guiding difference between system and environment, Tarde's is premised on a difference between the one imitating and the one (person, gesture, idea, etc.) being imitated.

This, Sampson continues, is widely recognisable today when 'corporate and political powers [...] tap into a tendency toward imitation–suggestibility by measuring, priming, and manipulating the collective mood' (2012: 14).

These examples make clear that a chief reference point for some of the scholars affirmatively interpreting Tarde's work is the centrality Tarde assigns the vocabulary of somnambulism, hypnosis and suggestion. The analytical importance of this vocabulary is displayed, for instance, in Tarde's pointed statement that '*Society is imitation and imitation is a kind of somnambulism*' (1962: 87, original emphasis), as well as in his assertion, 'I shall not seem fanciful in thinking of the social man [*sic*] as a veritable somnambulist', i.e. as someone who is thrown into a society constituted by somnambulistic imitations that endlessly crisscross individuals (1962: 76). Present-day scholars emphasise, against this backdrop, that Tarde's conception of the individual as a sleepwalker describes the individual as a piece of clay that can be formed in the hands of the *suggestionneur*. Testifying to the pervasiveness of this power of moulding, Tarde argues that suggestion is not merely a matter of injecting beliefs from the outside into the individual on a purely ideational level. Rather, it might even be a matter of reformatting the organism, evinced by his confirmatory reference to the French physiologist Charles Richet in *Laws of Imitation*:

'It is a curious sight,' says M. Charles Richet, 'to see a somnambulist make gestures of distaste and nausea and experience real suffocation when an empty bottle is put under his nose and he is told that it contains ammonia, or, on the other hand, to see him inhale ammonia without showing the least discomfort when he is told that it is pure water'. (Tarde, 1962: 81)

If we are to take such statements seriously, it hardly makes sense to speak of a distinctive individuality or an autonomous self. What Tarde seems to present here is the absence of fixed boundaries between self and other, as well as the ability of external *suggestionneurs* to produce the subject in their image. Ruth Leys neatly summarises this point:

By dissolving the boundaries between self and other, [Tarde's] theory of imitation-suggestion embodied a highly plastic notion of the human subject that radically called into question the unity and identity of the self. Put another way, it made the notion of individuality itself problematic. (1993: 281)

Finally, and relatedly, Tarde's theory dismantles the idea of a formative conscious individuality, according to the affirmative interpretation. Instead, individuals are captured by mimetic, quasi-hypnotic forces that annul their conscious, deliberate decision-making abilities. So, when they imitate beliefs and desires from others, individuals need not be consciously aware of these forces since the imitation process is tantamount to sleepwalking. In the words of Moebius, 'The processes of repeating are not an expression of conscious individuals who decide rationally but are essentially processes that carry on unconsciously, unintended and beyond purely rational calculations' (2004: 65).[6]

Challenging the Supposed Antagonism between Durkheim and Tarde

It might be surprising and perhaps even confusing that Tarde's textual corpus, especially his remarks on individuality and imitation, can give rise to such contradictory interpretations, with one group of commentators rejecting its sociological value today and another group celebrating the very same parts of his sociological thought for its timeliness and significance. While such incompatible assessments are not exclusive to the reception of Tarde's work, what remains peculiar here is the common ground identifiable between the differing readings offered by, say, King *contra* Latour and Deleuze. More specifically, it is striking that much of the controversy around Tarde's work starts from an exaggeration of the differences between his project and Durkheim's, an ostensible gulf the two scholars did much to widen through the insults they traded (many of their mutual jabs are collected in Tarde and Durkheim, 2010). However, as I demonstrate in this section, Durkheim and Tarde's analytical avenues for understanding the social might not be all that different. Bruno Karsenti similarly stresses this point (2010), taking some

---

[6] Some recent interpretations, especially Sampson's and Thrift's, situate Tarde's work in connection with present-day findings in neuroscience. According to the former, 'Tarde's appeal to somnambulism maps interestingly to current ideas expressed in cognitive neuroscience concerning the relation between thinking and the automatic processing of affect said to occur via mirror neurons or emphatic transmissions' (Sampson, 2012: 13). Although I appreciate that it is becoming increasingly popular to try to found social theory in neuroscience (see for an attempt to base crowd theory on neuroscience McPhail et al., 2015), I do not share this endeavour and will therefore not go deeper into this particular aspect of the recent affirmative adaptation of Tarde. My scepticism is based on two points: neuroscience findings on, say, mirror neurons are highly contested, even and especially among neuroscientists (for a damming insider critique of oft-referenced studies on mirror neurons, see Hickok, 2014). Further, I do not see a need for such a hard-science grounding of social theory. The questions social theorists should ask themselves when embarking on a search for neuroscience backing are these: What would such a search entail for social theory? What would it mean that a few sociological ideas might achieve substantiation via neuroscience? And what, especially, would it mean that other ideas might *not* find such support? Would we need to discard them? A new, damaging puritanism could easily emerge out of this, one far more restrictive than Durkheim's. That said, there are obviously interesting genealogical analyses that trace the ways in which present-day neuroscience findings echo concerns that date back to *fin-de-siècle* discussions of imitation and suggestion. See Lawtoo (2019) for one such genealogical analysis.

important steps towards rethinking the relation between Durkheim and Tarde in less antagonistic terms.

Karsenti's analysis belies several taken-for-granted claims about the ways in which Durkheim and Tarde analysed imitation. For example, he intervenes in their controversy about whether sociologically relevant imitation can take place between individuals who are not already socially knotted. Karsenti suggests that this disagreement can be circumvented, if not resolved, by recognising that Tarde's analytical model is less about the origin of the social and more about how the social unfolds:

[Tarde's theory of] imitation does not enquire into beginnings, but rather into the *vector of sociality*. The question it raises is not the origin of the relation, but simply what it consists in, what it is made of, what it is, precisely, that makes it a relation. (2010: 46–7, original emphasis)

So, Karsenti argues, from a Tardean point of view the sociological task is not necessarily to excavate some primordial imitation that initiated society. The task is rather to map, analyse and understand how sociality and social bonds are continuously generated and regenerated through imitative patterns.

Karsenti similarly questions Durkheim's assertion that Tarde's notion of imitation entails a kind of psychologism that should be banned from sociology. In what reads as an echo of Deleuze, albeit one with different grounds and implications, Karsenti argues that this damning claim rests on a misunderstanding of Tarde's project and its conception of interpsychology:

Tarde's interpsychology is not a psychology, insofar as it wishes to grasp what passes *between* individuals, to apprehend the relation itself. Interpsychology is not a sub-set of psychology; rather, it aims at studying psychic phenomena which are beyond the individual and yet are not subsumed into collective representations. (2010: 44, original emphasis)

Karsenti engages in a balancing act here that is not too different from Tarde's own. The central point he makes is that while Tarde's particular lexicon (especially the term 'interpsychology') might invite the sort of critique Durkheim expressed, the content of his theoretical work was sociological through and through. However, since he refers to 'psychic phenomena', Karsenti might fail to persuade faithful Durkheimeans that their master was misguided. Importantly, however, Karsenti demonstrates why sociologists should not be put off by this parlance. One reason relates to what he refers to as 'the concept of imitation's prime strength': it 'might allow us to grasp, not *the experience of the social milieu* so much as *the social experience of the milieu* – which Durkheim's approach tends to limit a priori' (2010: 48, original emphasis). Put differently,

Tarde's conception of imitation permits an analysis of how an individual's experience of the world, including the beliefs and desires that go into framing such an experience, is inherently social since such beliefs and desires circulate amongst individuals in imitative patterns.

Fashion serves as an illuminating example of this. The experience an individual has of articles of clothing is deeply affected by how particular seemingly individual desires ('psychic phenomena') are framed socially, a process aptly articulated in the following passage by novelist Karen Blixen:

> I have wondered why numb things placed aside in cupboards or on shelves, and in no way attacked by either moth or corrosion, in their unnoticed existence over the years suffer radical changes. I have seen it with my own dresses, bought in Europe but left in the wardrobe in Africa, when I, after two or three years, took them out to put them on, and they, without having stretched or shrunk, suddenly seemed to be too long or too short. They had not changed, and yet they were changed. Fashion and my own eyes caused this change. (Blixen quoted in Schiermer, 2016: 131)

In addition to demonstrating how the individual gaze is filtered through the social logic of fashion, the quotation addresses the role of objects and how socially distributed desires interact with objects. The role of objects will be further analysed in Chapter 4. For now, the important thing to recognise is the Tardean notion, already mentioned earlier, that much of what the individual considers singular to himself or herself (ideas, beliefs, desires, preferences, etc.) is inherited through imitation from others and therefore in fact social rather than strictly individual. This produces a particular *social epistemology* in which perception and knowledge are socially framed. The aim of Tarde's interpsychology is precisely to grasp the workings and constitution of this social epistemology, not by scrutinising the inner workings of the psyche but rather by analysing how that which is considered 'inside' (desires, thoughts, etc.) is intimately related to the 'outside': the desires, thoughts, etc. shared by and inherited from others.

This connection between the inside and the outside is an obvious place to leave Karsenti's analysis and look closely at how Durkheim and Tarde theorise this link, laying bare how the two sociologists' ways of theorising the social do not just conflict with one another but also demonstrate important overlaps. Recall that for Durkheim, social facts are characterised by the ways in which individual behaviour is shaped by external coercive influence. Accordingly, for Durkheim, the central sociological task is to understand how certain normative modes or schemas of 'acting, thinking and feeling' are not individual but rather 'external to the individual', though they impose themselves upon him or her in spite of 'existing outside the consciousness of the individual' (1982: 51). The underlying connection is that Durkheim and Tarde effectively concurred on this fundamental issue about the inside–outside dynamic between the thoughts, actions, beliefs, etc. of the individual and the extra-individual patterns that structure them. In other words, Durkheim and Tarde agreed that the individual is profoundly shaped by external forces. A series of observations from Durkheim's manifesto *The Rules of Socio-logical Method* (in which he argues how sociology can obtain autonomy as a scholarly discipline) further justify an attention to the similarities rather than the sense of an insurmountable gulf between his and Tarde's project. First, Durkheim states,

it is indisputable today that most of our ideas and tendencies are not developed by ourselves, but come to us from outside, they can only penetrate us by imposing themselves upon us. This is all that our definition [of social facts] implies. (1982: 52)

This core conception of social facts is startlingly in accord with Tarde's interpsychology-cum-sociology, which also aims to grasp how ideas and tendencies coming from the outside impose themselves on individuals.

A larger rupture between the two scholars consists in the ways they understood how ideas impose themselves on individuals. Inspired as he was by Immanuel Kant's moral philosophy (see, e.g. Presskorn-Thygesen, 2017), Durkheim emphasised 'law and custom' as motors which ensure that individuals direct their ideas and actions according to external constraints (1982: 50). Evoking Foucault's analytics of power, one can say that Durkheim's primary template for understanding the constraining power of social facts is therefore taken from a legalistic realm. More specifically, Durkheim's repeated stress on the supposedly 'coercive power' of social facts (e.g. 1982: 51, 53) aligns with what Foucault calls a 'juridico-political discourse', i.e. an essentially repressive conception of power 'centered on nothing more than the statement of the law and the operation of taboos' (Foucault, 1990: 85, 88).[7] Tarde's Bernheimian inspiration might suggest a parallel train of thought. After all, Bernheim's conception was partly indebted to similarly repressive elements (which, as mentioned in Chapter 1, was one of the reasons behind Freud's critique of suggestion theory). The pride Bernheim took in the ways in which the *suggestionneur* was ostensibly able to transform

---

[7] See, for example, Durkheim's clarification about social facts: 'While one might perhaps contest the statement that all social facts without exception impose themselves from without upon the individual, the doubt does not seem possible as regards religious beliefs and practices, the rules of morality and the innumerable precepts of law – that is to say, all the most characteristic manifestations of collective life' (1974: 25).

the *suggestionné* into an automaton and/or fix any laziness of the subject machine by speaking in an authoritative voice clearly evinces this (Bernheim, 1889: 29).

While Bernheim may therefore be tarred with the same juridico-political brush as Durkheim, Tarde's conception of imitation used a much less repressive vocabulary.[8] Here, imitation is not so much a matter of people imitating others out of fear of sanctions (Durkheim's model, see e.g. 1982: 51). Rather, imitation is said to rest on *prestige*, something that endows imitation with a more affirmative character. 'The magnetiser', Tarde stated, 'does not need to lie or terrorise to secure the blind belief and the passive obedience of his [*sic*] magnetised subject. He has prestige – that tells the story' (1962: 78). This conception is one of the central reasons why Tarde has been resuscitated in present-day social theory. His notion of imitation based on prestige renders it more compatible than Durkheim's coercive register with analytical frameworks (such as those of Sampson, 2012; Thrift, 2008b) that stress what Foucault terms governmental forms of power, i.e. ways of exercising power that rest on productive rather than repressive technologies and which operate in indirect fashion by structuring 'the possible field of action of others' (Foucault, 1982: 221).[9]

Of course, the reference to prestige only displaces the analytical problem, in a sense. Why would the *suggestionné* be led by the prestige of the *suggestionneur*? And what constitutes the latter's prestige in the first place? Tarde is not particularly clear on these matters, merely suggesting that people possess beliefs and desires which seek 'expression just as the water of a lake seeks an outlet': the *suggestionneur* produces an outlet for such beliefs and desires, and the *suggestionneur*'s prestige is constituted by the

---

[8] Tarde well recognised the centrality of coercion in Durkheim's conception of social facts: for Durkheim, 'it is not the more or less of generalization, of imitative propagation of a fact, which constitutes its more or less social character; it is the more or less of *coercivity*. Indeed, according to [Durkheim], the definition of the social fact is double. One of its characters, as we know, is [...] that it "exists independently of its individual expressions". But there is another character, no less important, which is to be coercive' (Tarde in Tarde and Durkheim, 2010: 32, original emphasis).

[9] While Tarde's notion of prestige is certainly less imbued with repressive undertones than Durkheim's definition of social facts, one might nonetheless argue that by invoking prestige as a guiding concept in explaining how imitation unfolds, Tarde unwittingly stirred up a notion that carries along the baggage of asymmetric delusions. 'Prestige' derives from *praestigiae*, which refers to deceptive tricks carried out, for instance, by jugglers. I am grateful to Brigitte Weingart for drawing my attention to this etymological aspect of the term; Weingart has demonstrated that the notion of fascination shares a similar conceptual history (Weingart, 2014). In his sociology of religion, Durkheim operated with the notion of respect in a manner somewhat parallel to Tarde's conception of prestige (Durkheim, 1995: 209).

ability to provide such an outlet (Tarde, 1962: 78). Again, these responses are only partially helpful. However, there are other ways of shedding light on Tarde's assertion that the magnetiser ensures obedience through prestige.

For example, since prestige may be seen as a particular form of authority, one analytical entry into understanding it (and what it is not) may be pursued via Weber's notion of charisma and charismatic authority. On the surface, charisma seems to bear some resemblance to prestige. Weber argued that the validity of charisma is based on the 'recognition' of those subjected to it and that 'Psychologically this recognition is a matter of complete personal devotion to the possessor of the [charismatic] quality' (1978: 242). However, in contrast to Tarde's model, Weber's account suggests that the belief in and recognition of the charismatic leader works as a 'duty' demanded by the leader, who sanctions non-submission (1978: 242). This reveals the strong repressive anchoring of Weber's analysis, much like Durkheim's own. Furthermore, Weber associated charisma with a religious-spiritual domain and argued that due to its religious undertones, charisma 'is specifically foreign to economic considerations'; indeed, 'From the point of view of rational economic activity, charismatic want satisfaction is a typical anti-economic force' (1978: 244, 245). By thus pitting charisma against economic logics, Weber effectively denied the possibility that the economy may also be characterised by charisma and charismatic features. Tarde's notion of prestige made no similar claims; it can be applied to any field, which reveals another, more important observation: perhaps inquiring into the origins of prestige misses the point. As discussed earlier, it is not so much *beginnings* and *origins* but rather *modi operandi* that are central to Tardean thought. What matters from Tarde's point of view is that suggestion involves some sort of asymmetry, which he named prestige: even in the absence of sanctions some people are willing or prone to submit to others regardless of the grounds of this prestige.

Returning to the connections between Tarde and Durkheim, one observes in Tarde's work contrasts to Bernheim's notion of suggestion which align him more with Durkheim than Tarde himself acknowledged. According to Durkheim, one of the central problems with Tarde's imitation theory is that by referring to how one individual imitates another, it never moves beyond a purely individual and therefore – in Durkheim's taxonomy – non-sociological level: 'an individual state which impacts on others none the less remains individual' (1982: 59, n. 53). Durkheim's objection gains some initial support from Bernheim's definition of suggestion. However, Bernheim's conception of suggestion is, in its clinical formulation, modelled around a two-person template:

that of physician and patient. By contrast, Tarde's notion of imitation is, qua its sociological ambitions, primarily a multi-person model; it is therefore not obvious that the influence exercised on particular individuals can be seen as the result of 'an individual state'. There are several testimonies to this in Tarde's writings. His observation that 'three-quarters of the time we obey a man [*sic*] because we see him obeyed by others' (1969: 314) suggests that imitative relations which seemingly assume a two-person character may be part of broader imitative patterns. Relatedly, even if an imitative relation commences in a two-person formation, it can leave behind this dyadic structure and become part of a much broader imitative current (Borch, 2005: 85). Tarde furthered this by identifying the crowd and the family as 'two distinct germs of societies', meaning that any societal order has 'one or the other as its principal source' (1968: 325). While admittedly rather speculative, this claim demonstrates how Tarde sought to base his analysis of societal imitation on multi-person conglomerations rather than reduce it to a two-person model.[10] And this multi-person perspective, in which imitation unfolds in a web of social entanglements, suggests that Durkheim was wrong in claiming that 'an individual state which impacts on others' can be meaningfully be considered as 'nonetheless remaining individual'. In fact, on this point, the similarities between Durkheim's project and that of Tarde are more profound than the former proposed.

Interestingly, and indicative of the considerable overlaps between Durkheim and Tarde foregrounded here, the latter's emphasis on crowds and families as sociological exemplars finds almost identical expression in the work of Durkheim, who interpreted them as manifestations of social facts. For Durkheim, the upbringing of children demonstrates the manifold ways in which the child is subjected to the 'pressure of the social environment which seeks to shape him [*sic*] in its own image, and in which parents and teachers are only the representatives and intermediaries' (1982: 54; see also 1961: 73–4). Tarde concurred but articulated this in terms of how the child is subjected to the influence of external rays of imitation, some being mediated via parents, some via teachers and some via still others.

Crowds also occupied a central role in *Rules*, Durkheim's methodological manifesto, with crowd behaviour as a paradigmatic example of

---

[10] This is, to follow up on the previous discussion of King's neglect of both the third volume of Sloterdijk's spheres project and of Tarde's emphasis on collective formations, also the reason why Sloterdijk takes a particular interest in Tarde's work in his sociological volume on foams – as opposed to in his volume on bubbles, which pivots around two-person constellations.

social facts not restricted to a legalistic logic. Durkheim's interest in crowds is no doubt a reflection of the intellectual climate at the time.[11] After all, *Rules* was published in 1895, the same year that Le Bon's treatise *The Crowd* came out and, hence, at the height of the crowd debates that preoccupied France at the end of the nineteenth century (with some of Tarde's key contributions on this matter published in 1892 and 1893). Evidently these debates were not lost on Durkheim, who argued:

In a public gathering the great waves of enthusiasm, indignation and pity that are produced have their seat in no one individual consciousness. They come to each one of us from outside and can sweep us along in spite of ourselves. [...] Hence we are the victims of an illusion which leads us to believe we have ourselves produced what has been imposed upon us externally. (1982: 52–3, see also 56)

While Durkheim recognised that such crowd behaviour is driven by collective emotions that gain a self-propelling force, operating more fluently and in less orderly ways than suggested by the narrow juridico-political discourse otherwise informing his conception of social facts, this juridico-political template nonetheless loomed in the background. 'If an individual tries to pit himself against one of these collective manifestations, the sentiments that he is rejecting will be turned against him' (1982: 53). In other words, though resistance against collective enthusiasm might provoke sanctions, people may not be aware of these before refusing to ride the collective wave.

Thus far, I have used this discussion of the individual in its relation to society and the social to demonstrate that much of the scholarly commentary on Durkheim and Tarde has unduly amplified their differences at the expense of recognising the important, even fundamental, similarities across their projects. By insisting on their antagonistic relationship, much of the existing reception of Durkheim and Tarde has engaged, uncritically, in a restaging of the late-nineteenth-century battle between the two sociological giants. I label it 'uncritical' because the adversarial statements by Durkheim and Tarde have been taken at face value

---

[11] Education and crowd phenomena were topics that continued to occupy Durkheim throughout his career, as is evident in his posthumously published lectures *Moral Education* (1961) as well as in his work on the sociology of religion (Durkheim, 1995). I return to the latter in Chapter 3. For now, the interesting thing to note is that a great deal of his subsequent work on crowd and collective formations is anticipated in the *Rules*, including the vocabulary of 'social "currents"', 'common emotion', 'special energy', 'collective drive', etc. (1982: 52, 53, 56, 58). For discussions of such thematic and conceptual continuities in Durkheim's work, see Arppe (2005), Schiermer (2019) and Torres (2014). I discuss aspects of Durkheim's later reflections on crowds, and their parallels to Tarde's work, in Borch (2012b: 70–6).

without an adequate examination of how their work, in spite of numerous self-positioning assertions, may contain broader commonalities in their conception of sociology and the social, particularly with respect to how they see individuals being influenced from the outside. Demonstrating this paves the way for Chapter 3, in which I go against the grain to treat Tarde and Durkheim as part of a somewhat common analytical enterprise. More precisely, I reinvigorate parts of Tarde's theorisation in tandem with Durkheim's and argue that a notion of social avalanching can be derived from their work. Before getting to that, however, I elaborate on the concept of individuality that can be distilled from Tarde's work.

The Tardean Individual: Tensional Individuality

Attending to Tarde's writings on individuality rapidly returns us to a critical juncture in his debate with Durkheim. If Tarde conceived of the individual as the *locus socialis*, the point from which the social derives and unfolds, then Durkheim's reservations about an implicit individualism or psychologism in the former's work would be confirmed. Countering this aspect of Durkheim's critique of Tarde, Karsenti argues that 'it is in no way self-evident that Tarde's conception of imitation denotes an individualist position' (2010: 44). Similarly, the poststructuralist interpretation of Tarde flatly rejects this Durkheimean proposition to insist that rather than being the locus of the social, the individual is better understood as one of its effects. This latter interpretation surely carries force. Given the somnambulistic constitution of the individual presented earlier, the search for an individualist origin of society appears an intractable endeavour. From this Tardean perspective, society is not founded on any one individual's ideas or behaviours; certain inventions may be attributed to specific individuals, and since others may subsequently imitate these inventions, in such cases some form of individualist origin might be said to exist. However – and this is a key reason why the Tardean model does not advance a pure individualist position – inventions, as Tarde (1899) conceives, often consist in utilising or bringing together existing imitative patterns in novel ways (e.g. smartphones, which combine functions that allow users to talk on the telephone, listen to music and search the internet). Truly understanding such inventions, therefore, entails excavating in a genealogical fashion the imitative patterns that they bring together – patterns therefore prior to what an individual inventor creates from them. Further, Tarde's sociological interest here does not focus on the identification of individuals as the source of particular imitative patterns. Rather, what is sociologically important is to scrutinise how people are interrelated through imitations and how this interrelation materialises even at an intra-subjective level.

For Tarde, therefore, the singular individual is not the building block of the social. Scholars such as Blackman, Sampson and Thrift are right to insist that Tarde's model is not characterised by methodological individualism, just as any form of rational-choice thinking – à la Berk – is entirely absent from his work. Instead, Tarde effectively proposed imitation as a *social suture* that binds individuals in ways that are difficult to disentangle analytically. This is so not only because of the sheer number of imitative ties but also because the stitching can take place without individuals fully recognising it – Blixen's quotation above illustrates this, suggesting that the social epistemology she deployed to assess her dresses had changed imperceptibly but with perceptible implications. It is this socially convoluted form of individuality that Tarde sought to capture.

Despite its obvious merits, the interpretation of Tarde's notion of individuality as found in the work of Sampson, Thrift and others nonetheless only tells part of the story, as it is possible to single out in Tarde's writings moments in which individuality is seen as less plastic and more substantive. These moments are identifiable at two different levels of his analysis: one concerns the intra-subjective, *intra-cerebral* constitution of the individual, the other the *inter-cerebral* mechanism of social relationality as effected through hypnosis. Together they make up Tarde's doubly socially entangled concept of the individual. I discuss each of these levels and their interconnections to demonstrate that while Tarde strongly emphasised the mimetic features of subjectivity (per Sampson, Thrift and others), he also retained a solid notion of individual substance as resilient to mimetic entanglements.

The Intra-Cerebral Constitution of the Individual

Tarde described the 'psychological individual [*l'individu psychologique*], the "myself," [as] an assemblage and a connection of states of consciousness or of *subconsciousness*, that is of information and impulses', internal as well as external (1968: 116, original emphasis). In pursuing this line of thought, he arrived at an essentially informational account of the brain as the place where the 'myself' is located. According to Tarde, the 'myself' is not to be conflated with the brain as such, and the latter is not constituted by or reducible to one 'myself'. Rather he argued, in a monadological mode,[12] that the brain is better conceived as a complex

---

[12] This is one of several manifestations of Tarde's pansocial monadology (for a discussion of this, see Lorenc, 2012). And yet, here as elsewhere, Tarde's relation to monadology is

composition of multiple 'myselfs',[13] each of which is relationally constituted (where each individual myself is 'an assemblage and a connection',
as the quotation above expresses). Tarde added that each 'myself' is,
more specifically,

localized within very narrow limits [in the brain], is simply an interweaving, but a
true and actual interweaving, of information and of influences, a *place* [*lieu*] and at
the same time a *bond* [*lien*] of instructions and of impulses, emanating from all the
neighboring cells [i.e. neighboring 'myselfs']. (1968: 124, original emphasis)

Two aspects of this conception are crucial. The first is that the individual
and its cerebral constitution are portrayed here as *inherently social*. Similar
to Tarde's definition of the social individual as a 'veritable somnambulist', as someone exposed to and in-formed (formed within) by instructions and impulses from others, the 'myself' is seen as a bond or
association of such instructions and impulses. In other words, each
'myself' is constituted relationally – namely, in its relation to other
'myselfs'. Second, no stable hierarchy exists amongst the many 'myselfs'
that inhabit the individual brain. Although one 'myself' may usually be
dominant, constituting the identity of the person, others might challenge
its authority. Tarde illustrated this social dynamism with explicit reference to the notion of free will, which he critiqued and found deeply
problematic. In *Penal Philosophy* (originally published in 1890), Tarde
presents his monadological alternative to free will and discusses how it is
useful when analysing whether liability can be ascribed to situations in
which free will is absent. Tarde's discussion deserves to be quoted at
length, as it nicely captures the sociality of the myself(s):[14]

The freedom of the 'myself' becomes its authority over the other 'myselfs' of the
brain. The extent of its freedom is the measure according to which it is well
informed and well seconded by the latter. It ceases to be free at the precise
moment when it is more opposed than served, more contradicted than
confirmed by them, that is to say when the information and the impulses which
it has already received from some of them and which it has appropriated and

---

more ambiguous than many recent interlocutors would have it. In contrast to, for
example, Latour (2002), I do not find it justified to see Tarde's reflections on
monadology as the key to understanding his thought. For example, in the sections
from *Penal Philosophy* I discuss here, Tarde himself voiced some concern about
framing his thinking monadologically (see 1968: 124, 126).

[13] This plural form, 'myselfs', is used in the English translation of Tarde and is retained
here despite being unusual. The French original simply uses 'moi', while the plural is 'les
autres moi' (1972: 125). Note also that the French original does not put *moi* in inverted
commas.

[14] That reflections on these matters preoccupied Tarde in *Penal Philosophy* (1968) testifies
to the centrality of questions of free will and liability under hypnosis in late-nineteenth-
century criminological debates (see Borch, 2015).

assimilated to itself by its adhesion, not free but necessary by virtue of its nature, are contrary to the suggestions which it receives from others, which cannot be appropriated, and as a consequence cannot be assimilated. In a case in which these latter should overpower it, it would no longer be the 'myself' which was *itself the cause* of the act carried out, and its responsibility would be released. (1968: 125, original emphasis)

While this suggests that there is no autonomous core in the 'myself', given that it is relationally constituted as a bond of instructions and influences, individuals do differ in terms of their compositions of 'myselfs'. In other words, personal identity is not merely a matter of which 'myself' is dominant but equally a question of which 'myselfs' are co-existing in the brain. It follows from this Tardean emphasis on individuality as the composition of 'myselfs' that any quest for an individualist origin of society is replaced by a search for myriad 'myselfs' cast in an ongoing interchange – sometimes combat – with one another (e.g. Tarde, 2012: 65). Equally important, the social struggle for dominance among the 'myselfs' does not take place on a secluded battlefield, confined within the boundaries of the brain. Rather, it evolves in a context of *inter-cerebral* dynamics, per Tarde's definition of imitation as the 'quasi-photographic reproduction of a cerebral image upon the sensitive plate of another brain' (1962: xiv). Hypnotism, hypnotic suggestion and somnambulism – notions used interchangeably by Tarde – are emblematic of these inter-cerebral dynamics: all point to this second dimension of Tarde's doubly socially entangled conception of the individual.

The Inter-Cerebral Constitution of the Individual: The Role of Hypnotic Suggestion

Hypnotism, Tarde explained, 'is the experimental junction point of psychology and sociology; it shows us the most simplified sort of psychic life which can be conceived of under the form of the most elementary social relation' (1968: 193).[15] What happens when one person hypnotises another – to commit certain criminal acts, for instance, seeing as Tarde was writing in a criminological context – amounts to a specific rearrangement of 'myselfs':

Our somnambulist is mistaken in believing that he [*sic*] was able not to have wished to do his act; but he is not mistaken in believing that *he* wished it and that consequently it really is *his*. Only this *he* is not his normal 'myself,' it is a quite

---

[15] This statement about the junction point of sociology and psychology confirms the observation made earlier: contrary to what Deleuze and Latour assert, Durkheim was not off-target in claiming that psychology had some leverage on Tarde's sociology.

Figure 2.1 The individual as automaton.
Note: Late-nineteenth-century automaton by George Moore: a fully mobile robot automaton powered by an internal steam engine.
Source: George Moore's steam man, 1893. © 2019. Photo Ann Ronan/Heritage Images/Scala, Florence

special 'somnambulistic myself,' which nevertheless retains the moral character of the other 'myself.' (1968: 194, original emphasis)

This quote asserts that hypnosis brackets the normally dominant 'myself' and temporarily replaces it with a new 'myself' – the 'somnambulistic myself' – which then serves as the new authority. This is in keeping with the affirmative reading of Tarde I presented earlier, according to which the Tardean individual is plastic and mouldable. However, the quote also complicates this interpretation in that it suggests the authority of the 'somnambulistic myself' is an incomplete one, because it is unable to take full command over the other 'myself(s)'. In particular, according to Tarde, certain moral features make their presence felt.[16]

---

[16] The emphasis on morality provides Tarde still more common ground with Durkheim. Resonating with some of the Kantian spirit of Durkheim's work, Tarde spoke of 'a moral duty', a wish that 'by means of a contagion of imitation […] little by little acquires […]

Tarde's insistence on this 'moral base' (1968: 194) demonstrates that he did not attribute to hypnotism the same power that Le Bon (2002: 8) would a few years later when suggesting that hypnotic-suggestible crowds are able to transform their members into veritable *automatons*. Tarde's conception of hypnosis conceived a layer of friction between the external instruction and the individual's submission to it, meaning that the Tardean individual is not quite as passive and malleable as the crowd subject identified by Le Bon. Tarde stressed that 'The hypnotized person, in fact, is not purely an automaton' (1968: 194), partly because the moral base of subjects allegedly impedes the hypnotist's influence over them.[17] More important, Tarde drew on the French philosopher Frédéric Paulhan to argue that the individual is characterised by some 'logic and finality' that curbs the force with which external hypnotic influence can exert itself on the person (1968: 198, see also 116, n. 2). This latter dimension also illustrates the limitations of using hypnotism as a core encapsulation of the social. As Tarde remarked, hypnotism may be seen as 'the most elementary social relation' (1968: 193), but in most cases only in a somewhat artificial and reduced form. What is social about hypnotism is that it establishes a bond of association between two individuals. More precisely, it portrays the social as centred around one imitative channel – that emanating from the hypnotist. However, from a sociological point of view, this is also where the artificiality lies, since hypnotism revolves around a two-person relationship. It merely illustrates how an individual is influenced by one other individual but not, more realistically, how an individual is enmeshed in an array of external influences (as per the earlier discussion). In this latter situation, Tarde argued, the 'logic and finality' of the individual comes to play an important role:

it is [...] certain, according to us, that the social relation being imitation, the most thoroughly social being is the most thoroughly imitative being. But we must

the authority of the categorical imperative' (1968: 24). Disentangling exactly what morality means for Tarde is not easy, though. What does seem clear is that rather than being founded in any kind of transcendental or a priori principles, morality is something imitatively disseminated – like most other parts of Tarde's system – which means it should be seen as part of monadological battles with competing ideas.

[17] According to Tarde, 'it has never been demonstrated by a single authentic example that hypnotism has transformed a good and straight nature into one which is cruel and false; and the thefts of watches and the blows which have been suggested to various honest and mild subjects have either only been carried out because the person hypnotized was conscious of playing a part in a comedy, or else could not be carried out because the moral base of the being has obstinately resisted this suggestion' (1968: 194). This evokes points consonant with Borch-Jacobsen's analysis of Bernheim and the volitional dimension of suggestion.

notice this very important point: absolute imitativeness, *the faculty of submitting to influences of all kinds and from every side*, and not merely from one single direction, as is the case with the hypnotic subject, *must essentially imply the faculty of resisting an isolated example, a particular influence*. A universal impressionability assumes an *extraordinary originality* which consists in a profound finality and logic, a regular combination of scattered impressions under the domination of one of them which the 'myself' has made its own and by means of which it incorporates all the others. (1968: 199, emphasis added)

It is here that the limitations to interpretations of Tarde by Sampson, Thrift and others like them manifest. In *Penal Philosophy*, Tarde makes clear that he does not conceive of the individual as a simple container of external influence, nor does he reduce it to a piece of modelling clay that can be endlessly reshaped. Certainly, he strongly emphasised that the individual is thrown into the world in a way that persistently brings it under the sway of external suggestions. But Tarde also attributed to the individual a form of buoyancy that enables it to navigate these suggestions and avoid becoming a straw in the wind. Indeed, Tarde argued that the malleability of the individual is *conditioned* by the latter's particular constitution – its substance or core, so to speak. Rather than suggesting a zero-sum game between an individual's malleability and core, Tarde proposed that the better defined their cores, the more individuals are capable of subjecting themselves to de-individualising suggestions from the outside.[18]

This is at the heart of his analysis of how the individual is constituted and how it relates to what is external to it. Tarde explicitly suggested that every individual is characterised by an 'original identity [*identité originale*]' based on 'the persistence of some first element' – the person's particular 'myself', or, in other words, the 'myself' that defines him or her (1968: 128). On an intra-cerebral level, there is one primary 'myself' that, in spite of any ongoing monadological struggle with other 'myselfs', fundamentally constitutes that person. That 'myself' may be challenged or temporarily replaced by a 'somnambulistic myself', as when under hypnosis, but such substitution suspends neither the moral stance nor the logic and finality of the primary 'myself'. Furthermore, should the primary 'myself' be permanently replaced by a new 'myself', 'this change

---

[18] This substantive layer of individuality is not entirely disregarded by Sampson, who notes that 'the somnambulist's vulnerability to hypnosis is located in the [...] inseparable relation between human volition (intention) and the involuntary mechanical habits of everyday life' and that Tardean individuality should therefore be 'grasped according to a hypnotic sleepwalk somewhere between unconsciousness and attentive awareness' (2012: 13). However, the specific analyses following this recognition tend to silence this in-betweenness and only pay attention to the somnambulist dimension.

is always a fall' (1968: 122–3). In other words, the primary 'myself' cannot be enduringly substituted without bringing about a serious identity crisis.

Despite its solidity when it comes to morality, logic and finality, the core identity exists in a state of continuous development due to its interaction with other 'myselfs'. It is 'influenced by others and even owing to their co-operation almost the whole of its stored-up power' (1968: 128). Here cooperation is understood as a matter of absorption. This dynamic is not too different from how an organism grows by absorbing nourishment, though Tarde likens this expanding nature of the 'myself' to how society itself develops:

> Thus the 'myself,' in its incessant changes from one perception to another, from one act to another, proceeds in the same way as does society in its transition from one discovery to another, from one invention to another. So long as a society absorbs more innovations favorable to its principles than innovations opposed to them, it strengthens its identity; under the opposite circumstances it alienates itself. (1968: 121)[19]

This comes close to what the Austrian novelist and crowd theorist Hermann Broch (1955) would later theorise as 'ego expansion' and 'ego contraction': an expanding modification of the ego takes place when it is able to incorporate that which is external to it, but a contracting modification occurs if the ego is deprived of some of its content. Tarde did not talk about contraction so much as alienation, positing a relative rather than absolute relationship between the primary 'myself' and the other 'myselfs'.

It is also clear that Tarde conceived of the intra-cerebral level as inherently social and that he did so in a twofold fashion: in regard to the dynamics between the 'myselfs' (their ongoing struggles and cooperation) and also because the 'myselfs' can be induced, imposed and influenced from the outside (from the interaction that takes place between individuals when ideas, beliefs, desires and the like circulate among them). The tight links between these two levels are highlighted by Tarde's penchant for comparing intra-cerebral dynamics to societal ones. Consonant with his monadological credo that '*everything is a society*' (2012: 28, original emphasis), he portrayed the inner life of the brain as a genuine sociological environment. Essentially, Tarde deployed his

---

[19] Combining this absorptive ability with a monadological framing is possible because Tarde's conception of the latter was based on a notion of 'open monads' endowed with a capacity to 'penetrate each other reciprocally, rather than being mutually external' (2012: 26, see also 34).

broader sociological and monadological frameworks to understand these intra-cerebral social dynamics.[20] In addition, he likened the 'myself' to a state apparatus: 'the "myself" is to the brain what the State is to the nation', describing the primary 'myself' and the state as 'the guiding personality which advises and commands' in each domain (1968: 129). While this can be interpreted as an (implicit) endorsement of a kind of conservative statism, Tarde did make plain that there are crucial limitations to the analogy. While he believed that the destabilisation of the primary 'myself' is likely to effect a deeper constitutional crisis for the individual, he noted that 'social revolutions sometimes constitute progress', suggesting that the overthrowing of the state need not be negative (1968: 123).

A final comment is warranted about the interaction between 'myselfs'. Tarde insisted that while the primary 'myself' undergoes some modifications due to interaction-based absorption,

the essential thing is to recognize in the brain the supremacy of a central element [the primary 'myself'], *always the same throughout its continual modifications*, and whose familiar states, an echo but not a result of the states belonging to the innumerable elements which surround and are subjected to it[,] constitute the normal person. (1968: 124, emphasis added)

This simultaneity of sameness and difference suggests that Tarde conceived of individuality as a matter of degree. Individuality, he proposed, can be seen on a scale. At one end, the primary 'myself' operates in near isolation and/or with little external influence; at the other end is a situation, such as hypnosis or collective forms of being-carried-away, in which the guiding power of the primary 'myself' is considerably reduced. The former reflects the 'maximum of identity', whereas the latter signifies the minimum. Tarde posed a challenging question: 'What is this maximum and what is this minimum of identity, between which our existence oscillates?' (1968: 119). He did not offer a full solution but instead – and I do insist on this – provided important pointers. His work

---

[20] Durkheim follows a similar path in 'Individual and Collective Representations' (1974). While he reiterated his standard critique of Tarde – namely, that it would be wrong to 'reduce sociology to nothing more than a corollary of individual psychology' (1974: 2), he too suggested that intra-cerebral dynamics could be analysed on the basis of an essentially sociological model. Of course, in Durkheim's case, that entailed a model which foregrounded the *sui generis* character of 'mental facts in relation to the cerebral cells' (1974: 25, 26). As Karsenti (2010: 54) notes, 'It is surprising to find Durkheim reincorporating sociology into the very heart of psychology, the discipline which still [in Durkheim's view] threatens its independence'. Yet, what is arguably more astonishing in this context is that Durkheim even referred approvingly to Pierre Janet and his work on hypnotic suggestion (1974: 20–1). This suggests, in line with my earlier discussion, that the divides between Tarde and Durkheim can be easily exaggerated at the expense of recognising their shared ideas.

clearly suggests that rather than paying attention to just one of the two poles of this spectrum, an analytical recalibration is needed in order to retain both ends as well as their tensional relationship. This latter observation is crucial to what I have tried to sketch here. Tarde's analysis of individuality is rather more complex than past commentators have recognised, and this complexity is evident in his simultaneous adherence to a profoundly relational understanding of the individual and to the notion of a core identity. Acknowledging this brings into relief the interpretative problem shared by both the Durkheim-inspired critique of Tarde's alleged individualism and the affirmative emphasis on his plastic notion of the individual. Each of these positions clings to only one end of the analytical spectrum and disregards the entanglement of its poles. By contrast, I suggest that the significance of Tarde's conception of individuality lies in its portrayal of the individual in a *tensional relationship* between some persistent features of the individual (its core) and its external co-constitution (its malleability). Specifically, I argue that Tarde conceptualises the individual as always cast in this *tension between mimetic and anti-mimetic dimensions*: some aspects of the individual, such as its 'logic and finality', are anti-mimetic, whereas the beliefs and desires that circulate from individual to individual are mimetically constituted. In some situations, anti-mimetic dimensions may dominate the individual; in others, mimetic ones are foregrounded. But overall, Tarde suggests that an entangled, Moebius-like tensional relationship plays out between the two poles, often placing them in a state of indeterminacy.

Tarde's conception of tensional individuality, especially that contained in his 1890 book *Penal Philosophy*, has largely escaped the attention of both those influenced by Durkheim and, more recently, those proposing an affirmative reception of Tarde. Yet, the same commitment to both a mimetic and a more substantive, anti-mimetic self is found in other better-known parts of Tarde's oeuvre, including his most famous book, *The Laws of Imitation*, in which he explores how new ideas may be imitated due to what he referred to as 'logical causes':

Logical causes operate whenever an individual prefers a given innovation to others because he [*sic*] thinks it is more useful or more true than others, that is, more in accord than they are with the aims or principles that have already found a place in his mind (through imitation, of course). (1962: 141)[21]

---

[21] While logical causes thus indicate that particular ideas are imitated because there are narrow, rational (e.g. economic or ideational) reasons to do so, so-called extra-logical imitation demarcates contexts in which imitation takes place without any such strictly

In some instances, therefore, the imitation of new ideas may occur 'isolated from any prestige' that may be attributed to the persons being imitated (1962: 141). Following this broad conception of imitative dynamics, Tarde asserts that 'imitation may be conscious or unconscious, deliberate or spontaneous, voluntary or involuntary' (1962: 192). At the same time, however – and further complicating matters – he also maintains that a purely conscious, deliberate and voluntary type of imitation is likely to be a rare occurrence, as even seemingly conscious decisions, such as those made by an apparently autonomous self, can be easily embedded in and co-shaped by external imitative currents. This point is present in the qualifier at the end of the quote above, in which Tarde observes that the aims and principles that inform an individual's decisions have infiltrated the mind through imitation, from some external source. Speaking generally, he claims that

man [*sic*] is wrong in thinking that he imitates because he wishes to. For this very will to imitate has been handed down through imitation. Before imitating the act of another we begin by feeling the need from which this act proceeds, and we feel it precisely as we do only because it has been suggested to us. (Tarde, 1962: 193)

What comes to the fore here, once again, is Tarde's understanding of the individual as captured in mimetic and anti-mimetic tension, oscillating between two extremes, neither of which fully disappears.

Acknowledging this tensional foundation of the individual does not exclude a broader diagnosis of how society or particular social configurations might tip the balance from anti-mimeticism to mimetic influence. This diagnostic layer is consistent with Tarde's analysis in *The Laws of Imitation*, in which the logical causes of imitation receive considerably less attention than 'extra-logical' influences such as fashion and prestige. It also accords with Tarde's answer to his own rhetorical question regarding the analysis of extra-logical vectors: '[Is it] true that as a people becomes civilised its manner of imitating becomes more and more voluntary, conscious and deliberate? I think the opposite is true' (1962: 192). Moreover, as Chapter 3 elaborates, the identification of social situations in which mimetic influences play a comparatively stronger role aligns with Tarde's analysis of crowds as settings of intensified mimesis.

There is one key respect, however, in which Tarde's tensional individuality does not neatly map on to later parts of his oeuvre. This applies in particular to ideas presented in his essay *Monadology and Sociology*

---

rational motives. Perhaps not surprisingly, it is these extra-logical dimensions that are associated with mimesis in Tarde's work.

Figure 2.2 Tensional individuality.
Source: Jakob Kolding (b. 1971), *Ansigt*, 2015. 76 × 56.6 cm. Collage on paper.
Unique. Courtesy: Jakob Kolding and Galleri Nicolai Wallner, Copenhagen.
Photo Anders Sune Berg

(Tarde, 2012), which plays an important role in some of the Latour- and Deleuze-inspired revitalisations of his work. Taking inspiration from a monadological interpretation, Sergio Tonkonoff argues that for Tarde,

> Individuals are not irreducible and compact elements [...]. Rather, they are open monads almost entirely made up of beliefs and desires. [...] An individual is, *most of all*, a passage and sedimentation zone of social flows that are repeated in him (or her) in the form of judgments, memories, wills, and habits. (2013: 271, emphasis added)

The reading I have proposed contests this monadological phrasing of individuality by questioning and qualifying the 'most of all' proviso. My point is that while this may be hard to digest for scholars of an anti-essentialist bent, Tarde's reflections on individuality in *Penal Philosophy* recognise some form of essentialism, some form of substantivism that should be acknowledged *alongside* the plastic conception from the monadological perspective. This is the challenge Tarde offers to present-day social theory: How to straddle two conceptions of the individual that are usually seen as opposites? As I have demonstrated, he answers this by accepting individuality as engaging in a tensional relationship between mimetic and anti-mimetic tendencies.

Tensional Individuality beyond Tarde

I have attended to Tarde's writings to demonstrate how the concept of tensional individuality can be identified in early French sociology. But as Chapter 1 argues, the set of ideas I have distilled from Tarde's work had wider currency in the late nineteenth and early twentieth centuries as well. Akin to how Le Bon and other crowd theorists offered a broader sociological version of Bernheimean micro-clinical endeavours, so too did the Tardean concept of individuality present a sociological variant of Bernheim's reflections on the *suggestionné*'s tensional constitution. Yet, the observation that individuality should be understood in terms of a tensional relationship between mimesis and anti-mimesis stretches considerably beyond the work of Bernheim and Tarde. A response to modernist experiences of the late nineteenth century, the notion of tensional individuality populated the work of a substantial number of thinkers – some very influential – in this period. This can be seen by attending to a set of broader modernist observations in Europe, sociological reflections by the likes of Georg Simmel and George Herbert Mead, and trends of thought in psychology both in the United States and in the twentieth century in general.

Modernist Reflections: Nietzsche

Nidesh Lawtoo's book *The Phantom of the Ego: Modernism and the Mimetic Unconscious* (2013) offers a good starting point. Lawtoo compellingly shows how in the late nineteenth century individuality was widely conceived of as a phantom. Seen as non-identical with itself, individuality was wrought in a complex mimetic relationship to others in a way that 'troubles the boundaries of individuation' (2013: 28). Lawtoo identifies this 'phantasmal' conception of the self, of mimetic rather than self-contained individuality, across the work of a range of (otherwise) disparate thinkers and writers such as Friedrich Nietzsche, Joseph Conrad, D. H. Lawrence and Georges Bataille. Particularly instructive, Lawtoo's analysis of Nietzsche zeroes in on what the latter calls a 'pathos of distance' (2013: 29). According to Lawtoo, this Nietzschean notion has two aspects:

On one side, it marks a critical, philosophical *distance* from forms of mimetic behavior Nietzsche – as well as other modernists after him – frequently denounces in modern subjects. His targets are often subjects he derogatively calls 'the many' or, more often, 'the herd': gregarious, unoriginal people who, in his view, are not in conscious possession of their egos and are, thus, easy prey to different forms of psychic dispossession. [...] On the other, less known side, the concept of 'pathos of distance' points towards Nietzsche's own emotional vulnerability to the mimetic *pathos* he so eloquently denounces in others. (2013: 3, original emphasis)

In other words, much like Le Bon, Nietzsche eagerly critiqued mimesis as a de-individualising force that undermines the bounded individuality of *others*. But devastatingly, and unlike Le Bon, *Nietzsche felt himself attracted to this mimesis* and, more than that, easily submitted to it himself. Lawtoo summarises: 'if Nietzsche is so passionately opposed to the affective force of pathos, it is because this force has already taken possession of him, in a mimetic way' (2013: 3).

The central achievement of Lawtoo's analysis is that it treats the writers he scrutinises as exemplars; their works serve as anchors that help establish the more general experience with modern society he diagnoses, wherein the individual in the modern social order is caught in mimetic and anti-mimetic oscillations. What Nietzsche, Conrad, Lawrence, Bataille and the host of other figures captured in Lawtoo's analytical cabinet share is the pervasive sense that modern society renders individuality problematic. In Hegelian terms, the individual is not given in and for itself; rather, it is intrinsically linked to others in ways that confuse interiority and exteriority, but which nonetheless retain traces of singular individuality. It is important to note this diagnosis does not simply anticipate – by half a century, albeit with other and more profound analytical tools – Riesman's famous notion of 'other-directed' people, characterised by their being deeply 'sensitized to the expectations and preferences of others' (Riesman, 1961: 8). More is at stake, since these modernist observers portrayed individuality as inherently tensional. In a nutshell, they suggested that other-directedness might appear problematic vis-à-vis a liberal tradition of self-contained, volitional individuality; yet this theoretico-ideological problematisation of other-directedness was followed, even undercut, by the experience of the attraction to and actual being-carried-away by mimetic currents.

Sociological Reflections: Simmel and Mead

The ideas Lawtoo identifies amongst this selection of modernist observers resonate with views expressed in German and American sociology. In Simmel, this materialised in his famous 1905 pamphlet 'The Philosophy of Fashion' (Simmel, 1997d).[22] My interest here begins with Simmel's fundamental observation about fashion as combining 'the need for integration on the one hand and the need for separation on the other' (1997d: 191). Indeed, Simmel's essay is one long exposé on collectivity, individuality and how fashion is an expression of – as well as a means of navigating – their interrelations.

According to Simmel, and echoing Tarde, the collective dimension of fashion is a function of 'the psychological tendency towards *imitation*' (1997d: 188, original emphasis). By imitating others, the individual obtains 'the assurance of not standing alone' and becomes a virtual 'vessel of social contents' (1997d: 188). However, fashion does not merely make people alike in a mimetic whirlwind. Its logic of differentiation appeals to an anti-mimetic counter-tendency: standing out. What is fascinating about fashion, according to Simmel's analysis, is that it brings together mimesis and anti-mimesis in one 'unified act' (1997d: 189). Furthermore, resonant with the Tardean analysis of tensional individuality, Simmel was well-aware that fashion's simultaneous 'impulse

---

[22] As David Frisby (1997: 13) notes, Simmel addressed the question of fashion on several occasions, beginning with his 1895 text 'Zur Psychologie der Mode. Sociologische Studie' (Simmel, 1992b). I limit my discussion to his 1905 essay since it provides the most extensive treatment of the topic. Note that Simmel's texts on fashion are largely overlapping and that the essay 'The Philosophy of Fashion' is almost identical to the 'Fashion' essay that first appeared in English in 1904, later republished in the *American Journal of Sociology* (Simmel, 1957). However, as the 'Fashion' essay omits certain sentences and emphases from the 'The Philosophy of Fashion' text, the latter is better suited to my analysis.

towards individualization and the drive for immersion in the collectivity' prompts questions about freedom and dependency (1997d: 196, 200). Simmel's conception of their interrelation recalls how Bernheim's work opens the possibility that submission to collective suggestion could be volitional, as well as Durkheim's positive connection between collectivity and individuality. Thus, Simmel argued for a plus-sum relationship between mimetic immersion in the collective and an affirmation of personal anti-mimetic freedom; portraying the individual as consisting of an inside self and an external appearance, fashion's role in external appearance allowed for an expansion of interiority.[23] In Simmel's words,

a triumph of the soul over the given nature of existence is achieved which, as least as far as form is concerned, must be considered one of the highest and finest victories: namely, that the enemy himself [*sic*] is transformed into a servant, that precisely that which seemed to violate the personality is seized voluntarily, because the levelling violation is here transferred to the external strata of life in such a way that it furnishes a veil and a protection for everything that is innermost and now all the more free. (1997d: 198–9)

Much like Tarde, who applied his overall sociological programme to the inner workings of the brain, Simmel suggested that the dialectical relationship between fashion's mimetic dimensions and anti-mimetic differentiations applies 'within the individual soul' as well (1997d: 200). What emerges out of this doubling of imitation and individualisation is a situation in which the 'needs for imitation, similarity, and for the blending of the individual into the mass, are here satisfied purely within the individuals themselves' via an imitation of 'their own self' (1997d: 201).

While Simmel's reflections on the inner mimetic and anti-mimetic dimensions of the soul remained somewhat opaque, the idea that the self is multiple would draw further attention in the work of George Herbert Mead. One of the main ideas in the tradition of symbolic interactionism, which Mead (co)pioneered, is the notion that the self is constituted by two central components: a 'me' and an 'I'. According to Mead, the 'me' represents the attitudes of others. These include, at least when the self is fully developed, those of the 'generalized other' – in other words, 'the attitude of the whole community' (Mead, 1934: 154). The 'me' orients itself towards attitudes that exist in society (or in those sections of society to which the individual belongs), and these become instrumental as internalised guidelines for a person's conduct. In Mead's words:

[23] I return to this relationship between surface and depth in Chapter 4.

It is in the form of the generalized other that the social process influences the behavior of the individuals involved in it and carrying it on, i.e., that the community exercises control over the conduct of its individual members; for *it is in this form that the social process or community enters as a determining factor into the individual's thinking*. (1934: 155, emphasis added)

Consequently, the 'me' is effectively portrayed by Mead as standing in a relation to the generalised other, one that recalls Durkheim's understanding of how social facts impose themselves on individuals as external constraints that condition how people think. In a mimetic vocabulary, Mead's 'me' therefore suggests a strong form of mimesis in which – as per Tarde's general model – external beliefs and desires shape the individual's internal beliefs and desires. Yet, Mead added to this a potential counter-dynamism, an anti-mimetic force summarised by the workings of the 'I'. The latter represents 'the response of the individual to the attitude of the community as this appears in his [*sic*] own experience' (1934: 196). While Mead argued that no self emerges until individuals take the attitude of some other as 'an essential part' of their behaviour, the 'I' can respond to the attitudes of society in ways that need not conform to whatever the 'me' has incorporated (1934: 195). The 'I' can, in other words, ensure innovation and therefore also bring an element of unpredictability into Mead's system, more generally. It further follows that the Meadean self is not a mimetic dupe which, like an automaton, executes and (thereby) reinforces society's dominant ways of thinking. Rather, Mead presupposed the existence of an individual's anti-mimetic core, which may be expressed through the 'I' (1934: 197).

Like Simmel, therefore, Mead's distinction between 'me' and 'I' is one between collectivity and individuality. As Tarde did, Mead depicted the individual as given in a tensional relationship between external mimetic conditioning and internal anti-mimetic aptitudes. Mead further agreed with Tarde that in some situations, the (mimetic) 'me' would play a relatively larger role than the (anti-mimetic) 'I', and vice versa in others (1934: 199). In other words, Mead, too, identified an oscillation between the two poles.

The fact that the ideas of Simmel and Mead have a certain affinity to the notion of tensional individuality is probably no coincidence, considering the specific historical situation and the landslide experiences they shared – along with Tarde, Nietzsche and others – described in Chapter1. But there is arguably another reason why the notion of tensional individuality resonated with Simmel and Mead, one which connects them to these other thinkers as well: the attempt to theorise in ways that showed a central inspiration from psychology. *Contra* Durkheim's mantra about the need to sharply separate sociology from psychology,

Simmel and Mead were proponents of a social-psychological tradition that moved comfortably between sociology and psychology, combining ingredients from each domain in their thinking.

This theoretical alignment between Mead, Simmel and Tarde notwithstanding, it is important to note that Mead did not phrase his ideas in the lexicon of mimesis and imitation. Indeed, Mead did not share Simmel's and Tarde's emphasis on these notions and surely would not grant imitation the same explanatory status the two Europeans did. He explicitly dismissed Tarde's work and asserted, in one of the lectures that formed the basis for his main work, *Mind, Self, and Society*, that 'imitation as a general instinct is now discredited in human psychology' – thereby also implicitly challenging Simmel's notion of a 'psychological tendency towards imitation' (Mead, 1934: 52, 53).[24] In fact, as Ruth Leys demonstrates in her careful deconstruction of his thinking, Mead based his theory on a 'resolve to defeat Tarde's theory of imitation-suggestion' and to replace it with one in which 'the self-identical ego or *subject* is silently presupposed' (Leys, 1993: 287, 292, original emphasis). However, regardless of this antagonism towards notions of mimesis and imitation, Mead nonetheless advocated a conception of the self strikingly similar to the tensional individuality portrayed in Tarde's work.

US Psychological Reflections: Sidis

I mentioned that Mead's, Simmel's and Tarde's commitment to a conception of tensional individuality might have to do with their insistence on the relevance of psychological ideas. Indeed, this notion of tensional individuality gained widespread traction within psychological quarters in both Europe and the US. The Ukrainian-American psychologist Boris Sidis's book *The Psychology of Suggestion* (1898) deserves particular attention as an illustration of the American situation. In it, Sidis pursues the

---

[24] Had he been more attentive to Simmel's work, Mead would have discovered that Simmel offered an answer to a question Mead himself posed but found no convincing answer to, at least none convincing enough to grant imitation a central analytical role: 'Is there any reason for imitation?' (1934: 52). Why, in other words, would people care to imitate? By way of an answer, Simmel suggested that imitation reduces complexity and embeds the individual in a collectivity: 'Imitation gives the individual the assurance of not standing alone in his or her actions. [...] Whenever we imitate, we transfer not only the demand for creative energy, but also the responsibility for the action from ourselves to another. Thus the individual is freed from choosing and appears simply as a creature of the group' (1997d: 188). Even though Simmel certainly saw greater analytical potential in the notion of imitation than Mead did, he did not buy into the full Tardean conceptual horizon of hypnotic suggestion. His ambivalence about this tradition is reflected in his reviews of the work of Tarde and Le Bon; see Simmel (1999a; 1999b).

broad agenda of understanding suggestion at the level of both the individual and the collective/crowd. The latter was especially important to Sidis's former colleague and mentor, the American psychologist and pragmatist philosopher William James, who wrote in his introduction to the book that one of its core accomplishments was how it discussed 'the very important matter of "crowd psychology" [...] almost for the first time in English. There is probably no more practically important topic to the student of public affairs' (1898: vii).[25]

Based on more than 3,000 experiments, conducted in part while Sidis worked at Harvard University, the book presents a careful analysis of the role of suggestion and the composition of the self. Sidis's analysis engaged in explicit dialogue with contemporaneous French debates – he often referred approvingly to the work of the Nancy School, for instance. The central idea Sidis developed is that the self should be seen as divided into two: the waking self and the subconscious self (also referred to as the primary and the secondary self, respectively).[26] The former was treated as an autonomous conscious self capable of independent thinking and decision-making. The latter, by contrast, referred to a hypnotic, highly plastic self, evinced by Sidis's observation (echoing Bernheim) that under hypnosis

you can do with the subwaking self anything you like. The subwaking consciousness is in your power like clay in the hands of the potter. The nature of its plasticity is revealed by its complete suggestibility. Unlike clay, however, it can not be hardened into any permanent and durable form. (1898: 246)

While this might suggest a strict separation between an anti-mimetic waking self and a subconscious self enmeshed in mimesis, Sidis's analysis in fact emphasised their entangled nature. He argued that no person is defined only by the waking self; the subconscious self always co-

---

[25] Testifying to Sidis's status as an important representative of crowd psychology, the American sociologist George Edgar Vincent referred to him as one of the authors who, alongside famous names such as Le Bon and Tarde, had 'made important contributions to the morbid psychology of the group, as displayed in mental epidemics and mob violence' (1904: 152).

[26] Somewhat related discussions of a dual self attracted significant attention throughout the nineteenth century under the conception of the brain as divided into two semi-independent (but nonetheless related) hemispheres, the left side and the right side. As Anne Harrington (1987) cogently details, these discussions became deeply entangled in debates about hypnosis and suggestion in France and beyond. Considering the overall point of my book, this link is hardly surprising, as the notion of the brain's two hemispheres suggests that the individual can be analysed as one stretched out, as it were, between two poles (the left side associated with volition, intelligence, reason, etc. – the right side with instinct, passion, unconsciousness, etc.) that stand in a complex relationship to each other.

constitutes the person. Indeed, Sidis took pains to demonstrate that 'the secondary self is part and parcel of our normal state' (1898: 158). His analysis thus pointed not only 'to a double self as constituting human individuality' but also to the idea that a tensional relationship between mimesis and anti-mimesis defines the default human condition (1898: 91). At a deeper level, Sidis sought to demonstrate that this tensional relationship plays out even *within* the subwaking self. Thus, for all the mimetic plasticity attributed to the subwaking self, a considerable part of *The Psychology of Suggestion* was devoted to identifying within this self 'the presence of a hidden agency [...]; an agency that possesses perception, memory, judgment, and even will', something that would speak in favour of the existence of an anti-mimetic dimension (1898: 92). Sidis referenced a number of experiments conducted both by others and himself in support of this claim (see also Blackman, 2012: 90). These include, for example, parallel work on double consciousness by the French psychologist Alfred Binet (see, e.g. 1896) in which experiments with automatic writing played a central role, i.e. writing without being conscious about it.[27] These experiments demonstrated, according to Sidis, that the subwaking self possesses a particular level of sensation, perception and reasoning that is not available to the waking self. Surprisingly, Sidis argued these experiments produce 'direct evidence of the reality of a secondary consciousness, of an intelligent, subwaking, hypnotic self concealed behind the curtain of personal consciousness' – behind the workings of the primary, waking self (1898: 99–100, see also 106). The central corollary of the double self is that instead of conceiving of hypnosis in de-individualising terms (as something undermining the conscious state of the individual), Sidis suggested that 'hypnosis is a conscious state' (1898: 120). Similar to Tarde, Sidis (1898: 96, 106) thus argues against likening the hypnotic self to an automaton.

One may object that Sidis developed his insights from types of experimentation, including automatic writing, to which today's scholars might not attribute much significance. Indeed, Sidis cited many experimental methodologies even more exotic than automatic writing. It is worth noting, however, that in his introduction to Sidis's book, William James praised the author's 'ingenious experiments' and believed they, while not always complete, 'open[ed] the way to a highly important psychological investigation' (1898: vi). Differently described, Sidis's experimental work was carefully situated within state-of-the-art research at the time but carried a touch of the *avant-garde*. For present purposes, however,

---

[27] For a fascinating analysis of the role of automatic writing in this tradition, see Blackman (2014).

I am more interested in Sidis's analytical template than his experimental validity. Crucially, Sidis's work arrived at a notion of tensional individuality that evokes themes also addressed by Bernheim, Tarde and others. Of course, Sidis's (1898: 106) notion of the double self is not entirely parallel to Bernheim's conception of it; the former assigns it more partial or 'rudimentary' volition than the latter (as per Borch-Jacobsen's interpretation). Similarly, Tarde's conception of the individual contains greater multiplicity in that it allows for many more cohabiting 'myselfs' than the two identified by Sidis.[28] More important, however, in keeping with the tensional relationship between mimesis and anti-mimesis proposed by Bernheim and adapted by Tarde, Sidis's notion of the self does not simply and neatly distinguish between a waking, anti-mimetic self and a mimetic, subwaking one. Instead, this distinction is reintroduced, in a convoluted manner, within the seemingly mimetic subwaking self, thereby rendering the initial separation between mimesis and anti-mimesis effectively indistinct.

I focus on Sidis's book as an exemplar of a broader type of research conducted in the United States at the end of the nineteenth century, which included, *inter alia*, James's work. It might be tempting today to write off Sidis's ideas as the dubious ruminations of an oddball. However, the kind of work he advocated did have widespread traction during his time and thus usefully illuminates the genealogy I chart here (for a positive appreciation of his work, see Bruce, 1923). James's endorsement of Sidis's book also bestowed it with scholarly legitimacy and demonstrated that the thoughts it put forth were analytically useful. James's recommendation of Sidis's work was no mere gesture: his interest in the book reflected his own expeditions into similar terrain. Among other things, James (2000: 58–9) wrestled with 'the ancient problem of "the one and the many"' – a problem that, as Lisa Blackman cogently demonstrates, also and especially manifests at the level of individuality. In Blackman's summary:

The topology of subjectivity that James presents is one which views the human subject as being akin to a channel or conductor of thought, open and permeable to the other, invoking a sense of a shared collective consciousness, rather than one closed and located within atomized subjects. (Blackman, 2012: 30)

---

[28] Although Sidis (1898: 136–8) did refer to experiments that demonstrate three selves, his main conception remained that of a dyadic or double self. Also, when Sidis recognised the existence of more than two selves, any such additional selves were analysed in a pathological register, whereas Tarde theorised the multiplicity of selves as the normal state of affairs.

Importantly, however, this view of the subject as channel does not entirely dispense with the individual to furnish a notion of pure plasticity – the subject as being multiple. Rather, James was well aware that the problem of the one and the many was not resolvable by analytically choosing either in the hope that the fundamental problem would then vanish like dew before the sun. Either extreme position can face critique if treated in isolation. The notion of an autonomous individual can be disputed with evidence brought up by Sidis and other scholars, which pointed to the profound entanglement of each subject with others. Similarly, the notion of pure individual plasticity and complete permeability can be contested by insights into the willpower allegedly at play even in suggestive processes. Consequently, in my reading, 'the problem of personality', as Blackman (2008) labels it, translates into an understanding that retains the simultaneous, if tensional, relationship between oneness and manyness.

Twentieth-Century Psychological Reflections

My final illustration of how the conception of a tensional relationship between mimesis and anti-mimesis resonates with ideas that went beyond the writings of Bernheim, Tarde and other *fin-de-siècle* theorists attends to its temporal, rather than merely geographical, relocation. In a series of penetrating genealogies of trauma, guilt and shame – thematised in the work of psychologists of trauma (Sigmund Freud, Morton Prince, Sándor Ferenczi, etc.) and psychologists of guilt and shame (Robert Jay Lifton, Terrence Des Pres, Eve Kosofsky Sedgwick, etc.) – Ruth Leys (2000; 2007) demonstrates that the questions of mimesis and anti-mimesis that emerged from discussions of trauma, for instance, were by no means confined to Bernheimean endeavours. Rather, they became foundational to how these phenomena were analysed throughout the twentieth century (see similarly Blackman, 2012). Several central points emerge out of the complexity of Leys's genealogies. Take, for instance, Leys's explanation of how, already in the work of Charcot and his contemporaries but extending well into the twentieth century,

Trauma was defined as a situation of dissociation or 'absence' from the self in which the victim unconsciously imitated, or identified with, the aggressor or traumatic scene in a condition that was likened to a state of heightened suggestibility or hypnotic trance. (Leys, 2000: 8)

While this suggests that mimesis was central to how trauma was conceived at the time, a counter-movement, 'a tendency towards the repudiation of mimesis[,] was from the start also at work in the field' (2000: 9).

In this '*antimimetic* tendency', as Leys calls it, trauma was conceived as 'a purely external event coming to a sovereign if passive victim' (2000: 10, original emphasis). In other words, within this counter-movement the individual was portrayed in terms of its alleged autonomy. Interestingly, and anticipating Lawtoo's parallel analysis of Nietzsche and other *fin-de-siècle* modernist observers, Leys notes:

> It is as though early theorists of trauma were simultaneously attracted to and repelled by the mimetic-suggestive theory, as though the basis of the latter's appeal – its ability to explain the victim's suggestibility and abjection – was also its chief defect – its threat to an ideal of individual autonomy and responsibility. (2000: 9)

Leys's genealogical work demonstrates that in spite of persistent efforts to the contrary, the anti-mimetic movement could not completely do away with mimesis. Accordingly, the central achievement of her historical reconstructions of trauma and guilt lies in her compelling demonstration that there has 'been a continuous tension or oscillation between the two paradigms, so that even the most resolutely anti-mimetic theory of trauma has tended to resurrect the mimetic theory itself' (2000: 10; 2007: 10–11).[29]

Reviving the Notion of Tensional Individuality

Thus far, I have sketched several articulations of a tensional relationship between mimesis and anti-mimesis. The majority of these were formulated at the turn of the nineteenth century, in both Europe and the United States, but as Leys's work makes plain, this tension remained foundational to important traditions in psychological thought throughout the twentieth century. While the traditions I have examined include well known, if controversial, figures such as Freud, Nietzsche and Tarde, I realise that some of the names associated with the tensional understanding of individuality might be unfamiliar in a twenty-first-century context. Many have certainly lapsed into obscurity, and they have chiefly surfaced from hibernation in specialist historical-genealogical investigations. However, what is important here is not whether the tensional notion of individuality is espoused by a set of renowned and highly regarded scholars: it is clear that we are dealing with a broad analytical repertoire,

---

[29] Considering the attentiveness with which Leys analyses the mimesis–anti-mimesis tension in trauma theory, it is somewhat surprising to note that in her otherwise brilliant analysis of Tarde, she disregards the anti-mimetic layers in his notion of individuality and presents the latter as if it entailed only a plastic-mimetic conception (see Leys, 1993).

the emergence of which is anything but coincidental. The tensional understanding of individuality took shape in response to and as a means of coming to terms with a particular modernist experience: that of being caught between a sense of one's independent self yet subsumed under external mimetic influence, the latter often in a profound experience of being-carried-away in a collective.

While a certain *fin-de-siècle* historicity therefore emerges in this experience of tensionality, Leys's genealogical work suggests that it would be wrong to dismiss tensional individuality as just another oddity from a distant past, an outlandish trace of an experience that is no longer ours. Rather, her work invites us to ponder if the persistent oscillation between mimetic and anti-mimetic conceptions – the stamina with which the tensional relationship makes itself felt in psychological thought – could have reasons irreducible to some ideational path dependency. Bluntly put, the tensional understanding of individuality recurs because it points to something fundamental about individuality, especially in a modern social order. It was clearly the central hunch of the *fin-de-siècle* observers that the tensional notion sheds important light on individuality as it was actually lived. I suggest that this conception should be revived in a present-day context, as its analytical salience has not diminished – even today, subject-centred approaches, including rationalist-individualist accounts of crowd and collective behaviour, face an analytical impasse they need to correct.

Others have argued along similar lines. For example, at the end of her genealogical examination of the late-nineteenth and early twentieth-century roots of today's affect theory, Lisa Blackman suggests that 'rather than existing as bounded, autonomous subjects, we exist in shared ecologies. We are perhaps characterized more by the paradox of being both one yet many, of being thoroughly singular-plural beings' (Blackman, 2012: 180). The paradox of being one yet many is, in essence, a rephrasing of the notion of tensional individuality I have examined. Moreover, like Leys's, Blackman's analysis attends primarily to various branches of psychological thought, reflecting how psychologists have been particularly attentive to – and entangled in – tensional notions of individuality. While this is hardly surprising given the strong late-nineteenth-century interest in these matters in French psychotherapy and beyond, it remains remarkable, from a comparative scholarly perspective, that *fin-de-siècle* sociological reflections left no similar imprint on sociology's subsequent development – at most, it did so only at its fringes. After all, much twentieth- and twenty-first-century sociology is indebted, in some way or other, to what is often seen as a Weberian commitment to methodological individualism that leaves little room for mimesis and touts a notion of self-contained individuality instead.[30] To be sure, a host of structuralist and, especially, post-structuralist theories have offered positions counter to key Weberian ideas. While several of these theories display some recognition of mimetic features (e.g. Deleuze, 1994), they have largely failed to acknowledge the more substantive aspects of individuality captured in the concept of tensionality, as the work of Judith Butler nicely illustrates. Butler strongly opposes a notion of gender as something pre-given and argues instead for analysing gender as the performative effect of various imitations of circulating ideals and socio-cultural pointers. Subjectivity, for Butler, is a matter of mimetic plasticity:

> *gender is a kind of imitation for which there is no original*; in fact, it is a kind of imitation that produces the very notion of the original as an *effect* and consequence of the imitation itself. In other words, the naturalistic effects of heterosexualized genders are produced through imitative strategies; what they imitate is a phantasmatic ideal of heterosexual identity, one that is produced by the imitation as its effect. (Butler, 1991: 21, original emphasis)

In keeping with this purely mimetic position – one at the mimetic extreme of the continuum I sketched – Butler rejects any notion of a 'volitional subject behind the mime' (1991: 24). Despite her references to Borch-Jacobsen and Leys, she misses their central insight into how mimesis is tensionally related to an anti-mimetic, substantive self.

In addition to sociological work which taps into either pole of the mimetic–anti-mimetic continuum, there is of course a diverse group of sociologists, including Pierre Bourdieu (Bourdieu and Wacquant, 1992), Anthony Giddens (1984) and Niklas Luhmann (1995), that has tried to bridge or circumvent the divide between methodological individualism and structuralism. However, such attempts have rarely been executed via solutions that revolve around the mimesis–anti-mimesis tension. Thus, the discipline of sociology and its development throughout the twentieth century until today remains characterised by a pronounced lack of attention to the tension between mimesis and anti-mimesis. The reasons, both overlapping and mutually reinforcing, behind this disremembering of a *problematique* so central to sociology's nascence include the discipline's marginalisation of crowd theory – the main propagator of mimetic thought – during the twentieth century (Borch, 2012b); the increasing separation between sociological theorisation and psychological thought,

---

[30] As I come back to in the next chapter, Weber himself actually seemed to grant imitation a significant sociological role, though this has escaped attention in much Weber commentary.

the latter a key base for recognising mimesis–anti-mimesis tensions; as well as the aforementioned stronghold that Weberian notions have held over the discipline and its development, a grip that has rendered mimetic notions of individuality analytically unpopular if not outright dubious.

As mentioned earlier, I advocate for an end to this forgetting of the notion of tensional individuality and for its subsequent revival. Much more than reflecting a widespread experience of a highly specific historical situation, an emphasis on tensionality is helpful in elucidating individuality and collectivity in diverse contexts from the metropolis to financial markets, as well as periods stretching from the early twentieth century to the twenty-first. More generally, tensional individuality serves an important theoretico-analytical purpose today: it offers an antidote to prevailing conceptions of individuality and collectivity that herald one end of the mimesis–anti-mimesis spectrum, disregarding not just the other end but also the mutual, if tensional, interconnections between these poles.

★★★

Tarde's sociological theorisation offers an interesting conception of tensional individuality that may be read as a response to the particular historical situation of the late nineteenth century, during which a widespread sense of mimetic turbulence gained traction. I have demonstrated that the conception of tensional individuality is present not only in Tarde's thought but also in the work of many of his contemporaries. Indeed, present-day rehabilitations of Tarde should not be obstructed by Durkheim's rebuttal of his work, as the two held positions not quite as dissimilar as they liked to claim. It is important for me to stress this, not merely to redeem Tarde's credibility but also because I extract an understanding of collective behaviour drawn from the work of Durkheim, Tarde and other scholars in Chapter 3.

The Tardean conception of tensional individuality I have developed may trigger two types of questions. The first concerns the origin of the core identity: If tensional individuality entails taking seriously the notion of a substantive identity, how then does this identity transpire? Did Tarde believe that a person is born with a specific identity that remains unchanged throughout life? Did he subscribe to some essentialist notion of individuality? This is one valid interpretation of his position. Alternatively, Tarde may have neither reflected deeply on this question in his deliberations of individuality nor considered the search for origins his primary preoccupation. Taking this inquiry further, it is plausible that he would have considered both the 'logic and finality' and the 'moral base' of the individual as necessarily developed in mimetic relation to others (no *deus ex machina* or spontaneous emergence here) but still insist on these assuming some stickiness: once mimetically developed, they change little and are resistant to new external mimetic influences. The other type of question, arguably of greater sociological pertinence, is whether there are conditions that impinge on where particular forms of individuality fall on the continuum – how tensional individuality is more precisely shaped in specific situations. Are certain conditions conducive to forms of individuality that swing more towards anti-mimesis? Are some conditions more likely than others to produce mimetic forms of individuality? And are there situations that increase the likelihood of rapid oscillations between the two poles?

Perhaps unsurprisingly, these questions return me to discussions of crowd and collective behaviour; Tarde, along with many other *fin-de-siècle* social theorists, would assert that the crowding and amassing of people constitutes a condition in which the pendulum of individuality moves towards the mimetic end. In the next chapter I draw upon the work of Tarde, Durkheim and others to develop the concept of social avalanching and examine, among other things, its effects on individuality. Regarding the influence of environmental conditions on individuality, Tarde further argued – akin to scholars such as José Ortega y Gasset – that the city constitutes a setting in which mimesis is likely to be especially predominant. I examine this suggestion in Chapter 4, which explores how urban life produces specific forms of social avalanching, with corresponding effects on individuality.

3   Social Avalanches

In a comprehensive examination of Weimar crowd thinking, Stefan Jonsson notes that the early-twentieth-century pressure on established forms of individuality gave rise to 'not only a post-individualistic idea of human subjectivity but also a post-individualistic notion of the masses' (Jonsson, 2013: 143). This post-individualistic idea of subjectivity resembles the mimetic layer I analysed in Chapter 2: the individual is neither fully autonomous nor sovereign but rather profoundly externally influenced, to the extent that it becomes difficult to separate inside from outside. As the previous chapter demonstrates, a host of modernist observers subscribed to this post-individualistic notion of subjectivity. They did so (and this is less emphasised by Jonsson) not by entirely abandoning a sense of sovereign self but by conceiving of these two conceptions as given in a tensional relationship. In the present chapter, the focus shifts from the subject or individual to what Jonsson fittingly calls a post-individualistic conception of the *masses* – one which does not reduce crowds to a more or less random agglomeration of individuals who each pursue particular goals. Rather than explaining collective behaviour by making recourse to singular individuals, a post-individualistic approach accords crowds a certain *eigendynamik* that goes beyond the level of the individuals who partake in them.

The emphasis on these inner dynamics of crowds was a defining feature of late-nineteenth-century French crowd psychology, as illustrated in Le Bon's work. His psychology of crowds has a certain Machiavellian pedigree since, in addition to providing a diagnosis and explanation of crowd behaviour, he also suggested a set of tools that politicians could employ in order to govern crowds to the former's advantage (Borch, 2009: 275; Moscovici, 1985: 58).[1] Such tools included making simple, blunt statements and repeating these over and over again (e.g. Le Bon, 2002: 77–81).

---

[1] Granted, Le Bon was ambivalent on this issue. While he did point to certain means of crowd government, he also stressed that politicians should lower their hopes for what could in fact be achieved: 'A knowledge of the psychology of crowds is to-day the last

Le Bon therefore recommended that politicians should utilise a main feature of crowds: the supposedly contagious nature of thought and feeling within them. 'Ideas, sentiments, emotions, and beliefs possess in crowds a contagious power as intense as that of microbes', he asserted (2002: 78). Precisely this dimension of contagion demonstrates that for Le Bon, the crowd is not merely an entity that can be formed in the hands of a clever leader. The crowd also contains *self-organising dynamics* that need to be taken seriously. In other words, from the point of view of Le Bon's theorisation, crowds are characterised by dynamics irreducible to the actions of either the leader or its individual members.

Just as the notion of individuals caught in a tensional relationship between mimesis and anti-mimesis gained traction in response to and resonated with the particular modernist experience of the late nineteenth and early twentieth centuries, so too did the idea that contagion dynamics are inculcated into crowd and collective behaviour. This is not to suggest that conceptions of contagion have their roots in the late nineteenth century. As Peta Mitchell convincingly demonstrates, for example, a long tradition of discussing contagious phenomena can be traced as far back as ancient Greek reflections on miasma (Mitchell, 2012: ch. 2). And yet, as Mitchell affirms, discussions of contagion nevertheless assumed a particular shape and intensity at the end of the nineteenth century. In response to 'modernization, urbanization and the development of mass media', a set of contagion vocabularies such as 'moral contagion' and the 'contagion of example' became popular tools with which to draw connections between physical contagion in disease and social forms of contagion such as revolutionary crowds and flashes of public outrage (Mitchell, 2012: 63).

Cities, in particular, were seen as sites where contagion proliferated in all its shapes; I discuss this in detail in Chapter 4. Following Priscilla Wald's formulation, the late nineteenth century marked an era in which 'Researchers and theorists used contagious disease both literally and metaphorically in the studies of urban space and national affiliation, of assimilation and ghettos, to explore the phenomenon of cultural contact' (2008: 116). In Le Bon's case, the discussion of contagion was not directly tied to urban developments, seeking as he did to capture a collective experience even more intense than that arising out of the changing urban fabric. This collective experience, the crowd experience, was one of *being carried away*, of losing one's sense of self as a result of collective de-individualising frenzy, regardless of whether the crowd

---

resource of the statesman who wishes not to govern them – that is becoming a very difficult matter – but at any rate not to be too much governed by them' (2002: xiv).

experience was located in the metropolis or elsewhere. As this crowd experience was widely portrayed as a specifically modern occurrence, the work of Le Bon and others writing about crowds at the end of the nineteenth century should be thought of as a response to and a means of grappling with this fundamental *fin-de-siècle* experiential layer.

In this chapter, I look closely at how this experience was conceptualised in late-nineteenth and early-twentieth-century social theory. I argue that it is possible to distil from a range of reflections on crowd behaviour a notion of *social avalanche*, or *social avalanching*, that accounts for the experience of being-carried-away in a manner that stresses particular self-organising dynamics of collective formations. Specifically, I establish the notion of social avalanching on the basis of a reading that traverses the work of a number of turn-of-the-nineteenth-century theorists, including scholars such as Durkheim and Tarde, who are usually seen as belonging to opposing camps. While such an endeavour faces the obvious risk of turning an array of disconnected propositions into an incoherent patchwork of ideas, my central point is that instead of insisting on the rift between these theorists and their alleged incompatibility, it makes more sense to interpret them as responding to similar modernist experiences.

Why add the notion of avalanching to an already large pile of sociological concepts? Why not simply adhere to 'crowds' and 'collective behaviour' if these are already centrally placed in the analytical repertoire revived in this chapter? I argue that the concept of avalanche was in fact deployed by a range of late-nineteenth and early twentieth-century social theorists to make sense of their experience of crowd behaviour and collective de-individualisation. In that sense, I am loyal to their conceptual choices and merely seek to foreground and clarify a notion already present in the social theory of this time period. I realise that some of the scholars to whom I refer (and their heirs) may not have been too comfortable with being labelled crowd theorists; in light of the critiques of crowd theory, avalanching might be a less-burdened conceptual choice. This may be a contestable assertion, as some might object even more strongly to the notion of avalanche, declaring that it exemplifies the type of metaphor of which social theory should rid itself. However, as I argue, the validity of this critique is not quite as straightforward as it might seem. I therefore claim that 'social avalanche' should have its place in the sociological lexicon, taking comfort in the fact that many established, sanctioned notions in sociology are no less metaphoric than that of avalanching.

Further, social avalanching as I define it has a broader scope than crowding; the latter is in fact better understood as a specific subset or embodiment of the former. What is significant about social avalanching is that it can refer to processes that need not involve human beings

Figure 3.1 Avalanche.
Note: Joseph Mallord William Turner (1775–1851), *The Fall of an Avalanche in the Grisons*. Exhibited 1810. London, Tate Gallery. Oil paint on canvas. Support: 902 x1200 mm. Accepted by the nation as part of the Turner Bequest 1856.
Source: © 2019. Tate, London/Photo Scala, Florence

directly. I stress this feature not to evoke late-nineteenth-century attempts to understand sociality via a medical-biological register and through phenomena such as contagion. Instead, I propose a sociological vocabulary with which we might begin to better understand how particular non-human processes produce recognizable forms of sociality. While the present chapter only briefly sketches this analytical possibility, Chapter 5 pursues it in greater detail in the context of algorithmic finance today and the interactions between fully automated computer algorithms. I contend that even if this is an emphatically non-human domain, it nonetheless displays signs of sociality in the form of social avalanching.

I begin by challenging the normative valence often associated with classical crowd theory. Since the crowd theory tradition of Le Bon, Tarde and others has often been taken by subsequent sociologists to represent an overly conservative horizon, in which crowds are seen as antithetical to society (again, pointedly summarised in McPhail's notion of the 'madding crowd'), resuscitating this tradition could appear an almost regressive endeavour. Nonetheless, while it is certainly true that aspects of crowd theory discourse at the end of the nineteenth century tended to depict crowd behaviour in an antagonistic relationship with society, it is also possible to identify more balanced or nuanced accounts within this discursive repertoire. I demonstrate this via a discussion of Tarde's work, deriving from it a *principle of extension* which holds that crowds can be seen as 'prosocial' entities – entities that do not undermine society and the social but may rather be expressions of sociality. More specifically, the principle of extension suggests that crowds and society are made of the same material, so to speak, and that their difference is therefore less of kind than of intensity. Having shown that classical crowd theory need not be normatively tainted, the next section takes a fresh look at classical social-theory reflections on crowd behaviour. Drawing upon Durkheim, Sidis, Simmel and Tarde, I argue that what happens in crowd and collective behaviour is a levelling process in which boundaries between individuals cease to exist, resulting in, among other things, a loss of self. I argue in favour of mobilising the notion of social avalanche to make sense of these dynamics.

Discussing the sociological value of metaphors such as social avalanche, I propose that not only are many famous sociological concepts grounded in similar types of metaphors but, more important, it is possible to work in a careful manner with metaphors turned into concepts, namely via the process of generalisation and respecification championed by Luhmann. I use this approach to offer a generalisation of the notion of avalanching inspired by complexity science as well as sociological respecifications of it that relate to the work of Durkheim, Sidis, Simmel and Tarde. The chapter ends with some implications from the discussion of social avalanches by reconsidering Weber's conceptualisation of social action and suggesting that it is unfit for capturing the types of experiences described as social avalanches.

Crowds and the Social: A Principle of Extension

A useful entry into reviving late-nineteenth-century crowd theory is the relationship between sociality and crowd behaviour. Le Bon, for one, would phrase this relationship in antagonistic terms. Labelling crowds barbarian and irrational, and associating them with socialism, he portrayed crowds as antisocial microbes mainly driven to undermine modern, civilised social order (2001; 2002). In this, Le Bon's voice was not alone. Tarde, too, subscribed to this view in some of his early writings. In these texts he analysed crowds from a criminological perspective, arguing that crowds are inherently criminal and irrational

(Tarde, 1892; 1893). Although this has been widely ignored (one exception being Stäheli, 2009), a more global look at Tarde's work, especially his later books and articles, reveals a far more balanced notion of crowds. I give two illustrations of this, one relating to what he wrote explicitly about crowds and the other inferable from his reflections on what constitutes society and the social.

In his 1898 essay 'Le Public et la foule', included in his 1901 book *L'opinion et la foule*, Tarde distinguishes between crowds and publics by arguing, as the standard interpretation goes, that crowds constitute unruly entities, whereas publics embody the kind of rational deliberation that would later be associated with Jürgen Habermas's work (Tarde, 1989). What has often escaped attention, however, is that Tarde was much less clear-cut in his dismissal of crowds and praise of publics in this essay than much subsequent commentary suggests (e.g. Katz, 2006; McPhail, 1991: 17). That such a biased reading emerged in an English-speaking context might be due to the fact that the portion of the 1898 essay included in Terry N. Clark's 1969 collection of Tarde writings, published under the Heritage of Sociology series at the University of Chicago Press, portrayed crowds uniformly negatively and publics essentially positively (Tarde, 1969). Now that an English translation of the final part of the 1898 essay (the part missing from Clark's collection) has appeared, Tarde's explicit reflections on crowds and publics cannot be neatly defined as a rebuttal of crowds and an endorsement of publics. Rather, as Abe Walker (2013: 229) rightly notes, 'Tarde is generally ambivalent on the relation between the public and the crowd' (for a similarly balanced account of Tarde's notion of publics, see Niezen, 2014). Not only did Tarde argue that publics can engage in criminal activity, he also submitted:

Though I hate to say it, there is a widespread type of devotion-motivated crowd that plays a critical and beneficial social role, and counteracts all the wrongdoing of other collectives. I am speaking about festival crowds, which are joyous, in love with themselves, and uniquely drunk on the pleasure of gathering for the sake of gathering. (2013: 233)

While this explicit recognition of the prosocial dimensions of crowds is, admittedly, a rare island in a sea of frightened and scornful remarks from *fin-de-siècle* crowd theorists, it anticipates Simmel's (1971) notion of sociability and its applicability to a crowd context (see also Borch, 2010; Stäheli, 2009: 411). Moreover, Tarde's affirmative conception of crowds here is consonant with a notion of imitation inferable from some of his more general reflections on sociality, a fact that becomes clear if one consults *The Laws of Imitation*. In it, Tarde devotes particular energy to answering the question of what society is (1962: ch. 3). As Chapter 2 illustrates, Tarde's answer to this query revolved around the notion that society and the social are nothing but imitation: in the act of imitating someone, we establish a social bond to that person in that we effectively pay respect to him or her. Importantly, Tarde added, this generally takes place in a somnambulist, sleepwalking manner. He further argued that crowds, the entities Le Bon casts in opposition to society, are also imitatively constituted. They too are milieus for imitative behaviour. In fact, Tarde asserted, crowds are social configurations in which intense, contagious imitation unfolds:

A *mob* [*foule*] is a strange phenomenon. It is a gathering of heterogeneous elements, unknown to one another; but as soon as a spark of passion, having flashed out from one of these elements, electrifies this confused mass, there takes place a sort of sudden organization, a spontaneous generation. This incoherence becomes cohesion, this noise becomes a voice, and these thousands of men crowded together soon form but a single animal, a wild beast without a name, which marches to its goal with an irresistible finality. The majority of these men had assembled out of pure curiosity, but the fever of some of them soon reached the minds of all, and in all of them there arose a delirium. The very man who had come running to oppose the murder of an innocent person is one of the first to be seized with the homicidal contagion, and moreover, it does not occur to him to be astonished at this. (1968: 323, original emphasis)

With this quote in mind, it makes sense to infer that when Tarde asserted in *Laws of Imitation* that the 'perfect and absolute' form of sociality would in 'its hypothetical form [...] consist of such an intense concentration of urban life that as soon as a good idea arose in one mind it would be instantaneously transmitted to all minds throughout the city' (1962: 70), he sees the crowd as embodying such a perfect and absolute form of sociality that ideas – good or bad – would 'soon reach the minds of all' its participants. In fact, Tarde's general sociology might be said to be *founded on a model of suggestible crowds*. Tarde simply deployed for crowds the same analytical template that he mobilised to understand the social. While I would not go so far as to propose that 'Tarde's entire sociology of imitation is a theory of crowd emergence' (Mazzarella, 2010: 723), there is enough evidence in Tarde's writings to suggest that he established a tight connection between crowds and society, with imitation a central feature of their social fabric. Recall also Tarde's assertion that the crowd constitutes one of two distinct germs of society, something which further suggests that crowds and society are affirmatively interlinked.[2]

---

[2] Accordingly, I disagree with Karsenti when he asserts that Tarde's sociological programme 'left behind crowd psychology' (2010: 53). Quite the contrary, crowd thinking is central to Tarde's conception of the social.

In more general terms, this points to a principle of extension which can be inferred from Tarde's writings. This principle asserts, *contra* Le Bon, that society and the crowd are not antagonistic entities. Rather, they are united via their shared imitative foundation. More than that, the sociality of crowds becomes a microcosmos of sociality more broadly: the crowd captures core dimensions of imitative sociality, and its *modus operandi* thus extends far beyond the crowd dynamic itself.

One of the central corollaries of conceiving of crowds and society within a relationship of extension (and hence continuity) rather than antagonism is that it invites a reassessment of the ways in which *fin-de-siècle* crowd theory has been associated with an air of pathological exceptionalism. Le Bon certainly described crowd behaviour in a vocabulary of pathology, but as the principle of extension identifiable in Tarde's writings makes plain, it is possible to detect a counter model within late-nineteenth-century discourse that does not portray crowds as pathological entities. Consequently, it is difficult to concur with Ralph Turner, a representative of the reconceptualisation of collective behaviour sociology that took place in the 1960s, when he asserts that classical crowd theory 'adopt[ed] the exceptional aberration as the model for collective behavior as a whole' (1964: 386). For some scholars, aberrant exceptionality surely did serve as the template for understanding crowds, but not for others. Tarde, for instance, saw crowds not as an exceptional aberration but rather, *contra* Turner's interpretation, the template with which to study society itself. Ignoring this counter-discourse means disregarding important analytical complexities in the *fin-de-siècle* tradition.

That sociality extends between crowds and society naturally does not entail that the two are identical, and Tarde did not suggest this either. A core difference lies in crowds being more prone than other social formations to the kinds of avalanching I explore below. As my interpretation above shows, the instantaneous transmission of ideas in the city – a homogenising phenomenon that captures the process of avalanching – is especially identifiable in crowds. The experience of being-carried-away generated by the instantaneous transmission of ideas (and the destabilisation of individuality that this entails) is a central aspect of crowds, according to the Tardean tradition; it is an experience, I argue, that deserves our analytical attention today.

Avalanching

I have used Tarde as an example that encapsulates ideas with widespread currency in the time period in which he was writing. In this section, I cast the analytical net wider, taking three examples from the vast pool of ideas circulating in France, Germany and the United States at the time to demonstrate how late-nineteenth and early-twentieth-century social theorists conceived of crowd and collective behaviour. I begin with Durkheim's reflections on collective effervescence as articulated in his 1912 book *The Elementary Forms of Religious Life* (Durkheim, 1995). In this study, Durkheim famously draws attention to the forms of collectivity that arise when certain Australian tribes organise religious ceremonies or hold a corroboree. Durkheim argues that these gatherings upend ordinary ways of life and the normative patterns guiding them: 'Everything changes when a corroboree takes place' (1995: 217). More specifically, he asserts,

Once the individuals are gathered together [in a corroboree crowd], a sort of electricity is generated from their closeness and quickly launches them to an extraordinary height of exaltation. Every emotion expressed resonates without interference in consciousnesses that are wide open to external impressions, each one echoing the others. The initial impulse is thereby amplified each time it is echoed, like an avalanche that grows as it goes along. (1995: 217–18)

Durkheim further noted that one of the effects of this collective effervescence is a loss of individuality on part of the people participating. Illustratively, he spoke about a metamorphosis of the individual: 'Feeling possessed and led on by some sort of external power that makes him [*sic*] think and act differently than he normally does, he naturally feels he is no longer himself' (1995: 220). Importantly, Durkheim argued, this feeling is not singular: it is shared throughout the crowd, enhanced by the ways in which 'the feelings evoked by one spread contagiously to the other' (1995: 221). The explanation for this being-carried-away has to do with what Durkheim describes as the alleged 'emotional and passionate faculties of the primitive' people, who are 'not fully subordinated to [their] reason and will', something that supposedly renders them particularly susceptible to being carried away in collective frenzy (1995: 217). This aspect of Durkheim's analysis lends an air of pre-modernity to the Australian collective effervescence, seemingly detaching it from the specifically modernist situation in France when he published the book. Even so, it makes sense to interpret Durkheim's examination of collective effervescence as a phenomenon that is also, and perhaps especially, modern.

This interpretation finds substantiation, first, through Durkheim's penchant for interpreting the collective effervescence of the Australian tribes in light of late-nineteenth-century concerns. Specifically, the discursive field of crowd psychology that Tarde represented permeates Durkheim's entire analysis of the corroboree, even though the latter remained highly critical of Tarde's work. For example, Durkheim was quick to relate effervescence to broader societal dynamics:

Under the influence of some great collective shock in certain historical periods, social interactions become much more frequent and active. Individuals seek one another out and come together more. The result is the general effervescence that is characteristic of revolutionary or creative epochs. (1995: 212–13)

Durkheim mentioned the French Revolution as a case in point, invoking one of the most significant historical events that, alongside the 1871 Paris Commune, inspired many crowd analyses in the late nineteenth century. Indeed, these events often figured centrally in the intellectual landscape of *fin-de-siècle* crowd psychology (Borch, 2012b: ch. 1). But in addition to such revolutionary eruptions, any observer of late-nineteenth-century urbanisation processes would immediately recognise the relevance of Durkheim's point and its relation to urban agglomeration. In fact, Durkheim's analysis of the collective effervescence of the Australian tribes closely resembles his remarks on collective emotions in the *Rules*. As mentioned in Chapter 2, in this work, Durkheim evoked a common, contemporaneous urban experience with 'public gatherings' and their alleged ability to 'sweep us along in spite of ourselves' (1982: 52, 53). He further remarked in his general account of social facts that

An outburst of collective emotion in a gathering […] is a product of shared existence, of actions and reactions called into play between the consciousnesses of individuals. If it is echoed in each one of them it is precisely by virtue of the special energy derived from its collective origins. (1982: 56)

In his later account of collective effervescence, Durkheim would return to this notion of a collective echo chamber, in which emotions quickly intensify through their mutual resonance and individuality is suspended as a result. While the concept of collective effervescence was coined in the context of his study of allegedly *premodern* rituals, the analytical template informing it was therefore developed in an attempt to come to terms with *modern* society. Consequently, the central point I am interested in here is not whether a certain anachronism lingers over Durkheim's analysis of the corroboree, but rather that this analysis can capture collective dynamics that also, and especially (according to the *Rules*), have a modern bent to them.[3]

---

[3] It is also through this connection to the *Rules* that Durkheim's analysis avoids the exceptionalism otherwise underpinning the discussion of the corroboree. While the corroboree certainly has an exceptional character, as it may only take place on rare occasions, the public gatherings examined in the *Rules* are endowed with a much more

Setting aside Durkheim and the French context, a set of ideas found in German and US circles of thought, beginning with Simmel's discussion of crowd dynamics, was also framed in response to distinctively modern experiences. Like Durkheim, Simmel did not see himself as part of the crowd theory community despite addressing issues relating to the crowd on several occasions.[4] One indication of his interest in crowd psychology manifests in his reviews of books by Le Bon, Tarde and the Italian crowd theorist Scipio Sighele (Simmel, 1999a; 1999b; 1999c). Further, Simmel addressed questions of crowd and collective behaviour directly in several of his own major writings. In the present context, I merely wish to emphasise one example of this in his masterpiece, *Soziologie*. In it, Simmel repeatedly referred to hypnotic crowd suggestion when accounting for collective behaviour (e.g. 1992a: 165, 206, 704). He also evoked the Le Bonian notion that crowds are particularly prone to submit to simple ideas (1950d: 93; 1992a: 69–70).

Most important, he argued that when people come together in a crowd, 'innumerable suggestions swing back and forth, resulting in an extraordinary nervous excitation which often overwhelms the individuals, makes every impulse swell like an avalanche, and subjects the crowd [*Menge*] to whichever among its members happens to be the most passionate' (1950c: 93, translation modified; 1992a: 70).[5] Elsewhere, he similarly remarked that

[Crowds] are characterized by casual stimuli making for enormous effects, by the avalanche-like growth of the most negligible impulses of love and hate, by an objectively quite understandable excitation in the throes of which the crowd [*Masse*] blindly storms from thought to deed – by an excitation that carries the individual without meeting any resistance. (1950a: 35, translation modified)

Indeed, he continued, the crowd brings about a 'fusion [...] under one feeling, in which all specificity and reserve of the personality are suspended', one in which 'the individual, by being carried away, carries away' (1950a: 35; 1950c: 93–4; 1992a: 70). Consonant with Durkheim, Simmel portrayed crowds as spatiotemporal configurations of mutually reinforcing impulses that include the loss of self as one of their main

---

regular status; their non-exceptional dimension better aligns them with the principle of extension I described earlier.

[4] For more detailed discussions of Simmel's contribution to crowd theory, see Borch (2010; 2012b: ch. 3).

[5] It seems that in most of the contexts in which he wrote about crowds, Simmel referred to their avalanching properties (in addition to what has been quoted here, see also 1989: 212; 1992a: 206).

effects.[6] A central founder of urban sociology, Simmel easily related his reflections on crowd phenomena to a metropolitan domain, an observation I return to in Chapter 4.

The resonance of Durkheim's and Simmel's ideas in the United States is most readily demonstrated in Sidis's work. A substantial part of Sidis's *Psychology of Suggestion* is devoted to collective phenomena and, specifically, to examining the importance and implications of suggestion in collective settings. Reflecting this interest, Sidis spends numerous pages in the book addressing the investigation of 'society', an examination that includes analyses of mental epidemics, stampedes, financial crazes, etc. Sidis's foray into these phenomena begins with a brief outline of his anthropological starting point:

> Suggestibility is a fundamental attribute of man's [sic] nature. We must therefore expect that man, in his social capacity, will display this general property; and so do we actually find the case to be. What is required is only the condition to bring about a disaggregation in the social consciousness. This disaggregation may either be fleeting, unstable – then the type of suggestibility is that of the normal one; or it may become stable – then the suggestibility is of the abnormal type. *The one is the suggestibility of the crowd, the other that of the mob.* (1898: 297, original emphasis)[7]

A similar conceptual separation between crowd and mob would not usually populate the work of French and German crowd theorists, for whom the two notions would be collapsed. Although Sidis was not consistent in treating crowds and mobs as distinct phenomena (he tended to use the terms synonymously), his conceptual differentiation allows for the observation that crowds can morph into mobs if the

---

[6] Similar ideas were expressed by other contemporaneous German scholars. One example is the philosopher and sociologist Max Scheler. In his book *The Nature of Sympathy*, the first edition of which was published in 1912, Scheler discussed the phenomenon of 'emotional infection': the contagion of a state of feeling among people in a group, where the happiness of one person spreads to others. In his analysis of this topic, Scheler quickly entered the domain of crowd theory, referring explicitly to Le Bon, Tarde and others. Scheler brings together infection, avalanche and crowd and collective behaviour thus: 'The process of infection is an involuntary one. Especially characteristic is its tendency to return to its points of departure, so that the feelings concerned *gather* momentum like an avalanche. The emotion caused by infection reproduces itself *again* by means of expression and imitation, so that the infectious emotion increases, again reproduces itself, and so on. In all mass-excitement, even in the formation of "public opinion", it is above all this *reciprocal effect* of a self-generating infection which leads to the uprush of a common surge of emotion, and to the characteristic feature of a crowd in action' (2008: 15–16, original emphasis).

[7] Further reflecting upon the anthropological foundation of his work, Sidis similarly remarked that 'Social life presupposes suggestion. No society without suggestibility. Man [sic] is a social animal, no doubt; but *he is social because he is suggestible*' (1898: 310, original emphasis).

conditions are right. In Sidis's words, crowds 'carry within themselves the germs of the possible mob' (1898: 300). Sidis did not portray in detail the exact processes responsible for effecting a transition from crowd to mob. He merely suggested that entrancement and the intensification of collective energy it enables are to blame. Referring to how a leader, or a 'master', of crowds can be involved in such dynamics, Sidis argued that

The suggestion given to the entranced crowd by the 'master' spreads like wildfire. The given suggestion reverberates from individual to individual, gathers strength, and becomes so overwhelming as to drive the crowd into a fury of activity, into a frenzy of excitement. As the suggestions are taken by the mob and executed the wave of excitement rises higher and higher. Each fulfilled suggestion increases the emotion of the mob in volume and intensity. Each new attack is followed by a more violent paroxysm of furious demoniac frenzy. The mob is like an avalanche: the more it rolls the more menacing and dangerous it grows. (1898: 303)

Further echoing Durkheim's and Simmel's observations of crowds as resonance spaces, Sidis similarly asserted that 'In the entranced crowd, in the mob; every one influences and is influenced in his [sic] turn; every one suggests and is suggested to, and the surging billow of suggestion swells and rises until it reaches a formidable height' (1898: 303).

The excerpts from Durkheim, Simmel and Sidis quoted here have several things in common. They all describe, at an experiential or de facto level, how being-carried-away is an essential part of this form of crowd sociality. In crowds, people experience a loss of self: strict boundaries between people disappear; a process unfolds, in which each person's resistance to others is suspended (Durkheim, Simmel), set in motion by suggestions that fluctuate rapidly between individuals (Simmel, Sidis) until a levelling collapse takes place.

Crucially, all three authors deploy the notion of the avalanche to account for the fast and uncontrollable growth of crowd suggestion. An avalanche can be defined as a process in which a system-wide levelling effect is triggered by a minor event. Tarde is on a similar track when arguing that:

When the flutter of a bird's wings triggers an avalanche, it is a very weak force compared to the force of gravity and the force of molecular cohesion, constant forces whose unstable balance has been disrupted by this small, accidental shock. Nevertheless, this small shock is the explanation for the avalanche. (1902: 1)

Importantly, in the crowd domain, the levelling effect is the collapse of individuality: while some form of individuality might be retained outside of collective formations (however tensionally it might be defined), the avalanche suspends individuality – anti-mimetic traces simply succumb to the mimetic flow. This is the core message in the work of Durkheim,

EMPORTÉS PAR UNE AVALANCHE

Figure 3.2 Being carried away by an avalanche.
Note: Carried by an Avalanche, 1901. Illustration published in *Le Petit Journal*, 23 June 1901.
Source: © 2019. Photo Art Media/Heritage Images/Scala, Florence

Sidis and Simmel, who arrived at accounts that concur with Tarde's phrasing of the matter: in crowds and collective formations, 'imitation-fashion effects its leveling and its changes, its assimilations of vast extent and its transformations in short periods of time', so much so that differences are momentarily shelved (1968: 326).

I take this likening of crowd suggestion with avalanches as my cue, arguing that this notion of avalanche is an appropriate account of how singular individuals are overwhelmed by collective forces in and during the crowd event. Yet, I go beyond Durkheim, Sidis, Simmel and Tarde in one respect: while their references to avalanche may be seen as analogical (suggestible crowds are *like* the kinds of avalanches we know from nature), I propose treating avalanching as equivalent to other, fully canonised sociological concepts. In other words, I argue for including social avalanche in the sociological lexicon. To successfully translate the avalanche from metaphor to concept, I use Luhmann's principles of generalisation and respecification.

Metaphors-Turned-Concepts via Generalisation and Respecification

The use of analogies and metaphors draws sociologists apart.[8] Some scholars treat these devices with hostility and argue for a sanitised sociology devoid of any metaphorical traces. For example, Donald N. Levine (1995: 260) notes that Weber was highly critical of the organic notions of society that populate the work of Herbert Spencer, Durkheim and others, who understood society with reference to how biological organisms work. Referring explicitly to the German social scientist Albert Schäffle's functional-organic approach, Weber acknowledged that some metaphors might be 'convenient for purposes of practical illustration and for provisional orientation', but he also noted that if such notions are 'illegitimately "reified"' they become 'highly dangerous', therefore needing elimination (Weber, 1978: 15).[9] Weber's dismissal of metaphors reverberates in contemporary discussions of financial markets. Some financial observers today liken markets to population ecologies and suggest that insights from evolutionary and ecological models provide fitting means

---

[8] But obviously not only sociologists. The pros and cons of deploying metaphors have been subject to heated debates in philosophy from Aristotle to Hobbes to present-day thinkers (see, e.g. Mitchell, 2012: ch. 1).

[9] From Weber's point of view, it must have been surprising that someone like Durkheim, who otherwise heralded a scientific puritanism, fell prey to analogies and metaphoric usage. For a discussion of analogies and metaphors in Durkheim's work, see Levine (1995) and Lukes (1985).

with which to understand the inner workings of markets, so much so that policy implications are sometimes derived from these models (e.g. Farmer and Lo, 1999; Haldane and May, 2011). These connections between biology and finance have prompted harsh critiques of how they produce a naturalisation of economic behaviour which, *inter alia*, removes attention from the genuinely social and political dimensions of markets (e.g. Cooper, 2011; Crosthwaite, 2013; see also Peckham, 2013a; 2013b).

Other sociologists, by contrast, find analogies and metaphors useful and challenge their poor reputation among some in the field. For example, in *Methods of Discovery*, Andrew Abbott characterises 'Analogy as the queen of heuristics' (2004: 118), and Richard Swedberg similarly emphasises the heuristic qualities of analogies and metaphors (2014: 82–92). Still other sociologists object to a strict separation between illegitimate metaphors and legitimate concepts, a division which assumes that the latter should reign over the former in a fixed terminological hierarchy. Niklas Luhmann, for one, has questioned such a partitioning. Luhmann has a particular stake in that debate: his social systems theory has often been accused of relying unduly on biological metaphors. Specifically, such accusations have targeted the notion of autopoiesis, which Luhmann developed with explicit inspiration from the biologists Humberto Maturana and Francisco Varela, for whom the concept referred to the self-reproduction of biological systems such as cells (e.g. Luhmann, 1990; Maturana, 1981). Luhmann is aware that 'sociologists are rather sensitive' when it comes to the risk of deploying a 'biological metaphor comparable to the organism metaphor that has been applied to social systems in an uncontrolled fashion and quite possibly with conservative intentions' (2013: 80). However, on closer inspection, such concerns are often misplaced, because what chiefly distinguishes metaphors from concepts is usage:

> If we return to Aristotle's *Politics* and to other traditional texts, we can say that all concepts are metaphors. Everything has come about in some metaphorical fashion and has become independent of such origins only through the technical use of language on the basis of the procedures of condensation, identification, and the increase of its possible applications. If one has in mind this wide sense of 'metaphorical', then there are no objections to a metaphor. [...] In the final analysis, everything is metaphorical. (2013: 80)

Luhmann illustrates this point with the idea of 'process'. A seemingly well-established sociological concept, it originated in chemistry, then travelled to law and then to philosophy before it finally arrived and gained traction in sociology (2013: 80). Similar trajectories may be identified for concepts such as 'mass' or 'atmosphere' (for a discussion of the latter, see

Löfgren, 2015), perhaps even 'structure' and 'power' – 'revolution', at least, originated in astronomy (Beniger, 1986: 7). Or take the conceptual pair of 'resonance' and 'dissonance', a set of concepts with a non-sociological, metaphorical origin that have enjoyed popularity in economic sociology (Beunza and Stark, 2012; Stark, 2009), which I return to in greater detail in Chapter 5. Examples are, in other words, legion. In the present context, I add further credence to Luhmann's observation about the ways in which well-established sociological concepts may have a meta-phorical background by focusing on another concept from economic sociology – namely, the notion of embeddedness, which has become one of the most hailed sociological concepts during the past decades.

The sociological popularity of embeddedness today owes a lot to Mark Granovetter and his seminal 1985 paper 'Economic Action and Social Structure: The Problem of Embeddedness', which for several reasons became synonymous with the research agenda of the 'new economic sociology' (Granovetter, 1985). In the paper, Granovetter deployed the notion of embeddedness to account for how the actions of economic agents are shaped by the 'concrete, ongoing systems of social relations' in which they take part or, in other words, are embedded (1985: 487). However, as Granovetter observed, the term embeddedness is not his invention. It has a longer history tied, in particular, to Karl Polanyi, for whom the term had a slightly different meaning. For Polanyi, embedded-ness referred to the overall connections between the economy and society (Polanyi, 2001). Though Granovetter's and Polanyi's conceptions of embeddedness differ, what is crucial here is that Granovetter's notion is explicitly indebted to Polanyi's and that, according to Fred Block,

it seems plausible that Polanyi drew the metaphor [of embeddedness] from coal mining. In researching English economic history, he read extensively on the history and technologies of the English mining industry that faced the task of extracting coal that was embedded in the rock walls of the mine. (2001: xxiv, n. 10).

In line with Luhmann's general observation, embeddedness, widely seen today as a core sociological concept, originated in a rather murky, non-sociological background as a metaphor taken from the mining industry. The transformation from metaphor to well-established sociological con-cept demonstrates the travails of 'condensation, identification, and the increase of its possible applications' that Luhmann points to.[10]

---

[10] Of course, transformations can also move in other directions. As an example from late-nineteenth-century psychological thought, Harrington relates how one of Charcot's colleagues, Amédée Dumontpallier of the Pitié Hospital, took inspiration from economic life when coining (no pun intended) a particular finding from experiments

Metaphors and analogies therefore need not be treated as sociological outcasts whose presence should not be tolerated in the mansions of established theorisation.[11] That said, two caveats are warranted. First, various terms have different evocative qualities.[12] While 'process' might be said to be fairly low in evocative content, as it mainly stirs up an image of non-stasis, 'embeddedness' and 'atmospheres' are arguably warmer terms that arouse a larger repertoire of images. Similarly, 'avalanche' is a highly evocative term rich in imagery. This perhaps explains why Durkheim, Sidis and Simmel deployed the metaphor: it evokes images of great forces beyond the control of individuals, with the capacity to bring about immense change and destruction. It is possible that terms low in evocative content are easier to transform successfully into concepts than those which evoke a richer set of images, which might partially explain why organismic metaphors encounter fierce opposition when translated into sociological concepts. If this is true, then one might expect the term 'avalanche' to face opposition as well.

The second caveat is that the condensation, identification and application of analogies and metaphors can be accomplished in rather different ways. Again, Luhmann is helpful with devising concrete strategies for ensuring that metaphors transform into concepts through practical use. He suggests deploying a two-phase model of *generalisation* and *respecification* to avoid what Renate Mayntz (1990: 5) has referred to as the challenges that come with 'theory transfer in the strict sense' from one domain to another. The problem with strict theory transfer is that

the application of a theory with proven descriptive and explanatory validity in a phenomenal field A to a different field B, presupposes a basic isomorphism of the

with hysterics – for some patients, bodily sensations followed a division of the body into left and right, and when the sensation of one side was activated through the use of metals, the sensation of the other side was suspended and only restored once the metal was again removed from the first side. According to Harrington, 'Dumontpallier, inspired by a visit to the bank in which he had moved funds from one account to another, christened [this finding] the *law of transfer*' (1987: 172, original emphasis).

[11] There is another, arguably deeper dimension to this which is not touched upon by Luhmann. Poststructuralist philosophers such as Jacques Derrida and Gilles Deleuze have argued that any use of a concept or metaphor in a domain outside of its original formation will automatically bring a change in its meaning. This idea has been nicely summarised by Paul Patton (2010: 27), who states that from the point of view of Deleuze, 'concepts developed in relation to one set of problems may be applied to another set of problems, thereby transforming the original concept', a statement that applies equally well if 'concept' is replaced by 'metaphor'. This type of observation sheds new light on the concern with metaphors. If Derrida and Deleuze are correct, the problem is no longer whether a particular metaphor from, say, a biological domain can be legitimately applied to account for a social phenomenon; this problem ceases to be fundamental if the meaning of a metaphor changes amidst its different applications.

[12] I thank Kristian Bondo Hansen for drawing my attention to this.

two fields, i.e. identity or close similarity of their structure – elements, forces, and relationships. (1990: 51)

By contrast, taking the route of generalisation and respecification has the advantage that no isomorphism need be postulated, no ontological and other similarities a priori assumed. For such an approach, 'The central issue is, rather, the specific differences existing between the original and the new field of application' (1990: 51).

In Luhmann's work, aimed at developing a sociological systems theory, this two-phase model entails first understanding in a generalised manner how systems operate (regardless of the specific type of system) – something that requires recourse to general systems theory – before respecifying these general systems traits in a sociological context. What, in other words, are the main insights into the *modus operandi* of systems that general systems theory offers? And how might these insights be respecified sociologically in a way that takes seriously the features specific to social systems? By following this approach, Luhmann avoids making any claims about the possible similarities between, say, biological and social systems while still retaining sensitivity to the specificities that pertain to a social domain (as compared to other types of systems).[13] Luhmann framed this approach explicitly as an alternative to 'the (highly controversial) direct analogy between social systems and organisms or machines [...] Analogy would mislead us into believing similarities to be essential. The longer path of generalization and respecification is more neutral' (1995: 14).

Luhmann made one important further addition to this approach. For this process to be truly constructive, it is important to tame generalisation to ensure that notions that are too generic are evaded: 'Generalities can be trivial. If one wants to check the fruitfulness of generalizations, one must position the concepts used at the most general level of analysis, not as concepts describing possibilities but as concepts formulating problems' (1995: 15). Consequently, for Luhmann's own project, proceeding via general systems theory was important not because of its ability to portray features that belong to all types of systems but because it could point to sets of problems that might find different solutions in different system types. This relates to the particular type of functional analysis Luhmann favoured, the basic objective of which is comparison: to demonstrate and examine the ways in which there might be different solutions to the same problem and how the same solution might produce

---

[13] As a result of this two-phase model, the notion of autopoiesis I mentioned earlier looks completely different in Luhmann's respecified adaptation as compared to its original formulation by Maturana and Varela (see Borch, 2011: 26–7; 2012a: 131–2).

different problems (see, e.g. Luhmann, 1964).[14] Applying this gesture to the *problematique* of the present chapter, the functional-comparative endeavour I examine here approaches the problem of how to understand crowd and collective behaviour in a way that avoids a rationalist-individualist account. Instead, it provides a functionally equivalent approach which takes into account the modernist experiential layer (of being carried away by collective formations) of the late nineteenth and early twentieth centuries and recognises a level of self-organisation in collective dynamics. This approach is consistent with the principle of extension while allowing for different degrees of intensification.

Against this background, I suggest examining the notion of social avalanche through a process of generalisation and respecification, taking into consideration the generalised reflections on avalanching found in complexity science and respecifying the avalanche in dialogue with sociological theory. By deploying this two-phase model, I seek to evade a one-to-one transplantation of complexity science concepts into a sociological register.

From Piles of Sand to Piles of People

In *How Nature Works* (1997), Per Bak, the late Professor of Theoretical Physics at the Niels Bohr Institute in Copenhagen, put forward a general theory of 'self-organized criticality'. Bak took the first steps towards this theory a decade earlier in an article published in *Physical Review Letters* (Bak, Tang and Wiesenfeld, 1987), and his 1997 book expanded upon and popularised these early insights. The theory of self-organised criticality belongs to a branch of complexity science that studies systems characterised by large variability, contingency and emergent properties. A physicist, Bak focused his interest on understanding dynamics that can be identified in nature, as the title of the book suggests, though he also deployed the theory of self-organised criticality in analyses of traffic jams and economic crises. Briefly put, Bak's central argument ran thus:

complex behavior in nature reflects the tendency of large systems with many components to evolve into a poised, 'critical' state, way out of balance, where minor disturbances may lead to events, called avalanches, of all sizes. Most of the changes take place through catastrophic events rather than by following a smooth gradual path. The evolution to this very delicate state occurs without design from any outside agent. The state is established solely because of the dynamical

---

[14] For discussions of Luhmann's functional approach, see Borch (2011; and especially 2012a).

Figure 3.3 The sandpile model.
Source: iStock by Getty Images

interactions among individual elements of the system: the critical state is *self-organized*. (1997: 1–2, original emphasis)

While this quote conveys Bak's main hypothesis in abstract terms, the majority of his book is devoted to demonstrating the theory's usefulness for reinterpreting complex dynamics in a variety of contexts, from earthquakes to the brain and to mass extinctions of particular species – all of which, Bak claimed, can be more fruitfully understood in terms of self-organised criticality.

Although Bak's theoretical model thus sought to describe a set of foundational dynamics identifiable in a wide and diverse array of systems (not unlike general systems theory), he accorded one recurrent instantiation particular illustrative importance. This 'canonical example' (1997: 32) is the model of the *sandpile*, which Bak thinks most intuitively captures the dynamics of avalanching. Imagine a clean, flat table: grains of sand are added, one by one, at one or more points. Gradually one or more piles take shape. From time to time, minor landslides may occur as more and more sand is added. Initially local in scale, these landslides are no longer so past a certain point:

As the slope [of the sandpile] increases, a single grain is more likely to cause other grains to topple. Eventually the slope reaches a certain value and cannot increase any further, because the amount of sand added is balanced on average by the amount of sand leaving the pile by falling off the edges. This is called a stationary state, since the average amount of sand and the average slope are constant in time. It is clear that to have this average balance between the sand added to the pile, say, in the center, and the sand leaving along the edges, there must be communication throughout the system. There will occasionally be avalanches that span the whole pile. This is the self-organised critical (SOC) state. The addition of grains of sand has transformed the system from a state in which the individual grains follow their own local dynamics to a critical state where the emergent dynamics are global. In the stationary SOC state, there is one complex system, the sandpile, with its own emergent dynamics. The emergence of the sandpile could not have been anticipated from the properties of the individual grains. (Bak, 1997: 51)

The sandpile model contains six elements essential to Bak's theory of avalanches and self-organised criticality. First, the model demonstrates that quantitative changes might have qualitative effects for the system in question (1997: 32). In the SOC state, the quantitative addition of more grains of sand will transform the system qualitatively, as the piles avalanche and their slopes break down. Second, the model entails a 'holistic description of the properties of the entire pile' rather than an account of the characteristics of individual grains (1997: 2). In sociological terms, Bak's model refuses methodological individualism and is instead committed to understanding emergent collective dynamics. Third, and relatedly, the sandpile model attends to the interactions between grains of sand. When Bak speaks of 'communication' in the sandpile system, this should not be understood literally. Instead, it refers to the notion that 'grains interact and may cause each other to topple' (1997: 54). Each grain of sand stands in relation to others, and the effect of each must be measured in terms of its consequences in a collective frame, which may be local at times and global at others. Fourth, although in the sandpile model new grains of sand are added by some outside person, the sandpile itself is seen as an operationally independent system which reaches its state of criticality via its self-organising dynamics. This is the reason for Bak's repeated emphasis that the emergent properties of the sandpile are not effects of an outside agent's deliberate design. Instead, the sandpile is conceived as an operationally autonomous system (which, as Luhmann never tired of explaining, does not rule out that the system is constitutively tied to its environment, see e.g. Luhmann, 1995).

Fifth, the gradual addition of more and more grains of sand indicates that the sandpile has a historicity to it. Due to the new sand added, the shape of the sandpile at t_n will differ from its shape at, say, t_{n+5}. This entails path dependency in the sense that the effects of adding a new grain of sand at t_{n+6} will depend on the particular shape that evolved from t_n to t_{n+5}. Historicity, however, should not be confused with predictability, as if the careful monitoring of new sand added would allow for a calculation of how the sandpile would evolve. Due to the emergent nature of the sandpile and its self-organised criticality, and in keeping with the qualitative transformations that may occur as a result of quantitative changes, 'The sandpile goes from one configuration to another, not gradually, but by means of catastrophic avalanches'; therefore, 'we must also abandon any idea of detailed long-term determinism or predictability' (1997: 60, 32). More correctly, while 'short time predictions' of a 'local environment' might be possible, large-scale avalanches cannot be foreseen (1997: 59). This is a crucial part of Bak's theory: instead of praising prediction and explanatory power, it is important to realise that avalanches can at best be traced ex post facto – by exploring the historical processes that led to certain slopes which then avalanched unpredictably (1997: 61).[15]

Sixth, it is central to Bak's sandpile model that its avalanching dynamics can be described using a power law of the Gutenberg-Richter type, which describes a relationship between the magnitude and frequency of earthquakes – small ones occur often, big ones rarely – but with their distributions following a clear common pattern. Applied to the sandpile, this means that small avalanches occur much more regularly than large ones, but also that large avalanches 'follow the same law' as small ones (1997: 14). More generally put, 'Large catastrophic events occur as a consequence of the same dynamics that produces small ordinary everyday events' (1997: 32). This might be described as the sandpile model's version of the principle of extension.

Aspects of Bak's analysis of avalanching systems might seem to echo discussions of, say, chaos theory or tipping points. Both of these describe how small events might have immense effects, most notably illustrated with chaos theory's butterfly effect, which resembles Tarde's comment on the effects of the flutter of a bird's wings. Bak spent considerable energy spelling out the differences between chaos theory and the theory of self-organised criticality in his book. In a nutshell, he argued that the similarity between the two is only apparent. For example, chaos theory has little understanding of the historicity of systems (1997: 30–1, 158–9). The notion of tipping points, popularised by Malcolm Gladwell (2000), similarly observes that small changes can have huge effects, though Gladwell's notion is not backed by a coherent theory of self-organisation like Bak's is. However, much like Gladwell – who demonstrates the ubiquity of tipping points in all sorts of examples, from the popularity of TV shows to crime rates to shoe fashion – Bak could not resist deploying his theory of self-organised criticality in social

---

[15] The lack of predictability Bak accorded to self-organised criticality may be difficult to digest for some. For one, Ted G. Lewis's popularised application of Bak's theory to a host of social phenomena, from terrorism to internet storms, reflects his constant search for ways in which catastrophes might be mitigated (Lewis, 2011). But such a search is predicated on avalanching catastrophes being predictable, which runs counter to Bak's model.

contexts. Specifically, he examined how economic phenomena and traffic may be better understood if their avalanching properties are
accounted for.

Bak justifies his foray into this more sociological domain – a domain
inhabited by interacting humans rather than grains of sand – by
remarking, 'After all, human behavior is a branch of biology' (1997:
183). This immediately raises suspicion about Bak's understanding of
both social processes and social (and cultural) theory, which is, regret-
tably, confirmed by Bak's actual analyses. For example, Bak argued that
economic fluctuations are difficult to accommodate within economic
equilibrium theory, whereas they can be understood through the theory
of self-organised criticality. Indeed, Bak may have a point here, although
he arrives at this via a highly abstracted and simplified model of the
economy that bears no resemblance to real-life economic phenomena.
Furthermore, when discussing fluctuations in the economy, Bak invokes
Marx, suggesting that

To him, the capitalist society goes from crisis to crisis. A centralized economy
would eliminate the fluctuations to the benefit of everybody, or at least the
working class. Marx argued that a large avalanche, namely a revolution, is the
only way of achieving qualitative changes. (1997: 192)

Elsewhere in the book, he similarly compares the dynamics explored in
the sandpile model to Marx's historical analysis of capitalism: 'Evolution
of the sandpile takes place in terms of revolutions, as in Karl Marx's view
of history. Things happen by revolutions, not gradually, precisely
because dynamical systems are poised at the critical state' (1997:
60–1). While this comparison might seem theoretically appealing, it
ignores that Marx's theory is based on dialectics; Bak's notion of self-
organised criticality has no similar dialectical process built into it.

The more general problem with Bak's attempts to distill sociological
implications from his theory is that what he presents here is, in
Luhmann's terms, an example of a respecification that fails. Bak assumed
that his general theory could be applied directly, in a one-to-one manner,
to domains outside its original formulation. He was, unfortunately, far
from the only one making this mistake. For example, Jaap van Ginneken
(2009) deploys complexity science, and even Bak's sandpile model, to
straightforwardly explain collective behaviour, arguing that these theories
from the natural sciences can account *directly* for social events (see,
similarly, Lewis, 2011). This is the kind of approach that Luhmann
cautions against when emphasising the need for generalisation *and*
respecification. Bak provided a generalised theory, but the sociological
*re*specification he offers is poor, and van Ginneken's is just as

problematic. I therefore suggest a different type of respecification, one better tailored to the *problematiques* of the present book.[16]

As mentioned earlier, the general principle of avalanching describes how after a gradual expansion of the system, a system-wide levelling effect can be triggered by a minor, local event. This can be respecified sociologically in three distinct ways. The first addresses crowd and collective behaviour in which people are psychically co-present. Durkheim, Sidis, Simmel and Tarde analysed this type of behaviour in their observations of collective forms of avalanching: they describe how the collective setting, the physical amassing of people, gives rise to specific self-organising dynamics in which the accumulation of more and more suggestions suddenly reaches a critical state. This critical state is characterised by 'an extraordinary height of exaltation' (Durkheim), 'an extraordinary nervous excitation' (Simmel) and 'a frenzy of excitement' (Sidis). In this critical state a new suggestion or minor disturbance may topple the other suggestions, producing a levelling effect throughout the crowd or collective formation. More specifically, the many differences that otherwise characterise the crowd – its compositional multiplicity and the diversity of ideas and suggestions that swing back and forth – collapse and give way to the dominance of only one or a few ideas (Simmel speaks of a 'one-sided exaggeration', see 1950d: 94; 1992a: 70). This materialises in a loss of individuality: each individual is 'overwhelmed' (Simmel, Sidis) and the thoughts of each are shaped by external suggestions. This toppling of individuality demonstrates that according to the sociological respecification of avalanching evident in the work of Durkheim, Sidis, Simmel and Tarde, as long as the avalanche goes on, individuality is no longer tensionally constituted. In avalanching, the pendulum swings to the mimetic pole such that each member of the crowd or collective formation is carried away by mimetic forces in a frictionless manner, 'without interference' (Durkheim) and 'without meeting any resistance' (Simmel).[17]

---

[16] My approach has commonalities with McPhail's (1991; 2006) attempt, via Tamotsu Shibutani, to draw a connection between complexity theory and Mead's theory of the act, arguing that the latter contains aspects later described in complexity theory. Importantly, however, McPhail (2006: 450) does not distinguish sharply enough between the agency of 'atoms, molecules, neurons', on the one hand, and sociality, on the other.

[17] This is one of several features that separate social avalanches from the threshold model of collective behaviour suggested by Granovetter (1978). Drawing on Berk's work, Granovetter's model proposes that people make decisions about whether or not to participate in, say, riots, based on the perceived costs and benefits of either alternative and according to the number of other people participating. Contrary to the notion of

The loss of self that takes place through avalanching and being-carried-away further demonstrates that quantitative changes, the addition of more and more people and suggestions, can produce qualitative effects in the crowd or collective formation. The other five elements in Bak's general model have similar respecified sociological equivalents. Durkheim's, Simmel's, Sidis's and Tarde's analyses of crowd and collective behaviour emphasise a holistic account of the gathering. They aim to accentuate the emergent properties of crowd behaviour rather than try to reduce such behaviour to a mere addition of individuals (à la Berk). They also all stress the interactive dynamics of crowd and collective behaviour, paying special attention to the ways in which suggestions interact with one another. Each suggestion '[echoes] the others' (Durkheim); they 'swing back and forth' (Simmel) and 'reverberate from individual to individual' (Sidis).

It is clear from their writings that Durkheim, Simmel and Sidis accord the crowd or collective formation specific independent dynamics irreducible to the design of any outside agent, a position that aligns with Durkheim's mantra to study society as a *sui generis* phenomenon. Moreover, Durkheim, Simmel and Sidis all describe avalanching against the backdrop of a particular historicity of crowds: being-carried-away occurs as a result of a gradual build-up, wherein the crowd or collective formation is brought into a state which can suddenly avalanche. Finally, while none of these social theorists subscribe to statistical power laws, they all deploy a uniform approach to avalanches big or small. In other words, Durkheim, Simmel and Sidis do not discriminate between small and big avalanches when it comes to accounting for their underlying dynamics.[18]

The second sociological respecification of the theory of self-organised criticality moves a step beyond the context of crowds of physically co-present individuals, although it shares several features with this first respecification. Evoking Tarde's analysis of imitation, it describes instead how sociality can avalanche regardless of its spatiotemporal instantiations. More specifically, a social avalanche can be understood, via Tarde, as a two-phase process in which more and more imitation-suggestions accumulate at the beginning. In Tarde's words, 'Terraces of consecutive and connected magnetisations are the rule' (1962: 84). It is this step-like terracing which can eventually, in the second phase,

---

social avalanche, the threshold model assumes that people's dispositions remain constant and unaffected by the collective amassing (1978: 1436).

[18] Sidis arguably offered the most nuanced view when suggesting a conceptual differentiation between crowds and mobs. However, this distinction relates not so much to the size or intensity of the avalanching but rather to whether some sedimentation of the social avalanche takes place.

collapse and give way to a system-wide levelling, in which differences between the various somnambulistic imitations are annulled and one imitation-suggestion achieves hegemony, at least temporarily, until a new phase of growth sets in. This avalanching process is therefore one of differences amongst imitations: a multiplicity of imitations is reduced to one dominant imitation, similar to what Tarde stated about the 'somnambulistic myself' gaining momentary authority over the other 'myselfs'. On an experiential level, this type of social avalanche may not be different from that described by Durkheim, Simmel and Sidis in their analyses of crowd and collective behaviour. In the Tardean respecification, too, social avalanche gives rise to a sense of loss of self and the experience that the various 'myselfs' are indeed being carried away by some specific, externally induced somnambulistic imitation. Here, too, tensional individuality is temporarily replaced by a frictionless state of mimesis.

The third sociological respecification moves further beyond classical reflections on crowds and collective behaviour. Indeed, it moves beyond conventional sociological accounts in the sense that it respecifies the notions of avalanche and self-organised criticality for an emphatically non-human domain, but in a way that does not revert to Bak's basic psychics approach. Rather, this respecification suggests that the Tardean two-phase process applies equally well to forms of avalanches amongst *fully automated algorithms*. While I elaborate on this analytical route in Chapter 5, the similarities between interactions among fully automated trading algorithms in financial markets and how suggestions float around in society, according to the Tardean sociological template, are apparent here. Singular trading algorithms each pursue individual strategies, though without necessarily seeking the kind of global dominance Tarde attributes to imitation in his more monadological moments – trading algorithms are often designed to leave few traces in order to avoid being traded against. Akin to how in human society the aggregation of an array of singular imitations might eventually collapse in a levelling avalanche, singular trading algorithms may occasionally enter a process in which their designers' expectations of them and their behaviour (the ways in which the algorithms are supposed to act and interact) are disappointed. The 'identities' of these algorithms – the singular ways they are designed to behave – are then temporarily suspended by an avalanching market maelstrom that sweeps these algorithms away, say, in a rapid price decline.

Social Action Reconsidered

One of the interesting implications of the notion of social avalanche is that it invites a reconsideration of established sociological concepts, such as that of social action. I demonstrate this through a discussion of Weber's conceptualisation of social action as outlined in his posthumously published magnum opus, *Economy and Society*. Parallel to how Durkheim defined the sociological discipline through the study of social facts, Weber argued that 'Sociology [...] is a science concerning itself with the interpretive understanding of social action and thereby with a causal explanation of its course and consequences' (1978: 4). Much has been written about this and other Weberian definitions during the past century, and my aim here is neither to revisit the many pros and cons that have been identified nor to do justice to Weber's complex attempt at founding an individualist theory of action. I limit myself to some principal observations about the ways in which the appreciation of social avalanches (and tensional individuality) questions a range of Weber's fundamental assertions and assumptions while pointing towards an alternative notion of social action – one a priori marginalised in his conceptual framework, as Weber was well aware.

According to Weber, social action has a dual definitional structure, reflecting that the term is in fact a pair. Thus, Weber stated,

We shall speak of 'action' insofar as the acting individual attaches a subjective meaning to his [*sic*] behavior – be it overt or covert, omission or acquiescence. Action is 'social' insofar as its subjective meaning takes account of the behavior of others and is thereby oriented in its course. (1978: 4)

When Weber goes on to elaborate on the term and its two dimensions ('action' being 'social') he demonstrates the considerable nuance characteristic of his work. However, this nuance notwithstanding, he also makes a number of conceptual decisions with devastating analytical implications, as they bar a range of phenomena – including those captured through the notion of social avalanches – from the domain of proper sociological analysis.

One of these conceptual decisions has to do with his definition of 'action'. As the quote above shows, Weber reserves the notion of action for describing situations in which subjective meaning can be identified. Indeed, his broader conception of 'explanatory understanding' calls for an investigation of the subjective meaning of action as it relates to the more general 'complex of meaning' in which action is embedded (1978: 8–9). What is attributed less significance for understanding social action are 'processes and phenomena which are devoid of subjective meaning, in the role of stimuli, results, favoring or hindering circumstances' (1978: 7). In line with this, Weber established a conceptual hierarchy with subjective meaning placed at the top and phenomena allegedly devoid of subjective meaning serving as a sort of filler that might contribute to the sociological account but never independently of references to sub-jective meaning. Put differently, Weber's approach distinguishes between 'meaningful action' – action to which subjective meaning can be attached – and 'merely reactive behavior to which no subjective meaning is attached' (1978: 4).

It follows from this conceptual hierarchy that although Weber recog-nised that clear lines between meaningful action and reactive behaviour might be difficult to establish *empirically*, the two terms should nonethe-less be treated as *analytically* separate. A key corollary of this move is that Weber ended up dismissing as sociologically unimportant a range of phenomena that *fin-de-siècle* social theorists accorded primary attention. For example, Weber explicitly argued that crowd behaviour of the sort portrayed by Le Bon does not count as social action. Weber submitted that crowd members may behave in particular ways because they are part of a crowd: the crowd exerts a certain influence on them. But he referred to this as an instance of 'reaction' or 'action conditioned by crowds', making clear that this is precisely a form of stimuli devoid of subjective meaning (1978: 23). In Weber's phrasing:

> It is not proposed in the present sense [i.e. according to Weber's definition] to call action 'social' when it is merely a result of the effect on the individual of the existence of a crowd as such and the action is not oriented to that fact on the level of meaning. (1978: 23)

However, it is not only crowd behaviour in the form analysed by Le Bon which fails to comply with Weber's understanding of social action – imitative behaviour, as articulated by Tarde, does as well. From Weber's point of view the problem remains the same: imitative behaviour is essentially reactive, showing 'no meaningful orientation to the actor imitated' (1978: 23). The key illustration he offered of such reactive imitation is of people putting up their umbrellas at the onset of a shower: 'This would not ordinarily be a case of action mutually oriented to that of each other, but rather of all reacting in the same way to the like need of protection from the rain' (1978: 23).[19] Weber admitted one exception to imitation as a merely reactive phenomenon – situations in which the imitation of others is based on a fashionable trend. In such cases, he stated, action is meaningfully oriented towards others (1978: 24).

Granted, Weber treated imitation and crowd behaviour as 'borderline' cases between reactive behaviour and social action (1978: 23), at least,

---

[19] He also ruled out contemplation and solitary religious activities from the domain of social action, since these activities are allegedly not oriented towards others (1978: 22). That said, from a Tardean point of view, even solitary activities may well be imitatively founded and thus social.

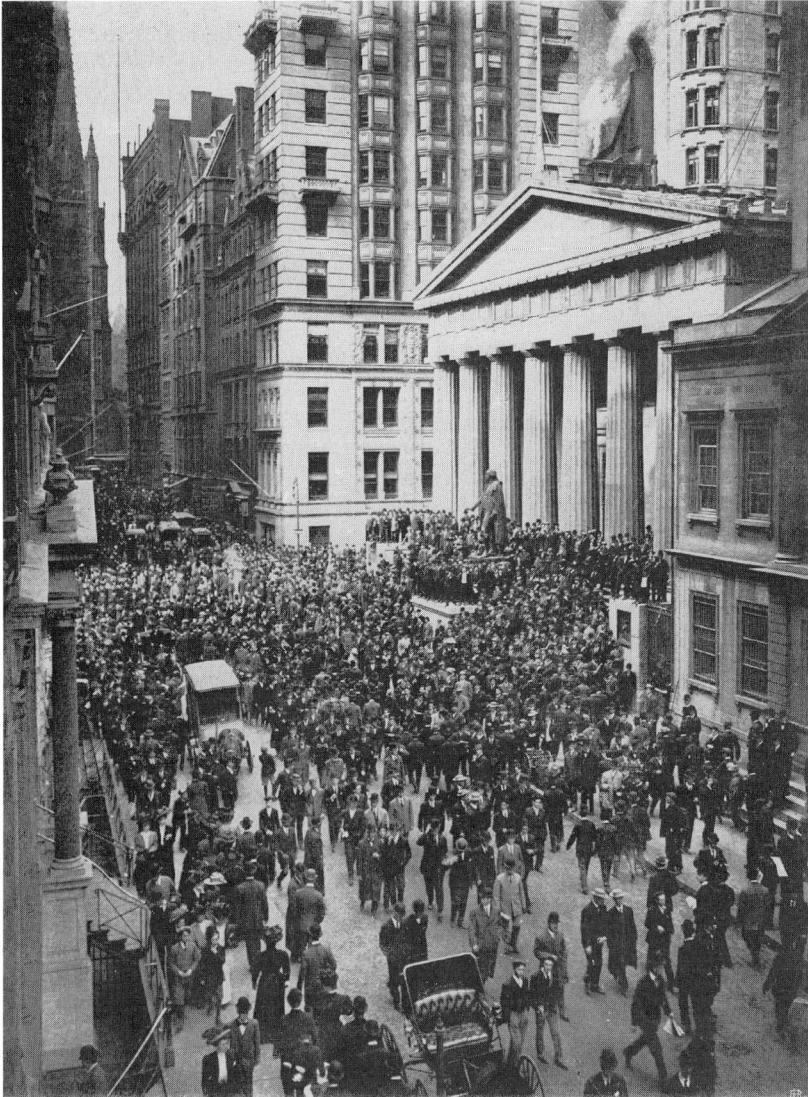

Figure 3.4 Crowd action.
Note: New York crowd in front of the Federal Hall (sub-Treasury building) on Wall Street during the financial crisis, United States of America, 1907 Bankers' Panic, photograph from *L'Illustration*, No 3376, 9 November 1907. Milan, Biblioteca Ambrosiana.
Source: © 2019. Veneranda Biblioteca Ambrosiana/DeAgostini Picture Library/Scala, Florence

though he clearly leaned towards labelling them merely reactive, seeing them as tipping away from the domain of social action (and hence sinking into the domain of sociologically unexciting phenomena). Unfortunately, it is not always obvious from his writings why some forms of imitation might be regarded as social action and others as merely reactive behaviour. It seems that Weber disregarded behaviour as non-social action if the actor's orientation to others and the potential meaning he or she accords to his or her behaviour are 'altogether unconscious' or 'seldom fully self-conscious' (1978: 24).

Dismissing crowd and imitative behaviour as merely reactive behaviour because it is not fully self-conscious is, in a sense, consistent with how Le Bon and other crowd theorists described such behaviour. Their discursive repertoire often conceived of crowd imitation in terms of hypnotic suggestion and stressed that due to the hypnotic force emanating from crowds, crowd members are not fully conscious of their behaviour. The notion of tensional individuality similarly suggests that the individual oscillates between conscious, anti-mimetic tendencies on the one hand and non-conscious, mimetic ones on the other. And, as mentioned, mimetic forces take over in social avalanches. Against this background, it follows from Weber's definition of basic sociological terms that a social avalanche is merely a form of reactive behaviour which does not count as proper social action, and that the notion of tensional individuality is difficult to digest from a Weberian point of view. Of course, the mimetic dimensions of tensional individuality might be to some extent aligned with Weber's notion of affectual social action, but in his perspective, even such action 'stands on the borderline of what can be considered "meaningfully" oriented, and often it, too, goes over the line' (1978: 25).

The more general implication is, therefore, that if Weber's conception of social action is accepted, treating social avalanches and tensional individuality as important phenomena falls outside the remit of sociology. This follows from his totalising assertion, similar to Durkheim's, that the study of social action – specifically the study of instrumental action, which is Weber's paradigmatic model – makes it legitimate to speak of sociology as a 'science' (1978: 24). According to Weber, this remains the discipline's distinctive trademark; consequently, the hierarchy between social action and reactive behaviour should be preserved if the discipline is to retain its scientific status.

This is Weber as he is often portrayed, the Weberian conception of social action as it has been retold time and again. However, his development of the notion of social action reveals another side, one which unfortunately has gone unnoticed in much standard commentary and which shakes the conventional interpretation of Weber's thought. For example, Weber conceded that sociology 'is by no means confined to the study of social action' (1978: 24, see also 27). In fact, although he insisted on a conceptual distinction between social action and merely reactive imitation of the type described above, Weber also observed that 'merely reactive imitation may well have a degree of sociological importance *at least equal* to that of the type which can be called social action in the strict sense' (1978: 24, emphasis added). So, to repeat my earlier point, empirically reactive imitation may be at least as dominant and significant as social action. Relatedly, Weber emphasised that while sociologists should try to identify the subjective meaning of an individual's action, the individual in question cannot be assumed to be aware of this subjective meaning. Indeed, 'In the great majority of cases actual action goes on in a state of inarticulate half-consciousness or actual unconsciousness of its subjective meaning' (1978: 21). Interestingly, both these points – the empirical relevance of reactive imitation and the general somnambulism of people – form the backdrop to a proposal Weber formulated in 1909–10 for a sociological study of the press, especially newspapers. In it, he argued for the importance of such a study by referring to 'The mode of constitution of the psychic means of suggestion through which modern society continually strives to assimilate and adapt individuals – the Press as one of the means of moulding the *subjective* individuality of modern man [*sic*]' (1998: 111, original emphasis).

What emerges out of these concessions is a striking difference between Durkheim and Weber.[20] It was of utmost importance to the early Durkheim to dismiss imitation unambiguously, rejecting its relevance as a concept and as an empirical phenomenon in its own right. In Weber's system, by contrast, imitation – 'on which Tarde has rightly laid emphasis' (1978: 23) – is accorded considerable real-life empirical importance. The same applies to the somnambulist state of 'inarticulate half-consciousness or actual unconsciousness' often associated with imitation. Weber essentially agreed with Tarde that in real life, people are often veritable somnambulists when it comes to subjective meaning. Taking these admissions seriously, one may argue that Weber might have regarded his own focus on conscious action as an *exception* to most of empirical social life. If this is indeed the case, one might see in Weber an invitation to develop a broader repertoire of concepts of social action, a

---

[20] I am grateful to Bjørn Schiermer for drawing my attention to this discrepancy.

repertoire better suited to address some of the many real-life phenomena that Weber's notion of social action strains off.

Weber's conceptual template entails that the types of experiential layers I have excavated in this book are exceptionally difficult to address analytically. More pointedly, if Weber's definitions are followed, sociology essentially becomes incapable of understanding the landslide events I have described: his conceptualisation of social action a priori dismisses as *analytically* irrelevant the forms of social avalanche that a host of late-nineteenth and early-twentieth-century observers found significant about modernity. These observers responded to the experience of a range of core societal transformations which cannot be neatly packed into a conceptual container focusing on social action in the Weberian sense. Consequently, if this experiential layer is to be taken seriously, a different conceptual apparatus is needed, one less preoccupied with 'social action in the strict sense' that Weber associates with the term.

A first gesture towards loosening the Weberian demarcation of what is included and excluded by the concept of social action is to note that in spite of Weber's analytical dismissal of Tarde's notion of imitation, the latter might be more aligned with a Weberian conception than suggested in *Economy and Society*. Tarde understands imitation with reference to hypnotic suggestion and does so in a way that resonates with Weber's definition of what counts as social: imitation is clearly seen as a matter of behaviour oriented towards the behaviour of another person. The relationship between the *suggestionné* and the *suggestionneur* brings that point home plainly. Weber would probably not disagree with this but merely assert that this relationship is one of reaction: the *suggestionné* simply reacts unconsciously to whatever the *suggestionneur* demands. However, as my discussion of both Tarde's tensional account of individuality and Borch-Jacobsen's reinterpretation of Bernheim's account of individuality demonstrates, there are reasons to challenge this purely reactive understanding of hypnotic suggestion. The volitional dimension at play in hypnotic suggestion shows that even according to a Weberian lexicon, some form of subjective meaning can be accorded to the *suggestionné* (see also Borch, 2019).

Allow me to proceed beyond the Weberian conception by critically discussing the role of non-human objects. Clearly, non-human objects are devoid of subjective meaning in the sense that they are not able to attach meaning to their own behaviour or effects on their behaviour. Yet, this does not preclude that their functioning is embedded in particular schemes of meaning. In Weber's words,

every artifact, such as for example a machine, can be understood only in terms of the meaning which its production and use have had or were intended to have.

[...] That which is intelligible or understandable about it is thus its relation to human action in the role either of means or of end; a relation of which the actor or actors can be said to have been aware and to which their action has been oriented. (1978: 7)

The design and use of various objects may thus serve specific means or ends, and it is in this sense that social action applies in relation to non-human objects. Subjective meaning is simply inculcated into objects which serve as dutiful servants, or proxies, of human beings. This might seem a straightforward approach to non-human objects, but things become more complex if social avalanches are recognised in, say, the non-human domain of interacting trading algorithms in financial markets. Such avalanching points to the possibility that non-human objects might be oriented towards the behaviour of other non-human objects, but in ways where their interactions are not necessarily guided by means or ends defined by humans. In other words, although this seems incompatible with – even unfathomable from the point of view of – Weber's conceptual framework, the avalanching interaction between fully automated trading algorithms seems indeed a form of social action, albeit one unrelated to subjective meaning. My point is that trading algorithms are designed to achieve particular means or ends, and as such they comply with Weber's reflections on how meaning might be inscribed into them. However, in the interaction patterns of these algorithms, forms of social action can arise which, given their emergent nature, cannot be understood with reference to predefined means or ends. What happens in avalanching moments is neither intended nor foreseen.

What this all suggests is that Weber's notion of social action needs to be replaced by a more minimalist conception, according to which social action is not defined with reference to subjective meaning but only in terms of whether behaviour is oriented towards the behaviours of others. If such a definition is accepted, then social avalanching would also count as social action, albeit as a specific form of the latter.

★★★

The notion of social avalanche I have developed in this chapter arises out of a series of late-nineteenth and early twentieth-century social theory reflections on crowd and collective behaviour. Despite its legacy in an existing theoretical tradition, it is important to me to make clear that the concept of social avalanche need not carry any of the negative undertones often associated with classical crowd theory, such as its alleged tendency to promote a 'myth of the madding crowd', as McPhail claims. The conception of collective formations presented in this chapter is one which does not pit crowds or collective formations as antagonistic to the social. It therefore steers clear of the charge, rightly raised against much classical crowd theory, that its observations of crowd behaviour were politically motivated when describing crowds as entities undermining society from within. Instead of endowing crowds, in a quasi-ontological manner, with threatening, revolutionary, emancipatory or other qualities, it makes more sense to say that whether the action that stems from collective formations is 'good', 'bad', 'just', or 'unjust' depends on the observer observing the action and cannot be determined a priori. So, contrary to both Le Bon's negative appraisal of crowds and the more positive estimation of collective behaviour found in much twentieth-century work (one being the alleged 'moral economy of crowds', see Thompson, 1971), *social avalanche itself entails no moral valorisation.* Social avalanches as such are neither strictly positive nor negative. That said, following Tarde's reflections, one may even say that crowd imitation is inherently social rather than antisocial, as imitation always establishes a social bond. Similarly, social avalanches are, indeed, social. They constitute particular social bonds and are thus prosocial. Furthermore, although a social avalanche cannot be a priori normatively judged, its levelling processes might be said to institute a particular form of normativity in the sense that it bestows one type of imitation with momentary hegemony – similar to how Tarde identified a 'myself' as having temporary authority over other 'myselfs'. This normativity is emergent in the sense that it cannot be predicted and that it arises from the internal dynamics of the avalanching process.

The principle of extension authorising this interpretation may be read as a move towards the *normalisation* of the crowd, similar to Berk's rational-choice model, which argues, too, for deploying the same analytical template to understand crowd and non-crowd phenomena. *Contra* Berk's approach, the conception presented here does not begin with an isolated, rationally optimising actor. Instead, while it makes sense to conceive of individuality as cast in a tensional relationship between mimesis and anti-mimesis, as Chapter 2 argues, this tensional constitution temporarily collapses in avalanche processes, giving rise to a profoundly imitative, and hence relational, constitution of the individual. Consequently, the collective being-carried-away in social avalanche is not an effect of individuals pursuing their own specific objectives. Indeed, given that a Tarde-inflected model of social avalanche operates on the level of somnambulistic imitation, the phenomenon amounts to a form of collectivity irreducible to any form of individualistic behaviour; the notion of social avalanche entails a *post-individualistic notion of crowding, massification and collectivisation.* To the extent that specific objectives are pursued, these would have to be explained in terms of imitation: social avalanches may entail the homogenisation of objectives in the sense that people start sharing the same objective(s). Importantly, however, such a shared objective would be spread through imitation without originating in or profoundly characterising the individuals partaking in it. In other words, the pursuit of similar objectives is an effect, rather than a trigger, of social avalanche (for a similar type of argument against taking objectives or interests for granted, see Hayden, 2003: 20–2).

Despite the principle of extension, something clearly happens in the process of social avalanching which differs from the normal workings of the social. In other words, a particularly intensive form of imitation can be identified in the form of social avalanching. This prompts the question of whether certain conditions render social avalanching more likely than others – a salient question even if social avalanches are characterised by self-organising features. After all, it is possible that self-organising processes are more predisposed to being set in motion in some situations than in others, regardless of their unpredictable results. To return to Bak's imagery, while avalanching in the sandpile is self-organising and undeterminable from the outside, such avalanching will only take place if a decent amount of sand grains is consistently added. A similar type of 'context' pertains to the first of the three sociological respecifications of Bak's model I discussed earlier: the avalanching that takes place in a crowd of physically co-present individuals. Durkheim, Sidis, Simmel and Tarde agree about how particular body-to-body situations may lead to social avalanching – the amassing of people seems to trigger this sort of collective avalanche. Yet, none of them digs deeper into the more specific features that might prompt social avalanching, despite the fact that since not every physical amassing produces social avalanching, it is to be expected that certain factors are more likely than others to activate it. Searching for such factors would be a valuable research exercise even if Bak is right to stress that avalanching processes can, at best, be traced retrospectively rather than in any predictive manner. I offer a few general reflections on the search for predisposing factors to avalanches in the book's conclusion. In the next two chapters, I pursue a different objective by demonstrating a number of ways in which the notions of tensional individuality and social avalanche have analytical purchase – beyond the context of late nineteenth-century crowd theory – as terms that can shed new light on empirical domains such as cities and financial markets, their respective dynamics as well as their interconnections.

4   Cities

'His works breathe love of cities'.

(Hughes, 1961: 558)

This is how Everett C. Hughes described Tarde in 1961, two years before being elected President of the American Sociological Association. Hughes was right; as sociology's master thinker of imitation, Tarde embedded his analysis of contagious imitative dynamics in an account of the changing role of cities in modern society (Borch, 2005). Several transformations of cities during the nineteenth century may be registered as plain statistical facts. Due to urbanisation, for example, 'London added nearly one million to its population each decade between 1871 and 1901, nearly doubling from 3.9 to 6.6 million' (Hall, Hardy and Ward, 2003: 3). Many other cities underwent similar experiences, and this dramatic degree of urbanisation produced a series of effects, which registered on Tarde's analytical radar.

The immense influx of people transformed cities into entirely new sites for human interaction, profoundly altering the ways in which everyday life unfolded and was perceived. In his wonderful account of the changes that Stockholm underwent in the twenty-year timespan from 1880 to 1900, Allan Pred meticulously demonstrates that the population of the Swedish capital almost doubled in size and that as a result of the massive arrival of new inhabitants, a veritable cacophony of tongues emerged – with multiple dialects existing next to one another, at times so different that common ground was difficult to establish (Pred, 1990). Tarde also recorded the internal, experiential changes of cities in his work. Writing in the 1890s, he noted the new sensory dimensions of the changing urban landscape and their effects: 'The noise and movement of the streets, the display of shop-windows, and the wild and unbridled rush of existence affect [city dwellers] like magnetic passes', transforming inhabitants into veritable somnambulists and rendering 'city life a concentrated and exaggerated type of social life' (1962: 84).

Importantly, Tarde argued that the magnetic influence of cities did not merely affect their urban inhabitants. In addition to changing the intra-urban milieu, cities acquired new and substantial prominence as places where innovations increasingly originated and from whence imitations spread more broadly. Where imitation was previously tied to nobility, with the lower classes imitating supposedly superior classes, imitation now centred on cities themselves:

Prelates and princes of the blood, monks and cavaliers, monasteries and chateaux have been suppressed to give place to publicists and financiers, to artists and politicians, to theatres, banks, bazaars, barracks, government buildings, and to the other monuments that are grouped within the circumference of a capital. (1962: 225)

Illustrating the ways in which the city in effect turned into an 'aristocracy of place' (1962: 225), hotbeds of new inventions facilitating their mimetic circulation and dissemination via novel technological advances, Tarde offered the following portrait of Paris:

Paris unquestionably rules more royally and more orientally over the provinces than the court ever ruled over the city. Every day the telegraph or the railroad distributes its readymade ideas, wishes, conversations, revolutions, its readymade dresses and furniture, throughout the whole of France. The suggestive and imperious fascination which it instantaneously exerts over this vast territory is so profound, so complete, and so sustained, that it no longer surprises anyone. This kind of magnetization has become chronic. (1962: 226)

Moreover, as a crowd scholar, Tarde easily linked the intense imitation dynamics of crowds to urban life more generally (recall the discussion of 'perfect and absolute' sociality in Chapter 3). It was clear to him that if crowds constitute occasional examples of avalanche sociality, in which individuality is beset by mimesis, then cities and urban life are everyday instantiations of these dynamics. Further, considering his French back-ground, Tarde was obviously well aware of the ways in which Paris in particular had been physically redesigned in order, in part, to curb the impact of revolutionary crowds. The Haussmannisation of Paris serves as the most notable illustration of this. Appointed prefect of the Seine by Napoleon III in 1853, Baron Georges Eugène Haussmann pushed through a dramatic transformation of the French capital in the second half of the nineteenth century (Tarde briefly mentions Haussmann in Tarde, 1962: 299). This included enforcing the building of new boule-vards and parks as well as the clearing of slum areas, which entailed displacing around 350,000 people from the affected areas (Donald, 1999: 46). While Haussmann's project brought fresh air to the city, it was driven as much, Benjamin argues (1999: 12), by a desire to 'secure

Figure 4.1 The Haussmannisation of Paris.
Note: A boat on Boulevard Haussmann, flood in Paris, France, photo from *L'Illustration*, No 3493, 5 February 1910. Milan, Biblioteca Ambrosiana.
Source: © 2019. Veneranda Biblioteca Ambrosiana/DeAgostini Picture Library/ Scala, Florence

the city against civil war' – in other words, against the eruptions of revolutionary crowds.

Haussmann's interventions suggest an underlying fear of the city that has little in common with the positive appraisal of urban life that Hughes rightly ascribes to Tarde. In some ways, however, Tarde's was a minority voice. In the late nineteenth and early twentieth centuries, the more dominant view was one that monitored the changing urban fabric with poorly disguised concern. While several observers agreed in their diagnoses that the urban individual is constantly bombarded by all sorts of sensory impressions which stem from the city's steady flow of people, the ebb and flow of traffic, constantly changing soundscapes, a ubiquitous display of advertisements, and so on, many also insisted that this colossal flux of the city – its currents, movements and transformations – rendered social avalanching a frequent yet undesirable occurrence.

In the present chapter, I discuss the plethora of ways in which late-nineteenth and early-twentieth-century observers saw urban life as permeated by social avalanches actual or potential, as well as how a notion of tensional individuality often undergirded these concerns. In line with the Tardean opening of the chapter, I begin with the concept of contagion to demonstrate that late-nineteenth-century debates about contagion established a connection between physical contagion (i.e. contagion through physical contact) and mental contagion (i.e. the contagion of ideas), and that this distinction acquired particular prominence in sociological reflections on modern urban life. With large numbers of people amassing in the same space, conditions were optimal for the spread of diseases and (dangerous) ideas. This, several observers argued, could lead to forms of avalanching mimesis detrimental to both individuality and democracy: forms of collective being carried away that, even if triggered by a minor event, could elicit a broader levelling effect.

I then zero in on the sensory bombardment often associated with cities and argue that the work of sociologists such as Simmel – more so than Tarde – provides important reflections on the tensional constitution of individuality that arises as a result of such sensory salvos. Moreover, as Simmel connected urban life to the modern money economy, I examine the links between contagion, cities and capitalism as they are thematised in the urban sociology of Robert E. Park. Importantly, Park suggested that stock exchanges are characterised by the same kind of avalanching dynamics often seen as key features of urban crowds. I then connect the work of the sociologists discussed in this chapter with a broader experience of early-twentieth-century society as one of constant flickering, a notion drawn from modernist literature. Among other things, this directs attention to the surface level of cities: the ways in which appearances acquire an increasingly important role in the modern urban habitat.

I end by discussing the rise of modernist architecture and urban planning, which favoured a critique of surface ornamentation and, akin to the Haussmannisation of Paris, argued for wholesale urban planning as a means to avoid the avalanching propensities of cities. I examine the critique of ornamentation and its links to concerns with avalanching and tensional individuality. Specifically, the architect Adolf Loos not only dismissed ornamentation as primitive and degenerate but also argued for the importance of immediacy to objects. Loos saw this as a bulwark against avalanching dynamics in the city, just as his critique of ornamentation was fuelled by a tensional conception of individuality.

Contagious City Spaces

In Chapter 1, I referred to Ortega's experience of the modern city as a place where the overload of human material made itself palpable.

Although the particular type of negative effects he associated with rapid urbanisation (the transformation from *select* to *mass* individuals) may be specific to his conceptual horizon, the overall sense that the urban influx of people triggered an array of novel *problematiques* had broader purchase. Some of these were epitomised in the discourse on urban contagion which gained footing at the end of the nineteenth century. I briefly mentioned in Chapter 3 that particular contagion vocabularies took shape at this time; for rather obvious reasons, the notion of contagion seemed highly appealing as a means of coming to terms with rampant urbanisation. After all, the term is derived from the Latin *contagio* – meaning contact or touch – and as the writings of observers such as Ortega made clear, physically touching and getting in contact with others was difficult to avoid in the new city spaces. Given that unoccupied space had developed into an increasingly scarce resource, people were literally rubbing shoulders with one another.

The contagion vocabulary deployed to account for the perils of the new urban situation had a dual character. On the one hand, it had a biological dimension, referring to how the amassing of bodies rendered the spread of viruses at once more likely and more dangerous, as more people could be affected in a short time. On the other hand, urban observers also pointed out the existence of particular forms of *mental* contagion, in which infection could take hold of people without leaving any physical traces – a phenomenon not necessarily related to any biological features. Such mental or 'psychic' contagion, whether categorised as 'moral contagion' or the 'contagion of example' (Mitchell, 2012: 63), has obvious affinities with the mimetic lexicon discussed in preceding chapters of this book. Indeed, this chapter makes clear that when urban observers were anxious about urban mental contagion in the late nineteenth and early twentieth centuries, this was not least because such contagion was believed to suspend individuality, laying bare that the individual can be subdued by external forces.

Although the biological and mental versions of contagion can be treated as analytically distinct, they were often conjoined in specific examinations of modern cities. This allowed for reinforcement logics in which biological contagion might prepare the ground for a more forceful mental contagion. Such links between biological and mental contagion were established by Le Bon, for whom the crowd and its alleged contagiousness of ideas and emotions was akin to the circulation of 'microbes' (2002: 78). As Peta Mitchell (2012: 98–99) notes, similar thoughts were expressed by the Russian psychologist Vladimir Bekhterev whose work was widely received in Germany in the early twentieth century (Borch, 2012b: 84–5). Bekhterev opens his 1903 book *Suggestion and Its Role in*

Social Life (the first ideas of which he presented at a lecture in St Peters-burg in 1897) by drawing a direct parallel between physical and psychic contagion:

> Nowadays people talk so much about physical infection through 'living contact' (*contagium vivum*) or so called microbes that I feel it is useful to consider 'psychic contact' as well (*contagium psychicum*), which causes a psychic infection, whose microbes, although invisible with a microscope, nevertheless function here, there and everywhere, similarly to physical microbes, and are transferred through words, gestures, and movements of surrounding people, through books, newspapers, etc. (Bekhterev, 1998: 1, original emphasis)

The problem Bekhterev and likeminded observers pointed to was not merely that such psychic contagion existed but that its societal import-ance was growing as a function of increasing urbanisation. So, with rapidly expanding cities, the seeds were planted for ever stronger forms of psychic contagion. This was deemed problematic because intense psychic contagion was associated with dangerous crowd and mob behav-iour and their supposed de-individualising effects. Illustratively, in his 1897 characterisation of 'The Mob Mind', the American sociologist Edward A. Ross defines the mob as '*a crowd of people showing a unanimity due to mental contagion*' (1897: 391, original emphasis). Ross considered such mental contagion the human equivalent to 'the contagion of feeling in a herd' of animals captured by anxiety or by a 'wave of excitement' (1897: 390). He argued that while mental contagion operates on a different plane than physical contagion, the psychic and the physical nonetheless intersect in important ways. Specifically, he suggested that crowds often exert 'a pressure on the body which prevents voluntary movement', and such limitations to voluntary movement help convey 'promptly to each all those electrifying swayings and tremors that express the emotions of the mass. The mere physical contact in the excited crowd, therefore, provides certain conditions of suggestibility' (1897: 392).

This connection between limitations to moving freely about and con-tagious suggestibility would also be identified by Boris Sidis (inspired by William James on this point). In *The Psychology of Suggestion*, Sidis argues that one's sense of self is intimately connected to one's ability to move freely ('We may say that the individual self grows and expands with the increase of variety and intensity of its voluntary activity', Sidis, 1898: 299) and that limiting one's voluntary movements constitutes a central way of inducing suggestion and hypnosis, as it makes a person more susceptible to suggestion (1898: 47, 59; see also Sidis, 1895). Following on with this, Sidis maintained that since crowds of co-present people, who amass together elbow to elbow, create a situation in which voluntary

Figure 4.2 Contagious city spaces.
Note: Main Street, Bulwell, Nottingham, Nottinghamshire, c. 1900–1911.
Procession and crowds on Main Street, perhaps for the coronation of Edward VII
in 1902 or George V in 1911, or an Empire Day event. London, North East
Midland Photographic Record.
Source: © 2019. Photo Scala Florence/Heritage Images

movements are strictly curbed, the selves of crowd participants are
greatly reduced. Sidis summarised this insight with the formula, '*Intensity
of personality is in inverse proportion to the number of aggregated men* [*sic*]'
(1898: 299, original emphasis).[1] Acknowledging that the many physical
contacts generated by urbanisation and modern cities would create a
fertile breeding ground for mental contagion was but a small step.[2] In
Ross's words,

It has long been recognized that the behavior of city populations under
excitement shows the familiar characteristics of the mob quite apart from any

---

[1] Bekhterev discussed this proposition as well. Yet, contrary to Sidis, he did not grant the
limitation of free movement a direct role in producing suggestibility. Bringing up the issue
of attention, Bekhterev argued instead that if a person's free movement is limited, that
person is better able to focus attention on a particular object; however, after a while 'such
concentration of active attention, as it is known, leads easily to its exhaustion, and with
that comes the favorable ground for suggestibility' (1998: 166). According to Bekhterev,
this process may materialise in both one-to-one hypnosis and crowd suggestion. Sidis
similarly considered attention an important aspect of inducing hypnosis (1898: 59).
[2] Drawing on both Sidis and Tarde, Edward Jones (1900: 204–5) made precisely that
argument.

thronging. Here we get unanimity, impulsiveness, exaggeration of feeling, excessive credulity, fickleness, inability to reason, and sudden alternations of boldness and cowardice. (1897: 393)

This account of mob characteristics resonates with Le Bon's negative appraisal of crowds. In addition to echoing Le Bon, Ross's explanation of why urban excitement elicits such features overlapped with what would become a popular urban sociological trope, particularly in Simmel's work. Thus, Ross asserted, it is not least due to the 'nervous strains of great cities' that urban inhabitants start acting as if they were part of a mob (1897: 393). Where Simmel held that the city's salvo of sense impressions leads to a blasé attitude in the urban dweller, Ross drew attention to a broader social pathology, keeping to the negative image of crowds and mobs he shared with Le Bon:

The continual bombardment of the attention by innumerable sense impressions is known to produce neurasthenia or hysteria, the peculiar malady of the city dweller. Then, too, there thrive in the sheltered life of the city many mental degenerates that would be unsparingly eliminated by the sterner conditions of existence in the country. But aside from this the behavior of city dwellers under excitement can best be understood as the result of mental contacts made possible by easy communication. While the crowd, with its elbow-touch and its heat has no doubt a maddening all its own, the main thing in it is the contact of minds. (1897: 393)

The reference to such a 'contact of minds' illustrates that, for Ross, the crowd was not merely a hotbed of physical contagion (through its elbow-touching and shared temperature) but equally one of mental contagion. This addresses a more general concern of his: cities and urbanisation bring together numerous people and thereby create fertile conditions for mental contagion to thrive in. The piling up of people living and moving about in physical proximity to one another is simply an optimal breeding ground for mental contagion – contagion of such intensity that interpersonal frictions are likely to disappear and a form of 'mental intimacy' may ensue (1897: 397). Even more than that, with the advent of new means of communication such as the telegraph and similar 'space-annihilating devices' (1897: 394), the kinds of mental contagion identifiable in crowd behaviour can in fact stretch far beyond the physical confines of any particular crowd or mob. In a mediatised age, Ross noted, 'Mental touch is not bound up with proximity' (1897: 394). This only exacerbates the problem of mental contagion. According to Ross, a person might normally be able to resist singular external suggestions and retain 'a sage Emersonian individualism' (1897: 398). However, 'when numerous identical suggestions beset one, one's power of resistance is gradually undermined' – and this was precisely the kind of effect he believed both crowds and modern mass media prompted (1897: 392). The consequence of this was immediately visible, showing itself in a swallowing up and sweeping away of individuality: 'Men who can readily throw off the thousand suggestions of everyday life will be quite swept away by the reiteration of a single idea from all sides' (1897: 392).

Ross effectively detailed some of the ways in which urban sociality is closely tied to avalanching dynamics: the quantitative amassing of humans engenders physical and mental contagion, meaning that when a 'wave of excitement' (1897: 394) is triggered in such fecund environments for contagion, it overpowers any barriers individuals might have against mimetic influence. In short, the increase in suggestibility and the manifold sense impressions of the city work together to render anti-mimetic individuality a highly fragile affair. Indeed, once absorbed by the city, individuals swing towards the mimetic pole of their tensional constitution. According to Ross, these dynamics are entangled with and further buttressed by mass-mediated mental contagion.

It should be clear that Ross's reflections on urban life and its various de-individualising contagion dynamics were described in a negative register, which emphasised that contagiousness was likely to generate an '*irrational unanimity of interest, feeling, opinion, or deed*' (1897: 395, original emphasis). Elaborating on this, Ross argued that when contagious fads and crazes take hold of urban populations, replacing reasoning individuals with imitative and other-directed ones, the very foundation of democracy is endangered: 'Democracy's ideal is a society of men [*sic*] with neither the "back"-look on the past nor yet the "out"-look on their fellows, but with the "in"-look upon reason and conscience' (1897: 398). Given his alarmist account of urban contagion's ability to unleash a social avalanche undermining individuality (and democracy), it is not surprising that Ross advocated as a kind of tonic against the metropolitan evils of mimesis any means that 'shall brace men to stand against the rush of the mass' (1897: 398). These included, as I have discussed elsewhere, particular architectural designs (Borch, 2012b: 138; 2013: 587–9). Since Ross believed physical proximity is conducive to mental contagion, and since many urban inhabitants were exposed to such proximity when being 'crowded into barrack-like tenement-houses' (1908: 88), it would be a significant step forward, he reasoned, if more elbow room and more physical space could be provided in and around people's houses and apartments. Specifically, he argued – in a somewhat Haussmannian fashion – broader streets, more parks and more space around houses (so that houses need not rub shoulders with one another) would all substantially contribute to reducing urban contagion.

I return to these reflections on how architectural interventions relate to avalanche sociality and tensional individuality later. For now, I wish to comment on neurasthenia, which Ross referred to in the previous quotation as a particularly urban malady. That this disease was mentioned in the context of a late-nineteenth-century American's problematisation of the perils of urban life is far from coincidental. While it is disputed who exactly coined the notion (Sukov, 1971: 2a–2b), it is certain that the American neurologist George Miller Beard played a crucial role in fuelling contemporary debates about neurasthenia (Schuster, 2011). It is similarly well established that Beard conceived of neurasthenia as the modern malaise per se – as *the* manifestation of the ways in which modernity generates particular forms of sickness. The basic line of reasoning behind Beard's assertion was that people possess a certain amount of energy in the nervous system. Since modern society puts a high strain on people's mental activity, this may lead to neurasthenia, defined as 'nervous exhaustion' (Beard, 1971). In other words, the more nervous energy consumed by people paying mental attention to, say, the rapidly changing impulses of the city, the more their overall reserves are taxed and the more likely they will come to suffer from anxiety, headache, fatigue and the many other symptoms Beard associated with neurasthenia.

Beard and his cohorts conceived of neurasthenia as 'an *American disease*', a malady not only of modern origin but also one that 'abound[s] especially in the northern and eastern part of the United States' (1971: 7, 31, original emphasis). Similarly, William James reportedly referred to neurasthenia as 'Americanitis' (Beck, 2016). However, considering the connection established between modern cities and neurasthenia that Ross demonstrated, it is not surprising that discussions of nervous exhaustion soon spread to Europe, where urbanisation was as much of an issue as it was in the United States (Gijswijt-Hofstra and Porter, 2001). In particular, as Joachim Radkau vividly demonstrates in *Das Zeitalter der Nervosität* [*The Age of Nervousness*], the notion of neurasthenia enjoyed a remarkably successful career in Germany in the late nineteenth and early twentieth centuries (Radkau, 1998). Akin to the United States, Germany was characterised by extensive industrialisation and urbanisation. The ruptures described in Chapter 1 contributed to elevating 'tempo' as a key concept through which to capture the present (1998: 190–215). Everything seemed to move at an accelerating pace, and this was nowhere as evident as in the metropolis. Accordingly, many observers suggested that neurasthenia was particularly virulent in cities, with their ever-changing impressions. Writing in a French context, Tarde made similar observations. He too described cities in ways that dovetailed with *fin-de-siècle* discussions of neurasthenia: 'The cities attract to themselves from all directions the most active brains and the most nervous organisms, the fittest to utilise modern inventions' (1962: 228).

Not surprisingly, the diagnosis of modern metropolitan neurasthenia was followed by an array of suggestions for cures and remedies. Some argued for putting 'nerve hygiene in the metropolis' at the top of the agenda (Radkau, 1998: 310). Others put faith in various forms of gymnastics, which were seen as a form of will and self enhancement (Rothe, 2019). Still others believed that hypnosis and suggestion constituted potent therapeutic tools with which to treat neurasthenics (Radkau, 1998: 357–75). Beard himself would discuss connections between trance, hypnotism, somnambulism and neurasthenia (1971: 172) – a constellation of concepts articulating the notion that neurasthenia comprises yet another manifestation of the ways in which urban life may bring people out of balance and render their inner compasses unreliable.

Tensional Individuality in the City

Although the term neurasthenia was not explicitly deployed by Simmel in his classic 1903 essay 'The Metropolis and Mental Life' (1997c), the condition it refers to plays an important role in the text (Bistis, 2005; Frisby, 2013: 72–7).[3] Contrary to Ross, Simmel did not accord contagion dynamics a principal role; like Ross, however, he attended to the city's allegedly de-individualising features, although in a more balanced fashion that better appreciates how the metropolitan inhabitant is cast in a tensional relationship between mimesis and anti-mimesis.

The central problem Simmel wrestled with in the essay was this: How can some form of individuality be maintained and expressed when the city itself harpoons that individuality, as evinced by its bombardment of sensory expressions and social avalanches? The factors contributing to this *problematique* are manifold. To begin with, there is a range of forces which, according to Simmel, render autonomous individuality an achievement increasingly difficult to obtain in the metropolis. For one, the city produces a genuine attack on the nerves of the urban inhabitant in several ways – an issue that placed Simmel squarely in discussions of neurasthenia. The frantic soundscape of the city, its flux of people and traffic, and its barrage of advertisements all generate a 'swift and

---

[3] Moreover, David Frisby (2013: 75) quotes some of Simmel's contemporaries, such as Ernst Troeltsch, who suggested that 'Simmel himself was afflicted with this modern neurasthenia which he so often describes'.

Figure 4.3 Urban de-individualisation.
Note: George Grosz (1893–1959), *Jacobstrasse*, 1920. Munich, Bayerische Staatsgemäldesammlungen. Papier Aquarell. Inv.: 13484.
Source: © 2019. Photo Scala, Florence/bpk, Bildagentur für Kunst, Kultur und Geschichte, Berlin. © George Grosz/VISDA

uninterrupted change of outer and inner stimuli', a situation with no equivalent in the serene life of the village, and which creates an immense '*intensification of nervous life* [*Nervenlebens*]' on part of the urban inhabitant (1997c: 175, original emphasis, translation modified). Simmel noted elsewhere that an increase in nervousness accelerates the fashion dynamics discussed in Chapter 2: 'The more nervous the age, the more rapidly its fashions change, simply because the need for the appeal of differentiating oneself [...] goes hand in hand with the weakening of nervous energy' (1997d: 192). This suggests that for Simmel, the city constitutes a place particularly liable to unleash social avalanches. Indeed, the metropolis and the crowd are homologous in their nervous excitation, although the fashion logics propelled in the city may assume a more mediated form and are not necessarily bound to physical proximity.

This emphasis on the multiple stimuli of the city is a trope that many other urban observers would repeat and lend credence. It is echoed, for instance, in Ortega's visual account of the city as well as in Pred's analysis of *fin-de-siècle* Stockholm and its cacophony of tongues. Both Ortega and Pred drew attention to the particularly intensive sensory landscape of cities. As mentioned at the beginning of the chapter, this claim also forms part of Tarde's analysis of the city, with its emphasis on the noise of the metropolis. While urban noise at Tarde's time of writing tended to stem from what Emily Thompson (2002: 117) refers to as 'traditional sounds: horse-drawn vehicles, peddlers, musicians, animals, and bells', the situation was radically different a few decades later when, during the Roaring Twenties, a machinic soundscape fully permeated modern cities (automobiles, loudspeakers, factories, etc.). As Thompson fittingly notes, 'the Roaring Twenties really did roar' (2002: 120). The German-born American psychoanalyst and philosopher Erich Fromm would later capture this changing urban sensory fabric with *Escape from Freedom* (1941), which painted an even more ornate image of the city and its sensory impressions than Simmel, Ortega and Tarde did. Alluding, *inter alia*, to the German sociologist Siegfried Kracauer's famous 1927 analysis of the so-called Tiller Girls as an expression of what he called the 'mass ornament' (Kracauer, 1975), Fromm wrote:[4]

Vastness of cities in which the individual is lost, buildings that are as high as mountains, constant acoustic bombardment by the radio, big headlines changing three times a day and leaving one no choice to decide what is important, shows in which one hundred girls demonstrate their ability with clocklike precision to

---

[4] Like Kracauer's, Fromm's analysis tapped into a broader critique of mass society, though this is a dimension I leave aside here (for a discussion of this, see Borch, 2012b: 206–16). I return to Kracauer's essay later in the chapter.

eliminate the individual and act like a powerful though smooth machine, the beating rhythm of jazz – these and many other details are expressions of a constellation in which the individual is confronted by uncontrollable dimensions in comparison with which he [*sic*] is a small particle. All he can do is to fall in step like a marching soldier or a worker on the endless belt. He can act; but the sense of independence, significance, has gone. (1941: 131–2)

Simmel's key contribution was to theorise the possible effects on individuality of this immense urban sensory bombardment that Fromm would later capture so eloquently. When social avalanches materialise, outside suggestions become so intense that individuals are inundated by an 'extraordinary nervous excitation' (1950c: 93). Yet these remain somewhat exceptional situations, and one of the immediate consequences of the city's routine sensory salvo is the development of a 'blasé attitude' in normal life: the 'incapacity […] to react to new sensations with the appropriate energy' (1997c: 178). With the predominance of the blasé attitude, the multiple and constantly changing stimulations from the urban environment 'are experienced as insubstantial. They appear to the blasé person in an evenly flat and grey tone; no one object deserves the preference over any other' (1997c: 178). What Simmel describes here anticipates Ortega's diagnosis in that Simmel too was interested in the relationship between quantity and quality. But where this relationship materialised for Ortega as a concern with how quantitative multiplicity can lead to qualitative personality changes (the lamented transformation from select to mass persons), Simmel sang a slightly different tune. For him, the central thing is how in the city, sensory bombardment – the quantity of impressions – leads to a vanishing of qualitative differences between these impressions. The colourfulness of urban life and the many differences the city affords are simply registered as an indistinct greyness.

Simmel's analysis has an additional affinity to what Ortega (1960: ch. 12) would later stress in his examination of the emergence of mass personality as an upshot of modern society and particular technological developments. In Simmel's work, this emerges in a more general discussion of modern culture, a topic he returns to repeatedly in his writings. Key to his analysis of culture is the distinction between its subjective and objective dimensions and how culture constitutes the back-and-forth mediation of these. Specifically, he argued that human subjects, endowed with an innovative spirit, develop ideas which crystallise in objects, broadly understood to include artworks, law, religion, science, technology, institutions and so on. These objects tend to assume a quality independent of their subjective origin. For example, law and science function in ways liberated, as it were, from specific individuals; they have a meaning and applicability that go far beyond the particular people who brought them about. Still, objects are connected to individual subjects in that they work back on the latter. According to Simmel, human subjects only fully develop via encounters with objects; in this dialectical game, 'Culture comes into being [...] by the coincidence of two elements, neither of which contains culture in itself: the subjective soul and the objective intellectual product' (1997b: 58). Consequently, culture arises out of the interplay between a 'subjectification of the object' and an 'objectification of the subject' (1997b: 58).

This conception entails that these diverse elements, the subject and object sides, converge in a synthesis called culture. Importantly, however, Simmel's critical diagnostic observation stated that *modern* culture works against such a happy marriage. Taking Marx's notion of the 'fetishistic character' of economic objects as an illustrative example, Simmel argued that in modernity, objects increasingly assume a life of their own after their invention, cutting loose from the purposes originally associated with them (1997b: 70).[5] What ensues is a situation, allegedly accelerated by the growing social division of labour, in which humans are increasingly estranged from objects. Instead of using objects as a means of inner growth, the subject 'becomes the mere bearer of the compulsion with which this logic rules developments' (1997b: 72). This, then, is the tragedy of modern culture according to Simmel: 'The formlessness of the objectified spirit as a totality grants it a developmental tempo which must leave that of the subjective spirit behind by a rapidly growing margin' (1997b: 75).

Returning to the objectives of this chapter, one observes that what Simmel portrayed in his discussion of the tragedy of modern culture was a development equally addressed by Ross, Ortega and the many scholars and writers analysed in Chapter 1 – namely, the sense that there is a growing pressure on individuality in modern society. In Simmel's terms, this was not least a function of objects becoming increasingly detached from subjective spirit and threatening to become a plain burden, something crushing individuality, rather than a means of subjective growth. Simmel argued that this development, particularly important to the present discussion, is especially prominent in cities:

The metropolis is the genuine arena of this [modern] culture which outgrows all personal life. Here in buildings and educational institutions, in the wonders and comforts of space-conquering technology, in the formations of community life,

---

[5] Simmel's example from the scientific domain flew in the face of the Durkheimean tradition; he argued that a 'fetishistic worship' had developed 'with regard to "method" – as if an [academic] achievement were valuable simply because of the correctness of its method' (1997b: 71).

and in the visible institutions of the state, is offered such an overwhelming fullness of crystallized and impersonalized spirit that the personality, so to speak, cannot maintain itself under its impact. (1997c: 184)

In spite of such pressure, and *contra* Ortega, Simmel insisted that attempts to establish distinct forms of individuality can and do material-ise. In other words, the growing importance of objective culture might not pull the rug entirely from under the individual but may well animate people to exert their individuality in ever-louder and ever-more-visual ways (more on this below).

Another feature that sets Simmel's investigation apart from Ortega's has to do with the former being more attuned to the intimate connections that exist between modern cities and capitalism. One of the many inter-esting features of Simmel's analysis is that it ties together the develop-ment of the blasé urban attitude with the modern money economy. 'The metropolis has always been the seat of the money economy', Simmel maintained (1997c: 176).[6] Yet the connection between the two is more profound than the one merely constituting a fertile ground for the other; in Simmel's analysis, cities and money are connected on several funda-mental levels.

Simmel believed each to be particularly oriented towards reason and intellect. In order for them not to be completely overwhelmed by the multiple and relentlessly shifting stimulations confronting them, urban inhabitants tend to foreground reason and intellect as opposed to emo-tion. For urban dwellers, an immunisation strategy, in which they main-tain an intellectual distance to the many sensory impressions so as not to be taken over by them, effectively becomes second nature. According to Simmel, a similar intellectual gesture characterises the money economy (2011: 470–8). Its calculative nature and matter-of-factness give priority to the intellect. Furthermore, by according primary importance to exchange value, money erases any qualitative differences between things; 'it reduces all quality and individuality to the question: How much?' (1997c: 176). Just as the bombardment of the senses greys out the experience of the urban fabric, so money renders indistinct the

---

[6] According to Simmel, the money economy also accelerates a dynamism he attributed to fashion, in which the upper classes use fashion as a means to differentiate themselves from the rest of society chasing behind them, imitating the former in ways which propel these to turn to new fashion objects, and so on. 'The prevalence of the money economy is bound to hasten this process considerably and render it visible, because the objects of fashion, embracing as they do the externalities of life, are particularly accessible to the mere possession of money, and therefore through these externalities conformity to the higher stratum is more easily acquired here than in fields which demand an individual proof of worthiness that money cannot secure' (1997d: 190).

phenomenological differences between things: everything is treated alike and measured with the same yardstick – its price.

Consequently, where Ross portrayed the city as a site with optimal breeding conditions for avalanching contagion due to people mingling physically with one another, Simmel stressed the city's manifold sensory impressions and its reliance on monetary circulation as key factors that constitute the urban habitat. And while Ross underlined the ways in which contagion can propel irrationality, Simmel suggested that urban flux helps nurture an intellectual, reason-based attitude. Though these might seem like stark differences – and there is no doubt that Ross and Simmel had dissimilar views on cities and their effects – their analyses may be more productively interpreted as shedding light on different aspects of avalanching and tensional individuality – or as approaching these with different accents. More to the point, the kinds of de-individualising avalanches Ross lamented are recognised by Simmel in his analysis of how the magnitude of the city's sensory bombardment can overwhelm the unprotected individual. However, according to Simmel, this external, mimetic de-individualisation is precisely counteracted by the cultivation of the intellect and a dispassionate approach to the force of mimesis. So, while the blasé attitude might suggest that urban inhabitants approach the city in a dispassionate fashion, Simmel in fact pointed to greater complexity on this point. On the one hand, urban dwellers are characterised by 'reserve' in their daily interactions, for the simple reason that it would be too psychologically exhausting for each person to engage deeply with everyone encountered in the city (1997c: 179). On the other hand, however:

the inner aspect of this outer reserve is not only indifference but, more often than we are aware, it is a slight aversion, a mutual strangeness and repulsion, which will break into hatred and fight at the moment of a closer contact, however caused. (1997c: 179)

Interestingly, in Simmel's reflections on metropolitan life, his reference to this underlying antipathy is not simply a basic anthropological assumption about people's psycho-social constitutions but just as much yet another manifestation of the immunity strategies at play in the city.[7] Therefore, Simmel argued, antipathy serves as a protection against 'these typical dangers of the metropolis, indifference and indiscriminate

---

[7] These are themes that have recently acquired new prominence in the spatial ontology of Sloterdijk. In Sloterdijk's work on foams, there is a strong emphasis on people experiencing the urban habitat as essentially dangerous, causing them to develop various immunity strategies (Sloterdijk, 2004). For discussions of this, see Borch (2008; 2013).

suggestibility' (1997c: 179). In other words, antipathy ensures some form of anti-mimetic individuality. Of course, antipathy is rarely a socially acceptable way to express individuality, and so alternative manifestations are needed. Simmel claimed that 'the specifically metropolitan extravagances of mannerism, caprice, and preciousness' constitute alternative ways to fulfil the desire 'of "being different"' (1997c: 183). Consequently, however difficult this is to accomplish, reserve and indifference towards others prompts urban inhabitants to stand out, to become visible or audible – in short, to attract attention (1997c: 184).

This points to another connection between cities and the money economy. In *The Philosophy of Money*, Simmel detailed how money, like the city, transforms the relationship between objective and subjective culture. He argued that the money economy contributes to the separation between objective and subjective culture: money emblematises a lack of subjective content, an alienation from human subjects. On the other hand, however, this estrangement may facilitate a new level of individualism:

Thus money, as an intermediate link between man [*sic*] and thing, enables man to have, as it were, an abstract existence, a freedom from direct concern with things and from a direct relationship to them, without which our inner nature would not have the same chances of development. If modern man can, under favourable circumstances, secure an island of subjectivity, a secret, closed-off sphere of privacy – not in the social but in a deeper metaphysical sense – for his most personal existence [...], then this is due to the fact that money relieves us to an ever-increasing extent of direct contact with things, while at the same time making it indefinitely easier for us to dominate them and select from them what we require. (Simmel, 2011: 509)

This set of reflections underscores Simmel's inclination towards a notion of tensional individuality. His analysis of the metropolis and its mental life suggests that urban individuality is cast in a tensional relationship. On the one hand, factors such as sensory bombardment and modern culture work towards overwhelming and minimising individuality, rendering the latter an effect of external forces. On the other hand, however, these de-individualising tendencies are counteracted by attempts to carve out, however extravagantly, expressions of autonomous individuality which render sovereign individuality recognisable to others and to the individuals themselves. Moreover, while Simmel's analysis of the predominance of modern culture might suggest that tensional individuality need not be restricted to the metropolis, his insistence that the tragedy of culture is especially pronounced in cities highlights that this tensionality is particularly visible in the urban context – in part due to the nature of modern cities and in part because of their embeddedness in the money economy (see also Simmel, 1997a).

Much of the content of Simmel's 1903 analysis would later become sedimented in the experiences and concerns that typified the Weimar years for many people. In his sweeping examination of Weimar philosophy, social theory and literature, Helmuth Lethen identifies a widespread discussion of what he calls the 'cool persona', which embodies central features of Simmel's tensional urban individual (Lethen, 2002). Lethen conceives of the cool persona less through Simmel and more via Riesman's vocabulary of the other-directed character type. In contrast to the inner-directed type, who is equipped with a 'gyroscope' (a device used for orientation) as an internal guide, the other-directed type is more like a 'radar' who 'receive[s] signals from far and near; the sources are many, the changes rapid' (Riesman, 1950: 25). Lethen's point is twofold: Riesman's lexicon aptly brings these character-type differences into relief, and the kind of other-directed radar type Riesman would popularise in mid-twentieth-century American sociology was already prominent in the cultural discourse of the Weimar era. Indeed, the multifarious urban stimuli Simmel described were only exacerbated in Berlin, which had grown into the third largest city in the world, with more than four million inhabitants, in the frantic Weimar years (Ward, 2001: 9). In this chaotic post-war situation, in which people lived face-to-face with revolutionary aspirations, the gyroscope effectively went 'out of order' collapsing and giving way to a radar-like scanning of and relation to events.

Lethen notes that although several Weimar cultural critics scorned the cool persona for being 'plastic in the hands of manipulators' (2002: 189), this does not produce the sense of a subject entirely bereft of autonomy. On the one hand, like Simmel suggests, the lack of an internal gyroscope may produce efforts on part of the individual 'to raise a shield, a reinforced ego, so as not to be invaded and ruined by [external] pressures' (Jonsson, 2013: 144). Relatedly, on the other hand, Lethen asserts that

Riesman dares to consider other-direction and personal autonomy as of a piece, without resorting to the figure of the armored subject. The autonomy of the radar type is never an all-or-nothing affair, but the result of a largely imperceptible struggle with varieties of conformity. (Lethen, 2002: 188)

In other words, even the radar type oscillates between the poles of a continuum stretching from autonomy to external determination.

While much of this echoes broader concerns with tensional individuality as traced through this book thus far, Lethen also makes clear that the Weimar situation added a number of specific features to this general image. Most important, it is crucial to realise that the cool persona or radar type gained traction not least as a response to the experiences of the

First World War. In Lethen's words, 'the war had demonstrated that inner-direction could be done away with by fiat. [...] Most of the post-war judgments pronounced against the "soul" and the "bourgeois psyche" appear to be reactions to the "failure" of inner-direction' (2002: 189). Testifying to its prominence, Jonsson (2013: 145) highlights that observers of different political leanings found common ground in their critique of the radar type. On the political left, the radar type was denigrated as being liable to tranquillising media and entertainment, perhaps even showing proto-fascist propensities – a kind of problematisation, in other words, which resembled Ross's claim that other-directed individuals were unfit for democracy. On the right, the radar type was seen as emblematic of a broader cultural decline, a symptom and expression of the consequences of a social avalanche that left Germany's cultural achievements in ashes.

What these critical observers shared, according to Lethen, was how 'they reacted like individuals who feel – as events take a sudden leap forward – that they are being run over' (2002: 193). The critics of the radar type were also united in their failure to fully appreciate that the cool persona might also carry an affirmative side. For example, Lethen (2002: 190) sees in this critique a generational conflict, in which the older generation fell short of recognising that the cool-persona generation could be at ease with and truly enjoy the new media landscape of which it was assumed a victim. Similarly, Jonsson notes that the radar type 'could provide the basis for a new human autonomy in its own right' (2013: 145). Jonsson develops this point by exploring the ways in which a new type of flâneur literature took shape during the Weimar years, referring especially to Anke Gleber's analysis of flânerie (Gleber, 1999). Mobilising the German writer Franz Hessel, Gleber argues that Hessel proposed a conception of flânerie as a textual reading of the city which became emblematic of Weimar culture. A genuine radar type, who functions as 'the registering medium of Weimar modernity, the flaneur embodies an intellectual and sensory disposition that records and responds to the new phenomena of the metropolis, the new sensations of its streets' (1999: 43). Capable of carrying out this careful recording, the flâneur is not marred by the sensory exhaustion and blasé attitude Simmel portrayed. At the same time, flânerie does not take place in a purely rational, unaffected manner. Rather, for Hessel, the flâneur enters a 'somnambulatory state', a 'dream state' which 'gives access, in its very undecidedness, to an entire spectrum of insights that awaken new senses of the familiar ways of observing the world' (1999: 68).

The central point here is that Hessel's account is indeed affirmative. Much like Charcot's and Bernheim's experimentation with cameras discussed in Chapter 1, Hessel drew attention to an excavation of dimensions of metropolitan life that would be unattainable without the flâneur's careful somnambulist recording. Moreover, Jonsson adds, 'In flâneur writing of the 1920s the flâneur does not master the city, nor does he survey it, but he lets himself get lost in it' (2013: 148).[8] While this volitional submission to a somnambulist position echoes discussions from Chapter 1, in the Weimar case it was given a special touch in that the city was seen as an arena where the behaviours and footprints of the masses were inescapable. Consequently, the Weimar flâneur and urban masses co-existed: the former was an ingrained part of the latter.

This reintroduces the themes of social avalanches and tensional individuality, as the flâneur seems to be engaged in a balancing act between surrendering to avalanching mass mimesis and retaining a registering distance from it. In Jonsson's words, 'it was the city itself that conquered the individual, and the flâneur surrendered by becoming one with the crowd while at the same time recording its changeable rhythm, velocity, and intensity' (2013: 148). As I return to in Chapter 5, this inside–outside relationship – the simultaneous immersion in and distancing from the crowd – is a theme that finds a unique adaptation in debates about financial markets and their contagious crowd dynamics. In order to prepare for that discussion, I dive into some of the connections between contagion, cities and capitalism here.

Bridging Contagion, Capitalism and Cities

I have argued that the writings of Ross and Simmel provide exemplary illustrations of the ways in which late-nineteenth and early-twentieth-century examinations of modern cities made prominent what I have analysed as avalanching contagion and tensional individuality. As demonstrated, Ross's investigation was tied to a discussion of modern mass media and the forms of mental contagion they engendered. By contrast, Simmel's investigation attended to modern capitalism's links to metropolitan life and the immunity strategies people develop in order to protect themselves against being inundated by sensory impressions. Instead of parcelling out these dimensions and treating them separately, other scholars sought to bring them into dialogue with one another. Such a combination was suggested, for example, by Robert E. Park, the central

---

[8] The gendering is deliberate here, as much of the flâneur literature indeed presumed a male perspective (Jonsson, 2013: 151–2). For a discussion of female flânerie, see Gleber (1999: chs. 9 and 10).

voice of the Chicago School of urban sociology and a former student of Simmel.

Park's first major intervention in these debates was his doctoral dissertation, *The Crowd and the Public*, which was published in German in 1904 – ten years before he moved to Chicago (Park, 1972). In it, he ventured beyond the Le Bon–Tarde tradition and its attempt to ground the analysis of crowd behaviour in hypnotic suggestion. Park did not buy into a fright-based model that saw crowds as the pure antithesis to society, as per Le Bon. Equipped with a good amount of Simmelian inspiration, he insisted instead that crowds also come with a liberating potential: they provide at times a means through which individuals can escape narrowing social bonds and develop new, less restricting ones (1972: 48, 79).

I have argued elsewhere that Park's discussion in *The Crowd and the Public* is undergirded by his strong interest in urban matters, developed years before when he was working as a journalist in New York City (Borch, 2012b: 141–2). The link between crowds and cities would assume a still stronger and more explicit role in Park's seminal 1915 article 'The City: Suggestions for the Investigation of Human Behavior in the City Environment' (Park, 1915). In this article, which set the tone for decades of important work in urban sociology, the connection between crowds and cities saw several incarnations. Most notably, Park devoted entire sections of the article to discussing issues such as 'The stock exchanges and the mob' and 'Temperament and social contagion' (1915: 591–3, 611–12). For example, Park made plain that cities are places where 'contagious intimacy' is likely to flourish, something that allegedly rendered notions such as 'suggestion', 'imitation' and 'suggestibility' pertinent means by which to understand urban dynamics (1915: 590, 612). While this bears some semblance to Ross's account, Park's reflections differ in two substantial respects. First, akin to how he did not fully accept the purely negative image of crowds often associated with the French *fin-de-siècle* tradition, he also did not share Ross's anxious concerns about cities and their alleged propensity to fuel crowd behaviour. Rather, though recognising that cities might give rise to, say, particular forms of crime, Park generally portrayed city life in an unmistakably positive and affirmative manner. In particular, he rejoiced that life in the urban habitat abounds with both 'confusion and excitement' and argued that this double-sided nature of cities works as a great lever of attraction (1915: 608).[9]

---

[9] This affirmative approach to city life is an echo of the enduring influence Walt Whitman exerted on Park (see Borch, 2012b: ch. 4; Cappetti, 1993: 24–6).

Second, as Priscilla Wald (2008: 128 ff.) has cogently demonstrated, the contagion vocabulary Ross subscribed to morphed into broader notions of communication and association in Park's writings. For Ross, the sociological importance of the contagion lexicon resided in its ability to shed light on *mental* dynamics, more specifically the ways in which individual minds are beset by mental mimesis. Given Ross's normative commitment to a strong notion of individuality, such mental contagion could but signify a corrosion of the social. By contrast, Wald argues, Park's conception of contagion had a much less pathological dimension. Reconceiving the term as *social* contagion, Park referred to processes that tie individuals together via communication and, in other words, rendered social contagion indistinguishable from communication by mobilising communication and suggestion terms in concert (1915: 598; Wald, 2008: 117). In addition to drawing from existing contagion vocabulary (suggestion, imitation, etc.) and retailoring it in communication attire, Park's reorientation also signalled contagion's normative implications: instead of being synonymous with the erosion of the social, as per Ross, social contagion may instead be seen as 'the primary mechanism of social cohesion' (Wald, 2008: 116, see also 136). Thus reformulated as communication, contagion transformed into an essentially positive and affirmative notion that describes the constitution of the social, including the ways in which associations come into being and develop.[10]

As mentioned, Park aligned the interest in contagious urban dynamics with a discussion of the connection between cities and capitalism, approaching this relationship from several angles. For example, in an inventory of urban 'vocational types' that he presented in 'The City', the 'stockbroker' was listed alongside 'the bartender', 'the ward boss', 'the cabman', and many others (1915: 586). Relatedly, Park conceived of the city as a marketplace – specifically as a 'market for the special talents' of

---

[10] This 'tactical polyvalence' of the contagion discourse – 'the shifts and reutilizations of identical formulas for contrary objectives' (Foucault, 1990: 100) – conceals important overlaps between Park and Ross. For example, Ross was deeply inspired by Tarde's work (see Borch, 2012b: 136–40), and a similar Tardean influence seems extant in Park's reformulation of the contagion vocabulary. Although Park tried to insert some distance between his conception and Tarde's, several of his observations had a strong Tardean flavour. In his discussion of communication, for example, Park deployed the notion of suggestion explicitly, arguing that one of the ways in which communication is a 'very subtle [mechanism]' materialises in how difficult it often is 'to conceive how suggestions are conveyed from one mind to another' (1915: 598). He similarly noted that communication may take place in a non-conscious manner. Given two persons, A and B, 'A may act upon the suggestions that emanate from B without himself [*sic*] being clearly conscious of the source from which his motives spring' (1915: 599). More generally, Park's *The Crowd and the Public* followed directly in the footsteps of discussions laid out in Tarde's *L'opinion et la foule* (Tarde, 1989).

people, a place where specialisation and division of labour can flourish in conjunction with industrialisation, the money economy and financial services. Stock exchanges especially attracted Park's attention and interest: they work as a kind of news barometer, a means of absorbing news from all over the world and translating them into prices and price movements. This, he continued, lends them an instability far more extreme than what characterises erratic crowds and mobs (1915: 591). In fact, Park argued that avalanching properties are perhaps immanent nowhere more than in the stock exchanges: 'It is true of the exchanges, as it is of crowds, that the situation they represent is always critical, that is to say, the tensions are such that a slight cause may precipitate an enormous effect' (1915: 591). Park referred to such situations of sudden change as 'psychological moments'. These, he suggested, 'occur more frequently in cities than in smaller communities', thereby epitomising a particularly urban kind of avalanching (1915: 592). In fact, avalanching crises assume such a frequency in crowds and stock exchanges that they constitute 'the normal condition' (1915: 592).

Like Simmel, Park established a close connection between cities and the modern economy. This applied both in a weak, homologous sense of the city as constituting a market of talents, as well as in a stronger sense, in which he saw exchanges as sites where urban crowd dynamics are particularly intensive and can be observed close at hand. However, by portraying exchanges as laboratories in which the crises and instabilities that allegedly characterise the urban domain can be studied in their more extreme manifestations, Park gave his analysis a twist that aligned it more with Ross's considerations than with Simmel's. Thus, the 'wave of excitement' Ross associated with urban contagion, as well as the 'impulsiveness, exaggeration of feeling', and 'inability to reason' he attributed to urban crowds (1897: 390, 393), all better describe Park's take on the psychological moment of stock exchanges than Simmel's emphasis on the money economy's intellectual attitude does. Park's account of the stock exchanges and their crisis-prone crowd-like nature simply leaves little room for the kind of reason and intellect Simmel insisted on.

Park was more Simmelian in his understanding of urban individuality and its tensional constitution. Thus, while the psychological moments of the crowded metropolis suggest a sweeping away of individuality in an avalanching maelstrom, Park also maintained that the city provides ample opportunities for individuality to develop and thrive. One facet of this, mentioned above, relates to Park's analysis of crowd behaviour, in which he asserted that collective behaviour might trigger 'a new social order' with redefined roles, conceptions and expectations of individuality (Park and Burgess, 1921: 867). In other words, paradoxically, the

Figure 4.4 Urban crowds.
Note: Crowds on Wall Street, New York City, 1918.
Source: London, Stapleton Historical Collection. © 2019. Photo Stapleton Historical Collection/Heritage Images/Scala, Florence

apparent letting go of individuality may be the means through which new forms of individuality can surface. Another way individuality may flourish in the city, Park argued, is tied less to crowd behaviour and more to the vastness of its socio-moral space – the city can accommodate any inhabitant and, like a greenhouse, allow individuals to grow in accordance with their inner (anti-mimetic) qualities:

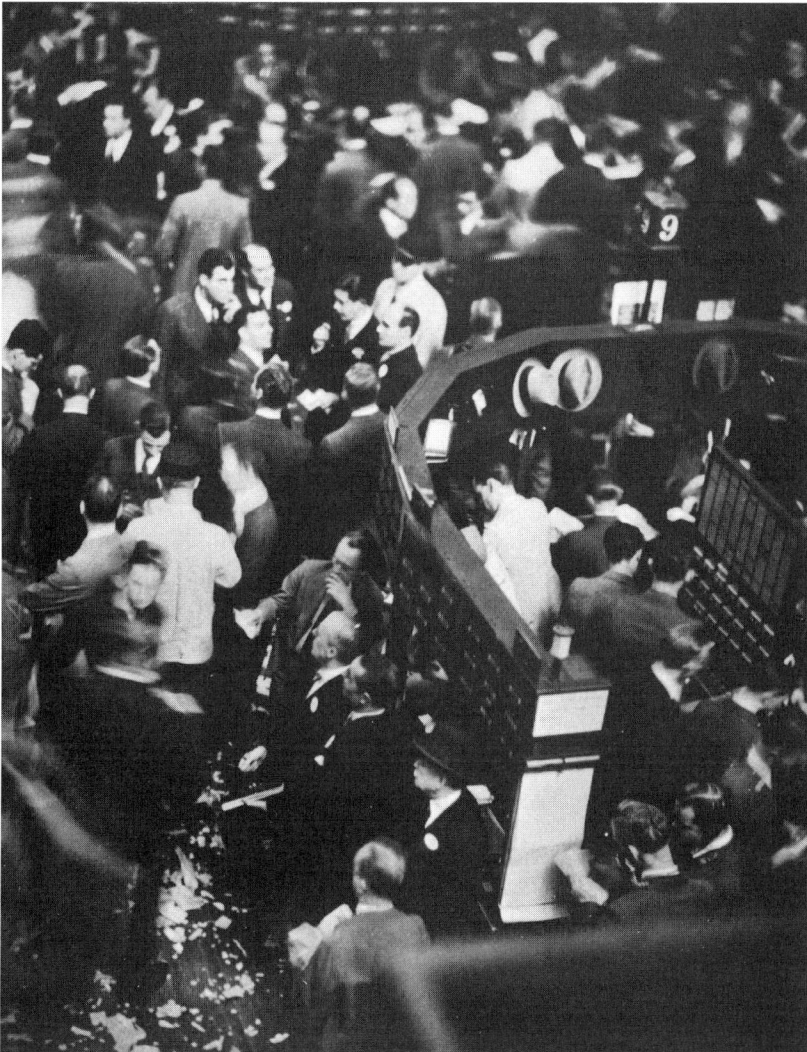

Figure 4.5 Trading crowds.
Note: Trading Post 9, New York Stock Exchange, early 1930s. Inside the horseshoe-shaped 'post' are the specialists' clerks and the tube attendants who receive orders and send reports.
Source: London, Stapleton Historical Collection. © 2019. Photo Stapleton Historical Collection/Heritage Images/Scala, Florence

The attraction of the metropolis is due in part [...] to the fact that in the long run every individual finds somewhere among the varied manifestations of city life the sort of environment in which he [*sic*] expands and feels at ease; finds, in short, the moral climate in which his *peculiar nature* obtains the stimulations that bring his *innate qualities* to full and free expression. (1915: 608, emphasis added)

What transpires here is not just a commitment to a tensional notion of individuality, in which individuality is seen as being stretched out between crowd mimesis and the coming into being or nurturing of anti-mimetic individuality. More than that, and more carefully elaborated than in Simmel's reflections on the metropolis, Park articulated individuality as a matter of surfaces and depths (for a discussion of these terms and their connections, see Brighenti, 2019). On the one hand, he suggested in a Simmelian tone that 'The lure of great cities is perhaps a consequence of stimulations which act directly upon the reflexes', to which he added, in a formulation that anticipates Erving Goffman, that in cities, 'the art of life is largely reduced to skating on thin surfaces and a scrupulous study of style and manners' (1915: 608). On the other hand, this attention to surfaces was accompanied by an appreciation of depths, specifically the depth of individuality – 'the original nature of the individual' (1915: 612) – that the city can shelter.

Constant Flicker

I would like to dwell on this surface level of urban life for a moment. Reading across the three main texts in this chapter so far – Ross's (1897), Simmel's (1903) and Park's (1915) – and assuming they can be seen as emblematic of broader academic currents and concerns, it does seem as if the attention to surfaces plays a prominent, perhaps even increasingly noteworthy, role in sociological reflections on the modern city that characterise this timespan of less than two decades. Ross's analysis addresses the surface level by depicting modern metropolitan individuals as being susceptible to 'fleeting impressions' due to their apparent shallowness: rather than being deeply grounded with a 'strong character', modern individuals have morphed into mere surface creatures who 'drift without helm or anchor at the mercy of wind and tide'; they are 'ripples [without] a real ground' (1897: 391, 397, 398). As a corollary of their openness to immediate impressions, 'the anchor of reason finds no "holding ground"' in them; there is no depth in these individuals to tie it to (1897: 395). In other words, in Ross's portrayal, the problem with the modern individual is that it does not strike root. Lacking verticality with a deep, solid base, the individual is reduced to empty can blowing about in the wind. No tensional co-constitution seems to exist between the surface individual Ross scorned and the Emersonian individual he idealised.

Simmel's urban sociology accords surfaces a higher status but via a more dialectical, back-and-forth movement. The most notable example of this is his emphasis on how surface-level sensory bombardment generates a blasé attitude that effectively transforms the role of the surface from one of variety into one of indistinct greyness. Further, much like in Park's work, Simmel outlined an ongoing dialectical movement between surface and depth: the urban individual's reserve and antipathy towards others suggests a certain depth, a root that – however delicate – protects against being carried away by urban surface commotion. But at the same time, Simmel argued, individuals strive to be appreciated as individuals, and to this end they engage in surface endeavours such as presenting themselves in extravagant ways. His considerations of fashion expressed similar ideas (1997d: 198–99).

Similarly, Park's programmatic article on the city ended by paying attention to the ways in which the urban individual is cast in a game of surface appearances – and a search for possible ways to ensure depth. The point I wish to make here is that regardless of how these urban sociologists, especially Simmel and Park, tied the surface level of urban life to their attempts to carve out depths, the attention to the surface, the façade, of the city gains importance in their work.[11] I suggest that their emphasis on urban surfaces echoed a broader modernist experience that was captured as well by other observers at the time. A prominent illustration of this is the way in which Ross's account of the urban inhabitant as an 'unsteady modern person whose ideas and preference *flicker constantly* in the currents of momentary popular feeling' (1897: 397, emphasis added) gained wider and increasingly stronger resonance within popular culture. Most notably, F. Scott Fitzgerald deployed the notion of a constant flicker in *The Great Gatsby* to depict the metropolis of the early twentieth century. In his 1925 novel, often described as the emblematic account of the Jazz Age (or the Roaring Twenties), Fitzgerald famously portrayed his protagonist Nick Carraway's encounter with the mysterious Jay Gatsby. Arguably, however, what lends the novel its characteristic flavour and exemplary status is less the tragic story it narrates than its depiction of the urban setting in which the narrative's

---

[11] By contrast, social theorists with a greater interest in the burgeoning field of psychoanalysis tended to focus more on the other side of the surface–depths relationship. One illustration of this is Walter Benjamin's comments on how film, a surface medium *par excellence*, is nonetheless also a window into the depths of human subjects.

events unfold. Significantly, Fitzgerald's account of the 1920s city was couched in language reminiscent of that of Ross, Park and Simmel. For example, in the novel Nick relates how, having accustomed himself to the city as a newcomer, he 'began to like New York, the racy, adventurous feel of it at night, and the satisfaction that the *constant flicker* of men and women and machines gives to the restless eye' (Fitzgerald, 2001: 37, emphasis added).

The literary scholar Guy Reynolds has argued that the phrase 'constant flicker', which appears elsewhere in the novel, is core to understanding *The Great Gatsby*. Reynolds points out that 'flicker' was 'a key word for modernist writers' and that Fitzgerald might have been especially inspired by Joseph Conrad's use of the term in *Heart of Darkness* (Reynolds, 2001: vi, n. 1). Yet,

Fitzgerald shifts 'the flicker' to the US, where it functions as the distinctive symbol of modernity, of the new. The flicker of electric light off a car; the flicker of an image as movie film clatters through a projector; the flicker of the distracted modern consciousness. (2001: vi)

The central point here is that Fitzgerald, born in 1896 during a time when a host of technological innovations were dramatically changing modern everyday life, articulated the urban experience that corresponded to their sedimentation. In particular, he offered a fictional rendition of the surface level analysed by Ross, Park and Simmel. An additional connection between *The Great Gatsby* and Park's and Simmel's reflections has to do with the links it established between urban flickering and capitalism. Consonant with Park's catalogue of urban 'vocational types', Nick, the protagonist, aims to make a living in financial speculation, which is connected to the city not merely through the physical anchoring of finance in Wall Street but also through the ways in which financial markets are, similar to the city, characterised by flickering – the constant flicker of quotes.

The salience of Fitzgerald's novel for the present discussion goes beyond its vindication in popular fiction of some of the main tenets of the urban sociology developed in the early twentieth century. From a theoretical point of view, the important observation discernible in the various writings on the constant flicker of cities and markets is that such flickering may fuel social avalanching or at least provide optimal conditions for avalanches to take place. In the language of Bak's sandpile model, a widespread condition of constant flicker is much like grains of sand loosely coupled to one another. In contrast to a wet pile of sand, characterised by stickiness, the constant flicker reflects a situation in which grains of sand can easily avalanche. The slightest puff can set in motion a larger chain reaction.

It is also worth noting that increasing attention to the surface level of urban life emerged in an array of Weimar writings as well. As Janet Ward has cogently detailed in *Weimar Surfaces*, a large reorientation towards surfaces took place in the Weimar era, especially during the 1924–9 time period, in which *Neue Sachlichkeit* (new objectivity) swept through architecture, art, design, etc. This movement hailed a modernist-functionalist approach to surfaces, bringing a rejection of ornamentation on the façades of buildings and a celebration of 'smooth, logical coolness' instead (Ward, 2001: 9). I discuss this reorientation in the following sections. What is important to note here is that this was more than an aesthetic recalibration or a mere shift in stylistic preferences. The surface level also became an object of study in attempts to capture the city and society more broadly. Emblematic of this analytical approach is Kracauer's aforementioned 1927 essay, 'The Mass Ornament', which opened:

An analysis of the simple surface manifestations of an epoch can contribute more to determining its place in the historical process than judgments of the epoch about itself. [...] the very unconscious nature of surface manifestations allows for direct access to the underlying meaning of existing conditions. (Kracauer, 1975: 67; see also Ward, 2001: 32)

In this somewhat topographic endeavour (Witte, 1977: 341), the inside-outside constitution of the flâneur I mentioned earlier assumes a vertical form. Rather than immersion versus distance, or being in versus out, Kracauer's analytical programme suggests that the surface should be analysed in order to better understand the depths of the city. He assumes, in other words, that if properly interpreted the surface level of the city offers an expression of its underlying depths.

The growing attention to surfaces identifiable across the urban sociological work of Ross, Simmel and Park may be seen as having paved the way for such Weimar ideas. However, the surface level was met with some resistance despite the popularity it enjoyed in the Weimar years. Ward mentions Stefan Zweig as an illustrative example. Writing in 1925 (the year *The Great Gatsby* was published) and defending a notion of 'inwardness', Zweig was deeply concerned about the increasing prominence of surfaces, seeing this as a problematic Americanisation of European life and arguing, in Ward's formulation, that it threatened to 'flatten out German individuality onto a single monotonous plane of surface' (2001: 38). While differently framed, this essentially rehearsed the concerns Ross articulated when the orientation towards surfaces was still in its infancy: the belief in and commitment to the notion of individual autonomy and the anxiety about flickering dynamics working against such autonomy.

The Plan

I have suggested that the three to four decades of urban sociological inquiry examined in this chapter – which overlaps with the time period of landslide events and the emergence of a sociological conception of avalanches and tensional individuality, as discussed in previous chapters – accorded immense importance to contagion, de-individualisation and re-individualisation, as well as the constant flickering of and connections between urban crowds and stock exchanges. Much of this was echoed in contemporaneous discussions of architecture and urban planning. Indeed, the rise of architectural modernism was largely a response to the types of concerns that Ross, Park and Simmel articulated: if only the recommendations of modernist architects and planners were followed, the perils of urban life would soon perish, including the allegedly imma-nent tendency of modern cities to generate social avalanches and de-individualisation. So, even though modernist architects conceived of entirely new ways of doing architecture and urban planning, their pro-grammatic plans nonetheless confirmed the (older) diagnosis of urban life penned by sociologists and the likes of Fitzgerald.

This was nowhere as lucidly expressed as in the work of Le Corbusier, the Swiss architect and urban planner who would become one of the leading figures of architectural modernism. Le Corbusier was born in 1887 amidst great social, industrial, urban, political and technological upheaval, and these sweeping changes did not go unnoticed in his architectural thinking. A central concern for Le Corbusier was the ways in which existing cities exerted enormous pressure on individuality. Similar to the urban sociologists' diagnosis of urban contagion and de-individualisation, he lamented,

In every one of these [contemporary] cities man [*sic*] is subjected to annoyance. Everything that surrounds him suffocates and crushes him. [...] A human crisis is raging in all the big cities and spreading its effects throughout the country. The city no longer serves its function, which is to shelter human beings and shelter them well. (Le Corbusier quoted in Conrads, 1970: 137)

In his chief manifesto, *Towards a New Architecture* (published in 1923),[12] Le Corbusier similarly portrayed the early twentieth century as suffering

---

[12] The French-language original is titled *Vers un architecture*, which literally translates as *Towards an Architecture*. While the English translation incorrectly included 'New' in the

from 'a moral crisis' where citizens were feeling as 'slave[s] of a frantic state of things' (1986: 271). The situation was so dire, he asserted, that the contemporaneous 'demoralization' and '[b]ewilderment' could easily end in revolution if no intervention were made. The kind of remedy Le Corbusier had in mind was, not surprisingly, architectural. Indeed, he saw the choice as one between 'Architecture or Revolution', with the implied addendum that 'Revolution [could] be avoided' only if architecture were to assume the form he prescribed (1986: 289). This alternative between architecture and revolution in Le Corbusier's project reflected a flash of Haussmann's legacy, something that further materialised in the totalitarian grandeur he shared with the Parisian prefect. Thus, Le Corbusier's call for a new approach to architecture was underpinned by a deeply felt dissatisfaction with how early twentieth-century architecture had developed. Barring a few notable exceptions from the design of, say, aeroplanes, cars and ships, Le Corbusier's underlying thesis was that the poor architectural situation was exacerbating the general moral crisis of his day.

As a way out of this predicament, Le Corbusier advocated a rationalistic, utilitarian architecture, the visual outline of which he accorded a most crucial role. Much like Ortega's lamenting of visual overflow in the city and Simmel's account of sensory bombardment, Le Corbusier decried the lack of order that rapid urbanisation had generated. More important, he wished to get to the root of the problem by eradicating the visual bewilderment of the modern city. One of the key means he proposed to this end was the *plan*: the careful arrangement of a city's many elements, in particular its buildings, their surfaces and the ways in which they stand in relation to one another. Such urban planning was no petty thing. 'A plan calls for the most active imagination', Le Corbusier stressed, as well as 'the most severe discipline. The plan is what determines everything; it is the decisive moment' (1986: 48). To emphasise its rationalistic nature, he likened it to 'an algebrization and a dry-looking thing' (1986: 49). However dry it may be, the plan would work tangible wonders once conceived and implemented. 'Harmony', a rhythm of equilibrium and the avoidance of the city's otherwise 'foul confusion', were some of the promises of urban planning Le Corbusier listed (1986: 48, 50, 57). The plan would generate order, and 'where order reigns,

book's title, this was not entirely unjustified in terms of content, as Le Corbusier did set out to define a novel type of architecture that better matched the conditions of the twentieth century. Indicative of this longing for a new beginning, the book contained essays Le Corbusier published in a magazine he had co-founded with Amédée Ozenfant in 1920, tellingly titled *L'Esprit nouveau* (Curtis, 1996: 168).

well-being begins' (1986: 54). Le Corbusier held this intimate connection between urban order and human well-being as a response to the city's visual bewilderment:

The eye of the spectator finds itself looking at a site composed of streets and houses. It receives the impact of the masses [of buildings] which rise up around it. If these masses are of a formal [i.e. rationalised] kind and have not been spoilt by unseemly variations, if the disposition of their grouping expresses a clean rhythm and not an incoherent agglomeration, if the relationship of mass to space is in just proportion, the eye transmits to the brain co-ordinated sensations and the mind derives from these satisfactions of a high order: this is architecture. (1986: 47)

Recall that Ross gestured towards similar ideas when arguing that dangerous mental contagion may be prevented through urban design. Le Corbusier effectively affirmed this suggestion, although he elaborated much further on it and bestowed it with specific physical content. Many of his proposed solutions to the problems of modern cities were predicated on emphatically modern innovations in construction – such as the combined use of steel and concrete, hailed by Le Corbusier for 'the exactitude with which these materials can be adapted to calculation' and hence to rationalist imagination (1986: 286). Similarly, he explicitly praised modern Fordist industrial production as a source of inspiration for how houses should be built. He did not fear that such mass-produced houses would sink into indistinct greyness. By contrast, he appreciated their de-individualised content and believed that they would cater to a demand he saw for regulating lines of visibility (1986: 264). Briefly put, modern technologies constituted a solution to the perils of modernity.

In a similar vein, Le Corbusier did not see urban density as a problem. While he believed that proper urban planning should bring more parks and open spaces to city centres and that traffic congestion must be relieved, he also argued in favour of augmenting urban density (1981: 170). In fact, according to Le Corbusier, de-congestion may be achieved through increasing density (Hall, 2002: 222). This was one of the central axioms guiding his 1922 proposal for 'A Contemporary City of Three Million Inhabitants', as well as his 1933 proposal for the Radiant City (Corbusier, 1981: ch. 11; Fishman, 1982: chs. 21, 24). Both portrayed a metropolis based on a dense centre of high-rise buildings, located in parks, surrounded by less dense areas in a grid structure; avenues would radiate outwards from the city centre so that traffic flowed in an orderly fashion. Interestingly, one of the implications – if an inadvertent one – of Le Corbusier's programmatic emphasis on a clear, geometric planning of the city was that it targeted the constant urban flicker identified by the likes of Ross, Simmel, Park and Fitzgerald. By bringing visual order to the urban habitat, Le Corbusieran planning promised to relieve the modern city of one of its most characteristic, if hectic, features; a key condition of social avalanches would thereby be eliminated.

Le Corbusier's ambition cannot hide the impression that an underlying, more totalitarian countercurrent can also be identified in his work. By proposing to bring order to the city through visual homogeneity and by doing so through modern production techniques, Le Corbusier effectively argued for a large-scale architectural manifestation of the type of mass ornamentation Kracauer analysed in 1927. Kracauer's investigation focused on the Tiller Girls, a then-popular dancing troupe of women dancers who, similarly dressed, lined up in rows and performed the same synchronised movements. Kracauer focused on this cultural phenomenon as an expression of something broader – namely, the embodiment of 'the aesthetic reflex of the rationality aspired to by the prevailing economic system' (1975: 70). Specifically, Kracauer argued that the Tiller Girls, carefully 'arranged in row upon ordered row', epitomised the de-individualising mass logic of the Fordist economy: like lines of factory workers, the dancing girls were reduced to mere bodily movements and, given their synchronicity, they lost all individual qualities (1975: 67). Precisely this type of mass ornamentation, this collectivistic aesthetic rendition of masses of de-individualised entities, seems a reference point in Le Corbusier's work, with its emphasis on orderly rows of high-rise buildings devoid of unique, individual characteristics.

Though I have focused on Le Corbusier here, the faith in architects and urban planners as not merely mitigators of small-scale problems but veritable master thinkers *and* doers whose interventions would eradicate the roots of urban malaise extended far beyond Le Corbusier. The British urban planner Ebenezer Howard and the American architect Frank Lloyd Wright expressed similar convictions about the force of architects and planners.

Howard's main contribution was his proposal for the Garden City, published in 1898 and conceived as a solution to the problems of the Victorian cities of his time (Howard, 2003). While Le Corbusier focused his planning on an intra urban level, Howard eschewed the existing city as a reasonable site for reform and argued instead for creating a new type of settlement, the scale of which departed from that of the vastly overcrowded cities. Specifically, he suggested a mediating layer between city and countryside, which would combine (lighter) industrial production from the city with the countryside's fresh air

Figure 4.6 The Tiller Girls.
Note: Morning rehearsal of the Tiller Girls at Scala Theatre in Berlin, 1927.
Source: © 2019. Photo Scala, Florence/bpk, Bildagentur für Kunst, Kultur und Geschichte, Berlin

and relative abundance of space. Howard conceived each such new settlement, each Garden City, as a set of concentric circles with a park at the centre (itself hosting civic institutions), surrounded by housing, factories, railways and an outer green belt of farms and forests – altogether making room for no more than 32,000 inhabitants (2003: 30). Upon reaching that limit, a new adjacent Garden City would be created. Eventually, a cluster of Garden Cities would ensue, producing agglomerations Howard dubbed 'Social Cities' (2003: ch. 13). Howard believed that since each Garden City would be carefully planned, the larger Social City would bring into being a well-functioning cosmos in which each inhabitant would benefit from both small-scale (Garden City) and medium-scale (Social City) order while avoiding the mass poverty of contemporary cities.

Similar to Howard, with whom he shared a deep-seated rejection of big cities as well as a 'populist antipathy to finance capital, and land-lordism' (Hall, 2002: 312), Frank Lloyd Wright argued for utilising the unbuilt land outside the existing metropolises. However, rather than striving for a collectivist vision that aligned city and countryside in a new and unique configuration – evidently centralised via its concentric structure – he proposed a radical de-centralisation of the city in a rural territory. This vision was prominently articulated in 'Broadacre City: A New Community Plan', published in 1935 (Wright, 2000). In it, Wright advocated a type of planning that would essentially transpose urban elements such as factories, cars, highways and high-rise buildings to the countryside, but in ways that did not transform the latter into a city. Rather, his vision amalgamated rural and urban structures, making them difficult to distinguish. Tightly linked to this physical reconfiguration was the redistribution of land, since in Broadacre City every citizen would be allotted at least one acre of land. This, Wright believed, was the central means towards avoiding the de-individualising consequences and rampant speculative capitalism of existing cities. Equipped with their own land, citizens would have enough possibilities to thrive as families while remaining connected to others via cars and telephones (or with their own helicopter or 'aerator', see, 2000: 348) – all of which would take place in a space that had none of the density of modern cities. In other words, isolation would be the starting point and main condition for this type of planning, and all interaction and collectivity would be products of purely voluntary outreach. While Wright certainly did not pin his faith on the Broadacre City as an immediate cure of the evils he associated with modern cities, he believed its results would eventually manifest:

Individuality established on such terms [i.e. of the Broadacre plan] must thrive. Unwholesome life would get no encouragement and the ghastly heritage left by over-crowding in overdone ultra-capitalistic centers would be likely to disappear in three or four generations. (2000: 349)

For all the differences in their specific plans, Howard, Wright and Le Corbusier shared the sense that comprehensive planning was the only way forward, the sole path to pursue if the problems with metropolitan disorder were to be alleviated.[13] This was underpinned by their shared commitment to emancipation. In Howard's proposal for the Garden City, emancipation materialised in a vision of individuals granted enough space and freedom to thrive while at the same time being closely tied to collective pledges and possibilities. In fact, Howard's suggestions were predicated on ideas about socialist community (Hall et al., 2003: 4).

---

[13] It is not my aim here to discuss the similarities and differences between Howard, Wright and Le Corbusier in any depth. For detailed accounts of their work and how they relate to one another, see Fishman (1982) and Hall (2002).

Wright held a stronger commitment to individualist ideals and believed that his plans for decentralisation would create suitable conditions for individuality to flourish (Fishman, 1982: 9, 93–6). For Le Corbusier, finally, urban planning ought to both liberate individuals and work towards a higher level of collective action. He articulated this point explicitly in the so-called Charter of Athens, which grew out of discussions among leading European architects at the 1933 meeting of the Congrès Internationaux de l'Architecture Moderne (CIAM). Le Corbusier formulated a substantial portion of the paragraphs presenting CIAM's recommendations for urban planning in the Charter. 'Town planning,' he insisted, 'must guarantee individual liberty at the same time as it takes advantage of the benefits of collective action' (Le Corbusier quoted in Conrads, 1970: 139). Establishing the proper balance between the individual and the collective was obviously no trivial feat. While the Charter did not specify in detail how this balance might be achieved, it did make the point that urban planners would have to take both dimensions into account. This exact stance defined Le Corbusier's own mediation of – or balancing act between – Howard's collectivist ideals and Wright's individualist approach: 'Left to himself [sic], man is quickly crushed by difficulties of all sorts which he has to surmount. On the other hand, if he is subjected to too many collective constraints his personality becomes stifled' (Le Corbusier quoted in Conrads, 1970: 145).

Collectivist ideals aside, Le Corbusier and Wright both saw the architect as raised above the collective and endowed with a preeminent level of individuality. Illustratively, in spite of his strongly pronounced individualism, Wright accorded the architect an immensely important role in establishing harmony in Broadacre City: 'The agent of the state in all matters of land allotment or improvement, or in matters affecting the harmony of the whole, is the architect. All building is subject to his [sic] sense of the whole as organic architecture' (Wright, 2000: 346). So much for Wright's individualism, in other words. At any rate, this individualism went hand in hand with the notion of 'the architect [as] a natural leader' (Fishman, 1982: 109). Le Corbusier expressed a similar elevation of the architect. Hailing Louis XIV, Louis XV and Napoleon for having produced wonderful places such as the Invalides, the Champ de Mars and the Tuileries, he invoked the distinction between leader and crowd so central to classical crowd theory: 'These works are a signal example of *creation*, of that spirit which is able to dominate and compel the mob' (1981: 282, original emphasis).[14] Again, a clear social and ideational

---

[14] For a discussion of Le Corbusier's 'quest for authority', see Fishman (1982: ch. 25).

hierarchy was at play here, with the architect, the source of creation, shining at the top.

A Tangible World: On Objects and Avalanching

Le Corbusier's emphasis on straight visual lines as a core feature of good urban planning – 'Geometry is the foundation' of town planning, he declared (1981: xxi) – indicates a broader commitment to visuality within modernist architecture. In addition to the geometrical principles in Le Corbusier's work, such as the consecration of the grid as a basic aspect of urban planning, early-twentieth-century modernist architects espoused several visual aspects of architecture. For one, they stridently discarded ornamentation and decoration as stylistic features of the past and argued that these had no place in the new type of architecture they advocated. The abandonment of ornamentation was formulated most programmatically and relentlessly by the Austrian architect Adolf Loos in his 1908 essay, 'Ornament and Crime' (Loos, 1998a). Loos argued that while ornamentation certainly had its place in the evolution of culture, it belonged to a primitive age, and any use of it in modern society was therefore 'a symptom of backwardness or degeneracy' (1998a: 170). In fact, he considered its modern-day use a veritable crime, asserting an evolutionary logic in his formula: '*the evolution of culture is synonymous with the removal of ornamentation from objects of everyday use*' (1998a: 167, original emphasis). Importantly, for Loos, the rejection of ornamentation was not just a matter of cultural or aesthetic judgement. He asserted too that 'in economic respects [ornamentation] is a crime, in that it leads to the waste of human labor, money, and materials' (1998a: 169). Without ornamentation, workers could spend their time on other, more important things to the dual betterment, Loos predicted, of their health and the national budget. While Loos was arguably the loudest proponent of this abandonment of ornamentation, others soon followed suit. Le Corbusier, for one, delivered a blistering diatribe against ornamentation in *Towards a New Architecture*:

Tail pieces and garlands, exquisite ovals where triangular doves preen themselves or one another, boudoirs embellished with 'poufs' in gold and black velvet, are now no more than the intolerable witnesses to a dead spirit. These sanctuaries stifling with elegancies, or on the other hand with the follies of 'Peasant Art,' are an offence. (1986: 91)

This harsh attack on ornamentation – and the call for more sanitised designs purified of any non-functional decoration – was not limited to a few isolated architects; it found backing in a widely shared international movement. The most prominent expression of this was Henry-Russell Hitchcock and Philip Johnson's 1932 book *The International Style*, which accompanied the New York City's Museum of Modern Art exhibition from the same year, entitled 'The International Style: Architecture Since 1922'. Counting a host of architects from several countries, including Le Corbusier, Walter Gropius, Ludwig Mies van der Rohe and others, Hitchcock and Johnson summarised three core design principles undergirding modernist architecture (which they called the International Style): the emphasis on volume rather than mass, regularity (which applied both to 'the use of standardized parts throughout' and to the 'orderliness of structure', see 1995: 70), and the absence of ornamentation. As for Loos, the rejection of ornamentation was presented by Hitchcock and Johnson as a function of 'an æsthetic as well as an economic desideratum' (1995: 83).

Further, in neither the 1932 exhibition nor the book were these visual principles penned down as mere abstract prescriptions. Rather, Hitchcock and Johnson demonstrated the ways in which these principles took material shape in the designs and actual buildings of the many architects whose work they covered. Interestingly, what emerged out of Hitchcock and Johnson's particular way of representing architecture was, as Schiermer notes, an approach that emphasised the 'purely *formal* conceptions of building structure and geometrical shape [...] This development increasingly turns the actual building into a detached object, only accessible through the gaze, bereft of tactile sensations and separated from its context' (2016: 139, original emphasis). In other words, Hitchcock and Johnson played no small role in establishing a tradition of architectural representation that has continued to this day, in which architecture is portrayed first and foremost visually. More precisely, architecture is reduced in this tradition to a stylised form in which a specific timelessness is the goal (buildings are pictured in their ideal appearance rather than with their wear and tear), with users, inhabitants or humans in general often absent.[15]

Loos's dismissal of ornamentation might have helped trigger this particular visual conception of architecture amongst modernist architects, including the specific visual representations of buildings that grew out of it. However, in actuality, Loos was more ambivalent on precisely this visual dimension. Instead of buying into the predominantly visual approach to (and representation of) architecture, which would later gain currency with the modernist movement he inspired, Loos advocated a

---

[15] Of the many images of buildings in Hitchcock and Johnson's book, only a few contain people.

much more tactile, embodied attitude. For example, referring to his own architectural designs, he counted it his 'greatest pride that the interiors which [he had] created are totally ineffective in photographs. [He has had] to forgo [*sic*] the honour of being published in the various architectural magazines' (Loos quoted in Colomina, 1994: 42). And rather than detailing every aspect of his designs with a pencil, he insisted that much of the architect's work could only be completed *in situ*, when walking through and experiencing in an immediate, multisensory way the specific room or building under construction (Colomina, 1994: 269). This immediacy with objects constituted for Loos the only way to finalise an architectural design. Yet such an immediate experience evades visual representation, according to Loos; visualisation would at best capture fragments of the actual (or planned) design, and not the most important ones.

Loos's object-oriented approach is significant for two reasons. First, Schiermer (2016) points out that a preoccupation with timelessness underpinned Loos's embodied attachment (rather than visual distance) to the objects he designed. Getting closer to the objects would entail a circumvention of the socio-temporal logic of fashion, described in the Karen Blixen quotation in Chapter 2. In Loos's own words, 'Fashion only moves so quickly because our relationship with things is out of synch. As soon as we have objects which possess the qualities of beauty and endurance, fashion will immediately come to a halt' (quoted in Stewart, 2000: 107). So, following Schiermer's interpretation, Loos believed that by enhancing object-directedness, one's immediacy to the object, any social influence on the ways in which the object is experienced would simultaneously be reduced. This was not merely a reconfiguration or better balancing of human subjects and objects, an attempt to alleviate the kind of modern estrangement from objects that Simmel diagnosed. Rather, regardless of whether Loos's vision may be highly difficult to achieve in practice – assuming as it does, *contra* Tarde's social epistemology, that the social framing of knowledge and perception can be bracketed – this sensory immediacy to the object was conceived as something of a bulwark against social avalanching. By escaping the visual representation of architecture in magazines, a form of representation at once fed by and further nourishing the dynamism of fashion, a detachment from fashion's mimetic logic seemed possible. In other words, immersion in the object was seen as a safeguard against being carried away by social collectives. As I return to in Chapter 5, this notion of using attention fixation on objects as a means of protecting the individual from social avalanches would later find its way into financial advice literature as well.

Second, Loos's approach revolved around a tensional conception of individuality, itself enveloped in a broader response to urban matters. Thus, Beatriz Colomina writes, 'The subject of Loos's architecture is the citizen of the metropolis, immersed in its abstract relationships and striving to assert the independence and individuality of its existence in the face of the leveling power of society' (1994: 273). Loos's thoughts on the relationship between independent individuality and external power mark a return to the connections between surfaces and depths, albeit architecturally restaged as a link between inside and outside. For example, he ended 'Ornament and Crime' by observing an inverse relationship between evolutionary progress and the degree to which ornamentation serves as a sign of individuality:

When [in earlier times] men followed the herd they had to differentiate themselves through color, modern man uses his dress as a disguise. His sense of his own individuality is so immensely strong it can no longer be expressed in dress. Lack of ornamentation is a sign of intellectual strength. (1998a: 175)

This touched upon Loos's more general reflections on fashion and how to dress, topics on which he had much to say.[16] The central element in his definition of a modern dress is that 'it does not attract any unwarranted attention' in the cultural setting in which the person wears it (2011a: 31). It is via this sense of blending into the environment that the dress serves as a disguise for the modern individual, according to Loos. The underlying credo of this clearly ran counter to Simmel's claims about how urban individuality might be developed through mannerisms (although it did echo Simmel's observation about 'the drive for immersion in the collectivity'; see 1997d: 196). For Loos, the less one stands out, the more modern one is. In Tardean terms this represented the most imitative gesture one could imagine, resulting in individuals essentially being one with the social environment, hence effectively

---

[16] A significant portion of the essays in *Ornament and Crime: Selected Essays* (Loos, 1998b) is about fashion. The same applies to the (partly overlapping) essays collected in *Why a Man Should Be Well-Dressed* (Loos, 2011b). Loos's analysis of the relationship between dressing, individuality and modernity has a normative bias to it (as well as class and gender biases, for that matter). That is, Loos did not establish the connection between inconspicuous dressing and modernity by observing, in an unaffected and objective manner, the ways in which changes in clothing patterns had evolved with the advent of modern society. Rather, he normatively committed to inconspicuous dressing and scorned the dandies of the world, 'for whom clothes serve only one purpose: to stand out from the crowd' (2011a: 31). Let me also note that there are considerable overlaps between Loos's general analysis of fashion dynamics (including the ways in which fashion trickles downs from 'the best circles', see 2011a: 32) and what Simmel (1957) articulates about fashion in a sociological domain. Connections between Loos and Simmel receive ample treatment in Stewart (2000).

dissolving into it and letting go of their individuality. Or rather, this was the case at a surface level. At a deeper level – in the interior of the person, as it were – individuality could prosper, argued Loos, not least because no energy needed to be reserved for external conspicuousness. With less invested in the surface, more could be invested in the interior. Loos established a direct analogy from this notion to his architectural designs, stating that 'The house has to look inconspicuous' and 'The house does not have to tell anything to the exterior; instead, all its richness must be manifest in the interior' (Loos quoted in Colomina, 1994: 274). Again, there is an echo in this of the broader urban condition, as Colomina rightly observes:

> [In his architecture] Loos seems to establish a radical difference between interior and exterior, which reflects the split between the intimate and the social life of the metropolitan being: 'outside,' the realm of exchange, money, and masks; 'inside,' the realm of the inalienable, the nonexchangable, and the unspeakable. (Colomina, 1994: 274)

Colomina goes on to demonstrate, in a critical deconstruction of some of the buildings Loos designed, that the separation between an inconspicuous exterior of non-individuality and a rich interior in which individuality asserts itself is rather more blurred than his programmatic statements may initially suggest. While parts of her analysis are, in my view, stretched – such as when she declares in a discussion of a specific interior that 'the threat of modernity, how to master the uncontrollability of the metropolis, is that of castration' (1994: 277) – her observation of the ways in which Loos's actual designs seemed to emphasise the membrane, the connections, between interior and exterior is nonetheless helpful. It highlights that if there is indeed a homologous relationship between the modern individual and Loos's architecture, the tensionality of the latter reflects back on the former.

Let me round off this foray into Loos's work by recapitulating two important features that relate directly to the analytical framework of the present book. The first is the alternative he offered to the modernist tradition he otherwise inspired: his break from the commitment to visuality that would become so prominent in the hands of Le Corbusier and others. By stressing immediacy and the tactile experiences of architecture, Loos proposed his own solution to the problem of social avalanches. Rather than visual order as the central fix in architecture, nearness to the object under design became a safeguard against being carried away in collective mimesis. Of course, this might be said to mainly affect the architect walking through a room under construction and not so much the urban inhabitant. However, Loos's attention to objects also registered in his emphasis on the interior of buildings as the true centre of architecture, and this dimension catered to all urban dwellers. The point of this inward-looking gesture was, second, to stress the existence of some core individuality beneath or behind exterior appearance. Loos insisted that an inconspicuous outside enabled a flourishing individuality to grow on the inside. What materialises in this conception is not just a zero-sum play between inside and outside. An essentially tensional notion of individuality equally surfaces, in which Loos intimately connects the two opposite poles: the Tardean imitative becoming one with the environment is the condition of possibility for the independent autonomous individual. As a result, Loos reintroduces a Bernheimean theme of wilful submission to suggestion, although this time approached from the opposite direction. The point is less that suggestion and mimesis are only imaginable because of a positive decision to let go of individuality but that mimesis (of surfaces) becomes the means through which the individual can develop (within).

★★★

Social avalanche is woven into the fabric of modern cities, and urban inhabitants are cast in a tensional relationship between mimesis and anti-mimesis. Such is the message touted by the many urban observers I have discussed above. Some of these observers are renowned sociologists, whereas the names of others may be less familiar to today's ears. Regardless of their status in the canon of sociological thinking, the works covered in this chapter amply suggest that late-nineteenth and early-twentieth-century reflections on modern cities were wedded to the analytical horizon I have excavated in the preceding chapters. Beyond such an alignment of ideas, however, the urban focus in sociology added new dimensions and accents to the framework derived from ruminations on crowds and collective behaviour. For example, and perhaps unsurprisingly, considerations revolving around architecture tend to attribute to objects a more critical role for understanding the subtleties of social avalanching and tensional individuality, with Loos's work assuming a particularly crucial role in this respect.

   More generally, by attending to the thoughts of seminal architects and urban planners, the analysis of a historical archive of sociological theory is supplemented by a more practical dimension. In addition to sharing the overall diagnosis of modern city life that found expression in the writings of urban sociologists, leading early-twentieth-century architects and urban planners offered something sociologists did not provide: equipped with plans and design skills, they presented meticulous proposals for how to radically re-think the layout, structure and organisation of cities. The motivation driving this grand planning endeavour was to fix the alleged de-individualising and de-moralising effects of existing cities and to create fresh conditions for an emancipation of urban inhabitants, which included ensuring their well-being. This programmatic reorientation of urban planning was clearly undergirded by a wish to keep in check any avalanching forms of being-carried-away that might arise from urban disorder. As demonstrated, this did not preclude an interest in collective dimensions. However, in the eyes of several of these architects and planners, not only were the collective aspects of the city malleable, they also should be shaped in ways that would further bolster or emancipate individuals. This suggests that in the work of these master planners, too, the individual was portrayed in a tensional relationship between external forces and internal autonomy. For example, Le Corbusier remained caught in a tensional conception of individuality in that the emancipation of individuals for which he advocated could only be ensured through the external intervention of the master architect. In other words, just as the medical hypnotist sought to liberate patients from their sicknesses, so too the active, sovereign individuality of the urban inhabitant could only come into being if the structural conditions that made them passive were transformed by the genius architect.

Yet, compared to sociologists such as Simmel and Park, the architects and urban planners were deficient in one important respect: while several brought up issues about capitalism and the modern economy, they did not treat these themes with much analytical care. Although Simmel put greater emphasis than Park on the alienating aspects of the money economy, both seized on the idea that urban dynamics are intimately connected to market logics and that social avalanching may be of particular import when it comes to appreciating the links between crowds, cities and financial markets. Precisely this type of connection, and the types of developments it may be undergoing today, occupy me in the next chapter.

5   Financial Markets

On Thursday, 6 May 2010, US financial markets experienced one of the biggest intraday declines in the history of the Dow Jones Industrial Average – a drop of 998.5 points (more than 9 per cent), equivalent to around $1 trillion in value. The greater part of the decline took place over just *four-and-a-half minutes*, but the markets, after having been temporarily suspended, recovered almost as quickly. The trading day began with a dip due to the sovereign debt crisis in Europe, but the subsequent rapid market decline was triggered, at least according to the official report published jointly in September that year by the two main US regulatory authorities – the Commodity Futures Trading Commission (CFTC) and the Securities and Exchange Commission (SEC) – when a large asset management firm executed a sizeable sell order that was initially partly absorbed by so-called high-frequency trading algorithms, which then 'aggressively sold' their position in a manner that rapidly drove down prices (CFTC–SEC, 2010: 3). The asset management firm in question was the Kansas City-based Waddell & Reed Financial Inc. (Lauricella, Scannell and Strasburg, 2010; MacKenzie, 2015: 647). While asset management firms often pursue a long-term investment perspective, the Waddell & Reed order attracted attention because of its instantaneous, short-term effects. Thus, what ensued after high-frequency trading algorithms responded to the sell order was a situation of extreme market volatility, in which some stocks were traded at prices far from their normal value, at 'irrational prices as low as one penny or as high as $100,000' (2010: 5). A large proportion of these trades were later cancelled by the exchanges due to being 'clearly erroneous' (2010: 6).

The event was soon dubbed the 'Flash Crash' due to this rapid decline and rebound of prices. What caused the Flash Crash? What characterised its dynamics? And what might be its broader implications for financial markets? These questions have been the subject of much subsequent inquiry, controversy and discussion by the public, media and scholars, and a range of explanations and perspectives have been offered. Notably, for example, US regulators changed their account of the event over time.

While the CFTC–SEC report from September 2010 saw the Flash Crash as a confluence of factors, albeit one triggered by the Waddell & Reed order, the regulators later identified a British trader, Navinder Singh Sarao, as the main culprit. In 2015, Sarao was arrested and charged with fraud and market manipulation, including playing a critical role in the Flash Crash, allegedly bringing down US markets from his parents' home in Hounslow on the outskirts of London. The two explanations were tied to different moral and legal registers. Where the Waddell & Reed order was seen as belonging to the domain of legitimate (though somewhat unusual) market behaviour, Sarao was charged with intentionally manipulating markets. However, neither explanation entailed that the intent to generate a big market collapse existed. Instead, according to both regulators' explanations, the Flash Crash was characterised by some trigger (legal or not) that unleashed a complex set of unanticipated interactions between trading algorithms.

In line with this, much of the commentary on the Flash Crash has seen the event as emblematic of the allegedly innate risks and challenges that come with a market configuration in which fully automated computer algorithms – rather than human beings – are behind the vast majority of market activity. Indeed, the Flash Crash seems to constitute more than a caesura in the ongoing life of financial markets, which have always been characterised by instabilities, booms and busts. The high rate of recurrence with which the Flash Crash is evoked in discussions about present-day markets and the importance it is attributed in these accounts suggest that it almost figures as a trauma, a shock that installed an unmistakable before and after, one that portends what might be in store as markets become increasingly dominated by algorithms. However, as I argue in this chapter, the Flash Crash should not merely be seen as a science-fiction-like narrative about technology taking over and demolishing the pillars of markets or of society. Rather, and arguably more interesting, existing accounts of the Flash Crash tend to conjure up tropes that associate it with classical modernist ideas about social avalanching.

That sci-fi and modernist tropes can and are being conjoined in discussions of the Flash Crash is evident in popular representations of markets, such as the British novelist Robert Harris's *The Fear Index* (2012). In this book, the protagonist Dr Alexander Hoffmann, an algorithmic hedge-fund manager, is the mastermind behind a new machine-learning trading algorithm which eventually spirals out of control as it assumes a life of its own and starts making independent decisions beyond human influence. The algorithm ultimately brings down US markets in a disruptive event that closely mirrors the 2010 Flash Crash. In fact, the novel explicitly references the September 2010 CFTC–SEC report on the Flash Crash, and much of the narrative follows this official report and its portrayal of the event (2012: 317–18).

In one sense, the emphasis of *The Fear Index* on technology makes it yet another novelistic adaptation of a Frankensteinian plot to the present; still, it is also more than just that. One of the book's exciting facets lies in the way it evokes arguments often articulated in academic debates about algorithmic trading. At one point, for example, Hoffmann celebrates algorithms because they 'don't have an imagination. They don't panic. And that's why they're so perfectly suited to trade on the financial markets' (2012: 112) – a statement often repeated by advocates of algorithmic trading and its alleged ability to excise human emotions to create a hard-nosed, rational trading environment. Another interesting feature of the novel, one that speaks directly to the themes of this book, concerns its blend of high-tech algorithmic developments and classical social theory about crowd behaviour. The latter surfaces in references to key crowd scholars such as Le Bon and Elias Canetti (1984), whose work constitutes important building blocks in the protagonist's intellectual inventory (e.g., 2012: 35, 109). Most crucial, though, this intellectual horizon is tied to the Flash Crash when Hoffmann, observing markets crash because of his algorithm, notes, 'We started it. [...] Set off an avalanche' (2012: 367).

While the reference to avalanching in *The Fear Index* might be somewhat casual, it nonetheless testifies to an important way in which the novel stirs up a larger discursive repertoire often evoked in discussions of the Flash Crash. From a theoretical point of view, the deployment of this conceptual register is at once thought provoking and consequential in that it effectively musters a set of notions, initially formulated for inter-human relationships, and mobilises this lexicon for the understanding of an emphatically non-human inter-algorithmic domain: the realm of fully automated algorithms observing and trading with one another. In other words, what is sociologically interesting about accounts of the Flash Crash is not least the ways in which they suggest that algorithms, too, can be swept away, avalanche and be captured in tensional relationships between mimesis and anti-mimesis. I realise that bringing this sociological conceptual register to bear on non-human interaction patterns might raise eyebrows. Does it really make sense to talk about social interaction between algorithms? Can theorisation that originates in concerns with human crowding be meaningfully applied to account for non-human dynamics? I assert that both questions can be answered in the affirmative and substantiate this claim in the course of the chapter.

I appreciate that the Flash Crash might seem like a somewhat fringe illustration of how financial markets operate, even if it constitutes for

many observers an emblematic specimen of the inherent risks of algorithmic trading. After all, financial markets are such big and complex
animals that to zero in on one dimension of this elephant is bound to miss
most of its other parts – not to mention the creature in its entirety. There
is really no way around this problem, especially not given the confines of
a single chapter. However, I nonetheless suggest that the vocabulary of
social avalanching and tensional individuality is indeed salient when it
comes to examining financial markets. Consequently, in addition to
focusing on the Flash Crash, I demonstrate that the notions of avalanche
and tensional individuality have, in fact, long been central to conceptions
of financial markets. From the late nineteenth century to the Flash Crash
(and beyond), observers have repeatedly stressed that the *modus operandi*
of financial markets closely resembles the dynamics I have analysed with
these notions.

In keeping with the time period that has occupied me so far in the
book, this chapter begins with a discussion of the ways in which late-
nineteenth-century financial markets became intertwined with issues of
crowding and cities, as well as the kinds of negative effects they were
believed to engender. For example, I discuss how financial exchanges
were architecturally designed to avoid the avalanching crowd behaviour
that contemporary urban scholars associated with the metropolis.
Similarly, I analyse contrarian investment advice, which proposed techniques for resisting the lure of markets: the potential sweeping-away of
investors that, according to the contrarians, always exists as an underlying current and an ever-present peril. What is particularly interesting
about contrarian literature is that its diagnosis of the avalanching propensity of financial markets and its suggestions for how to withstand their
de-individualising pressure rest on a tensional understanding of the
individual investor.

Against this more historical backdrop, I then make some considerable
temporal jumps to present key points in the growing computerisation of
financial markets that has taken place since the 1960s. This includes the
emergence of electronic 'click' or 'screen' trading, which gained momentum in the 1990s and is characterised by humans placing orders in
markets on their computers rather than on the bustling floors of traditional exchanges.[1] Interestingly, in spite of vastly reducing the (inter)
human element of trading, screen-based trading nonetheless seems to
face the same types of avalanching challenges that previous observers,

---

[1] Click or screen trading owes its name to the fact that traders, sitting in front of their
screens, place orders on their computers by actively clicking their mouse or stroking their
keyboard.

such as the contrarians, attributed to human traders in a more classical (non-computerised) setting. Equally interesting, practitioners' observations of the lure of markets, the ever-present danger of being carried away by the emotional maelstrom of markets, have found somewhat contemporaneous corroboration in the academic literature of behavioural finance.

Next, I outline how the move towards fully automated computerised trading in the early 2000s was, among other things, a response to this perceived human deficiency. Transitioning into automated, dehumanised trading was seen as a means to resist the avalanching mimesis of markets. To paraphrase Hoffmann in *The Fear Index*, algorithms may help create more stable and efficient markets because they are not subject to human biases or panicking behaviour. I argue that algorithmic finance does indeed eliminate core human elements as this form of trading takes place at speeds that far exceed the bandwidth of human perception, marking the entry of what might be called sub-perceptual, or subsensory, finance.

I then return to the Flash Crash as an emblematic event in the landscape of this sub-perceptual algorithmic finance, as it provides at first blush a perhaps surprising connection between present-day high-tech financial markets and the late-nineteenth-century framework of social avalanche and tensional individuality. Events such as the Flash Crash suggest that the experience with avalanching and tensional individuality should not be buried as obsolete. It may be an experience that still registers today, albeit with the significant addendum that market avalanches can now take place at the level of algorithms. I discuss some of the ways in which the Flash Crash has been seen by observers as an important event, especially significant for how it testifies to the normality with which flash crashes emerge in present-day markets. I also suggest that in spite of the importance attributed to the event, the economic impact of the Flash Crash was relatively restricted. This forms the backdrop for my claim that the strong interest the event generated might therefore reflect how the Flash Crash sheds light on dynamics of social avalanching in a contemporary setting. I discuss the implications of this analysis, including the suggestion that the interaction of fully automated algorithms generates a particular form of sociality.

My discussion of present-day algorithmic finance and the Flash Crash is primarily based on written sources such as journalistic accounts, government reports and academic papers. However, my analysis is also informed by interviews I have conducted with market participants involved in various forms of algorithmic finance, including high-frequency trading. The majority of these interviews (sixty in total) were conducted between April 2016 and November 2018; they focus on CEOs, CTOs, traders, developers, regulators, exchange officials and other finance professionals, many from London, New York, Chicago and San Francisco. While these interviews have provided me with insights into the field of algorithmic finance and hence constitute a backdrop to this analysis, I only refer to them lightly in the chapter.

Crowded Trading

If we follow Alex Preda in conceiving of stock exchanges as 'the core of financial markets' (2009b: 12), that core experienced a number of important changes in the late-nineteenth to early-twentieth-century. These changes were not merely an effect of boom-and-bust forces such as the 1873 and 1907 panics (e.g. Fraser, 2005: 108–9; Nations, 2017) but rather of the types of technological and architectural advances that have garnered attention elsewhere in this book. That stock exchanges would undergo considerable transformations in the late nineteenth century is hardly surprising given the turbulence that characterises their colourful history, which cannot be comprehensively recounted here. Suffice it to say that back in the eighteenth century, before formal exchanges became common, coffee houses constituted the main sites of financial transactions.[2] This might suggest a highly fragmented market structure, but this was only partially the case. For example, Bruce Carruthers reports that 'physically, the English stock market was highly centralized. It was located in the coffee houses in Exchange Alley, a small area near Lombard Street in Central London', with trading activity gravitating towards two coffee houses in particular, Jonathan's and Garraway's (1996: 169). Similarly, in New York the centre of action was made up by coffee houses such as Merchants and subsequently Tontine, the latter of which Fraser describes, in his cultural history of Wall Street, as 'the informal site of the [city's] first stock exchange' (Fraser, 2005: 23; see also Preda, 2009b: 60–61).

Formal exchanges took shape only gradually. According to David Kynaston, a formal London-based stock exchange, with an entry fee, replaced coffee-house trading in 1773 (2012: 14). The New York Stock and Exchange Board was established several decades later in 1817, and with its institutionalisation 'one could now truly speak of the floor of the exchange' (Fraser, 2005: 33), although this did not completely eliminate market fragmentation (Preda, 2009b: 123–6; Sobel, 1965: ch. 5). In

---

[2] A notable exception is Amsterdam, where the Hendrick de Keyser Exchange had been inaugurated as far back as 1611 (Petram, 2014: 103–8).

Figure 5.1 Wall Street.
Note: Financial District, Wall Street, in the background the US Sub-Treasury Building. New York City, 1951.
Source: Photographer: W. Fischer. Inv.: IfA 87554. © 2019. Photo Scala, Florence/bpk, Bildagentur für Kunst, Kultur und Geschichte, Berlin

Chicago, which would evolve to become the main centre for agricultural commodities and futures trading, market activities were more dispersed. When the Chicago Board of Trade (CBOT) was established in 1848, the hope was that it would be able to centralise trading at one location; it even offered refreshments such as cheese and ale in order to attract traders. However, 'Chicago's grain market continued to be as decentralized as ever, with traders conducting their transactions in offices, warehouses, and streets all around the city' (Cronon, 1991: 115). It took almost a decade to change this, but by then its trading floors – or trading 'pits', as they were named in Chicago – had become main hubs for financial transactions in the city.

A range of mid- and late-nineteenth-century technological innovations significantly changed the ways in which exchanges operated. Some had been invented for non-financial purposes but were quickly adopted for exchange-related uses. Telephones, for instance, were introduced to Wall Street in 1878, although for a while old-fashioned letters continued to be a major communication channel between brokers and their clients (Preda, 2009b: 121–2). Earlier, telegraphs were deployed as a valuable means of communication of financial information. William Cronon reports that the first telegraph lines reached Chicago in 1848 and that they dramatically reduced the time it took to send information back and forth to New York. An important consequence of this was that 'eastern and western markets began to move in tandem much more than before'; 'those with the best access to telegraph news were often in the best position to gauge future movements of prices' (Cronon, 1991: 121). This connection between Chicago and New York remains of utmost importance to today's financial markets, as I elucidate later, although of course telegraphic communication has long been supplanted by much faster data transmission infrastructures.

Other technologies were invented with the aim of responding to specific challenges in financial markets. The stock ticker, especially, was one such innovation – one whose history has been explored in several fascinating studies (Preda, 2006; 2009b: ch. 4; Stäheli, 2013: ch. 7). Invented in 1867, the stock ticker was a device that allowed price information from the exchange floor to be distributed in a fast and reliable fashion. Initially, the ticker printed price quotes of individual securities, but after a few years, additional information such as traded volume was also included (Preda, 2009b: 115). Providing such data made the stock ticker exceptionally popular amongst brokers and others who appreciated a more immediate and orderly flow of information – accompanied by the ticking noise to which the machine owes its name. Indeed, Preda suggests that for Edward Calahan, the inventor of the stock ticker, its main purpose

Figure 5.2 Stock ticker.
Source: Getty Images

was less a matter of enhancing informational efficiency (although it certainly did that) than 'eliminating the disorder' that otherwise characterised markets at this time, a lack of order Calahan knew well from his experience as a messenger boy who would hurry back and forth between the exchange and brokerage offices, adding to the chaotic and bustling sense of the market (2006: 764). Urs Stäheli similarly quotes Calahan, stressing the need to dispense with the 'noise and confusion' that characterised financial markets in the 1860s (Calahan, in Stäheli, 2013: 198).

The swift and widespread use of the stock ticker contributed to creating a more homogenous and tightly connected market, a development similar to but also more intense than that previously achieved with the telegraph. Thus, the disarray and informational fragmentation that had previously characterised financial markets was greatly reduced with the advent of the ticker. Among other things, a better 'reciprocal temporal coordination' ensued: 'From the perspective of the brokerage house, [the ticker] helped orient the participants' time and rhythm to that of Wall Street' (Preda, 2009b: 128). More than that, as Preda aptly notes, the ticker also produced an important change in the ways market participants approached markets. Any person who wanted a quick sense of the market and its movements now had to pay careful attention to the ticker tape. In fact, the market was increasingly being captured on the tape. Stäheli (2013: 209–12) argues that a corollary of this was the democratisation of markets. Previously, exchanges had been active in trying to protect the price information they generated, seeking to reserve it for their members. With the popularisation of the stock ticker, such information now quickly left the interior of the exchange and was widely disseminated. Consequently, Preda summarises, it is fair to say that with the rise of the ticker, 'The observer of the market was the observer of the tape. In this sense, the ticker contributed to a radical abstraction and reconfiguration of the visual experience of the market' (2009b: 131).

As mentioned earlier, the CBOT developed into a central exchange during the 1850s. At the end of the 1860s, it had become so popular – counting more than 2,000 members – that it was on the verge of over-crowding (Falloon, 1998: 72). As a means of facilitating a more orderly trading space, a new physical layout of octagonally shaped trading pits, with descending steps in the middle, was introduced in 1870 as a substitute for the flat trading floors previously used. While this design might have eliminated some of the chaos of trading, Reuben Jennings of Chicago nonetheless proposed an amended design, which he patented in 1878 under the title 'Improvement in Trading-Pits' (Jennings, 1878). Though similar to the existing pits, Jennings's design sought to replace flat trading floors with a three-dimensional design, consisting of a series of stepped platforms arranged octagonally around, and descending towards, a centre.

Jennings ascribed several advantages to his design. For example, it allegedly facilitated ventilation, since hot and cold air pipes could be inserted in designated air chambers under the steps. This aspect of the design seemed to suggest that the temperatures of the market could be regulated in tandem with the temperature of the room. A further benefit of Jennings's design was that it would allow for more efficient communication between traders. The stepped architecture permitted each trader to 'see over the heads of those in front of him', so that 'persons may stand and conveniently trade with persons in any other part of the pit' (1878: 1). This all touched upon the more fundamental achievement of order that Jennings's patent was supposed to deliver: as Kristian Bondo Hansen (2017: 57–8) notes, Jennings's design especially aimed at eliminating crowding in trading pits and the open-outcry trading they accommodated. If correctly implemented, Jennings believed, his design would ensure that 'the pit may be filled without inconvenience in the way of crowding' (1878: 1). In his underlying vision, the noise of trading pits, their incessant bustle and commotion, would all vanish and be replaced

R. S. JENNINGS.
Trading-Pit

No. 203,837.   Patented May 21, 1878.

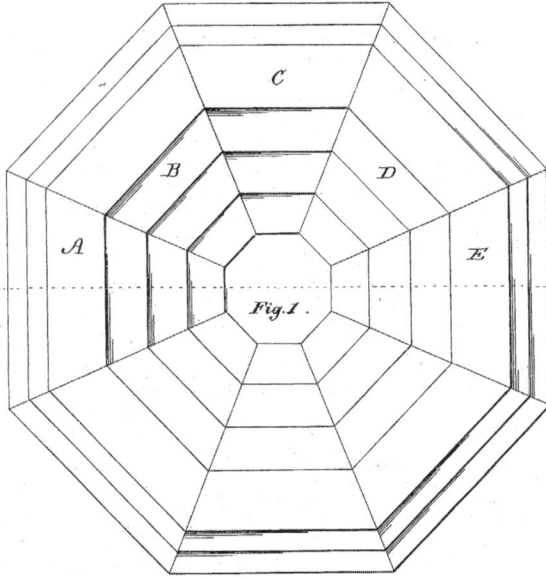

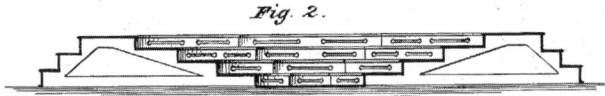

Figure 5.3 Jennings's trading-pit design.
Source: US Patent No. 203,837. Patented 21 May 1878

by a quiet, orderly space of financial transactions between traders who could easily see and hear their peers in the pit.

Trading platform designs similar to that proposed by Jennings would soon become commonplace at the CBOT and elsewhere, such as the Milwaukee Chamber of Commerce, although amended such that the steps rose above the floor of the room rather than sank below it, as Jennings had imagined. Jennings's contribution to the popularisation of octagonal trading pits was more contested. Once he had the patent in his hands, Jennings addressed both the CBOT and the Milwaukee Chamber of Commerce, claiming that they had infringed on his patent and demanding royalties for the use of his design. While the latter flatly rejected his claim, the CBOT paid him a handsome sum to settle the controversy (Falloon, 1998: 73–7). Some sources suggest that the court eventually annulled his patent (Hartman, 2006: 9, n. 7; Lukken, 2004).

Regardless of whether Jennings's impact was at best ephemeral, the basic problem he identified with the confused nature of existing markets resonated with what other observers noticed. While the stock ticker might have helped produce a more orderly flow of information from the exchange to the rest of the market, the interior of the exchange, its floors, or pits, remained loci of turmoil.[3] More precisely, the problem with the pits was that they reflected the urban exterior of the exchanges too much in spite of their interior character. This was exactly what Park (1915) had in mind when drawing connections between exchanges, crowds and cities, arguing that they were all captured by avalanching propensities. It therefore does not seem coincidental that pit traders would refer to themselves as 'crowds'. This emic term suggests that in spite of designs such as Jennings's, which sought to create a strong, architecturally anchored demarcation between allegedly disorderly urban

---

[3] The American novelist Frank Norris's *The Pit*, published in 1903, captured this nicely. Partly inspired by real events, the novel depicted a speculator trying, unsuccessfully, to corner the wheat market at the CBOT. This is how the pit was portrayed at the end of the novel when the corner breaks down: 'The roar was appalling, the whirlpool was again unchained, the maelstrom was again unleashed. And during the briefest of seconds [the protagonist] could fancy that the familiar bellow of its swirling, had taken on another pitch. Out of that hideous turmoil, he imagined, there issued a strange unwonted note; as it were, the first rasp and grind of a new avalanche just beginning to stir, a diapason more profound than any he had yet known, a hollow distant bourdon as of the slipping and sliding of some almighty and chaotic power' (1994: 326). While Norris's account was fictional, it nonetheless lends force to the notion that irrespective of Jennings's design, the pit continued to be associated with immense disorder. I thank Kristian Bondo Hansen for drawing my attention to this example. Norris's work is also discussed by Zimmerman (2006), who offers a fascinating account of how fiction picked up on the significant changes that financial markets were undergoing in the late nineteenth and early twentieth centuries.

life and orderly market behaviour, such a differentiation may not be easily established and maintained.[4] The blizzard of the metropolis – so key to the diagnosis proposed by the urban sociologists and architects discussed in 4 – seemed to not only parallel the frenzy and excitement of markets but also connect to it by way of their underlying avalanching dynamics. In a Simmelian vocabulary, the problem seemed to be that in spite of their embeddedness in both the money economy and urban logics, the pits had not yet developed the kind of firm intellectual attitude which Simmel otherwise associated with cities and markets. Rather, the pits seemed susceptible to those emotional pulls against which the intellectual attitude was supposed to deliver some protection.

While Park established connections between crowds, cities and financial markets from the vantage point of crowd theory and urban sociology, similar links would be drawn by early-twentieth-century observers, for whom financial markets constituted their natural home turf. Before examining a prominent example of this, it should be noted that the idea of seeing financial markets as emblematic of avalanching properties was nurtured by the fact that late-nineteenth-century crowd psychology was soon adopted beyond its original frame of reference – specifically, criminal and political crowds – as well as by the rise of a broader interest in mobilising psychological notions to better understand markets. Some of the key crowd scholars were instrumental in promoting these developments. For example, Tarde conceived of stock exchanges as veritable 'laboratories of collective psychology' (Tarde quoted in Hansen, 2017: 60). And not unlike Park, who characterised exchanges as news barometers, Tarde referred to them as 'special thermometers' that measure the sentiments of traders (Tarde, 2012: 43; see also Ross, 1908: 58–9; Weber, 2000: 325). Sidis, for his part, devoted a chapter of *The Psychology of Suggestion* to 'Financial Crazes', arguing that the kinds of suggestibility that could be observed in social life generally materialised equally in financial markets. Indeed, referencing examples such as the seventeenth-century Dutch tulip mania, he stated, 'The enthusiasm of speculative mania and the abject fear of financial panics are epidemical. Men [*sic*] think in crowds, and go mad in herds' (1898: 343). Further, bearing in mind his assertion that people become more suggestible if their free movement is curbed, Sidis arguably lent implicit support to the

---

[4] This sense of a lack of separation would haunt trading pits and floors for several decades. For example, Zaloom relays concerns in the late 1920s about the noise of the trading pits, specifically the trouble traders had hearing and being heard amidst 'the continual uproar and noise in the trading hall' (2006: 41). The frantic soundscape of the metropolis was, in other words, mimicked inside the exchanges.

kind of pit design Jennings advocated. The latter's architectural reorganisation of the trading space sought to ensure that traders would 'avoid occupying the same space', instead standing neatly next to one another and 'one behind the other' (Jennings, 1878: 1), thereby curtailing the otherwise allegedly epidemic nature of financial panics and the propensity of traders to be captured in suggestive avalanching (see also Hansen, 2017: 85).

Several economists and financial-market observers, writing in the early twentieth century, would soon pick up on this repertoire of ideas from crowd psychology. Hansen, in his detailed analysis of how ideas of crowd behaviour travelled from crowd psychology to financial economics as well as informed a broader investment literature between 1890 and 1940, fittingly refers to this as a '*psychologisation* of the markets': a mobilisation of psychology for the purpose of coming to terms with basic market dynamics (2017: 138, original emphasis). In particular, he argues, 'Psychology was indiscriminately used to explain alleged economic irrationality' (2015: 625). Hansen recognises that the deployment of ideas from crowd and collective psychology often happened in a rather eclectic and cursory fashion, without too much care for deep academic substantiation, although this certainly did not diminish the traction they gained at this time. To mention just a few examples, publications such as George C. Selden's *Psychology of the Stock Market* (1912), Henry Howard Harper's *The Psychology of Speculation: The Human Element in Stock Market Transactions* (Harper, 1926) and Fred C. Kelly's *Why You Win or Lose: The Psychology of Speculation* (1930) illustrate this psychological tide. These books all formed part of a subset or tradition of financial advice literature known as contrarianism, which drummed up particular tropes from crowd psychology.

Although the contrarian tradition was characterised by the pick-and-choose approach to academic findings I gestured to above, it nonetheless nurtured a set of core ideas. Contrarian writers argued that financial markets are indeed laboratories of collective sentiment and crowd thinking as per Tarde's and Sidis's portrayals. Furthermore, according to the contrarians, the kind of irrationality and stupidity attributed to crowds by the likes of Le Bon is also a characteristic feature of market participants. This generated an image of financial markets as made up of crowds of market actors who, since they are easily carried away by market sentiments, are often unable to retain their sound judgement and behave in irrational ways instead. Importantly, as Stäheli (2006; 2013) has demonstrated in his original analyses of contrarian thinking, this diagnosis of financial markets and their crowd-like behaviours was not debunked by the contrarians (see also Borch, 2007; Hansen, 2015). In contrast to Le

Bon, for whom crowds were emblematic of more or less everything detestable, the contrarians' observation of market crowds was at once more neutral and instrumental. On the one hand, they registered the crowd dimensions of financial markets in a neutral manner, as if delivering a disinterested, analytical account of any other phenomenon. On the other hand, they sought to exploit the alleged crowd features of markets and devised a set of investment strategies to that end. This is precisely where the name of the contrarian approach originates: since market participants tend to behave as crowds, they make irrational investment decisions; consequently, the most sensible investment approach is to monitor the market crowd closely and invest *contrary* to it. Selden elegantly captured the coolness this approach required, arguing that the trader or investor should 'endeavor to hold himself [*sic*] in a detached, unprejudiced frame of mind, and to study the psychology of the crowd, especially as it manifests itself in the movement of prices' (1912: 67).

What comes to the fore here is a complex interplay between mimesis and anti-mimesis. It might appear, from an immediate point of view, that contrarians treated financial markets in a purely mimetic fashion, arguing that market participants entirely (or mostly) submit to an imitative whirlwind and follow their peers, whether in a buy or sell direction. Much of the contrarian literature lends support to such a conception. Fred C. Kelly, for instance, affirmed in *Why You Win or Lose* that given that 'the natural behavior of the average person is likely to be wrong', 'there is one fairly safe guide to prudent procedure – to do exactly the opposite from what the majority of other people are doing. If one would win he [*sic*] must be contrary' (1930: 51). Nonetheless, contrarian investment advice was not simply a matter of advocating 'counter-mimicry' (Stäheli, 2006: 278) as a means to overcome the allegedly devastating avalanching believed to arise from crowd mimesis in markets: the sudden becoming-one with the market crowd, an experience of being carried away by the pull of the market and losing one's sense of self in a rapidly triggered levelling process. Rather, what was needed was an ingenious attachment to and detachment from crowd mimesis, an understanding of what the crowd is doing without simultaneously becoming part of it. The latter requirement in particular demanded the cultivation of a particular set of skills, and contrarian literature therefore focused extensive attention to studying *how* to achieve a distance from the threatening mimesis of the market. How could investors make sure that they would not succumb to the pressure of the market crowd and follow its stupid decisions? How to keep an analytical distance to its supposed nonsense?

Figure 5.4 Market chatter.
Note: Edgar Degas (1834–1917), *Portraits a la Bourse: representation d'Ernest May (1845–1925), financier et collectionneur.* C. 1878–79. Paris, Musee d'Orsay.
Source: © 2019. Photo Josse/Scala, Florence

According to Stäheli, the specific techniques the contrarians con-cocted to this end revolved around 'a whole program of disciplining and individualizing a speculator firmly positioned against the crowd' (2006: 279). In other words, these techniques were tasked with securing the individual an anti-mimetic stance vis-à-vis the market crowd. One technique aimed at what Stäheli refers to as affect control. In order to create a bulwark against, say, the epidemic nature of financial panics that Sidis identified, individual investors were advised to work hard on themselves. The contrarian Henry Howard Harper noted in the conclusion to his 1926 book *The Psychology of Speculation* that this included 'a complete mastery over one's impulses, emotions and ambitions under the most heroic tests of human endurance' (Harper, 1926: 106; see also Stäheli, 2006: 285). Another technique concentrated on isolation. Such isolation could assume a spatial form – for instance, by escaping the contagious nature of cities and the many market rumours that proliferated in them. A way to accomplish this was to retreat to smaller places or to the countryside. However, as Stäheli correctly notes, this technique suffered from two problems. First, 'it presupposes what it is supposed to produce: a highly self-disciplined speculator' (2006: 285). The decision to withdraw from the contagious buzz of the metropolis itself requires a good deal of individual autonomy and self-discipline. Second, given the popularity of stock tickers as well as the financial news reporting that became increasingly popular in newspapers throughout the nineteenth century (Poovey, 2008), attempts at spatial isolation in even seemingly remote places were no guarantee against being caught in the vortex of market information. This essentially harks back to the issue of mediatised contagion that Ross identified and its ability to sweep away people at a distance (see Chapter 4).

Humphrey B. Neill, a leading American contrarian, offered a response to this problem, detailing a more attention-oriented form of isolation.[5] Being in cities in which contagious market information circulates rapidly is not itself a major problem, Neill argued. However, in order to establish and retain a cool detachment from market information, the investor must master particular techniques. Specifically, Neill suggested that the investor always remember to bring paper and pencil and use writing as a means of fixating analytical attention on market movements without being caught in contagious gossip: 'Use pad-and-pencil since it will occupy your mind and concentrate your attention. Try it; you will not be able to chatter and keep track of trades at the same time' (Neill quoted in Stäheli, 2006: 286). In other words, and parallel to Loos's argument about the ways in which object-attention fixation may offer a bulwark against social avalanching, Neill believed that the individual can establish strong boundaries against collective forces.

---

[5] Neill's contribution to contrarian investment philosophy is discussed extensively in Hansen (2015; 2017) and Stäheli (2013).

This also suggests that while Neill's recommendations for some form of communicative isolation might have pleased Loos, they are tarred by the same paradox that applies to spatial isolation: they assume the autonomous investor type they are intended to generate. This is in fact a paradox that haunts all contrarian literature. It is never quite clear how the underlying Emersonian ideal of individual autonomy and self-reliance vis-à-vis crowd behaviour – an ideal the contrarians shared with Ross (Stäheli, 2006: 415, n. 442) – is to be squared with basic insights from crowd psychology. Taking the one seriously seems to automatically undermine the other. That is, unless one accepts that the two can co-exist as poles along the same continuum. This returns me to the notion of tensional individuality. In their attempt to devise strategies for how to avoid being caught in avalanching financial markets, which produce massive herding and sweep away any ability on part of the investors to make autonomous investment decisions, the contrarians were toying with an essentially tensional conception of the individual investor. While exposed to the crowd nature and mimetic pulls of markets, investors nevertheless possess individualistic cores that, if correctly nurtured through the right self-disciplining techniques, can develop some anti-mimetic fortification against mimetic currents, however forceful they may be. Cultivating such fortified individuality would not merely secure a sense of self but equally – and more decisively, for the contrarians – lay the foundation for profitable market behaviour.

Interestingly, central parts of the contrarian ruminations – on the need for discipline and emotional detachment to market developments, as well as their diagnosis of and concern with the potentially avalanching, de-individualising features of markets, in which market participants are swept away – constitute tropes that can be identified far beyond the early-twentieth-century circuit of contrarian investment-advice literature. These are tropes which seem intrinsically linked to the oper-ational logics of modern financial markets and are therefore also identifi-able today. But before moving from contrarianism to the present, let me illustrate the prominence of these tropes by returning to debates about the stock ticker, a technological instrument that prompted the same types of reflections and concerns that the contrarians put forth.

As mentioned earlier, the advent of the stock ticker generated a new type of market orientation in that observing the market increasingly entailed reading the ticker tape rather than, say, following exchange-floor dynamics from the visitors gallery. On one level, the ticker thereby seemed to secure the kind of distance to crowd behaviour that Jennings had in mind with his pit design (Stäheli, 2013: 199, 226). While the trading pit was allegedly marred by frantic movements and the ever-present risk of transforming into an avalanching blizzard, the ticker tape could be observed at a physical distance from the trading pit, say, while sitting in a comfortable chair in a quiet room. Stäheli demonstrates that this anti-crowd conception of the ticker – as an instrument enabling 'the individualized capitalist financier' to be safely detached from the agitated crowd – would be picked up in popular representations of markets, such as in movies (2013: 199). On another level, however, ticker-tape reading seemed to generate its own set of concerns remarkably similar to those advanced in debates about crowds and collective behaviour: the late-nineteen-century discussions of attention I touched upon in Chapter 1 were soon weaved into reflections on how to deal with the stock ticker. 'The ticker firmly bound investors and brokers to its ticks. Constant presence, attention, and observation were explicitly required by manuals of the time' (Preda, 2009b: 132). This constant attention easily lent itself to excess, as the circulation of notions of 'ticker trance' and 'tickeritis' well demonstrated (see Preda, 2009b: 133; Stäheli, 2013: 217). What they pointed to was an experience that aligned tape reading, and hence market observation, with hypnotic suggestion: the more attentive investors were to the ticker tape, the greater the risk of entering a hypnotic, trance-like state in which the tape reader effectively becomes 'an automaton that submitted to the tape, blindly carrying out its orders' or responding automatically to the price movements it relayed (Stäheli, 2013: 229).

Since constant attention to the tape was strongly recommended, and since the deliberate decision on the part of the individual to concentrate on the ticker tape could be accompanied by a loss of self (due to the letting go of individuality that would follow from the ticker trance), an essentially Bernheimian trope arose: the attentive tape reader 'had *to will to have no will*' (Stäheli, 2013: 233, original emphasis). So, while it might appear as if the stock ticker (and the object-attention fixation on it) did not, after all, secure solid protection against the de-individualising avalanching dynamics associated with the crowd behaviours of floor traders, it did not entail a complete suspension of individuality either. Rather, tape readers were attributed a tensional form of individuality, being consciously in charge of their submission to the flow of market information. The central difference with the Bernheimian template, here, lies in how the *suggestionneur* of the clinic had been replaced, in the market setting, with a machine that spat out price data. This de-humanisation of the *suggestionneur* constitutes one important move away from Bernheim's own framing and conceptual horizon. With the rise of algorithmic finance, in which fully automated computer algorithms place orders in markets, another arguably more controversial move is introduced, in which the *suggestionné* is de-humanised as well.

Figure 5.5 Tickeritis.
Note: Diego Rivera (1886–1957), *Wall Street Banquet (El banquete de los ricos)*. Mexico City, Secretaria de Educacion Publica.
Source: © 2019. Photo Schalkwijk/Art Resource/Scala, Florence. © Banco de México Diego Rivera & Frida Kahlo Museums Trust, México D.F./VISDA

Towards a Computerisation of Markets

The road from late-nineteenth-century open-outcry trading to present-day algorithmic finance is long and bumpy. As my aim here is not to trace it in any historical detail, I gloss over a significant amount of complexity – but let me single out just a few steps on this path. Throughout most of the twentieth century, exchange transactions continued to revolve around the kind of pit/floor trading that rose to prominence in the nineteenth century, in which human traders flocked to the floors of the exchanges, rubbing shoulders with one another in an often hectic, roaring market setting. However, especially from the 1960s on, the idea that computers could serve an important function in trading gained traction. One key milestone in this was the establishment of Institutional Networks in 1969 (rebranded as Instinet in 1985), which enabled the automated execution of block trades: trades of more than 10,000 shares (Castelle et al., 2016: 174). Another landmark development was the establishment of Nasdaq in early 1971, which introduced a centralised electronic platform for over-the-counter (OTC) dealer quotations. While OTC trading used to consist of (and in some markets is still made up of) a large non-centralised network of dealers who engage in bilateral relations in order to buy or sell their assets, the Nasdaq system created a trading place for dealers in which a host of market participants could constantly check prices and volumes on their computer screens – all they needed was a connection to the electronic network. Later in 1971, the financial economist Fischer Black published a two-piece article, 'Toward a Fully Automated Stock Exchange', in which he argued for pushing automation still further (Black, 1971a; 1971b). He argued that rather than being restricted to the electronisation of OTC, which Nasdaq had ushered into existence, the kinds of trading that were familiar to the New York Stock Exchange (NYSE) would also benefit from being automated. Such computerised automation could take place, he added, 'without introducing any additional instability in stock prices' (1971b: 87).

Although the full scope of Black's vision would long remain unrealised, computers were nonetheless soon making considerable inroads into financial markets. In 1973, the NYSE introduced their Designated Order Turnaround system, which allowed smaller orders to be routed electronically from member firms to the floor (Buck, 1992: 205). In 1976, the Cincinnati Exchange spearheaded a transition that would later become the norm: it shut down its trading floor and went completely electronic. A few years later, in 1978, the Intermarket Trading System was introduced in the United States as an early implementation of a national market system, which established a computer network that linked nine markets together (Buck, 1992: 210; MacKenzie, 2018: 1664). In 1981, Reuters introduced its Reuter Money Dealing services, which enabled direct electronic trading between banks (MacKenzie, 2015: 656; Wansleben, 2015: 30). Throughout the 1980s, computers were increasingly

Figure 5.6 Towards market computerisation.
Note: Henrik Plenge Jakobsen (b. 1967), *Nasdaq forever*, 2000. Inkjet on canvas 130 x 220 cm.
Source: Photo: Planet foto

introduced to the trading floors of exchanges, giving traders a faster and more accurate display of market movements. A further push towards the computerisation of financial markets took place in the 1990s, when several exchanges implemented electronic trading. For example, the French futures exchange Marché à Terme International de France (MATIF) moved from floor trading to electronic trading in 1998; the London International Financial Futures and Options Exchange (LIFFE) did the same in 1999–2000; and in 1999, the Chicago Mercantile Exchange (CME) decided that its 'futures [contracts] could be traded electronically, whether or not the pits were open' (MacKenzie, 2015: 664; see also Pardo-Guerra, 2010). As a result of this market reconfiguration, trading could now be conducted in front of computer screens in banks, proprietary trading firms, and the like. The shift from trading *floors* of human traders to electronic trading *rooms*, in which traders would engage markets via their screens, entailed a number of important transformations, some latent and others actual.

For example, the types of intimate connection between cities and markets discussed in Chapter 4 seemed increasingly fragile. With trading loosening its ties to the physical trading floors of the exchanges, the status of cities as hubs for financial transactions threatened to crumble. After all, computers can be linked to electronic markets from virtually anywhere. Nonetheless, while the 'formal' connection between markets and cities as mediated via exchanges has therefore been under pressure (further changes in that direction will be discussed below), the major financial players that pursue electronic trading, whether banks or proprietary trading firms, nonetheless tend to congregate in particular cities such as London, Chicago, New York, Frankfurt, Tokyo and Hong Kong (Cassis, 2012; Cassis and Wójcik, 2018; Sassen, 2005). This has secured cities a continued, prominent role even after the advent of electronic markets.

Another consequence of the move towards electronic trading concerns the skills required to be a good trader. In my fieldwork, I have come across a number of former pit/floor traders, all of whom relay that for a trader to be successful in open-outcry settings, the level of required math skills was not immense (it simply required performing basic calculations in the head). Due to the bodily nature of open-outcry trading, it was more important to have a solid physical stature in order to be seen and heard. With the rise of electronic trading, particular physical traits ceased to be of any importance. Instead, the need for an entirely different approach to markets came to the fore, an approach well captured by Caitlin Zaloom (2006) in her fascinating ethnographic study of the shift from pit to electronic trading. According to Zaloom, the people who do electronic screen trading often have academic backgrounds and possess more sophisticated math skills. The underlying hope driving this reorientation of trader competence is that 'the academic approach of the new traders would help them to see new ways to interpret market activity' (2006: 74). This emphasis on visuality is not coincidental. 'In the pits, the traders lived the markets in their bodies and voices. On the screen, traders *observe* the market and work *on* it' (2006: 141, original emphasis).[6]

While this suggests that electronic trading inaugurates a less embodied approach to markets, Zaloom's work makes plain that electronic traders seem to struggle with market dynamics strikingly similar to those which floor and pit traders had faced for generations. Thus, even when the balance tilted in favour of electronic trading, these markets, too, are often described in tropes reminiscent of discussions of de-individualising avalanching. In Zaloom's analysis, this materialises in statements about electronic markets being 'mesmerizing' (2006: 4) as well as in the ambition she unearths on the part of electronic traders to discipline themselves so that they do not become overly emotionally attached to markets.

---

[6] To help ease the transition from open-outcry to screen-based trading, software was invented in the 1990s which would create a synthetic representation of the information contained in the pits' noise and rumble. By activating such software and its simulation of 'sounds of a virtual open outcry floor based on the information from the electronic system', screen traders regained a semi-bodily feel for the market (Arnoldi, 2006: 389). According to Zaloom, however, such software was little used in practice (2003: 266).

The underlying lure of markets, the risk of being swept away in an avalanching market maelstrom in which autonomous decision making is suspended, seems, in fact, to have guided much of the training that both pit/floor and screen traders underwent (2006: ch. 6).

The rise of electronic trading therefore did not make emotions disappear from markets. It is more correct to say that the kinds of energy and excitement that generations of traders had experienced in the pits and on the floors assumed new shapes and expressions under the regime of electronic trading. This is a point forcefully corroborated by Karin Knorr Cetina in her study of electronic traders (Knorr Cetina and Bruegger, 2000; 2002). Knorr Cetina followed the electronic trading room of a global investment bank, specifically a group of traders specialising in foreign exchange. Not only were these traders 'strongly, even obsessively, engaged' with the market, their 'emotional engagement with the market' was profoundly mediated via their computer screens, so much so that one could justifiably speak about traders engaging in a 'postsocial relationship' with their screens (Knorr Cetina and Bruegger, 2002: 162, 176). In other words, while pit/floor traders developed an inter-human form of sociality with one another, electronic traders became socially attached to the market via their screens. To the extent that such attachment developed into highly intense forms, electronic trading reintroduced the *problematique* of 'ticker trance' and 'tickeritis' I described above (see also Preda, 2009b: 135). This is precisely the reason why the electronic traders Zaloom followed were carefully instructed to discipline themselves vis-à-vis the lures of the market.

Curiously, electronic-trading practitioners' recognition of market attachment, the binding of self to some non-human phenomenon (the market) or object (the screen) and the loss of autonomy this entails, largely coincided with the revival of a late-nineteenth-century mimetic conception of markets within financial economics. Thus, parallel to the rise of electronic screen trading, a group of financial economists argued with increasing vigour that markets cannot be fully comprehended if their (mass) psychological dimensions are not accounted for. Essentially (but seemingly unwittingly) readapting in a contemporary context the analytical horizon championed by the likes of Tarde, Sidis, Selden and Harper – but bestowing its basic ideas with greater, or at least freshly minted, academic prestige – these economists launched the new research programme of behavioural economics or behavioural finance, which gained momentum in the 1980s and 1990s.[7]

---

[7] I will only provide a rough sketch of behavioural finance and its links to mimetic thought here. For fuller discussions, see Borch and Lange (2017b) and Hansen and Borch (2019).

A principal proponent of behavioural finance is the American economist Robert J. Shiller, who in 2013 received the Sveriges Riksbank Prize in Economic Sciences in Memory of Alfred Nobel for his contributions. Some of Shiller's central ideas were articulated in his 1984 paper 'Stock Prices and Social Dynamics', in which he famously argued that 'mass psychology may well be the dominant cause of movements in the price of the aggregate stock market' (1984: 459).[8] Interestingly, this argument was embedded in reflections on suggestibility and associated with the broader claim that while investors are often seen as atomistic, independent decision-makers (in other words, as essentially anti-mimetic individuals), they are in fact subjected to all sorts of mimetic fads and fashions which render their investment decisions anything but independent. Other economists, drawing from the same well of late-nineteenth-century social theory, place greater emphasis on notions such as 'contagion' (Orléan, 1989) or 'herding' (Scharfstein and Stein, 1990). Common to them – and herein lies my central observation – is that they all breathe new life into the idea that there is a strong mimetic component to financial markets and that the practical challenge of trying to avoid being swept away by market avalanches or being captured by market pulls (as per Zaloom's and Knorr Cetina's analyses) is therefore not only very real but perhaps even insurmountable.

I do not want to exaggerate the connections between electronic screen trading and behavioural finance literature. They are in many ways disconnected, running as they do on parallel tracks. Nonetheless, in light of the overall argument of this chapter, the similarity between the practical concerns of electronic screen traders and the key message of behavioural finance theory is striking: both lend support to the notion that late-nineteenth and early-twentieth-century concerns about investors or traders caught in a tension between submitting to market pulls and resisting such attachments remain salient to late-twentieth-century financial markets.

Algorithmic Finance

The rise of electronic trading did not immediately replace open-outcry trading. For a long while the two forms of trading co-existed, albeit in a somewhat antagonistic relationship. Conducting her fieldwork in the late 1990s, when the balance was tipping in favour of electronic trading, Zaloom was exposed to arguments for and against each form of trading

---

[8] This notion has been a key lead for Shiller ever since and underpins most of his later work, including the bestseller *Irrational Exuberance* (2015).

configuration. Not surprisingly, traders working in the pits saw this type of trading as superior (see also MacKenzie, 2015). They insisted that open-outcry trading curbed market disorder and potential eruptions of irrational herding, 'since people working face-to-face could maintain stability in turbulent times' (Zaloom, 2006: 53). They further asserted that a transition to electronic trading would dry up market liquidity and decried that a well-known feature of financial markets, 'the energy and excitement that could only come from face-to-face competition', would vanish with electronic trading (2006: 53). Advocates of electronic trading pointed to similar facets but inverted these implications. The immense energy and excitement of open-outcry trading was, in their view, one of its major drawbacks and precisely the kind of feature that could unleash market instability. Electronic trading, they argued, would introduce a much cooler approach that would dampen market irrationality substantially and, by downplaying the face-to-face networks of traders, ensure a 'purer' and fairer market environment (2006: ix).

As the transition from pit/floor trading to electronic trading gradually consolidated in the late 1990s, a further escalation of the computerisation of trading was already under way. In contrast to electronic trading, in which humans place orders on their computers, the new type of computerised trading gaining traction in the new millennium delegates the actual trading, the actual placing of orders, to fully automated computer algorithms. The predominance of this type of *algorithmic finance*, or algorithmic trading, varies between markets. Donald MacKenzie reports that high-frequency trading, a particular form of algorithmic trading, makes up around half of the traded volume in shares, futures and benchmark US Treasurys, whereas the presence of high-frequency trading algorithms in spot foreign exchange markets is merely around 10 per cent (2018: 1639). Given that high-frequency trading is only a subset of the field of algorithmic finance, the algorithmic portion of any of these markets is likely to be significantly larger than these numbers suggest.

The field of algorithmic finance covers a lot of internal complexity. Most notably, it includes high-frequency trading, which utilises exceptionally fast technological infrastructure to exploit price differences in and across trading venues lasting less than a second. Further, as is obviously the case for many other domains as well, machine learning has made considerable inroads into financial markets and is now often combined with high-frequency trading. While the latter used to be strictly rule-based and deterministic ('if X happens in markets, do Y'), machine learning has introduced more adaptive approaches to automated trading, just as it seeks to create a machine-based rather than human-based detection of tradable patterns. Testifying to the ways in which the use of fully automated algorithms is proliferating, high-frequency trading algorithms, formerly associated with proprietary trading – firms trading on their own account rather than on behalf of clients – are now being used increasingly by brokers who execute orders on behalf of their clients. When an institutional client such as a pension fund sends an order to its broker today, the latter would either fill the order internally by pairing it with its other order flow (a process known as 'internalisation': the internal matching of orders *before* they ever reach a trading venue) or, if the order is sent to an exchange, execute the order algorithmically. This would often be done by slicing the 'parent' order into a number of smaller 'child' orders and submitting them to the market in ways that leave as little a market footprint as possible (if a big order is sent to the market, prices are likely to move against it). Efficient execution may entail randomisation of both the size and the interval of the orders. Consequently, institutional order flow, too, dons algorithmic attire today due to the ways in which brokers work.

Algorithmic finance was brought into being by a multifarious set of conditions (for a fuller discussion of these, see Castelle et al., 2016; Lange, 2020; MacKenzie, 2015; 2018). For example, the 1990s saw an increase in the number of Electronic Communication Networks (ECNs), of which Instinet was one (for a historical sociology of another ECN, Island, see MacKenzie and Pardo-Guerra, 2014). ECNs were invented as computerised broker-dealer systems that facilitated an electronic matching of buyers and sellers – much like an electronic exchange but, at least initially, placed under a different regulatory regime. With ECNs becoming popular, the space in which automated trading could evolve was considerably expanded. Furthermore, registered exchanges increasingly began catering to algorithmic trading, although this was sometimes met with fierce resistance. Echoing Zaloom, MacKenzie has demonstrated that the decision by the CME to move towards auto-mation was ridden with internal debates and contestation for decades (MacKenzie, 2015).

The overall automation of markets was also boosted by various pieces of market regulation. In the United States, this includes, especially, the Regulation National Market System (Reg NMS) from 2005, which stipulates among other things that a trade cannot be filled at a price worse that the so-called National Best Bid and Offer (NBBO), regardless of the trading venue to which it is sent. If one firm sends an order to, say, the NYSE, that order can only be filled at the NYSE if no other exchange offers a better price; otherwise, the order needs to be routed to the venue offering the best price. Reg NMS was invented in part to protect customers from sub-optimal prices. In effect, this regulatory framework helped consolidate automated trading, since firms specialising in this type of trading can exploit price differences that may exist across trading venues. That such price differences exist is a corollary of US markets being highly fragmented, with thirteen registered exchanges for shares trading and a host of alternative trading venues, including so-called dark pools, living and competing with one another (MacKenzie, 2018: 1651).

With algorithmic finance gaining traction, the skills traders need have once again been redefined. Algorithmic traders need to be both math and computer savvy, and people occupying such positions often have PhD degrees in physics, math, engineering, computer science, etc. (Borch and Lange, 2017a). The difference to pit traders is stark, but algorithmic traders are also an altogether different breed than screen traders. While the latter were assisted by computerised tools, their approach neither coalesced with computers nor pursued the science-like approach of algorithmic traders. This transition indicates a broader shift that has taken place within trading firms. Throughout the 1990s and early 2000s, it became increasingly popular to hire 'quants', people who bring a quantitative approach to finance. Such quants could have backgrounds in physics and math, but in contrast to present-day algorithmic finance, they often served a more back-office function in firms then. This means that rather than being in charge of the development of trading strategies, they functioned as research support for screen traders (for a lively first-hand account of this early phase of quants, see Derman, 2004). Contrary to the first-generation, the present generation of quants has moved centre stage in trading operations; today's quants do not merely assist traders but rather have become traders themselves.

The rise of algorithmic finance exacerbated the emptying of the trading pits/floors that electronic trading inaugurated, and even the iconic futures pits in Chicago have now been ousted, while a few options pits remain operational for complex contracts (Borch and Lange, 2017a: 283–4). In fact, it seems as if the deployment of fully automated algorithms for trading purposes would finally make all the hopes previously invested in electronic trading come true. Specifically, algorithmic trading promises to eliminate the human element of markets, as it were. Part of the reason why this has been seen as desirable has to do with collusion charges levelled against human intermediaries (e.g. MacKenzie, 2015: 654). Algorithms are believed to alleviate these concerns. Moreover, human traders working in open-outcry settings were notoriously susceptible to market panics (for discussions of market panic, see also Preda, 2009b: ch. 8; Zimmerman, 2006). But as the studies by Zaloom and Knorr Cetina have demonstrated, electronic traders too develop emotional attachments that prohibit the emergence of an allegedly pure, non-affected and unbiased approach to markets. By contrast, according to some of its proponents, algorithmic trading at long last secures a space for market efficiency, in which trading can take place unaffected by human fads and fashions. In what reads like an echo of Hoffmann in *The Fear Index*, one book on high-frequency trading articulates this argument:

An important part of algorithmic trading is that it takes out the human emotional aspect of trading. Trading decisions made by algorithms are based solely on the data analysed and not the whims, fear and greed of an individual trader. (Vaananen, 2015: 210)

So, although algorithms are obviously developed by humans, their 'virtue' is that once they operate in markets, they do so without human intervention. A hoped-for upshot of this is that avalanching dynamics and de-individualising tendencies would be finally relegated from markets and that an orderly terrain of actors and market behaviours would evolve as a result. Perhaps not surprisingly, reality does not look quite as neat as this slightly ideal image suggests. For starters, emotional attachments do creep into the ways in which trading algorithms are designed and deployed – despite the fact that with the rise of algorithmic trading, the emphasis is much less on market intuition than on bringing complex math and coding skills to productive use. The role of emotions shows, for example, in the ways in which people who develop trading algorithms sometimes struggle with retaining the delegation of decision-making power to their algorithms. When facing losses, one might be inclined to tweak the parameters of the algorithm instead of letting it pursue its pre-set strategy. A strong dash of discipline is therefore required to avoid interfering with the algorithms, and for that reason algorithmic traders relay that they need to develop techniques which deter them from overreacting to particular market swings, even if this may be 'emotionally complex' (Borch and Lange, 2017a: 296). So, while algorithmic trading is often described as a strict 'hands off' or 'no touch' approach to markets – in which algorithms should be left to do their work – it appears that the desire to interfere in them can be exceedingly strong. However, emotions can also have the opposite effect of making traders put too much faith in their algorithms. A person specialising in high-frequency trading describes this:

You get attached to the algorithms that you have developed. Like, if you see that it's not working as you expected it to, you want to make it work. You know, rationally, it won't. All the science tells you it won't. But still you think, 'If I can tweak it a little bit it might work'. (Quoted in Borch and Lange, 2017a: 298)

These are all indications that emotional attachments have not completely vanished, even though trading is increasingly conducted by fully automated algorithms. Rather, the issues traders have always faced – regardless of the overall market configuration – when it comes to emotions and the need for discipline are also identifiable in the algorithmic space (for a systematic discussion of this, see Borch and Lange, 2017a). While the risk of emotional overattachment and the quest for discipline may assume new accents in algorithmic trading, their presence suggests that for the human beings developing and monitoring these fully automated algorithms, the challenge of retaining decision-making autonomy vis-à-vis the lure of the markets continues to exist. That otherwise fully automated trading contains a human component is of course important to stress. After all, to repeat, these trading algorithms are developed by humans. At the same time, this human facet should not overshadow the fact that algorithmic finance profoundly reconfigures financial markets since the actual order flow – the orders being entered (or modified or cancelled) in markets as well as the various types of response they trigger – are increasingly being algorithmically generated. In that sense, humans have clearly been left behind. Indeed, the technological infrastructure of present-day financial markets is now so complex, and permits for such high-speed trading, that it has been effectively decoupled from human perception.

Sub-Perceptual Finance

Niklas Luhmann distinguishes between operations and observations (2013: 101–4), describing the former as the building blocks of a system – elements through which the system reproduces itself. He argues that the basic and distinctive type of operation of social systems is communication (not action), and these communicative operations are the elements that make up social systems (1995). Luhmann defines observations as particular operations, which draw a distinction and indicate one side and not the other (1993: 485). Observations are a subset of operations (namely, as operations within an observing system) and are not reducble to operations – though they may certainly observe the latter. The technical and analytical subtleties that ensue from the difference between the two need not concern us here – I am interested in the distinction simply because it helps elucidate some core features of present-day algorithmic finance. Thus, algorithmic trading increasingly separates the operational domain of finance from its observational layer. Specifically, when viewed at an operational level, much of what goes on in contemporary algorithmic finance takes place in ways that defy ordinary observation and human sensory perception, in particular. The operations of algorithms simply take place at such speeds that they cannot be observed directly; only their traces are observable.

This sub-sensory or 'sub-perceptual' (Coombs, 2016: 282) dimension is particularly apparent in the field of high-frequency trading, which exploits timescales that cannot be sensed by humans. The connection between the Chicago futures market and the stock markets in New York illustrates this point. While these specific markets have been tightly linked since the mid-nineteenth century (through the telegraph lines discussed earlier, for one) they are today more intimately coupled than ever, to the extent that related products are traded *almost* simultaneously. For instance, futures are traded at the CME in Chicago, with the E-mini (ES) futures contract being a particularly popular financial product 'with something like $150 billion worth of contracts' being traded every day, amounting to 'roughly twice as much as the entire stock market' (Durbin, 2010: 86). The ES tracks the Standard & Poor's 500 index (S&P 500), which is made up of stocks of the five hundred largest companies traded at the NYSE and Nasdaq. Since the ES tracks the S&P 500, the two are expected to move in tandem. Yet since the futures contract is traded in Chicago and its underlying shares in New York, prices can be slightly out of sync. Discrepancies of this kind are the stuff that arbitrage opportunities are made of. In order to take advantage of such opportunities, it is critical to have fast connections between the markets in Chicago and New York. In practice, however, and as an upshot of the shift to automation, the CME no longer matches orders in downtown Chicago (as it did during pit trading) but rather does so in a data centre in Aurora, Illinois. Similarly, the Nasdaq and the NYSE match orders at data centres located in New Jersey – their main centres are in Carteret and Mahwah, respectively – at considerable distance from where the two exchanges are headquartered in Lower Manhattan.[9]

That the 'engine room' of financial markets, the place where orders are placed and matched, has moved from the city centre to suburban areas (Aurora has a population of around 200,000; Mahwah's is less than 30,000) is yet another indicator of the loosening, or at least recalibration, of the traditional ties between cities, crowds and markets. More important for the present discussion, however, high-frequency trading firms invest heavily in getting appropriately wired up to the exchange data centres. First, in order not to lose important time when it comes to entering orders and receiving feedback and data feeds from the

---

[9] Other cities in New Jersey host financial data centres as well. This includes places such as Weehawken and Secaucus (MacKenzie, 2018: 1636).

individual exchanges, high-frequency trading firms co-locate their own servers in close physical proximity to the servers of the exchanges. Such co-location is often tied to hefty fees, and, not coincidentally, offering co-location has turned into a profitable side business for exchanges – as has selling market data, for that matter.[10]

More directly related to ES–S&P 500 arbitrage opportunities, high-frequency trading firms put a lot of effort and money into securing the fastest data transmission lines between the data centres in Aurora and New Jersey. The American journalist Michael Lewis's book *Flash Boys* (2014) captivatingly relates how in 2008–9, a firm, Spread Networks, invested some $300 million in laying a straighter line of fibre-optic cables along the roughly 1,100 km beeline between Aurora and New Jersey, an endeavour that included 'drilling through the Allegheny Mountains' (MacKenzie et al., 2012). Prior to the Spread Networks line, fibre-optic data transmission between Aurora and New Jersey followed a zigzag pattern, which made a roundtrip of data transmission as slow (!) as 17 milliseconds.[11] The Spread Networks line reduced this latency to 13 milliseconds (Lewis, 2014: ch. 1). By leasing access to the line for a monthly fee around $300,000, trading firms prevented themselves from being slower than their most ambitious competitors, who easily saw the benefit of gaining a 4 millisecond advantage. However, just as interesting as Lewis's account of Spread Networks's efforts is his conclusion, in which he observes that it took only a few years before fibre optics were superseded by microwave transmission (Lewis, 2014: 267–70). Indeed, as MacKenzie (2017: 66) has detailed, with current microwave infra-structures the time it takes to send information back and forth from the Aurora and New Jersey data centres is down to 8.02 milliseconds, only slightly longer than the 7.86 milliseconds it would take for light to travel the distance in a vacuum.

With long-distance data transmission approximating the speed of light and with trading algorithms being able to respond to market develop-ments at the level of nanoseconds (billionths of a second), finance has clearly entered a sub-perceptual era. The basic operational layer of algorithmic finance simply evades human perception, however uncanny that may sound. The difference to former market configurations is stark. Human pit/floor traders enacted an embodied market setting in which

---

[10] Illustratively, the NYSE's 2019 price list for its various services has more than ten out of thirty-five pages devoted to co-location services, with fees reflecting various types of connection, bandwidth, and so on. See www.nyse.com/publicdocs/nyse/markets/nyse/NYSE_Price_List.pdf (accessed 29 March 2019).

[11] A millisecond is a thousandth of a second. For comparison, it takes the human eye somewhere between 100 and 400 milliseconds to blink.

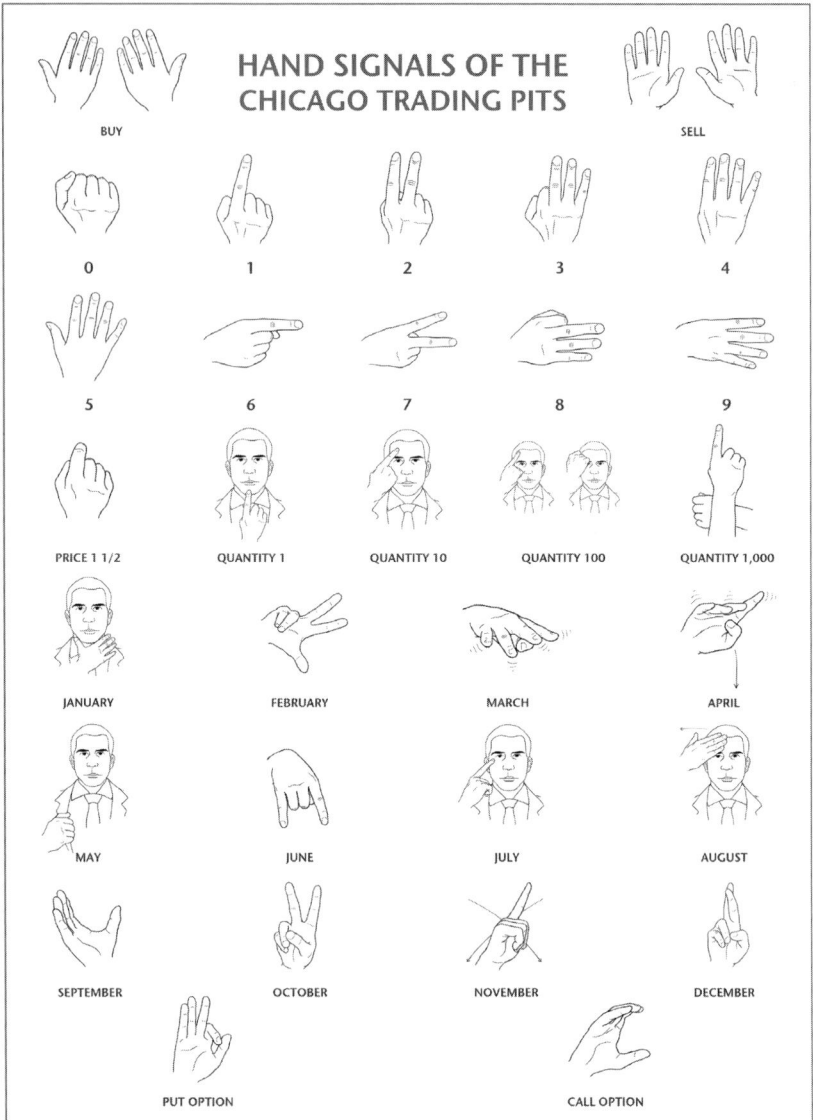

Figure 5.7 Hand signals.
Source: Courtesy: Mike Nudelman tradingpithistory.com

observing one another was crucial. Indeed, the hand signals invented for efficient open-outcry trading obviously relied on visibility.

Similarly, electronic screen trading was, as Zaloom and Knorr Cetina have pointed out, about traders observing the market on their screens, the underlying notion being that markets could indeed be visually monitored in real time. This ability of humans to be simultaneous with markets and follow market movements synchronically is precisely what has disappeared with algorithmic finance. Human observation and the algorithmic operations of markets have gone out of sync, and their discordance is only growing. What Simmel declared a tragedy of modern culture therefore penetrates the core of the diagnosis of financial markets today: 'The formlessness of the objectified spirit [present-day algorithms] as a totality grants it a developmental tempo which must leave that of the subjective spirit behind by a rapidly growing margin' (1997b: 75).

To give a further sense of this, in 2000 the US securities markets witnessed 'on average about 5 million trades and quotes per *day*; in the fall of 2012, at peak times there were up to 5 million trades and quotes per *second*', a dramatic increase due to the intensification of algorithmic trading (Malinova, Park and Riordan, 2013: 1, original emphasis). This increase in market activity is evidence of the impossibility of humans observing markets in anything resembling real time. One immediate implication of this is that human oversight of markets becomes ever thornier. Although the algorithmically entered orders are all registered electronically by the exchanges, the cumulative amount of data this generates is so vast that it takes massive effort to peel them apart and fully understand them.

While the human observation of markets is thus increasingly left behind by the mounting operating speed of trading algorithms, the connection between operations and observations has not been entirely cut. With humans excised from the operational domain, algorithms have taken over the core observational function that humans previously occupied. Thus, algorithms are to a large degree being developed to observe and respond to the behaviours of other algorithms. Speaking directly to this issue, traders relay that their algorithms are often designed to lower the likelihood that they will be recognised *as* algorithms *by other* algorithms.

Evoking Goffman's work, MacKenzie (2019) fittingly analyses such inter-algorithmic relationships under the term 'dissimulation', suggesting that the types of dissimulation that can be identified in the human interaction order, as per Goffman, find striking parallels in the emphatically non-human domain of interacting algorithms. Indeed, MacKenzie notes, 'we see in that interaction echoes of how we humans interact' (2019: 54). Whereas pit traders register each other's shouting, hand signals and facial expressions, the attention of algorithms is specifically focused on the *electronic order book*, which offers a visual listing of any pending, non-matched orders in the market at any given time. With a separate order book at every exchange and with the capacity of algorithms to place and cancel large numbers of orders at lightning speed, keeping track of order-book changes – for singular instruments but also, in case of arbitrage strategies, for related ones – is a non-trivial task for which the slow and limited perception spans of humans are ill suited, but one at which algorithms excel.[12] This orchestration of present-day markets also means that algorithms are not observing one another *directly*, as was the case for human traders in the pits or on the floors, but rather *indirectly* from market data as they enter or exit markets by placing, modifying or cancelling orders in the order book.[13] This is precisely what occurred during the Flash Crash of 6 May 2010.

---

[12] Trading algorithms may also attend to data that are neither visible in nor derived from the order book, such as news or Twitter feeds. There are indeed examples of algorithms whose market behaviours have been triggered by particular tweets (Karppi and Crawford, 2016). However, my interviews with algorithmic traders suggest that data from, say, social media constitute an insignificant fraction of the information that the algorithms mull over.

[13] The organisation of the electronic order book has features that bring to mind the aforementioned discussion about connections between cities, markets and crowds. In most cases, the order book's basic organising principle is that of a queue, which is also the emic term used. The queue of an order book means that orders that arrive first will also typically be matched first, provided that counterparties exist. Consequently, it is often considered of utmost importance to be 'on top of the book' – in other words, to be first in line – and this is one reason why investing in fast technological infrastructures can be rewarding. MacKenzie has analysed the role of order-book queuing with reference to Goffman's reflections on the queues of ordinary, non-financial situations (Goffman, 1983: 16; MacKenzie, 2019: 47–8). What MacKenzie does not notice is that queuing has a clear metropolitan backdrop that probably also informs Goffman's interest in the phenomenon. This urban resonance is better recognised by Barry Schwartz, who, in *Queuing and Waiting*, goes back to Simmel, the scholar credited with appreciating the ways in which 'punctuality' and calculable orderliness became central to modern metropolitan life as ways to counter the otherwise chaotic buzz of the city (Schwartz, 1975: 161, 187–8; Simmel, 1997c: 177). The point I wish to make here is that the electronic order book serves as a functional equivalent to the design of the trading pits, which, too, sought to address the kind of chaotic crowding attributed to cities. Where these pits have almost disappeared, the electronic order book seeks to ensure orderliness by making algorithms wait in line. Note that not all order books are organised around a queue principle of the sort described here. For example, instead of matching orders on the basis of time priority, some exchanges use so-called 'pro-rata matching, in which new executable orders are matched against existing orders in proportion to the size of the latter' (MacKenzie, 2019: 58). After I completed the manuscript for the present book, Juan Pablo Pardo-Guerra's *Automating Finance* came out (2019), i.e. at a stage that prevents me from discussing it at any length here. Let me just note that Pardo-Guerra's book carefully details the history behind the automation of financial markets. Further, at the end of the book, he analyses order-book queuing, drawing on Goffman and Schwartz, among others.

Figure 5.8 Urban queueing.
Note: The Metropolitan Museum of Art, exterior, during the exhibition
'The Mona Lisa by Leonardo da Vinci', 7 February–4 March, 1963; view
facing south showing crowds lined up on Fifth Avenue and on the front steps
of the Museum; photography date: 1963. New York: The Metropolitan
Museum of Art.
Source: © 2019. Photo the Metropolitan Museum of Art/Art Resource/Scala,
Florence

The Flash Crash: A Window into High-Frequency Trading

Beyond its inescapably spectacular nature, the Flash Crash is interesting
because it seems to offer an immediate invalidation of Fischer Black's
insistence in 1971 that trading could be fully automated without this
'introducing any additional instability in stock prices' (1971b: 87). In
fact, many refer to the Flash Crash as support for the assertion that
algorithmic finance opens a can of worms that can adversely affect the
stability of markets. Some observers connect the event to other famous
catastrophes from the domain of algorithmic finance, such as the case of
Knight Capital, a major player in the US financial markets, which lost
around $460 million in just 45 minutes in August 2012 due to an error in
its trading algorithm (Kenett et al., 2013; Kirilenko and Lo, 2013). With
such rehearsals, the Flash Crash continues to attract attention even
though it occurred back in 2010 (examples of a sociological interest in

the event include Lange, Lenglet and Seyfert, 2016; Thompson, 2017). In addition to academic interest in the event, the Flash Crash garnered renewed media attention in 2015 due to the arrest that year of Sarao, the British trader working out of Hounslow.[14]

The Flash Crash is often invoked by commentators as a window into the workings and potential effects of present-day algorithmic finance in general and high-frequency trading in particular. Interestingly, observers tend to see rather different things through that window. One reason for this is that there is considerable confusion as to what exactly constitutes the Flash Crash. There are, in other words, conflicting accounts about its 'eventness', a phenomenon not specific to the Flash Crash. As Robin Wagner-Pacifici argues, events are often 'intrinsically restless' (2010: 1356): there are different ways of delineating events (including their beginnings and endings, the main actors and processes involved, etc.), and event contestation is likely to revolve around such delineation and framing.

I shall be brief here on the ways in which the media have contributed to framing the Flash Crash event (I discuss this at more length in Borch, 2016). What is noteworthy is that the media coinage of the event as a 'flash crash' was almost instantaneous. The most dramatic market drop took place between 2:41 pm and 2:45:27 pm, at which point trading was suspended for five seconds. When trading resumed, 'broad market indices recovered', but individual securities still saw considerable price fluctuations. At approximately 3:00 pm, 'prices of most individual securities significantly recovered and trading resumed in a more orderly fashion' (CFTC–SEC, 2010: 9). At 2:58 pm, CNBC published an online article describing how the 'selloff is feeding on itself, bringing down almost all stocks' (Melloy, 2010). And at 4:15 pm, Michael Corkery, writing for the *Wall Street Journal*, published a post entitled 'The Stock Market's Flash Crash: How to Destroy $1 Billion in 60 Minutes' (2010). The term 'Flash Crash' gained traction within an hour, meaning that it only took a couple of hours for it to crystallise as the phenomenon's central point of reference.

The term's catchiness might be part of the reason why the event has attracted so much attention. But beyond that, its narrative quality consists equally in describing the swiftness of the market drop and recovery,

---

[14] Sarao eventually pleaded guilty to charges of market manipulation. Regardless of whether Sarao did in fact generate the full-scale of the algorithmic flash-crash herding he was accused of setting in motion, the case is noteworthy for how it testifies to the reconfiguration of cities and markets I mentioned earlier: it suggests that markets might no longer be embedded in essentially metropolitan dynamics (the crowding of urban life); rather, herding at central financial markets might now be triggered from places such as Hounslow.

as well as the immediate suspicion that high-frequency traders, who can send orders to the market in a flash, were profoundly implicated in the event. Reflecting this, the Flash Crash plays a critical role in what is arguably the most famous journalistic account of high-frequency trading: Lewis's *Flash Boys*, the title of which obviously alludes to the Flash Crash and flash – or high-speed – trading. Lewis describes this event as follows (though he mistakes the timing):

At 2:45 on May 6, 2010, for no obvious reason, the market fell six hundred points in a few minutes. A few minutes later, like a drunk trying to pretend he hadn't just knocked over the fishbowl and killed the pet goldfish, it bounced right back up to where it was before. (2014: 80)

The notion that the Flash Crash was an exceptional event runs through his account. It happened 'for no obvious reason' and appeared to be triggered by a minor event that eventually, but with extreme speed, spiralled both downwards and upwards. Indeed, in order to stress the exceptional, arguably even traumatic nature, of the event, Lewis draws a parallel between the Flash Crash and the crash of October 1929, in effect suggesting, therefore, that later generations might look back upon the Flash Crash as one of our era's defining moments (2014: 81).

Lewis's rendering of the event's exceptionality and singularity finds support in the academic literature to which I now turn. One illustration of this is an article by MacKenzie entitled 'Mechanizing the Merc: The Chicago Mercantile Exchange and the Rise of High-Frequency Trading' (2015). This article offers a fascinating and thorough analysis of the historical backdrop to high-frequency trading, but it also proposes an interesting discussion of the Flash Crash. The first sentence of Mac-Kenzie's article reads, 'At 2:40 p.m. on 6 May 2010, the US financial markets went into spasm' (2015: 646). The subsequent pages narrate the events of the day and how the Flash Crash, which began in Chicago, eventually spilled over, such that 'the sell pressure began to swamp the stock markets' in New York (2015: 648). For MacKenzie, then, the Flash Crash cannot be reduced or limited to what happened in Chicago; the ramifications on the New York markets equally form part of the event. This spill-over logic makes MacKenzie characterise the Flash Crash as the 'first generalized crisis' of the 'new world of automated high-frequency trading' (2015: 648); it was the first illustration of how vulnerable tightly interconnected markets are to this type of trading. Since the Flash Crash is seen in MacKenzie's text to embody a particular type of crisis intimately tied to high-frequency trading, the event plays an important role as a window into the new world of automated trading and its consequences.

While MacKenzie's analysis presents the Flash Crash as a window into present-day financial markets, he also treats it as an exceptional event, a rare occurrence. Other scholarly accounts question the exceptional status accorded to the Flash Crash, instead conceiving the event as a window into the now-normal workings of algorithmic finance, exemplified by high-frequency trading (thereby unwittingly rehearsing Park's early-twentieth-century observation about the normality with which markets, and crowds, enter into avalanching crises). One example of this is a paper jointly written by Susanne von der Becke and the physicist and co-director of the Financial Crisis Observatory, Didier Sornette, entitled 'Crashes and High Frequency Trading: An Evaluation of Risks Posed by High-Speed Algorithmic Trading' (a shorter version of the paper appeared in the UK Foresight report 'The Future of Computer Trading in Financial Markets'). In the paper, Sornette and von der Becke set out to find answers to the following question: 'Can high frequency trading lead to crashes?' (2011: 3). The article answers in the affirmative, with the Flash Crash serving as a key example throughout the analysis; it is immediately mentioned in the paper's opening paragraph:

The May 6 flash crash in 2010, which saw the Dow Jones lose about 1 trillion USD of market value and individual stocks trading at fractions or multiples within minutes, put increased focus on HFT. Even though high frequency traders were subsequently mostly cleared from having caused the crash, doubts remain as to whether this new form of trading bears potentially destabilizing risks for the market. (2011: 4)

Two things are interesting about this quote. One is that while MacKenzie presents an expansive account of the Flash Crash, linking the initial price movements in Chicago to subsequent developments in New York, Sornette and von der Becke offer a narrow demarcation. In their analysis, the Flash Crash event is reduced to the price drop, with no mention of the fact that prices quickly recovered, and therefore that the overall $1 trillion losses were rapidly regained. This narrow delineation of the Flash Crash adds weight to another interesting feature of the quote: that the event is linked directly to the 'potentially destabilizing risks' that high-frequency trading is said to introduce to financial markets (for similar accounts, see Lange, Lenglet and Seyfert, 2016; Snider, 2014: 754). This is indeed how Sornette and von der Becke invoke the Flash Crash throughout their paper: it serves the strategic function of exemplifying what might go wrong with algorithmic financial markets and how these are allegedly prone to crashes. So, while the Flash Crash may appear to be a singular and exceptional event, it should in fact rather be seen as illustrative of a destabilising, crash-prone dynamic inherent to present-day high-frequency-trading-dominated financial markets (see also Leal et al., 2014). In other words, its exceptionality is only apparent.

A similar conclusion is reached by other commentators who argue that the Flash Crash constitutes an important event because it captures something that is increasingly typical and representative of current financial markets. One example of such a reconfiguration of the Flash Crash – from an exceptional to an increasingly typical or representative event – is apparent in the research conducted by Nanex, a financial data provider. Nanex has not only been an outspoken critic of the 2010 CFTC–SEC report on the Flash Crash but also devoted a substantial part of its research to demonstrating the repeated recurrence of flash crashes in algorithmically dominated markets. Nanex has identified more than 100 flash crashes in 2013, and more than 40 between January and June 2014. According to the Nanex definition, a (down) flash crash occurs when the following applies to a stock price (the definition implies that flash events can also refer to rapid *positive* price changes):

(i) it has to tick *down* at least 10 times before ticking *up*,
(ii) price changes have to occur within 1.5 seconds,
(iii) price change has to exceed −0.8%. (Quoted from Golub, Keane and Poon, 2012: 5, original emphasis)

Several academic papers have adopted this definition in their analysis of algorithmic markets' allegedly flash crash–prone nature. One example is the article 'Financial black swans driven by ultrafast machine ecology', by the physicist Neil Johnson et al. (Eric Hunsader, a co-author of the article, is also the founder of Nanex). In it, the authors examine what they refer to as 'ultrafast black swan events' or 'black swan' crashes (Johnson et al., 2012: 1, 3; see also Johnson et al., 2013). They refer to the 2010 Flash Crash as a critical, destabilising event that illustrates the need for further understanding of such financial black swans. Thus, they argue:

Society's drive toward ever faster socio-technical systems means that there is an urgent need to understand the threat from 'black swan' extreme events that might emerge. On 6 May 2010, it just took five minutes for a spontaneous mix of human and machine interactions in the global trading cyberspace to generate an unprecedented system-wide Flash Crash. (2012: 1)[15]

Specifically, Neil Johnson et al. identify a total of 18,520 ultrafast black swan events in a dataset comprising stock-price movements from

---

[15] David Golumbia (2013: 295) similarly characterises the Flash Crash as a black swan event.

3 January 2006 to 3 February 2011. They take the notion of black swans from the work of Nassim Taleb, according to whom a black swan event has three attributes:

First, it is an *outlier*, as it lies outside the realm of regular expectations, because nothing in the past can convincingly point to its possibility. Second, it carries an extreme impact [...]. Third, in spite of its outlier status, human nature makes us concoct explanations for its occurrence *after* the fact, making it explainable and predictable. (2010: xxii, original emphasis)

The exceptional nature of black swan events, and how Johnson et al. relate to this, is especially interesting for present purposes. Referencing the work of sixteenth-century philosopher Francis Bacon, Johnson et al. noted that 'the scientific appeal of extreme events [such as ultrafast black-swan events] is that it is in such moments that a complex system offers glimpses into the true nature of the underlying fundamental forces that drive it' (2012: 3). At the same time, however, the sheer number of black swan events analysed undermines the notion of their being exceptional or outliers. Johnson et al. seem aware of this, noting, 'We uncovered 18,520 such black swan events, which surprisingly is more than one per trading day on average' (2012: 3). This, is, however, a vast underestimation. If we say that there are about 261 trading days per year (holidays excluded), then the period under scrutiny includes around 1,325 trading days in total, meaning that there are, on average, close to fourteen black swan events per trading day. Of course, to get a full picture of the relative frequency of these events, one would have to compare them to the actual number of orders placed – a number that is much higher in present-day algo-financial markets than in pre-algorithmic markets. Still, if about fourteen black swan events can be identified per trading day on average, it hardly makes sense to speak of them as exceptional events (see similarly Golub, Keane and Poon, 2012).

These different accounts suggest that the Flash Crash is indeed a restless event. While its demarcation in time and space is contested, there is nonetheless widespread agreement about the event's importance. In fact, much of the scholarly commentary explicitly asserts that the event signifies a major change in financial markets in the sense that it represents a crashing tendency now inherent in algorithmically dominated markets, and/or in the sense that it constituted a significant crisis. The latter interpretation is visible both in MacKenzie's characterisation of the Flash Crash as the 'first generalized crisis' in the world of high-frequency trading and in Johnson et al.'s likening the Flash Crash to a black swan event that has 'extreme impact'. Similarly emphasising the alleged impact of the Flash Crash, Andrei Kirilenko, former Chief Economist of the

CFTC, has argued, 'the algorithmic nature of HFT can cause significant impact. The pre-eminent example of this, of course, is the Flash Crash of May 6th of 2011 [*sic*]' (Kirilenko, Sowers and Meng, 2013: 59).

Flash Crash Avalanching

Interestingly, however, it is not quite clear what the actual impact of the Flash Crash was. While the humans watching the algorithms might have been terrified by what they saw, the economic repercussions of the event are difficult to pin down. Some firms are likely to have lost money during the Flash Crash, but, as I have argued elsewhere (Borch, 2016: 361–5), the overall economic losses were probably relatively slight – in part because markets quickly rebounded and in part because many trades during the downward move were cancelled by the exchanges. The somewhat insignificant economic impact of the Flash Crash has not lessened interest in the event; it continues to attract attention as an important event, both in the media and in scholarly circles. This discrepancy is curious. Why does the Flash Crash figure so centrally in discussions of algorithmic finance if the economic impact of the event was in fact rather limited? I suggest that the Flash Crash continues to fascinate because it conjures up two concerns, both of which have late nineteenth-century antecedents.

One such concern has to do with the fear of technology and its unanticipated forces – specifically, the concern that technological innovations are opaque to humans and may go astray (as per *The Fear Index*). In discussions on the phenomenon, references to the Flash Crash's technological aspects materialised in media reports pondering if the 'market swoon was caused by technical factors' such as a 'technical glitch' (Phillips, 2010a; 2010b). Concerns about technology also loom large in accounts of algorithmic trading's allegedly inbuilt propensity to run amok in an unanticipated frenzy. Sornette and von der Becke mobilise this image in their claim regarding the supposedly 'endogenous self-excitation nature' of high-frequency trading (2011: 11). Here, one hears echoes of late-nineteenth-century discussions of technological advances and how these radically reshaped society, leading to a reformatting of markets, their interconnectedness and the ways in which they were experienced. Concerns with the risky experiential effects of algorithmic trading surface in depictions of the perils that come with the 'nontransparency of computerized trading' (Golumbia, 2013: 286–7); in the asynchronicity between the operations and observations of sub-perceptual algorithmic finance; as well as in discussions of how the complexity and speed of high-frequency trading have outmanoeuvred

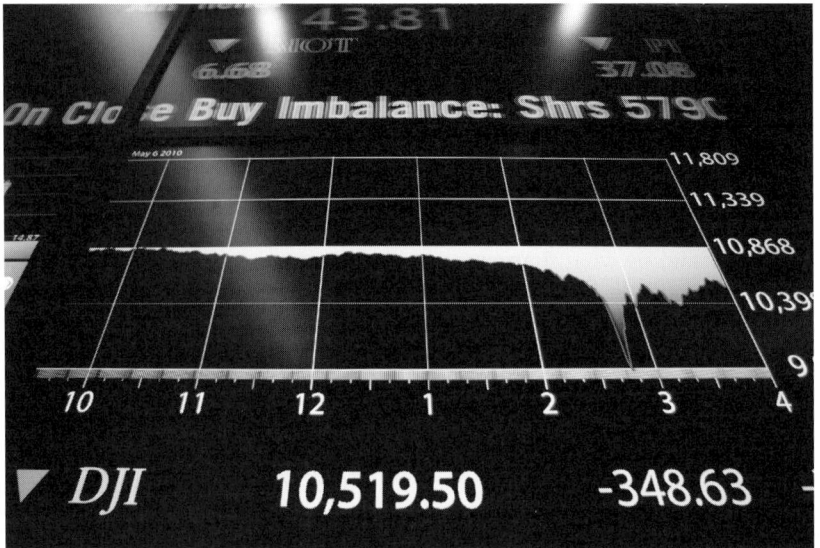

Figure 5.9 The Flash Crash.
Source: Photo Lucas Jackson/Reuters/Ritzau Scanpix

regulators and overwhelmed their capacity to effectively monitor modern markets (Lewis, 2014; Malmgren and Stys, 2011; Snider, 2014).

A different concern invoked in discussions of the Flash Crash revolves around crowds, herding and the social avalanches they might produce. Indeed, I argue that the Flash Crash continues to attract attention not simply because it was spectacular but also because it associates a modern experience with the field of algorithmic finance – the experience of being carried away in an avalanching, de-individualising process. In other words, the Flash Crash features so prominently in accounts of present-day markets because it echoes a broader, modern experience of the rug being pulled rapidly from under people, thereby undermining, if only momentarily, what is perceived as the normal state of affairs.

To illustrate, for several observers, the Flash Crash symptomises new types of systemic risk associated with algorithmic finance which point far beyond any immediate economic aftermath to 6 May 2010. In the words of Torben B. Andersen and Oleg Bondarenko, the Flash Crash is important as an example of 'highly erratic market dynamics' which might propagate 'into systemic disruptions to the financial systems' (2015: 2; see also Ivanov, 2011; Knight, 2012). This observation is echoed by scholars such as Johnson and Sornette, who essentially analyse the market as a complex system or ecology in which Flash Crash–type events constitute an immanent risk. For Johnson et al., the Flash Crash is significant as an illustration of the transition into a fully automated, machinic 'population of adaptive trading agents' as well as of the 'systemic risk' looming in such an ecology (Johnson et al., 2013: 3, 5).

A similar image is conveyed by Sornette and von der Becke, who describe financial markets as 'truly "complex systems" in a technical sense. As such, they are intrinsically characterized by periods of extremity and by abrupt state-transition and spend much time in a largely unpredictable state' (2011: 15). It is due to such unpredictable states, they argue, that high-frequency trading can produce 'Pro-cyclicality mechanisms, also known as positive feedbacks', something which allegedly 'leads to unsustainable regimes, ending in crashes and crises' (2011: 16). In other words, if markets are already unstable, as they were on the morning of 6 May 2010 in the light of the Greek debt crisis, this instability can be exacerbated by high-frequency trading algorithms herding one another and thereby transforming instability into widespread crashes (a view also expressed by Kirilenko et al., 2014).

What emerges out of these and similar accounts is a notion of the Flash Crash as an avalanche event: it was triggered by a minor event (the Waddell & Reed order) which – occurring at a time when markets were in a critical state – set in motion a self-organising dynamic in which algorithms started interacting in unanticipated ways. Similar to Durkheim's emphasis on the exultant effervescence of the corroboree (in which each emotion '[echoes] the others'; 1995: 217–18) and the contrarians' concern with contagious crowd dynamics in markets (in which the market crowd's avalanching impulses easily sweep away individual investors), the Flash Crash is portrayed as an event in which it is no longer humans but rather fully automated algorithms which echo each other in a rapid feedback loop. This is the central point of Lewis's explicit likening of the Flash Crash to 'a deadly avalanche' (2014: 82) and of Sornette and von der Becke's emphasis on the crash-prone nature of algorithmic herding (2011: 10–12). Sornette and von der Becke, in particular, stress a set of features I have associated with avalanches. Akin to how Bak describes the sandpile model, they see the Flash Crash event as 'rooted fundamentally [in] the existence of an intrinsic instability that has matured progressively, preparing the field for major disruptions that are triggered by local or proximate causes' (2011: 11). They further highlight the levelling process that can be triggered in such avalanche events, where the distinctiveness of algorithms ceases to exist and is replaced by homogeneity as algorithms start behaving similarly: 'adaptive and learning algorithms interacting by buying and selling on the same market tend to develop collective dynamical modes that are prone to large moves' (2011: 15). Despite initially following separate strategies, the avalanching, self-organising aspects of complex financial markets mean that algorithms 'tend to crowd in with similar strategies' (2011: 15).

Consequently, while concerns regarding crowds and their social avalanches have usually been framed as a primarily, if not exclusively, inter-human affair (by Durkheim, Simmel, Tarde, and the like), the mobilisation of crowd/herding tropes to understand the Flash Crash essentially implies the deployment of this human-oriented trope to a non-human, algorithmic domain. What had been previously reserved for human beings is now attributed to trading algorithms that operate independently and without direct human intervention. Contrary to the notion that technology/machines and humans exist in an antagonistic relationship (with the former challenging the latter), the portrayal of the Flash Crash as a matter of herding behaviour suggests that algorithms possess some form of sociality – namely, that of interacting actors captured in an avalanching maelstrom (more on this below). Accordingly, one corollary of these representations of the Flash Crash is that individual algorithms, too, can be swept away in a social avalanche. Relatedly, and in keeping with this explanatory horizon, the Flash Crash presents a reconfiguration of the classical *suggestionneur–suggestionné* relation. Rather than being a matter of a human *suggestionneur* affecting a human *suggestionné*, and rather than the model in which the human *suggestionné* is affected by a non-human *suggestionneur* (as in the case of the investor being carried away by reading the tape of the stock ticker), the Flash Crash suggests that under algorithmic finance both 'parties' are made up of fully automated algorithms. This mimetic dynamism is one that takes place between algorithms that oscillate between being one another's *suggestionneurs* and *suggestionnés*.

There is one important respect in which the algorithmic herding on 6 May 2010 is not quite equivalent to the avalanches and experiences of being-carried-away described by modernist observers such as Durkheim, Sidis, Simmel and Tarde. At least according to the 2010 CFTC–SEC report, 'a significant number [of automated trading algorithms] withdrew completely from the markets' during the downward-spiralling part of the Flash Crash, as they were programmed to exit markets in cases of extreme volatility (2010: 5). So, while some algorithms were caught in an avalanching process, others were instructed to stand aside, to seek refuge from the homogenising movement like well-trained contrarians, albeit without trading during the isolation. This ability to stand aside is rarely ascribed to humans within the classical sociological literature on crowds (e.g. Tarde, 1968). As demonstrated in previous chapters, late-nineteenth-century crowd theory instead tended to portray individuals as being entirely swept away and unable to evade the frenzy.

The Sociality of Algorithms

So far, I have mainly treated discussions of the Flash Crash from the perspective of second-order observation, meaning that I have observed how different observers observed the Flash Crash and how they conceived of it as an event. Luhmann (2012) separates such second-order observations from first-order observations, the latter being direct observations about 'something', such as the causal logics allegedly inherent to modern markets. Luhmann's sociological project was characterised by a strong preference for second-order observations since, according to Luhmann, they bracket ontological assumptions about the world. More precisely, by observing how other observers observe, sociologists need not make any ontological claims about how social reality is constituted – they can instead bring into relief the ontological assumptions of other observers. Despite Luhmann's reservations about them, first-order observations can be of analytical value (indeed, they are not entirely absent from his work). In that spirit, I now raise what observations of the Flash Crash might entail for economic sociology and social theory if they are taken seriously as first-order observations about how present-day algorithmic markets actually operate. This permits me to further elaborate on the perhaps controversial suggestion I made earlier: the Flash Crash hints at not just the crash-prone nature of fully automated algorithms but also their *sociality*, their capacity to engage in social interaction with one another. I substantiate this point via an analysis of the roles of herding behaviour and black swan events, both of which were central to discussions of the Flash Crash. Specifically, I discuss Daniel Beunza and David Stark's (2012) examination of dissonance and resonance in quantitative, computerised finance.

Beunza and Stark's analysis focuses on quantitative merger arbitrageurs who make investment decisions based on whether they expect a merger to take place between two corporations. To this end, arbitrageurs deploy a set of quantitative socio-technical devices which enable them to develop estimates of particular factors and to 'check their own estimates against those of their rivals': competing merger arbitrageurs (2012: 384). This factoring in of social cues amounts to, in Beunza and Stark's terms, a modelling endeavour turned 'reflexive'. Importantly, reflexive modelling is deployed here as a means through which traders incorporate *dissonance* into their trading: if the models indicate that rival traders estimate important variables differently, this is an invitation to scrutinise matters more carefully instead of following other traders blindly. While dissonance thus plays a productive role for quantitative traders, Beunza and Stark stress the risk that the incorporation of other market participants' assessments can generate calamitous 'cognitive interdependence', with traders making unprofitable decisions based on inaccurate social cues (2012: 410). For example, the trading community might collectively ignore important features of a potential merger or be overconfident about other features, meaning that individual traders might make investment decisions without being exposed to any real dissonance. In such cases, the dissonance one hopes for is replaced by *resonance*. In this way, 'Reflexive modelling amplifies individual errors when a sufficiently large number of arbitrage funds have a similar model. Whereas reflexive modelling improves trading on the basis of *dissonance*, it can lead to financial disaster in the presence of *resonance*' (2012: 410, original emphasis).

According to Beunza and Stark, the concept of reflexive modelling is superior to notions of herding and black swans. Referencing Nassim Taleb, among others, they argue that accounts of black swan events do have merit in pointing to how crises might occur if market participants deploy models that significantly 'underestimate uncertainty', e.g. by assuming that stock returns follow normal distributions rather than (more realistic) fat-tailed ones (2012: 386). That said,

the black swan is ultimately an under-socialized explanation of the risks created by models. The black swan presents financial actors as hopelessly unreflexive about the limitations of their models. Confronted by uncertainty about the model, we would expect market actors to rely on the social cues around them. (2012: 386)

Beunza and Stark acknowledge that these cues are included in herding models. However, in their view, these models allegedly 'do not account for the existence of technology in the decision-making process' (2012: 387). While herding and imitation might have offered 'a realistic portrayal of financial actors before the 1980s', 'the introduction of computers, equations and models into financial markets' has rendered herding behaviour irrelevant since, Beunza and Stark assert, traders prefer to adhere to their technological tools instead of imitating others (2012: 387). Beunza and Stark therefore consider reflexive modelling superior because it better accounts for the incorporation of social cues and the socio-technical reality of quantitative finance.

Beunza and Stark's article is based on ethnographic fieldwork conducted between 1999 and 2003. At that time, as the authors report, while human traders considered quantitative tools important and helpful, quantitative finance had not yet developed into the type of fully auto-mated trading that dominates current financial markets. To pointedly emphasise (and slightly simplify) this difference, it might be said that in the early 2000s, quantitative tools supported human traders and their decision-making, whereas human traders support fully automated algo-rithms today. As the discussions of the Flash Crash suggest, this shift has significant implications for the ways in which present-day quantitative finance generates and relates to dissonance and resonance.

For starters, present-day algorithmic finance, including high-frequency trading, is far more high-tech driven than the kind of quanti-tative finance analysed by Beunza and Stark. While Beunza and Stark pay considerable attention to the merger arbitrageurs's use of (rather low-tech) spreadsheets and phone calls, high-frequency trading is based on sophisticated forms of high-speed data processing such as server co-location, microwave transmission and so on. In this reality of extremely sophisticated technology and deeply interwoven markets, particular forms of 'cognitive interdependence' seem to take shape not so much among human actors (as per Beunza and Stark's analysis) but rather among algorithms. This is precisely what the Flash Crash laid bare, according to the accounts analysed above: the event demonstrated that human oversight and human cognitive interdependence have become both less feasible and less important in present-day financial markets, which are dominated by tightly entangled algorithms operating at extreme speeds beyond human perception. Their entanglement is based on – and further reinforces – the cognitive interdependence between algorithms.

Further, discussions of the Flash Crash do not seem to suggest that the kind of mature quantitative finance epitomised by high-frequency trading is based on reflexive modelling. Contrary to Beunza and Stark's example of merger arbitrageurs, high-frequency traders do not seek to systematic-ally incorporate the observations of rivals *in order to check their own strategies*. While they certainly take into account the actions of others in the market, they do not do so in order to critically question their own practices. Rather, high-frequency traders do this to predict the direction in which the market is moving and to profit from such predictions (see Lange, 2015; 2016).

This inter-observational dimension and the interactions it prompts between algorithms leads to the question of herding and avalanching. Sornette and von der Becke emphasise that high-frequency trading algo-rithms can engage in herding, which runs counter to Beunza and Stark's dismissal of herding as irrelevant today. This contrast stems in part from the significant difference between their conceptualisations of herding.

Beunza and Stark discuss herding with reference to financial economics literature (e.g. Scharfstein and Stein, 1990) and neoinstitutionalist accounts (DiMaggio and Powell, 1983) in which herding is conceived as a form of instrumental action; it makes sense to imitate others in situations of information uncertainty, as they might have better information than oneself. By contrast, for Sornette and von der Becke, the notion of herding has more in common with traditional sociological tropes of people being carried away in a social avalanche, a concept ignored in Beunza and Stark's instrumental rendering. Nonetheless, the discussions of the Flash Crash suggest that precisely such forms of non-instrumental herding might best account for what happened on 6 May 2010. In other words, the high-speed trading algorithms' mimicking of each other is not necessarily due to instrumental reasons but to their resonance-oriented design instead: the inter-observational ways in which they are programmed. Therefore, Beunza and Stark's finding that quantitative merger arbitrageurs 'were emphatically not mimicking their rivals' (2012: 402) cannot be applied to the Flash Crash. On 6 May 2010, algorithms were emphatically and intensively mimicking their rivals, both downwards and upwards.

The discussions of the Flash Crash may further challenge Beunza and Stark's assertion that 'arbitrageurs can collectively be wrong' (2012: 391), a point central to their analysis of how collective ignorance or overconfidence might lead to disastrous resonance. However, perhaps being right or wrong offers a false dichotomy here. Most observations of the Flash Crash, at least, forego such a distinction: neither the market drop nor its subsequent recovery was seen as a matter of algorithms being 'right' or 'wrong'. Neither part of the process can be adequately understood in those terms. What accounts of the Flash Crash point to – especially those inspired by Nanex's research – is simply that herding can go both ways: resonance can spiral downwards, generating massive instantaneous market drops, as well as upwards, leading to instantaneous price rises or market recoveries.

I therefore argue, based on these discussions of the Flash Crash, that Beunza and Stark's interesting analysis of reflexive modelling in early phase quantitative finance needs qualification when applied to the mature field of quantitative finance, today characterised by fully automated algorithmic trading. However, their analysis aptly understands one important aspect of algorithmically dominated financial markets: it recognises that quantitative finance might produce particular forms of sociality not easily understood by existing approaches in economic sociology. Specifically, the sociality of quantitative finance bridges its sociotechnical aspects with social cues. In the words of Beunza and Stark:

Reflexive modelling thus brings quantitative finance full circle: whereas the introduction of models and information technology in the capital markets brought in anonymity and a semblance of objectivity in the data, reflexive modelling makes it clear that traders are modelling not just the economic but also the social. Although anonymous and impersonal, quantitative finance brings back the interdependence among the actors – and, for that reason, its social aspect. But this form of sociability around models does not easily fit existing frameworks in economic sociology – it is disembedded yet entangled; anonymous yet collective; impersonal yet, nevertheless emphatically social. (2012: 412)

Interestingly, the final part of this quote reads as an encapsulation of urban sociality (e.g. Simmel, 1997c): life in the modern city is manifestly characterised by being 'disembedded yet entangled; anonymous yet collective; impersonal yet, nevertheless emphatically social'. The Flash Crash suggests that something similar can be said about fully automated trading algorithms despite their not being based on reflexive modelling; these algorithms, too, are 'disembedded yet entangled; anonymous yet collective; impersonal yet, nevertheless emphatically social'.

   This social dimension of an otherwise emphatically non-human domain – the realm of fully automated algorithms operating without human intervention – might appear controversial. As MacKenzie well notes, our 'intuitions may […] rebel' when faced with the claim that algorithms can have social bonds with one another (2019: 42). He makes this observation in an analysis, inspired primarily by Goffman's (1983) notion of the 'interaction order', of the relationship between fully automated trading algorithms. MacKenzie remarks that its potentially counter-intuitive facets notwithstanding, an existing branch of literature has long argued compellingly for the existence of sociality in electronic markets. This tradition includes Knorr Cetina's aforementioned work on the postsocial relationships electronic traders develop with markets through their screens. It includes Preda, who has made productive use of Goffman's notion of the interaction order in studies of the ways in which online traders engage with anonymous others via their screens (Preda, 2009a; 2017). Like MacKenzie, I argue for taking Knorr Cetina's and Preda's work one consequential step further to *analyse the interactions between fully automated algorithms as a form of sociality*. However, instead of mobilising Goffman for such an analysis, I suggest that the Flash Crash might be better understood by evoking an older sociological horizon. Specifically, this particular event demonstrated that imitation plays a central role in present-day algorithmic finance. In the Flash Crash, algorithms imitated one another, whether in the case of downward sell pressure (crashes) or upward buy pressure (recoveries). As per Tarde, since imitation is a form of sociality because it establishes a bond between the one imitating and the one(s) being imitated, the imitative interaction and 'interdependence' (Beunza and Stark) of fully automated algorithms materialised in a distinct and genuine form of algorithmic sociality.

More specific, while the usual algorithmic interactions in the electronic order book may be said to embody a particular form of algorithmic sociality, the Flash Crash event demonstrates that if conditions are right, algorithms can avalanche both upwards and downwards, just like human sociality. As in the general discussion of social avalanches in Chapter 3, I leave unanalysed the question of when suitable conditions are in place (and whether, say, the Greek debt crisis was a sufficient condition, as some accounts of the Flash Crash claimed), although I offer a few reflections on this in the conclusion.

The Tensional Individuality of Algorithms

As per the theoretical framework developed in this book, it is important also to address the question of tensional individuality when discussing algorithmic trading and the Flash Crash. The notion of tensional individuality – whether materialised in the thought of Bernheim and Tarde or in the pages of contrarian investment advice literature – arguably intimates that the submission to mimetic pulls is differentially distributed: some people get carried away entirely, some surrender in a volitional act and still others learn to resist external suggestions. This type of differentiation may equally be applied to algorithms during the Flash Crash. While some algorithms reportedly succeeded in withdrawing from markets, fleeing the turbulence in time, many others clearly did submit to avalanching pressure by participating in rapidly homogenising downwards and/or upwards turns. Since these algorithms tended to be deterministic in nature – at least at the time of the Flash Crash in 2010 – meaning that they were pre-programmed to respond in particular ways to specific market developments, it makes sense to conceive of their participation in the avalanching event as a volitional act: a consequence of positive algorithmic agency, albeit one with its own unanticipated consequences.

Talking about the volitional acts and positive agency of algorithms evokes the notion of 'instrumental action', famously defined by Weber as action 'determined by expectations as to the behavior of objects in the environment and of other human beings; these expectations are used as "conditions" or "means" for the attainment of the actor's own rationally pursued and calculated ends' (1978: 24). The electronic order book constitutes the relevant environment of the algorithms, in which others' behaviour (the behaviour of other algorithms or the human screen traders still active) allows the algorithms to form expectations about future market movements. If, say, buy orders suddenly pile up, this will likely trigger the expectation that prices will soon rise, and the algorithms will adjust their strategic behaviour accordingly.

When viewed as technological materialisations of instrumental action, algorithms are essentially portrayed as autonomous entities; their actions are not subsumed under a mimetic pull. Inspired by this kind of Weberian reasoning, Nicholas Gane has argued in *Max Weber and Contemporary Capitalism* that to the extent that financial algorithms engage in imitative strategies, such imitation is precisely strategic-instrumental (2012: 68), a notion reminiscent of the instrumental conception of herding to which Beunza and Stark subscribe. Gane's analysis is interesting for several reasons. He explicitly discusses the Flash Clash and, similar to the approach presented here, is keen on demonstrating that events such as the Flash Crash are not devoid of sociality. Mobilising Weber's conceptual register, he carefully attends to what the German sociologist has to offer such an analysis and where the limitations of a Weberian framework lie. Both dimensions are illuminating. The alleged analytical benefits echo the point about the role of instrumental action. Using the September 2010 CFTC–SEC report and its discussion of the Waddell & Reed order as a blackcloth, Gane states,

> the events of the Flash Crash suggest that wild market movements do not result simply from the irrational, affective decisions of crowds but can be caused by the deliberate and strategic actions of major market players, such as, in this case, the selling of a large number of contracts within a very short time-frame. (2012: 69)

Continuing from this, Gane interprets the Flash Crash as a matter of algorithms striving for power in the market (2012: 69–71). However, it is a power by proxy, as Gane – following Weber – sees algorithms as the delegates of humans, meaning that the supposed fight for power between algorithms in financial markets is in fact one between the various human beings who have designed them. Gane acknowledges that this is also where the limitations to a Weberian analysis of present-day markets become apparent. When Weber wrote about financial markets and stock exchanges, open-outcry trading constituted the natural centre of attention (e.g. 2000), and he could not have anticipated the transition into algorithmic, non-human markets. However, contrary to Gane, I argue against the Weberian temptation to reduce algorithms to mere delegates for humans, to a technological acting out of the power and instrumental rationality humans might pursue. In my view, such an approach severely underestimates the independent qualities of algorithms and their potential to be carried away by mimetic market pulls.

Simmel offers a more useful approach. Reflecting upon the relation between subjective and objective culture, he observed that in modern society, with its high degree of division of labour, 'a certain autonomous mobility of parts of the objects' can be identified, a central consequence of which is that 'Objects and people have become separated from one another' (2011: 499). Applied to financial algorithms, this observation assumes a new and radical meaning, opening an analysis that grants these algorithms a certain independence. Acknowledging this independence prepares the way for taking seriously the surplus, or emergent, element that the Flash Crash made manifest: while financial algorithms may in many cases be seen as an incarnation of autonomous decision-making, in which others' behaviour constitutes a factor that is taken into account but that does not nullify their sovereignty, the May 2010 event laid bare that interaction dynamics amongst algorithms can set in motion imitative and imitation-generated patterns neither anticipated nor designed. In such situations, it becomes clear that, like that of humans, the 'individuality' of algorithms is caught in a tension between mimesis and anti-mimesis, with avalanches pulling them towards the mimetic pole.

★★★

Financial markets look markedly different today than they did just fifteen to twenty years ago, not least because their advanced technological infrastructure sets them radically apart from their late nineteenth-century ancestors. Yet considerable continuities have survived. Financial markets have always been characterised by a race in which market participants seek to obtain market information faster than others. In that sense, present-day high-frequency trading is merely an extension of the age-old ambition to utilise speed advantages in markets. Similarly, as I have demonstrated in this discussion stretching from nineteenth-century exchanges to the 2010 Flash Crash, questions of tensional individuality and social avalanche persist whether markets are populated by human traders or fully automated algorithms. That said, the sociality of markets has undergone significant transformations, from the inter-human sociality of open-outcry trading to the postsocial relationships between electronic traders and their screens to an inter-algorithmic form of sociality. I have focused attention on the Flash Crash because it provides an entry into understanding such an inter-algorithmic sociality and its connection to social avalanches and tensional individuality. Let me close with a few reflections on the Flash Crash analysis I have offered and, in particular, some possible objections to it.

One important corollary of the Flash Crash that I have not addressed so far concerns the regulatory responses to the event. For example, in order to avoid future flash crashes of a scale similar to that of May 2010, US regulators introduced automatic 'circuit breakers', which come in various guises and are activated if market volatility increases too much too quickly (Borch, 2018). Since these mechanisms are designed to suspend trading if predetermined volatility thresholds are exceeded, it might be expected that flash crashes would turn into a thing from the past, a type of event that cannot occur again. This would simultaneously suggest that the emphasis accorded to the Flash Crash in this chapter is outdated, since algorithms would not be able to interact in ways that could produce similar avalanches again. Testifying against this, and punctuating the relevance of the May 2010 Flash Crash as an exemplary entry into understanding present-day market avalanches, are the several flash crashes which have been identified since 2010, some in analyses of the mini flash crashes cited earlier. Others have attracted more attention, such as a flash crash in the US Treasury market on 15 October 2014 (US Department of the Treasury et al., 2015). The point is that in spite of the measures regulators promote to avoid them, these types of events seem to recur nonetheless.

Moreover, the 'crash' terminology attached to the Flash Crash event and the notion that this amounted to an example of social avalanching might lend the impression that, to the extent that a vocabulary of sociality is salient, the dynamism of the Flash Crash signified a *collapse* or eclipse of the social rather than its positive (re)production. However, Tarde's sociological work serves as a useful reminder that even if social avalanching may appear as a breakdown of the social, it should in fact be seen as a particular instantiation of sociality in which, in this case, algorithms effectively created a social bond (however temporary) with each other.

Even so, to paraphrase Jonsson (2001: 3, 21), one might downplay the sociality of algorithms that surfaced in the Flash Crash as merely – or at most – a 'degree zero' of sociality, a sociality 'as yet without meaning and direction' or a 'glimpse of the social body as it exists prior to the emergence of either individuals or masses'. Certainly, the algorithmic sociality I am talking about here is absent *human* individuals or masses; it contains no (subjective) meaning in any Weberian sense. However, as scholars such as Knorr Cetina, Latour and others have argued, there is little reason why sociality should be restricted to a purely human domain, inhabited only by humans (Knorr Cetina and Bruegger, 2002; Latour, 2005); as I argued in Chapter 3, there is little reason why human meaning should be a key attribute of social action. The algorithms that were part of the Flash Crash – even those that left the scene – were certainly orienting their behaviour to the behaviour of others, but they did so without being impregnated with human-subjective meaning.

Arguably more powerful than the aforementioned objections so far, it is admittedly difficult to say whether particular algorithms entertained *recurrent* imitation-based social bonds with other particular algorithms or whether their interactions were merely isolated. Without a detailed analysis of the order book, it is difficult to assess whether, say, algorithm X interacted repeatedly with algorithm Y. Some algorithms might have traded a lot with certain others, while other algorithms might have engaged in only a few interactions. In any event, these specific interactions are likely to have been short lived, characterised by a quickly completed matching of orders in the order book. Since the response time of high-frequency trading algorithms is measured in fractions of a second, one might object that even if particular algorithms were interacting over a couple of seconds, the ephemeral nature of this hardly qualifies as proper sociality. That is to say, the lack of temporal sedimentation renders it impossible for algorithms to develop the many traits sociologists usually attach to sociality, such as norms, rituals and the like. Truly, it makes little sense to search for norms and rituals emerging out of the interaction of algorithms. However, the mere speed with which they operate does not disqualify algorithms for engaging in proper social relations. Substantiating this point recalls Chapter 2's discussion of Durkheim's critique of Tarde, as well as sociological discussions of metropolitan life and the connections between cities and financial markets.

Durkheim's dismissal of imitation as a key sociological conception was based in part on the assertion that people who are mutually related only by 'a chance, momentary association' are not properly socially connected. Urban sociology offered a counterargument to this claim, suggesting that the metropolis is the site *par excellence* of fleeting encounters with strangers and that these ephemeral meetings do not preclude sociality. For example, Simmel talked about the 'brevity and scarcity of the interhuman contacts granted to the metropolitan' inhabitant, arguing that these 'brief metropolitan contacts' in particular create the need for mannerism, for appearing different than others (1997c: 183). He also made clear that such constellations testify to the 'elemental forms of socialization' in the city (1997c: 180). However transitory these encounters, however unique the urban inhabitant strives to appear – all are inscribed in sociality and enact it. The point of this is to stress that the lack of temporal expansion or sedimentation per se is not a good argument against conceiving of fully automated financial algorithms as engaging in social relations with one another. Quite the contrary, 'brief encounters' may simply be the primary form that sociality assumes in anonymous electronic markets (Preda, 2009a). Interestingly, and despite developments that otherwise weaken the intimate relationship between cities and financial markets, this brings the discussion full circle: while the trading of financial instruments today does not take place in the urban buzz of the open-outcry pits of financial exchanges, the trading algorithms that dominate present-day markets engage in inter-algorithmic forms of sociality that – given their fleeting nature – have a strikingly metropolitan character.

Conclusion

Contingency is a leitmotiv in modern society – in fact, perhaps, its 'defining attribute' (Luhmann, 1998). According to Luhmann, 'Anything is contingent that is neither necessary nor impossible. The concept is therefore defined by the negation of necessity and impossibility' (1998: 45). That life in modern society is contingent and hence can be different is a message that has been central to the discipline of sociology since its inception in the late nineteenth century (Isenberg, 2018). Institutions can be different, customs may shift and meaning horizons can change. In this book, I have argued for going a step further than seeing modern society as tied to the experience that things *could* be different. What much *fin-de-siècle* social theory sought to capture was not an experience with contingency dressed as possibility. Rather, late-nineteenth and early-twentieth-century theorists tried to grasp an experience of things *actually* transforming – of society, in its big and small manifestations, being subject to a massive flow of change, which at times gave rise to a sense of radical rupture that soon rendered particular ways of life barely recognisable.

The point of reverting to the late nineteenth century was partly to correct the presentist inclination that haunts much of sociology: while the twenty-first century is certainly characterised by several significant changes – including massive urbanisation, an overflow of new technologies making substantial imprints on people's everyday lives, and sweeping transformations of tightly connected financial markets in which local instabilities can generate vastly negative consequences – many twenty-first-century transformations nonetheless pale in significance beside the profound disruptions that *fin-de-siècle* citizens lived through. However, going back to the late nineteenth century also serves another, perhaps more important purpose: it unearths a theoretical tradition of crowd theory that, if not entirely forgotten, has suffered a poor reputation amongst generations of sociologists. I have argued that this tradition deserves renewed attention because it encapsulates a theoretical response to the colossal transformations that European societies, especially, underwent during 1870–1930, and also because it offers important insights into sociality, collectivity and individuality which merit present-day analytical attention.

One of the key notions I have derived from the work of classical sociologists is that of tensional individuality: the idea that individuality is cast in a tensional relationship between external mimetic influence and inner anti-mimetic autonomy. The notion of tensional individuality at once negates and mediates between methodological individualism, on the one hand, and an extreme poststructuralist conception of individuality as entirely plastic, on the other. It negates the view that individuality is reducible to either end of this continuum. Instead, it stresses their coexistence. The insistence that some anti-mimetic individual autonomy exists and persists while mimetic forces work in the opposite direction – effectively seeking to annul individual differences and forms of autonomy – is captured in Tarde's dictum about ideas, beliefs and desires: 'Heterogeneity, not homogeneity, is at the heart of things. [...] Things are not born alike, they become alike' (1962: 71). The same applies to individuality. Through imitation, people resemble one another more and more but without thereby necessarily losing their heterogeneous cores. So, rather than analytically evading this dual composition of individuality, and rather than ironing out the friction and discord it obviously entails, the conception of individuality I have distilled from classical sociological theory insists on its paradoxical constitution.

Tensional individuality did not emerge out of thin air in the late nineteenth century: it was precisely predicated on the landslide events that took place at this time. In the light of technological and scientific advances, an upending of established political frameworks and institutions, as well as other similarly deep-seated societal changes, the conception of tensional individuality presented itself as a suitable analytical model for capturing the ways in which the belief in individual autonomy was challenged by a veritable flooding of individuality. Such flooding was not least associated with the types of crowd behaviour that attracted a deluge of scholarly attention at the end of the nineteenth century. It is against this backdrop of reflections on crowd behaviour that I derived social avalanches – this book's other central notion – as situations in which heterogeneity is temporarily replaced with homogeneity. People who may usually act differently start acting in concert; the typical multiplicity of ideas and imitations momentarily collapses and is substituted by uniformity. Social avalanches are self-organising processes in which a gradual build-up of elements suddenly produces a system-wide transformation. Experientially, the effect of this is a sense of being carried away and losing one's self, a mimetic undermining of differences between individuals.

Importantly, the notion of social avalanches does not invalidate the conception of tensional individuality. Rather, where the notion of tensional individuality points to the coexistence of mimetic and anti-mimetic dimensions, however paradoxical this seems, the analysis of social avalanches gives analytical weight to mimetic pushes: it emphasises that the mimetic dimension of individuality can rapidly escalate and that forces which produce a de-individualising subsumption under external mimesis can be set in motion. More than that, the self-organising dynamics of social avalanches and their irreducibility to the actions of particular individuals actually renders them post-individualistic phenomena.

Since the notion of social avalanche is founded on ideas from the repertoire of late nineteenth-century crowd theory, it has been important for me to stress that the main charges levelled against this theoretical tradition thus far have not been entirely justified, and that the analysis of social avalanche here steers free from such standard critiques. I am thinking, in particular, of the critique of the supposedly ideological undertones of classical crowd theory and its pathological account of collective behaviour. *Contra* such critiques, I have presented a re-evaluation of *fin-de-siècle* crowd theory, demonstrating that, as per the principle of extension, crowds and social avalanches are not antagonistic to society and the social. Rather, they bring to life a specific form of sociality, a social bond characterised by a particular intensity. Along similar lines, I have argued that social avalanches should not be assessed in a pathological register, nor should any a priori moral valence be attached to them. Social avalanches per se are neither good nor bad.

In order to demonstrate the analytical salience of the notions of tensional individuality and social avalanches, I have explored two empirical terrains: cities and financial markets. A host of late nineteenth and early twentieth-century sociologists and architects have portrayed social avalanches as an immanent feature of modern cities. Though urban planners asserted that the ever-lurking risk of rapid mimetic de-individualisation can be alleviated through the architectural overhauling of metropolitan spaces, the tensional constitution of urban individuality that underpins it does not disappear quite as easily. As urban sociologists have explained, the city produces a setting and atmosphere in which people are constantly exposed to external mimetic influence while at the same time carving out a space for themselves, in which they stand out and thereby both secure and assert some individual anti-mimetic autonomy. I make a similar point about financial markets. In the late nineteenth and early twentieth centuries, observations of financial

markets emphasised the avalanching propensities of markets, the imminent risk traders and speculators confront of being carried away by the
market. There, too, an image of tensional individuality gained traction,
exemplified by the advice to market participants about the need to
develop techniques that would ensure autonomous decision-making
even when faced with heavily mimetic market pulls.

In addition to separately examining tensional individuality and social
avalanches as they pertain to cities and financial markets, I also wanted to
use this theoretical framework as a lever for exploring the interconnectedness of cities and financial markets. While there are certainly more
links between these two domains than I have addressed here, I find it
important to stress the urban qualities of financial exchanges: the apparent indistinction between the dynamics of urban life as portrayed by
classical urban sociologists and the *modus operandi* of the trading pits/
floors of late nineteenth and early to mid-twentieth-century stock and
commodity exchanges. Briefly put, the social avalanches of the metropolis always only seemed a small step away from the trading pits/floors, and
in fact often inundated these too. I have argued that this type of link has
not become obsolete even if exchanges and financial markets more
broadly have moved towards computerised automation in recent
decades. While trading floors busy with physically co-present traders
have been largely replaced by automated trading, in which algorithms
interact with one another, the medium through which such interactions
take place – namely, the electronic order book – has a certain urban feel
to it. Trading algorithms are anonymous. They interact fleetingly, like
people passing one another in the street. Moreover, echoing the discussion of urban surfaces and depths, these algorithms are designed to
present a certain surface self to the trading public (especially to other
algorithms in the market) and may engage in acts of dissimulation and
camouflage in order to conceal their underlying strategies (Borch, 2017;
MacKenzie, 2019).

That said, the transformation of financial markets into automated
trading has nevertheless produced one clear change in the extent to
which these markets are characterised by urban features: humans have
been relegated to the background and algorithms have taken the front
seat. While the core concerns of classical urban sociology have pivoted on
the ways in which human beings act and interact in the city, a sociological
understanding of present-day markets must come to terms with the fact
that humans play second fiddle at best. Sure, humans do design and
programme trading algorithms, but as demonstrated earlier, humans are
utterly left behind once these algorithms start operating in markets. This
development prompts the question of whether the sociological insights

into urban dynamics apply equally well to all levels of a non-human, algorithmically dominated setting. I have suggested that it is in fact justified to invoke a theoretical vocabulary of urban sociality when analysing algorithmic markets. Specifically, I have argued that the theoretical framework of social avalanche I deploy to examine cities has analytical purchase in ongoing discussions of algorithmic interactions – or algorithmic sociality – within financial markets as well. As events such as the Flash Crash demonstrate, algorithms too can be carried away by the mimetic pull of the market. Despite their public presentation of self and their attempts to secure a level of autonomous decision-making, they too can submit to a de-individualising avalanche that makes each act like the others. So, while it might be a stretch to suggest that the inclination to imitation that sociologists like Simmel and Tarde have highlighted as a human propensity (a *Homo imitatus*) can be conferred upon algorithms (an *Algo imitatus*, as it were), Flash Crash events do illustrate that trading algorithms can be caught in mimetic whirlwinds.

This analysis and the assertion that sociality can legitimately be accorded to non-human algorithms point to one of the chief theoretical advantages of the reassessment of classical crowd theory proposed in this book. As mentioned in the introduction, this tradition has weathered severe blows throughout the twentieth century, particularly in the years after the late 1960s, which marked the birth of social movement studies. Social movement studies pushed for an analytical reorientation that left behind a range of conceptual baggage from the crowd and collective behaviour traditions, not least to rid itself of their supposed shortcomings. While this may have produced progress in terms of our understanding of social movements, cutting ties with the older tradition of classical crowd theory also entailed disconnecting from more general analytical ambitions and commitments. After all, in addition to responding to a particular historical situation of landslide events, classical crowd theory was deeply embedded in broader theoretical concerns about sociality, individuality and collectivity, growing out of and contributing to discussions about these themes. This is also what makes it possible to distil new theoretical frameworks from this tradition, as I have done here. The richness of this tradition generates an abundance of possibilities for generalisation and re-specification, including deploying late-nineteenth-century ideas to domains with which they otherwise appear to have little in common, such as algorithmic trading. Social movement studies, it seems to me, has fewer options in that regard. While that branch of research offers insights into its object of study, extending beyond its ken may require stretching the sociological imagination. Without pushing this point too far, one may say that it is difficult to conceive of trading algorithms from the point of view of social movement studies. Algo-rithms do not assemble in order to express and pursue a common political goal, but they do engage in behaviour that can be captured analytically via a reassessment of classical crowd theory.

Future Research

With the notions of tensional individuality and social avalanche as well as their analytical significance for understanding not just crowd and collect-ive behaviour but also cities and financial markets well established, new questions naturally arise. What lines of future research do the ideas put forth in this book invite? The most important task is arguably to flesh out in greater theoretical and empirical detail the circumstances under which social avalanches are likely to occur – both in a human and in a non-human, algorithmic domain – as well as the conditions under which individuality, in spite of its tensional constitution, tends to swing towards either pole of the mimesis–anti-mimesis continuum. Two ways of addressing these themes appear particularly promising to me.

The first consists in cross-fertilising the theoretical framework pre-sented here with the 'interaction ritual chain' model proposed by Randall Collins (2004). The basic objective of Collins's model, which also goes by the more formal title of 'the mutual-focus/emotional-entrainment' model, is to provide a theory of why particular social situations unfold as they do. What explains social interactions, their course, why people are attracted to them, gain emotional energy from them, and so on? These questions, among others, are at the core of Collins's theoretical work, developed through a mobilisation of insights from Durkheim's analysis of collective effervescence and Goffman's microsociology – a theoretical gesture similar to this book's aim to revisit the classics for contemporary theoretical purposes. In keeping with Durkheim's legacy, Collins pays considerable attention to crowd situations, settings characterised by the collective effervescence of people gathered at the same time and space. As with social avalanches, the social interactions Collins examines can quickly transform; for example, unleashed emotional energy may change the collective situation from one moment to the next. What Collins's theory offers through its Goffman-inflected microsociological interest, and what may be brought into dialogue with the notion of social ava-lanches, is a preoccupation with outlining a model of the 'fine-grained flow of micro-events that build up in patterns of split seconds and ebb away in longer periods of minutes, hours, and days' (2004: 47). In other words, Collins's approach offers a potential starting point for better understanding both the situational circumstances that may prompt, for all their unpredictability, social avalanches and their temporal extension.

Collins's theory is tied to an analysis of individuality and, on the face of it, its congeniality with the notion of tensional individuality is remarkable. Collins, too, suggests that individuality is stretched out on a continuum, in his case between axes of power and solidarity (2004: 347–50). Against this background, Collins develops an extensive typology of types of individuality, with some more prone to engage in crowded situations than others, for example. Such a typology may add to the examination of tensional individuality and an understanding of those situations in which one pole plays a comparatively larger role. However, one should also note that as with typologies in general, Collins's is rather schematic and somewhat absent of the phenomenological feel that otherwise characterises his work. More important, upon closer inspection, his analysis of individuality differs from mine in that for Collins, individuality is purely a product of social situations: he grants no individual core existence, nor does he acknowledge any non-situationally defined residue. As a result, Collins's theoretical model is only of limited use when it comes to fleshing out the concept and analysis of tensional individuality.

Other limitations are more pronounced. For example, Collins's theory has a strong analytical preference for face-to-face situations. While it does recognise that much sociality takes place in distanced and mediated contexts, such as over the phone or the internet, his theory's focus is nonetheless on situations in which people are physically, bodily co-present. Social avalanches, by contrast, need not be confined to face-to-face settings; they can be mediated as well. This touches upon a further limitation regarding the humanistic anchoring of Collins's model. *Contra* his claim that interaction ritual chain 'theory can be universally applied' (2004: 15), it is actually difficult to see how the model may be generalised and re-specified for situations of non-human, inter-algorithmic behaviour. Such situations fall outside the remit of interaction ritual chain theory. This is understandable if one is committed to a human-oriented research programme, which much of today's sociology continues to be. However, this humanistic emphasis has been severely critiqued in recent decades. Most notably, scholars such as Latour have argued for downplaying the role of humans or, at least, rethinking humans in a fashion that takes non-human objects and materiality much more seriously in social theory (e.g. Latour, 2005). Specifically, Latour champions a so-called symmetric approach: 'To be symmetric, for us, simply means *not* to impose a priori some spurious *asymmetry* among human intentional action and a material world of causal relations' (Latour, 2005: 76, original emphasis). It follows that how humans and non-humans interrelate is an empirical matter, not something that can be decided in advance.

If Latour's and others' invitation to grant non-human objects more analytical prominence is to be taken seriously, a general theory of social situations will have to go further than Collins's humanistic bias allows. This is particularly evident if the objective is to understand interactions in financial markets, as these are becoming less and less dominated by humans and increasingly controlled by non-human algorithms. But the example of financial markets and their sometimes-avalanching algorithms also indicates that perhaps Latour's principle of symmetry can become a straitjacket in that it assumes both humans and non-humans are of some significance, whatever their comparative importance in real life may be. The empirical reality of present-day financial markets suggests otherwise: some of the most fascinating and consequential forms of action and interaction taking place there are in fact those which assume a purely algorithmic configuration.

This realisation prompts a new question: How may such inter-algorithmic behaviours and their avalanching propensities, as evinced by flash crashes, be analysed? As I mentioned in Chapter 5, algorithms act and interact in markets via the electronic order book, and whatever they do in terms of placing, modifying or cancelling orders can, in principle, be analysed through the traces these actions leave in the order book. I say 'in principle' because trading venues carefully protect their order-book data – at least in their most granular form – and they are required by regulators to do so in order not to reveal by some mishap the identities of their market participants. That said, some research access to order-book data can and has been obtained, though until now this has mainly been an option pursued by financial economists. Still, even with such access, distilling the mechanisms that give rise to Flash Crash-like avalanches remains a non-trivial and cumbersome affair. This is where the second promising avenue for future research emerges: in addition to examining actual order-book data and the information they reveal about real-life algorithmic behaviours, one may study these behaviours through *agent-based modelling* (ABM).

ABM aims to understand and model the interaction of agents (variously defined) in specific contexts, which can shed light on emergent interaction dynamics, critical phenomena (crashes) and spontaneous pattern formation. ABM has been deployed in a variety of settings, such as urban traffic planning, disease contagion models and financial markets. In recent years, a growing number of scholars have successfully deployed ABM for sociological analysis (e.g. Cederman, 2005; Epstein, 2006; Gilbert and Abbott, 2005; Goldberg and Stein, 2018; Macy and

Willer, 2002; Squazzoni, 2012). ABM has proven particularly useful for studying contagion dynamics, and there is a rich history of simulation frameworks that share close ties to the late nineteenth-century tradition of crowd and contagion theory (Vehlken, 2019). This feature is one of the reasons why simulation may serve an important analytical function when it comes to analysing algorithmic avalanches. After all, conventional qualitative methods in sociology for studying financial markets face a methodological impasse when transposed to the domain of algorithmic behaviour. It is not possible to do fieldwork on the ground which tracks the real-time behaviours of algorithms. Nor, obviously, can algorithms be interviewed. While the humans who programme the algorithms can be observed and interviewed about the algorithms' underlying assumptions, these programmers often openly admit that they have limited insight into the ways their algorithms behave once the latter engage in inter-algorithmic behaviours (MacKenzie, 2019). Through ABM, by contrast, it is possible to simulate the interactions of trading algorithms. An appropriately sophisticated simulation framework may offer insights into the conditions likely to generate algorithmic avalanches as well as, relatedly, the situations in which algorithms are prone to mimic others.[1]

An ABM-based analysis of these conditions may be linked further to discussions about 'normal accidents' in markets, following in the footsteps of Charles Perrow's analysis of such accidents in the field of industrial production (Perrow, 1994). According to Perrow, normal accidents are likely to take place in systems characterised by highly complex interactions and tight couplings. This notion has later been adapted in analyses of financial markets (Mezias, 1994; Schneiberg and Bartley, 2010). It should come as no surprise by now that today's algorithmically dominated markets are a prime illustration of these two conditions being in place. The current interactions between trading algorithms are of such complexity that not even the designers of individual algorithms have a good sense of their interaction dynamics. The Flash Crash exemplifies the devastating effects that may result from these complex interactions and makes plain the consequences of the tight coupling of markets: a disruption in one market (in this case, Chicago) may quickly spill over to others (New York). The notion of normal accidents proposes a stronger focus on the role of organisational dimensions in a high-risk technological setting. Mobilising it alongside an ABM framework might prove a productive way forwards when it comes to examining the minute mechanisms likely to generate avalanches in financial markets.

---

[1] This is exactly one of the things we are working towards in my current research project on Algorithmic Finance.

Of course, the two analytical avenues I have highlighted here do not exhaust the ways in which the ideas I have presented in this book can be further explored and connected to other theoretical and analytical traditions. The potential for connectivity should be rich. What I offer, by dusting off a stock of partially forgotten late-nineteenth and early-twentieth-century social theories, is a new agenda for understanding individuality, collectivity and their entanglements, one that will hopefully galvanise a fresh theorisation of stale conceptions. I hope to have demonstrated that tensional individuality and social avalanches can certainly inspire a productive rethinking of crowd behaviour, sociality and a range of topics central to urban sociology and economic sociology. May other fields now join in.

References

Abbott, A. 2004. *Methods of Discovery: Heuristics for the Social Sciences*. New York and London: W. W. Norton & Company.

Alliez, E. 2004. 'The Difference and Repetition of Gabriel Tarde', *Distinktion* 9: 49–54.

Andersen, T. G. and Bondarenko, O. 2015. 'Assessing Measures of Order Flow Toxicity and Early Warning Signals for Market Turbulence', *Review of Finance* 19(1): 1–54.

Andriopoulos, S. 2008. *Possessed: Hypnotic Crimes, Corporate Fiction, and the Invention of Cinema*, trans. P. Jansen and S. Andriopoulos. Chicago and London: University of Chicago Press.

Arnoldi, J. 2006. 'Frames and Screens: The Reduction of Uncertainty in Electronic Derivatives Trading', *Economy and Society* 35(3): 381–99.

Aron, R. 1967. *Main Currents in Sociological Thought 2: Durkheim, Pareto, Weber*, trans. R. Howard and H. Weaver. London: Penguin Books.

Arppe, T. 2005. 'Rousseau, Durkheim et la constitution affective du social', *Revue d'Histoire des Sciences Humaines* 13(2): 5–32.

Ash, M. G. 2013. 'Weimar Psychology: Holistic Visions and Trained Intuition', in P. E. Gordon and J. P. McCormack (eds.), *Weimar Thought: A Contested Legacy*. Princeton, and Oxford: Princeton University Press, pp. 35–54.

Bak, P. 1997. *How Nature Works: The Science of Self-Organized Criticality*. Oxford: Oxford University Press.

Bak, P., Tang, C. and Wiesenfeld, K. 1987. 'Self-Organized Criticality: An Explanation of the 1/f Noise', *Physical Review Letters* 59(4): 381–4.

Barrows, S. 1981. *Distorting Mirrors: Visions of the Crowd in Late Nineteenth-Century France*. New Haven, CT, and London: Yale University Press.

Bauman, Z. 2000. *Liquid Modernity*. Cambridge: Polity Press.

Beard, G. M. 1971. *A Practical Treatise on Nervous Exhaustion (Neurasthenia): Its Symptoms, Nature, Sequences, Treatment*. New York: Kraus Reprint Co.

Bech, H. 1998. 'Citysex: Representing Lust in Public', *Theory, Culture & Society* 15(3–4): 215–41.

Beck, J. 2016. '"Americanitis": The Disease of Living Too Fast', *The Atlantic*: www.theatlantic.com/health/archive/2016/2003/the-history-of-neurasthenia-or-americanitis-health-happiness-and-culture/473253/.

Bekhterev, V. M. 1998. *Suggestion and Its Role in Social Life*, trans. T. Dobreva-Martinova. New Brunswick, NJ, and London: Transaction Publishers.

2001. *Collective Reflexology. The Complete Edition*, trans. E. Lockwood and A. Lockwood. New Brunswick: Transaction Publishers.

Beniger, J. R. 1986. *The Control Revolution: Technological and Economic Origins of the Information Society*. Cambridge, MA: Harvard University Press.

Benjamin, W. 1999. *The Arcades Project*, trans. H. Eiland and K. McLaughlin. Cambridge, MA: The Belknap Press of Harvard University Press.

2008. 'The Work of Art in the Age of Its Technological Reproducibility: Second Version', in *The Work of Art in the Age of Its Technological Reproducibility, and Other Writings on Media*, trans. E. Jephcott and H. Zohn. Cambridge, MA: The Belknap Press of Harvard University Press, pp. 19–55.

Bergson, H. 2001. *Time and Free Will: An Essay on the Immediate Data of Consciousness*, trans. F. Pogson. Mineola, NY: Dover Publications.

Berk, R. A. 1974. 'A Gaming Approach to Crowd Behavior', *American Sociological Review* 39(June): 355–73.

Berman, M. 2010. *All That Is Solid Melts into Air: The Experience of Modernity*, New Edition. London and New York: Verso.

Bernheim, H. 1889. *Suggestive Therapeutics: A Treatise on the Nature and Uses of Hypnotism*, trans. C. Herter. New York and London: G. P. Putnam's Sons.

Beunza, D. and Stark, D. 2012. 'From Dissonance to Resonance: Cognitive Interdependence in Quantitative Finance', *Economy and Society* 41(3): 383–417.

Binet, A. 1896. *On Double Consciousness: Experimental Psychological Studies*. Chicago: Open Court Pub. Co.

Bistis, M. 2005. 'Simmel and Bergson: The Theorist and the Exemplar of the "Blasé Person"', *Journal of European Studies* 35(4): 395–418.

Black, F. 1971a. 'Toward a Fully Automated Stock Exchange (Part I)', *Financial Analysts Journal* 27(4): 28–35, 44.

1971b. 'Toward a Fully Automated Stock Exchange (Part II)', *Financial Analysts Journal* 27(6): 24–8, 86–7.

Blackman, L. 2007. 'Reinventing Psychological Matters: The Importance of the Suggestive Realm of Tarde's Ontology', *Economy and Society* 36(4): 574–96.

2008. 'Affect, Relationality and the "Problem of Personality"', *Theory, Culture & Society* 25(1): 23–47.

2012. *Immaterial Bodies: Affect, Embodiment, Mediation*. London: SAGE.

2014. 'Affect and Automaticity: Towards an Analytics of Experimentation', *Subjectivity* 7(4): 362–84.

Block, F. 2001. 'Introduction', in K. Polanyi, *The Great Transformation: The Political and Economic Origins of Our Time*. Boston: Beacon Press, pp. xviii–xxxviii.

Borch, C. 2005. 'Urban Imitations: Tarde's Sociology Revisited', *Theory, Culture & Society* 22(3): 81–100.

2007. 'Crowds and Economic Life: Bringing an Old Figure Back In', *Economy and Society* 36(4): 549–73.

2008. 'Foam Architecture: Managing Co-isolated Associations', *Economy and Society* 37(4): 548–71.

2009. 'Body to Body: On the Political Anatomy of Crowds', *Sociological Theory* 27(3): 271–90.

2010. 'Between Destructiveness and Vitalism: Simmel's Sociology of Crowds', *Conserveries mémorielles* 8.

2011. *Niklas Luhmann (Key Sociologists)*. London and New York: Routledge.

2012a. 'Functional Eclecticism: On Luhmann's Style of Theorizing', *Revue Internationale de Philosophie* 66(1): 123–42.

2012b. *The Politics of Crowds: An Alternative History of Sociology*. Cambridge: Cambridge University Press.

2013a. 'Crowd Theory and the Management of Crowds: A Controversial Relationship', *Current Sociology* 61(5–6): 584–601.

2013b. 'Spatiality, Imitation, Immunization: Luhmann and Sloterdijk on the Social', in A. La Cour and A. Philippopoulos-Mihalopoulos (eds.), *Luhmann Observed: Radical Theoretical Encounters*. Houndmills, Basingstoke: Palgrave Macmillan, pp. 150–68.

2014. 'Gabriel Tarde (1843–1904)', in J. Helin, T. Hernes and R. Holt (eds.), *The Oxford Handbook of Process Philosophy and Organization Studies*. Oxford: Oxford University Press, pp. 185–201.

2015. *Foucault, Crime and Power: Problematisations of Crime in the Twentieth Century*. London and New York: Routledge.

2016. 'High-Frequency Trading, Algorithmic Finance and the Flash Crash: Reflections on Eventalization', *Economy and Society* 45(3–4): 350–78.

2017. 'Algorithmic Finance and (Limits to) Governmentality: On Foucault and High-Frequency Trading', *Le Foucaldien* 3(1): http://doi.org/10.16995/lefou.16928.

2018. 'Cool Trading', *Limn* 10: 84–8.

2019. 'The Imitative, Contagious, and Suggestible Roots of Modern Society: Toward a Mimetic Foundation of Social Theory', in C. Borch (ed.), *Imitation, Contagion, Suggestion: On Mimesis and Society*. London and New York: Routledge, pp. 3–34.

Borch, C. and Lange, A.-C. 2017a. 'High-Frequency Trader Subjectivity: Emotional Attachment and Discipline in an Era of Algorithms', *Socio-Economic Review* 15(2): 283–306.

2017b. 'Market Sociality: Mirowski, Shiller, and the Tension between Mimetic and Anti-mimetic Market Features', *Cambridge Journal of Economics* 41(4): 1197–212.

Borch, C. and Stäheli, U. (eds.). 2009. *Soziologie der Nachahmung und des Begehrens. Materialien zu Gabriel Tarde*. Frankfurt am Main: Suhrkamp.

Borch-Jacobsen, M. 2009. *Making Minds and Madness: From Hysteria to Depression*. Cambridge: Cambridge University Press.

Bourdieu, P. and Wacquant, L. D. 1992. *An Invitation to Reflexive Sociology*. Cambridge: Polity Press.

Brighenti, A. M. 2019. 'The Reactive: Social Experiences of Surface and Depth', in C. Borch (ed.), *Imitation, Contagion, Suggestion: On Mimesis and Society*. London and New York: Routledge, pp. 194–210.

Broch, H. 1955. 'A Study on Mass Hysteria. Contributions to a Psychology of Politics. Preliminary Table of Contents', in *Erkennen und Handeln. Essays, Vol. 2*. Zurich: Rhein-Verlag, pp. 257–82.

Bruce, H. A. 1923. 'Boris Sidis – An Appreciation', *Journal of Abnormal Psychology and Social Psychology* 18(3): 274–6.

Buck, J. E. 1992. *The New York Stock Exchange: The First 200 Years*. Essex, CT: Greenwich Publishing Group.

Buk-Swienty, T. 2008. *The Other Half: The Life of Jacob Riis and the World of Immigrant America*, trans. A. Buk-Swienty. New York: W. W. Norton.

Butler, J. 1991. 'Imitation and Gender Insubordination', in D. Fuss (ed.), *Inside/ Out: Lesbian Theories, Gay Theories*. New York and London: Routledge, pp. 13–31.

Böckenförde, E.-W. 2002. 'Forord til den danske udgave', in C. Schmitt, *Det politiskes begreb*, trans. L. B. Larsen and C. Borch. Copenhagen: Hans Reitzels Forlag, pp. 7–11.

Canetti, E. 1984. *Crowds and Power*, trans. C. Stewart. New York: Farrar, Straus and Giroux.

Cappetti, C. 1993. *Writing Chicago: Modernism, Ethnography, and the Novel*. New York: Columbia University Press.

Carruthers, B. C. 1996. *City of Capital: Politics and Markets in the English Financial Revolution*. Princeton: Princeton University Press.

Cassis, Y. 2012. *Capitals of Capital: The Rise and Fall of International Financial Centres, 1780–2009*, trans. J. Collier. Cambridge: Cambridge University Press.

Cassis, Y. and Wójcik, D. (eds.). 2018. *International Financial Centres after the Global Financial Crisis and Brexit*. Oxford: Oxford University Press.

Castelle, M. et al. 2016. 'Where Do Electronic Markets Come From? Regulation and the Transformation of Financial Exchanges', *Economy and Society* 45(2): 166–200.

Cederman, L.-E. 2005. 'Computational Models of Social Forms: Advancing Generative Process Theory', *American Journal of Sociology* 110(4): 864–93.

CFTC–SEC. 2010. *Findings Regarding the Market Events of May 6, 2010: Report of the Staffs of the CFTC and SEC to the Joint Advisory Committee on Emerging Regulatory Issues*. Washington, DC: The CFTC and the SEC.

Chamberlain, J. 1933. 'Books of The Times: Review of Joseph Roth, Radetzky March', *The New York Times* 17 October.

Chertok, L. and Stengers, I. 1992. *A Critique of Psychoanalytical Reason: Hypnosis as a Scientific Problem from Lavoisier to Lacan*, trans. M. Evans. Stanford, CA: Stanford University Press.

Clark, T. N. 1969. 'Introduction', in G. Tarde, *On Communication and Social Influence. Selected Papers*. Chicago and London: University of Chicago Press, pp. 1–69.

Collins, R. 2004. *Interaction Ritual Chains*. Princeton and Oxford: Princeton University Press.

Colomina, B. 1994. *Privacy and Publicity: Modern Architecture as Mass Media*. Cambridge, MA: The MIT Press.

Conrads, U. 1970. *Programs and Manifestoes on 20th-Century Architecture*. Cambridge, MA: The MIT Press.

Coombs, N. 2016. 'What Is an Algorithm? Financial Regulation in the Era of High-Frequency Trading', *Economy and Society* 45(2): 278–302.

Cooper, M. 2011. 'Complexity Theory after the Financial Crisis: The Death of Neoliberalism or the Triumph of Hayek?', *Journal of Cultural Economy* 4(4): 371–85.

Corbusier, L. 1981. *The City of To-morrow and Its Planning*, trans. F. Etchells. Mineola, NY: Dover Publications.

1986. *Towards a New Architecture*, trans. F. Etchells. Mineola, NY: Dover Publications.

Corkery, M. 2010. 'The Stock Market's Flash Crash: How to Destroy $1 Billion in 60 Minutes', *Wall Street Journal* 6 May: Retrieved from http://blogs.wsj .com/deals/2010/2005/2006/the-stock-markets-flash-crash-how-to-destroy-2011–billion-in-2060–minutes/.

Crary, J. 1999. *Suspensions of Perception: Attention, Spectacle, and Modern Culture*. Cambridge, MA: The MIT Press.

2013. *24/7: Late Capitalism and the Ends of Sleep*. London and New York: Verso.

Cronon, W. 1991. *Nature's Metropolis: Chicago and the Great West*. New York: W. W. Norton.

Crosthwaite, P. 2013. 'Animality and Ideology in Contemporary Economic Discourse: Taxonomizing Homo Economicus', *Journal of Cultural Economy* 6(1): 94–109.

Curtis, W. J. R. 1996. *Modern Architecture since 1900, third ed.* London: Phaidon.

Darnton, R. 1968. *Mesmerism and the End of the Enlightenment in France*. Cambridge, MA: Harvard University Press.

Deleuze, G. 1994. *Difference and Repetition*, trans. P. Patton. London: The Athlone Press.

Derman, E. 2004. *My Life as a Quant: Reflections in Physics and Finance*. Hoboken, NJ: John Wiley & Sons.

DiMaggio, P. J. and Powell, W. 1983. 'The Iron Cage Revisited: Institutional Isomorphism and Collective Rationality in Organizational Fields', *American Sociological Review* 48(2): 147–60.

Donald, J. 1999. *Imagining the Modern City*. London: The Athlone Press.

Durbin, M. 2010. *All about High-Frequency Trading*. New York: McGraw-Hill.

Durkheim, E. 1961. *Moral Education: A Study in the Theory and Application of the Sociology of Education*, trans. E. Wilson and H. Schnurer. New York: The Free Press.

1974. 'Individual and Collective Representations', in *Sociology and Philosophy*, trans. D. Pocock. New York: The Free Press, pp. 1–34.

1982. *The Rules of Sociological Method. And Selected Texts on Sociology and Its Method*, trans. W. Halls. London: Macmillan.

1995. *The Elementary Forms of Religious Life*, trans. K. Fields. New York: The Free Press.

2006. *On Suicide*, trans. R. Buss. London: Penguin.

2013. *The Division of Labour in Society*, trans. W. Halls. Houndmills, Basingstoke: Palgrave Macmillan.

Durkheim, E. and Fauconnet, P. 1982. 'Sociology and the Social Sciences (1903)', in E. Durkheim, *The Rules of Sociological Method and Selected Texts on Sociology and Its Method*, trans. W. Halls. New York: The Free Press, pp. 175–208.

Ellenberger, H. F. 1970. *The Discovery of the Unconscious. The History and Evolution of Dynamic Psychiatry*. London: Allen Lane The Penguin Press.

Epstein, J. M. 2006. *Generative Social Science: Studies in Agent-Based Computational Modeling*. Princeton: Princeton University Press.

Falloon, W. D. 1998. *Market Maker: A Sesquicentennial Look at the Chicago Board of Trade*. Chicago: Board of Trade of the City of Chicago.

Farmer, J. D. and Lo, A. W. 1999. 'Frontiers of Finance: Evolution and Efficient Markets', *Proceedings of the National Academy of Sciences of the USA* 96: 9991–2.

Fisher, M. S. 2012. *Wall Street Women*. Durham and London: Duke University Press.

Fishman, R. 1982. *Urban Utopias in the Twentieth Century: Ebenezer Howard, frank Lloyd Wright, and Le Corbusier*. Cambridge, MA: The MIT Press.

Fitzgerald, F. S. 2001. *The Great Gatsby*. Hertfordshire: Wordsworth Editions.

Foucault, M. 1982. 'The Subject and Power', in H. Dreyfus and P. Rabinow (eds.), *Michel Foucault: Beyond Structuralism and Hermeneutics*. Chicago: University of Chicago Press, pp. 208–26.

  1990. *The History of Sexuality, Vol. 1: An Introduction*, trans. R. Hurley. New York: Vintage Books.

Fournier, M. 2013. *Émile Durkheim: A Biography*, trans. D. Macey. Cambrige: Polity Press.

Fraser, S. 2005. *Wall Street: A Cultural History*. London: Faber and Faber.

Freud, S. 2004. 'Mass Psychology and the Analysis of the "I"', in *Mass Psychology and Other Writings*, trans. J. Underwoord. London: Penguin Books, pp. 15–100.

Friedman, M. and Friedland, G. W. 1998. *Medicine's 10 Greatest Discoveries*. New Haven and London: Yale University Press.

Frisby, D. 1997. 'Introduction to the Texts', in D. Frisby and M. Featherstone (eds.), *Simmel on Culture: Selected Writings*. London: SAGE, pp. 1–31.

  2013. *Fragments of Modernity: Theories of Modernity in the Work of Simmel, Kracauer and Benjamin*. London and New York: Routledge.

Fromm, E. 1941. *Escape from Freedom*. New York: Rinehart & Company.

Fukuyama, F. 1989. 'The End of History?', *The National Interest* 16: 3–18.

  1992. *The End of History and the Last Man*. London: Hamish Hamilton.

  2013. 'The "End of History" 20 Years Later', *New Perspectives Quarterly* 30(4): 31–9.

Gane, N. 2012. *Max Weber and Contemporary Capitalism*. Basingstoke: Palgrave Macmillan.

Giddens, A. 1984. *The Constitution of Society: Outline of the Theory of Structuration*. Cambridge: Polity Press.

Gijswijt-Hofstra, M. and Porter, R. (eds.) 2001. *Cultures of Neurasthenia: From Beard to the First World War*. Amsterdam and New York: Rodopi.

Gilbert, N. and Abbott, A. 2005. 'Introduction', *American Journal of Sociology* 110(4): 859–63.

Girard, R. 1977. *Violence and the Sacred*, trans. P. Gregory. Baltimore and London: The Johns Hopkins University Press.

  1987. *Things Hidden since the Foundation of the World*, trans. S. Bann and M. Metteer. London: The Athlone Press.

Gladwell, M. 2000. *The Tipping Point: How Little Things Can Make a Big Difference*. London: Little, Brown.

Gleber, A. 1999. *The Art of Taking a Walk: Flanerie, Literature, and Film in Weimar Culture*. Princeton: Princeton University Press.

Goffman, E. 1983. 'The Interaction Order', *American Sociological Review* 48(1): 1–17.

Goldberg, A. and Stein, S. K. 2018. 'Beyond Social Contagion: Associative Diffusion and the Emergence of Cultural Variation', *American Sociological Review* 83(5): 897–932.

Golub, A., Keane, J. and Poon, S.-H. 2012. 'High Frequency Trading and Mini Flash Crashes'. Available at SSRN: http://ssrn.com/abstract=2182097 (accessed 20 October 2014).

Golumbia, D. 2013. 'High-Frequency Trading: Networks of Wealth and the Concentration of Power', *Social Semiotics* 23(2): 278–99.

Granovetter, M. 1985. 'Economic Action and Social Structure: The Problem of Embeddedness', *American Journal of Sociology* 91(3): 481–510.

Hacking, I. 1983. *Representing and Intervening: Introductory Topics in the Philosophy of Natural Science*. Cambridge: Cambridge University Press.

Haldane, A. G. and May, R. M. 2011. 'Systemic Risk in Banking Ecosystems', *Nature* 469(7330): 351–5.

Hall, P. 2002. *Cities of Tomorrow: An Intellectual History of Urban Planning and Design in the Twentieth Century, third ed.* Oxford: Blackwell.

Hall, P., Hardy, D. and Ward, C. 2003. 'Commentators' Introduction', in E. Howard, *To-morrow: A Peaceful Path to Real Freedom*. London and New York: Routledge, pp. 1–8.

Hansen, K. B. 2015. 'Contrarian Investment Philosophy in the American Stock Market: On Investment Advice and the Crowd Conundrum', *Economy and Society* 44(4): 616–38.

  2017. *Crowds and Speculation: A Study of Crowd Phemomena in the U.S. Financial Markets, 1890–1940*. Frederiksberg: Copenhagen Business School, the Doctoral School of Organisation and Management Studies.

Hansen, K. B. and Borch, C. 2019. 'Market Mimesis: Imitation, Contagion, and Suggestion in Financial Markets', in C. Borch (ed.), *Imitation, Contagion, Suggestion: On Mimesis and Society*. London and New York: Routledge, pp. 91–106.

Harper, H. H. 1926. *The Psychology of Speculation: The Human Element in Stock Market Transactions*. Boston, MA: Henry Howard Harper.

Harrington, A. 1987. *Medicine, Mind, and the Double Brain: A Study in Nineteenth-Century Thought*. Princeton: Princeton University Press.

Harrington, A. 2002. 'Robert Musil and Classical Sociology', *Journal of Classical Sociology* 2(1): 59–76.

Harris, R. 2012. *The Fear Index*. London: Arrow Books.

Hartman, S. R. 2006. 'Sword, Shield, or Simply a Constitutional Right? Patents in the Futures Industry', *Futures & Derivatives Law Report* 26(8): 1–9.

Hayden, C. 2003. *When Nature Goes Public: The Making and Unmaking of Bioprospecting in Mexico*. Princeton and Oxford: Princeton University Press.

Hegel, G. W. F. 1991. *Elements of the Philosophy of Right*, trans. H. Nisbet. Cambridge: Cambridge University Press.

Hickok, G. 2014. *The Myth of Mirror Neurons: The Real Neuroscience of Communication and Cognition*. New York and London: W. W. Norton & Company.

Hitchcock, H.-R. and Johnson, P. 1995. *The International Style*. New York: W. W. Norton.

Hitler, A. 1992. *Mein Kampf*, trans. R. Manheim. London: Pimlico.

Hofmann, M. 2002. 'Translator's Introduction', in J. Roth, *The Radetzsky March*. London: Granta Books, pp. v–xvi.

Howard, E. 2003. *To-morrow: A Peaceful Path to Real Reform*. London and New York: Routledge.

Hughes, E. C. 1961. 'Tarde's *Psychologie économique*: An Unknown Classic by a Forgotten Sociologist', *American Journal of Sociology* 66(6): 553–9.

Isenberg, B. 2018. 'A Modern Calamity – Robert Musil on Stupidity', *Journal of Classical Sociology* 18(1): 55–75.

Ivanov, S. I. 2011. 'The Effects of Crisis on the Cointegration between the S&P 100 and the S&P 500 Indexes', *International Journal of Finance* 23(2): 6783–97.

James, W. 1898. 'Introduction', in B. Sidis, *The Psychology of Suggestion*. New York and London: D. Appleton and Company, pp. v–vii.

2000. 'The One and the Many', in *Pragmatism and Other Writings*. London: Penguin Books, pp. 58–73.

Jasper, J. M. 1998. 'The Emotions of Protest: Affective and Reactive Emotions in and around Social Movements', *Sociological Forum* 13(3): 397–424.

Jennings, R. S. 1878. *Improvement in Trading-Pits*. Chicago, IL: United States Patent No. 203,837.

Johnson, N., et al. 2012. 'Financial Black Swans Driven by Ultrafast Machine Ecology': http://arxiv.org/abs/1202.1448 (accessed on 16 June 2015).

et al. 2013. 'Abrupt Rise of New Machine Ecology beyond Human Response Time', *Scientific Reports* 3: Article number: 2627.

Jones, E. D. 1900. *Economic Crises*. New York: The Macmillan Company.

Jonsson, S. 2000. *Subject without Nation: Robert Musil and the History of Modern Identity*. Durham and London: Duke University Press.

2001. 'Society Degree Zero: Christ, Communism, and the Madness of Crowds in the Art of James Ensor', *Representations* 75(1): 1–32.

2013. *Crowds and Democracy: The Idea and Image of the Masses from Revolution to Fascism*. New York: Columbia University Press.

Karppi, T. and Crawford, K. 2016. 'Social Media, Financial Algorithms and the Hack Crash', *Theory, Culture & Society* 33(1): 73–92.

Karsenti, B. 2010. 'Imitation: Returning to the Tarde–Durkheim Debate', in M. Candea (ed.), *The Social after Gabriel Tarde: Debates and Assessments*. London and New York: Routledge, pp. 44–61.

Katz, E. 2006. 'Rediscovering Gabriel Tarde', *Political Communication* 23(3): 263–70.

Kelly, F. C. 1930. *Why You Win or Lose: The Psychology of Speculation*. Boston, MA: Houghton Mifflin.

Kenett, D., et al. 2013. 'How High Frequency Trading Affects a Market Index', *Scientific Reports* 3: Article number: 2110.

King, A. 2016. 'Gabriel Tarde and Contemporary Social Theory', *Sociological Theory* 34(1): 45–61.

Kirilenko, A., et al. 2014. *The Flash Crash: The Impact of High Frequency Trading on an Electronic Market*. Washington, DC: The CFTC.

Kirilenko, A. and Lo, A. 2013. 'Moore's Law versus Murphy's Law: Algorithmic Trading and its Discontents', *Journal of Economic Perspectives* 27(2): 51–72.

Kirilenko, A., Sowers, R. and Meng, X. 2013. 'A Multiscale Model of High-Frequency Trading', *Algorithmic Finance* 2: 59–98.

Kittler, F. A. 1990. *Discourse Networks 1800/1900*, trans. M. Metteer, with C. Cullens. Stanford, CA: Stanford University Press.

  1999. *Gramophone, Film, Typewriter*, trans. G. Winthrop-Young and M. Wutz. Stanford, CA: Stanford University Press.

Knight, W. 2012. 'Watch High-Speed Trading Bots Go Berserk', *MIT Technology Review*: Retrieved from www.technologyreview.com/s/428756/watch-high-speed-trading-bots-go-berserk/.

Knorr Cetina, K. and Bruegger, U. 2000. 'The Market as an Object of Attachment: Exploring Postsocial Relations in Financial Markets', *Canadian Journal of Sociology* 25(2): 141–68.

  2002. 'Traders' Engagement with Markets: A Postsocial Relationship', *Theory, Culture & Society* 19(5/6): 161–85.

Kracauer, S. 1975. 'The Mass Ornament', *New German Critique* 5(Spring): 67–76.

Kynaston, D. 2012. *City of London: The History*. London: Vintage Books.

Lange, A.-C. 2015. '*Crowding of Adaptive Strategies: Swarm Theory and High-Frequency Trading*'. Frederiksberg: Copenhagen Business School, unpublished manuscript.

  2016. 'Organizational Ignorance: An Ethnographic Study of High-Frequency Trading', *Economy and Society* 45(2): 230–50.

  2020. 'High-Frequency Trading and Spoofing', in C. Borch and R. Wosnitzer (eds.), *The Routledge Handbook of Critical Finance Studies*. London and New York: Routledge.

Lange, A.-C., Lenglet, M. and Seyfert, R. 2016. 'Cultures of High-Frequency Trading: Mapping the Landscape of Algorithmic Developments in Contemporary Financial Markets', *Economy and Society* 45(2): 149–65.

Latour, B. 2002. 'Gabriel Tarde and the End of the Social', in P. Joyce (ed.), *The Social in Question: New Bearings in History and the Social Sciences*. London and New York: Routledge, pp. 117–32.

  2005. *Reassembling the Social: An Introduction to Actor-Network-Theory*. Oxford: Oxford University Press.

Lauricella, T., Scannell, K. and Strasburg, J. 2010. 'How a Trading Algorithm Went Awry: Flash-Crash Report Finds a "Hot-Potato" Volume Effect from

Same Positions Passed Back and Forth', *Wall Street Journal* 2 October: Retrieved from www.wsj.com/articles/SB10001424052748704029304575526390131916792.

Lawtoo, N. 2013. *The Phantom of the Ego: Modernism and the Mimetic Unconscious.* East Lansing, MI: Michigan State University Press.

2019. 'The Mimetic Unconscious: A Mirror for Genealogical Reflections', in C. Borch (ed.), *Imitation, Contagion, Suggestion: On Mimesis and the Social.* London and New York: Routledge, pp. 37–53.

Le Bon, G. 1974. *The Psychology of Peoples.* New York: Arno Press.

2001. *The Psychology of Socialism.* Kitchener, Ontario: Batoche Books.

2002. *The Crowd: A Study of the Popular Mind.* Mineola, NY: Dover.

Leal, S. J., et al. 2014. 'Rock around the Clock: An Agent-Based Model of Low- and High-Frequency Trading': http://arxiv.org/abs/1402.2046 (accessed on 15 June 2015).

Lepenies, W. 1988. *Between Literature and Science: The Rise of Sociology*, trans. R. Hollingdale. Cambridge: Cambridge University Press.

Lethen, H. 2002. *Cool Conduct: The Culture of Distance in Weimar Germany*, trans. D. Reneau. Berkeley, CA: University of California Press.

Levine, D. N. 1995. 'The Organism Metaphor in Sociology', *Social Research* 62 (2): 239–65.

Lewis, M. 2014. *Flash Boys: Cracking the Money Code.* London: Allen Lane.

Lewis, T. G. 2011. *Bak's Sand Pile: Strategies for a Catastrophic World.* Williams, CA: Agile Press.

Leys, R. 1993. 'Mead's Voices: Imitation as Foundation, or, the Struggle against Mimesis', *Critical Inquiry* 19(2): 277–307.

2000. *Trauma: A Genealogy.* Chicago and London: University of Chicago Press.

2007. *From Guilt to Shame: Auschwitz and After.* Princeton and Oxford: Princeton University Press.

Lofland, J. 1982. 'Crowd Joys', *Urban Life* 10(4): 355–81.

Lombroso, C. 2006. *Criminal Man*, trans. M. Gibson and N. Rafter. Durham and London: Duke University Press.

Loos, A. 1998a. 'Ornament and Crime', in *Ornament and Crime, Selected Essays*, trans. M. Mitchell. Riverside, CA: Ariadne Press, pp. 167–76.

1998b. *Ornament and Crime: Selected Essays*, trans. M. Mitchell. Riverside, CA: Ariadne Press.

2011a. 'Men's Fashion', in *Why a Man Should Be Well-Dressed.* Viena: Metroverlag, pp. 28–36.

2011b. *Why a Man Should Be Well-Dressed*, trans. M. Troy. Viena: Metroverlag.

Lorenc, T. 2012. 'Afterword: Tarde's Pansocial Ontology', in G. Tarde, *Monadology and Sociology.* Melbourne: re.press, pp. 71–95.

Luce, E. 2017. *The Retreat of Western Liberalism.* New York: Atlantic Monthly Press.

Luhmann, N. 1964. 'Funktionale Methode und Systemtheorie', *Soziale Welt* 15: 1–25.

1980. 'Gesellschaftliche Struktur und semantische Tradition', in *Gesellschaftsstruktur und Semantik. Studien zur Wissenssoziologie der modernen Gesellschaft.* Frankfurt am Main: Suhrkamp, pp. 9–71.

1982. 'Durkheim on Morality and the Division of Labor', in *The Differentiation of Society*, trans. S. Holmes and C. Larmore. New York: Columbia University Press, pp. 3–19.

1989. 'Individuum, Individualität, Individualismus', in *Gesellschaftsstruktur und Semantik, Vol. 3*. Frankfurt am Main: Suhrkamp, pp. 149–258.

1990. 'The Autopoiesis of Social Systems', in *Essys on Self-Reference*. New York: Columbia University Press, pp. 1–20.

1993. 'Observing Re-entries', *Graduate Faculty Philosophy Journal* 16(2): 485–98.

1995. *Social Systems*, trans. J. Bednarz, Jr., with D. Baecker. Stanford, CA: Stanford University Press.

1998. 'Contingency as Modern Society's Defining Attribute', in *Observations on Modernity*, trans. W. Whobrey. Stanford, CA: Stanford University Press, pp. 44–62.

2012. *Theory of Society*, trans. R. Barrett. Stanford, CA: Stanford University Press.

2013. *Introduction to Systems Theory*, trans. P. Gilgen. Cambridge: Polity Pres.

Lukes, S. 1969. 'Durkheim's "Individualism and the Intellectuals"', *Political Studies* 17(1): 14–30.

1985. *Emile Durkheim: His Life and Work: A Historical and Critical Study*. Stanford, CA: Stanford University Press.

Lukken, W. (2004). 'Patent Pending: The Role of the CFTC in Intellectual Property Disputes Chicago, IL: Intellectual Property Panel at FIA Expo': www.cftc.gov/sites/default/files/opa/speeches04/opalukken-10.htm#fnB2 (accessed 20 August 2018).

Löfgren, O. 2015. 'Sharing an Atmosphere: Spaces in Urban Commons', in C. Borch and M. Kornberger (eds.), *Urban Commons: Rethinking the City*. London and New York: Routledge, pp. 68–91.

MacKenzie, D. 2015. 'Mechanizing the Merc: The Chicago Mercantile Exchange and the Rise of High-Frequency Trading', *Technology and Culture* 56(3): 646–75.

2017. 'Capital's Geodesic: Chicago, New Jersey, and the Material Sociology of Speed', in J. Wachman and N. Dodd (eds.), *The Sociology of Speed: Digital, Organizational, and Social Temporalities*. Oxford: Oxford University Press, pp. 55–71.

2018. 'Material Signals: A Historical Sociology of High-Frequency Trading', *American Journal of Sociology* 123(6): 1635–83.

2019. 'How Algorithms Interact: Goffman's "Interaction Order" in Automated Trading', *Theory, Culture & Society* 36(2): 39–59.

et al. 2012. 'Drilling through the Allegheny Mountains: Liquidity, Materiality and High-Frequency Trading', *Journal of Cultural Economy* 5(3): 279–96.

MacKenzie, D. and Millo, Y. 2003. 'Constructing a Market, Performing Theory: The Historical Sociology of a Financial Derivatives Exchange', *American Journal of Sociology* 109(1): 107–45.

MacKenzie, D. and Pardo-Guerra, J. P. 2014. 'Insurgent Capitalism: Island, Bricolage and the Re-making of Finance', *Economy and Society* 43(2): 153–82.

Macy, M. W. and Willer, R. 2002. 'From Factors to Actors: Computational Sociology and Agent-Based Modeling', *Annual Review of Sociology* 28(1): 143–66.

Maffesoli, M. 1996. *The Time of the Tribes: The Decline of Individualism in Mass Society*, trans. D. Smith. London: SAGE.

Malinova, K., Park, A. and Riordan, R. 2013. Do Retail Traders Suffer from High Frequency Traders? Unpublished manuscript.

Malmgren, H. and Stys, M. 2011. 'Computerized Global Trading 24/6 A Roller Coaster Ride Ahead?', *International Economy* 25(2): 30–62.

Marcuse, H. 1991. *One-Dimensional Man: Studies in the Ideology of Advanced Industrial Society*. London: Routledge.

Marshall, G. (ed.) 2007. *The Cambridge Companion to the fin de siècle*. Cambridge: Cambridge University Press.

Marvin, C. 1988. *When Old Technologies Were New: Thinking about Electric Communication in the Late Nineteenth Century*. Oxford: Oxford University Press.

Marx, K. and Engels, F. 2012. *The Communist Manifesto*. New Haven and London: Yale University Press.

Maturana, H. 1981. 'Autopoiesis', in M. Zeleny (ed.), *Autopoiesis: A Theory of Living Organization*. New York and Oxford: North Holland, pp. 21–33.

Mayer, A. 1981. *The Persistence of the Old Regime: Europe to the Great War*. New York: Pantheon Books.

Mayntz, R. 1990. *The Influence of Natural Science Theories on Contemporary Social Science*. Cologne: MPIfG Discussion Paper, No. 90/7, Max-Planck-Institut für Gesellschaftsforschung.

Mazzarella, W. 2010. 'The Myth of the Multitude, or, Who's Afraid of the Crowd?', *Critical Inquiry* 36(4): 697–727.

  2017. *The Mana of Mass Society*. Chicago and London: University of Chicago Press.

McAdam, D. 2007. 'From Relevance to Irrelevance: The Curious Impact of the Sixties on Public Sociology', in C. Calhoun (ed.), *Sociology in America: A History*. Chicago and London: University of Chicago Press, pp. 411–26.

McCarthy, J. D. 1991. 'Foreword', in C. McPhail, *The Myth of the Madding Crowd*. New York: Aldine de Gruyter, pp. xi–xviii.

McClelland, J. S. 1989. *The Crowd and the Mob: From Plato to Canetti*. London: Unwin Hyman.

McPhail, C. 1991. *The Myth of the Madding Crowd*. New York: Aldine de Gruyter.

  2006. 'The Crowd and Collective Behavior: Bringing Symbolic Interaction Back In', *Symbolic Interaction* 29(4): 433–64.

McPhail, C., et al. 2015. 'The Dynamic Complexity of Collective Action in Temporary Gatherings'. Unpublished manuscript.

Mead, G. H. 1934. *Mind, Self, and Society: From the Standpoint of a Social Behaviorist*. Chicago and London: University of Chicago Press.

Mellers, W. and Hildyard, R. 1989. 'The Cultural and Social Setting', in B. Ford (ed.), *The Cambridge Cultural History of Britain, Volume 8: Early Twentieth-Century Britain*. Cambridge: Cambridge University Press, pp. 3–44.

Melloy, J. 2010. 'Traders See Black Hole Effect as Sell-off Feeds on Itself', *CNBC* 6 May. Retrieved from eww.cnbc.com/id/36997706.

Mezias, S. J. 1994. 'Financial Meltdown as Normal Accident: The Case of the American Savings and Loan Industry', *Accounting, Organizations and Society* 19(2): 181–92.

Mitchell, P. 2012. *Contagious Metaphor*. London: Bloomsbury.

Moebius, S. 2004. 'Imitation, Repetition and Iterability: Poststructuralism and the "Social Laws" of Gabrial Tarde', *Distinktion* 9: 55–69.

Moscovici, S. 1985. *The Age of the Crowd: A Historical Treatise on Mass Psychology*. Cambridge: Cambridge University Press.

Mucchielli, L. 2000. 'Tardomania? Réflexions sur les usages contemporains de Tarde', *Revue d'Histoire des Sciences Humaines* 3: 161–84.

Murray, D. 2017. *The Strange Death of Europe: Immigration, Identity, Islam*. London: Bloomsbury.

Müller, J.-W. 2011. *Contesting Democracy: Political Ideas in Twentieth-Century Europe*. New Haven and London: Yale University Press.

2016. *What Is Populism?* Philadelphia: University of Pennsylvania Press.

Nations, S. 2017. *A History of the United States in Five Crashes: Stock Market Meltdowns That Defined a Nation*. New York: Willian Morrow.

Niezen, R. 2014. 'Gabriel Tarde's Publics', *History of the Human Sciences* 27(2): 41–59.

Nisbet, R. A. 2017. *Sociology as an Art Form*. London and New York: Routledge.

Norris, F. 1994. *The Pit: A Story of Chicago*. London: Penguin Books.

Orléan, A. 1989. 'Mimetic Contagion and Speculative Bubbles', *Theory and Decision* 27(1–2): 63–92.

Ortega y Gasset, J. 1960. *The Revolt of the Masses*. New York and London: W. W. Norton & Company.

Pardo-Guerra, J. P. 2010. 'Creating Flows of Interpersonal Bits: The Automation of the London Stock Exchange, c. 1955–90', *Economy and Society* 39(1): 84–109.

2019. *Automating Finance: Infrastructures, Engineers, and the Making of Electronic Markets* Cambridge: Cambridge University Press.

Park, R. E. 1915. 'The City: Suggestions for the Investigation of Human Behavior in the City Environment', *American Journal of Sociology* XX(5): 577–612.

1972. *The Crowd and the Public and Other Essays*. Chicago and London: University of Chicago Press.

Park, R. E. and Burgess, E. W. 1921. *Introduction to the Science of Sociology*. Chicago, IL: University of Chicago Press.

Patton, P. 2010. *Deleuzian Concepts: Philosophy, Colonization, Politics*. Stanford, CA: Stanford University Press.

Peckham, R. 2013a. 'Contagion: Epidemiological Models and Financial Crises', *Journal of Public Health* 36(1): 13–17.

2013b. 'Economies of Contagion: Financial Crisis and Pandemic', *Economy and Society* 42(2): 226–48.

Perrow, C. 1994. *Normal Accidents: Living with High-Risk Technologies*, revised ed. Princeton: Princeton University Press.

Petram, L. 2014. *The World's First Stock Exchange*, trans. L. Richards. New York: Columbia University Press.

Phillips, M. 2010a. 'Stock Market Fear Gauge up 60%, and Staying There', *Wall Street Journal* 6 May: Retrieved from http://blogs.wsj.com/marketbeat/2010/2005/2006/stock-market-fear-gauge-up-2060–and-staying-there/.

2010b. 'Stock Tumble: What Have You Heard Explain the Selloff?', *Wall Street Journal* 6 May: Retrieved from http://blogs.wsj.com.escweb.lib.cbs.dk/marketbeat/2010/2005/2006/stocktumblewhathaveyouheardexplaintheselloff/.

Polanyi, K. 2001. *The Great Transformation: The Political and Economic Origins of Our Time*. Boston: Beacon Press.

Poovey, M. 2008. *Genres of the Credit Economy: Mediating Value in Eighteenth- and Nineteenth-Century Britain*. Chicago and London: University of Chicago Press.

Pred, A. 1990. *Lost Words and Lost Worlds: Modernity and the Language of Everyday Life in Late Nineteenth-Century Stockholm*. Cambridge: Cambridge University Press.

Preda, A. 2006. 'Socio-Technical Agency in Financial Markets: The Case of the Stock Ticker', *Social Studies of Science* 36(5): 753–82.

2009a. 'Brief Encounters: Calculation and the Interaction Order of Anonymous Electronic Markets', *Accounting, Organizations and Society* 34(5): 675–93.

2009b. *Framing Finance: The Boundaries of Markets and Modern Capitalism*. Chicago and London: University of Chicago Press.

2017. *Noise: Living and Trading in Electronic Finance*. Chicago and London: University of Chicago Press.

Presskorn-Thygesen, T. 2017. *The Significance of Normativity: Studies in Post-Kantian Philosophy and Social Theory*. Frederiksberg: Copenhagen Business School, the Doctoral School of Organisation and Management Studies.

Radkau, J. 1998. *Das Zeitalter der Nervosität: Deutschland zwischen Bismarck and Hitler*. Munich: Carl Hanser Verlag.

Reich, W. 1971. *The Function of the Orgasm*, trans. T. Wolfe. New York: World Publishing.

1975. *The Mass Psychology of Fascism*, trans. V. Carfagno. Harmondsworth: Penguin Books.

Reynolds, G. 2001. 'Introduction: The "Constant Flicker" of the American Scene', in F. S. Fitzgerald, *The Great Gatsby*. Hertfordshire: Wordsworth Editions, pp. v–xix.

Riesman, D. 1950. *The Lonely Crowd: A Study of the Changing American Character*. New Haven, CT: Yale University Press.

1961. '*The Lonely Crowd*: A Reconsideration in 1960, with the Collaboration of Nathan Glazer', in S. M. Lipset and L. Lowenthal (eds.), *Culture and Social Character: The Work of David Riesman Reviewed*. New York: The Free Press, pp. 419–58.

Rosa, H., Dörre, K. and Lessenich, S. 2017. 'Appropriation, Activation and Acceleration: The Escalatory Logics of Capitalist Modernity and the Crises of Dynamic Stabilization', *Theory, Culture & Society* 34(1): 53–73.

Ross, E. A. 1897. 'The Mob Mind', *Popular Science Monthly* July: 390–8.

1908. *Social Psychology: An Outline and Source Book*. New York: Macmillan.

Roth, J. 2002. *The Radetzsky March*, trans. M. Hofmann. London: Granta Books.

2003. *What I Saw: Reports from Berlin, 1920–33*, trans. M. Hofmann. London: Granta.

2015. 'His K. and K. Apostolic Majesty', in *The Hotel Years*, trans. M. Hofmann. London: Granta Books, pp. 91–7.

Rothe, K. 2019. 'Mimesis as a Social Practice of Self-Education', in C. Borch (ed.), *Imitation, Contagion, Suggestion: On Mimesis and Society*. London and New York: Routledge, pp. 73–88.

Runciman, D. 2018. *How Democracy Ends*. New York: Basic Books.

Sampson, T. D. 2012. *Virality: Contagion Theory in the Age of Networks*. Minneapolis, MN: Minnesota University Press.

Sánchez, R. 2016. *Dancing Jacobins: A Venezuelan Genealogy of Latin American Populism*. New York: Fordham University Press.

Sassen, S. 2005. 'The Embeddedness of Electronic Markets: The Case of Global Capital Markets', in K. Knorr Cetina and A. Preda (eds.), *The Sociology of Financial Markets*. Oxford: Oxford University Press, pp. 17–37.

Scharfstein, D. S. and Stein, J. C. 1990. 'Herd Behavior and Investment', *American Economic Review* 80: 465–79.

Scheler, M. 2008. *The Nature of Sympathy*. New Brunswick, NJ, and London: Transaction Publishers.

Schiermer, B. 2016. 'On the Ageing of Objects in Modern Culture: Ornament and Crime', *Theory, Culture & Society* 33(4): 127–50.

2019. 'Durkheim on Imitation', in C. Borch (ed.), *Imitation, Contagion, Suggestion: On Mimesis and the Social*. London and New York: Routledge, pp. 54–72.

Schmitt, C. 1996. *The Concept of the Political*, trans. G. Schwab. Chicago and London: University of Chicago Press.

2003. *The Nomos of the Earth in the International Law of the Jus Publicum Europaeum*, trans. G. Ulmen. New York: Telos Press.

Schneiberg, M. and Bartley, T. 2010. 'Regulating or Redesigning Finance? Market Architectures, Normal Accidents, and Dilemmas of Regulatory Reform', in M. Lounsbury and P. M. Hirsch (eds.), *Markets on Trial: The Economic Sociology of the U.S. Financial Crisis: Part A*. Bingley: Emerald Group Publishing, pp. 281–307.

Schuster, D. G. 2011. *Neurasthenic Nation: America's Search for Health, Happiness, and Comfort, 1869–1920*. New Brunswick, NJ: Rutgers University Press.

Schwartz, B. 1975. *Queuing and Waiting: Studies in the Social Organization of Access and Delay*. Chicago and London: University of Chicago Press.

Scott, W. D. 1908. *The Psychology of Advertising: A Simple Exposition of The Principles of Psychology in Their Relation to Successful Advertising*. Boston: Small, Maynard & Company.

Selden, G. C. 1912. *Psychology of the Stock Market*. New York: Ticker Publishing Company.

Shiller, R. J. 1984. 'Stock Prices and Social Dynamics', *Brookings Papers on Economic Activity* 2: 457–510.

2015. *Irrational Exuberance, third ed.* Princeton and Oxford: Princeton University Press.

Sidis, B. 1895. 'A Study of the Mob', *Atlantic Monthly* 75: 188–197.

1898. *The Psychology of Suggestion: A Research into the Subconscious Nature of Man and Society.* New York and London: D. Appleton and Company.

Simmel, G. 1950a. 'Fundamental Problems of Sociology (Individual and Society)', in *The Sociology of Georg Simmel*, trans. K. Wolff. New York: The Free Press, pp. 1–84.

1950b. 'The Metropolis and Mental Life', in *The Sociology of Georg Simmel*, trans. K. Wolff. New York: The Free Press, pp. 409–24.

1950c. 'On the Significance of Numbers for Social Life', in *The Sociology of Georg Simmel*, trans. K. Wolff. New York: The Free Press, pp. 87–104.

1950d. *The Sociology of Georg Simmel*, trans. K. Wolff. New York: The Free Press.

1957. 'Fashion', *American Journal of Sociology* 62(6): 541–58.

1971. 'Sociability', in *Georg Simmel on Individuality and Social Forms. Selected Writings.* Chicago and London: University of Chicago Press, pp. 127–40.

1989. 'Über sociale Differenzierung: Sociologische und psychologische Untersuchungen', in *Georg Simmel Gesamtausgabe, Vol. 2.* Frankfurt am Main: Suhrkamp, pp. 109–295.

1992a. *Soziologie. Untersuchungen über die Formen der Vergesellschaftlichung.* Frankfurt am Main: Suhrkamp.

1992b. 'Zur Psychologie der Mode. Sociologische Studie', in *Georg Simmel Gesamtausgabe, Vol. 5.* Frankfurt am Main: Suhrkamp, pp. 105–14.

1997a. 'The Berlin Trade Exhibition', in D. Frisby and M. Featherstone (eds.), *Simmel on Culture: Selected Writings.* London: SAGE, pp. 255–8.

1997b. 'The Concept and Tragedy of Culture', in D. Frisby and M. Featherstone (eds.), *Simmel on Culture: Selected Writings.* London: SAGE, pp. 55–75.

1997c. 'The Metropolis and Mental Life', in D. Frisby and M. Featherstone (eds.), *Simmel on Culture: Selected Writings.* London: SAGE, pp. 174–85.

1997d. 'The Philosophy of Fashion', in D. Frisby and M. Featherstone (eds.), *Simmel on Culture: Selected Writings.* London: SAGE, pp. 187–206.

1999a. 'Book Review: Gabriel Tarde, *Les lois de L'imitation*', in *Georg Simmel Gesamtausgabe, Vol. 1.* Frankfurt am Main: Suhrkamp, pp. 248–50.

1999b. 'Book Review: Gustave Le Bon, *Psychologie des Foules*', in *Georg Simmel Gesamtausgabe, Vol. 1.* Frankfurt am Main: Suhrkamp, pp. 353–61.

1999c. 'Book Review: Scipio Sighele, *Psychologie des Auflaufs und der Massenverbrechen*', in *Georg Simmel Gesamtausgabe, Vol. 1.* Frankfurt am Main: Suhrkamp, pp. 388–400.

2011. *The Philosophy of Money*, trans. D. Frisby and T. Bottomore. London and New York: Routledge.

Simpson, G. 2002. 'Editor's Introduction: The Aetiology of Suicide', in E. Durkheim, *Suicide: A Study in Sociology*, trans. J. Spaulding and G. Simpson. London and New York: Routledge, pp. xiii–xxxii.

Sloterdijk, P. 2004. *Sphären III. Schäume: Plurale Sphärologie*. Frankfurt am Main: Suhrkamp.

Snider, L. 2014. 'Interrogating the Algorithm: Debt, Derivatives and the Social Reconstruction of Stock Market Trading', *Critical Sociology* 40(5): 747–61.

Sobel, R. 1965. *The Big Board: A History of the New York Stock Market*. New York: The Free Press.

Sornette, D. and von der Becke, S. 2011. *Crashes and High Frequency Trading: An Evaluation of Risks Posed by High-Speed Algorithmic Trading*. Zurich: Swiss Finance Institute, Research Paper Series No 11 – 63.

Spencer-Brown, G. 1969. *Laws of Form*. London: George Allen and Unwin.

Spengler, O. 1980a. *The Decline of the West, Vol. I: Form and Actuality*, trans. C. Atkinson. London: George Allen & Unwin.

1980b. *The Decline of the West, Vol. II: Perspectives of World-History*, trans. C. Atkinson. London: George Allen & Unwin.

Squazzoni, F. 2012. *Agent-Based Computational Sociology*. Chichester: Wiley.

Stark, D. 2009. *The Sense of Dissonance: Accounts of Worth in Economic Life*. Princeton and Oxford: Princeton University Press.

Stewart, J. 2000. *Fashioning Vienna: Adolf Loos's Cultural Criticism*. London and New York: Routledge.

Stäheli, U. 1997. 'Exorcising the "Popular" Seriously: Luhmann's Concept of Semantics', *International Review of Sociology* 7(1): 127–45.

2006. 'Market Crowds', in J. T. Schnapp and M. Tiews (eds.), *Crowds*. Stanford, CA: Stanford University Press, pp. 271–87.

2009. 'Übersteigerte Nachahmung – Tardes Massentheorie', in C. Borch and U. Stäheli (eds.), *Soziologie der Nachahmung und des Begehrens: Materialien zu Gabriel Tarde*. Frankfurt am Main: Suhrkamp, pp. 397–416.

2013. *Spectacular Speculation: Thrills, the Economy, and Popular Discourse*, trans. E. Savoth. Stanford, CA: Stanford University Press.

Sukov, M. 1971. 'Introduction to Reprint Edition', in G. M. Beard, *A Practical Treatise on Nervous Exhaustion (Neurasthenia): Its Symptoms, Nature, Sequences, Treatment*. New York: Kraus Reprint Co, pp. 2a–2e.

Swedberg, R. 2014. *The Art of Social Theory*. Princeton and Oxford: Princeton University Press.

Taleb, N. N. 2010. *The Black Swan: The Impact of the Highly Improbable, revised ed*. London: Penguin Books.

Tarde, G. 1892. 'Les crimes des foules', *Archives de l'Anthropologie Criminelle* 7: 353–86.

1893. 'Foules et sectes au point de vue criminel', *Revue des Deux Mondes* 332: 349–87.

1899. *Social Laws: An Outline of Sociology*, trans. H. Warren. New York: The Macmillan Company.

1902. *L'invention considérée comme moteur de l'évolution sociale*. Paris: V. Giard & E. Brière.

1903. 'Inter-Psychology, the Inter-Play of Human Minds', *International Quarterly* 7: 59–84.

1962. *The Laws of Imitation*, trans. E. Parsons. Gloucester, MA: Peter Smith.

1968. *Penal Philosophy*, trans. R. Howell. Montclair, NJ: Patterson Smith.

1969. *On Communication and Social Influence: Selected papers*. Chicago and London: University of Chicago Press.

1972. *La philosophie pénale*. Paris: Éditions cujas.

1989. *L'opinion et la foule*. Paris: Presses Universitaires de France.

2012. *Monadology and Sociology*, trans. T. Lorenc. Melbourne: re.press.

2013. 'Conviction and the Crowd', *Distinktion: Scandinavian Journal of Social Theory* 14(2): 232–9.

Tarde, G. and Durkheim, E. 2010. 'The Debate (Script by Eduardo Viana Vargas, Bruno Latour, Bruno Karsenti, Frédérique Aît-Touati and Louise Salmon)', in M. Candea (ed.), *The Social after Gabriel Tarde: Debates and Assessments*. London and New York: Routledge, pp. 27–43.

Taussig, M. 1993. *Mimesis and Alterity: A Particular History of the Senses*. New York and London: Routledge.

Thomassen, B. and Szakolczai, A. 2011. 'Gabriel Tarde as Political Anthropologist', *International Political Anthropology* 4(1): 41–60.

Thompson, E. 2002. *The Soundscape of Modernity: Architectural Acoustics and the Culture of Listening in America, 1900–1933*. Cambridge, MA: The MIT Press.

Thompson, E. P. 1971. 'The Moral Economy of the English Crowd in the Eighteenth Century', *Past and Present* 50(February): 76–136.

Thompson, G. F. 2017. 'Time, Trading and Algorithms in Financial Sector Security', *New Political Economy* 22(1): 1–11.

Thrift, N. 2008a. *Non-Representational Theory: Space, Politics, Affect*. London and New York: Routledge.

2008b. 'Pass It On: Towards a Political Economy of Propensity', *Emotion, Space and Society* 1(2): 83–96.

Tickner, L. 2000. *Modern Life & Modern Subjects: British Art in the Early Twentieth Century*. New Haven and London: Yale University Press.

Tonkonoff, S. 2013. 'A New Social Physic: The Sociology of Gabriel Tarde and Its Legacy', *Current Sociology* 61(3): 267–82.

Torres, E. C. 2014. 'Durkheim's Concealed Sociology of the Crowd', *Durkheimian Studies* 20: 89–114.

Tratner, M. 2008. *Crowd Scenes: Movies and Mass Politics*. New York: Fordham University Press.

Turner, R. H. 1964. 'Collective Behavior', in R. Faris (ed.), *Handbook of Modern Sociology*. Chicago, IL: Rand McNally & Company, pp. 382–425.

US Department of the Treasury et al. 2015. *Joint Staff Report: The U.S. Treasury Market on October 15, 2014*. Washington, DC: The U.S. Department of the Treasury, Board of Governors of the Federal Reserve System, the Federal Reserve Bank of New York, the U.S. Securities and Exchange Commission and the U.S. Commodity Futures Trading Commission.

Van Ginneken, J. 1992. *Crowds, Psychology, and Politics, 1871–1899*. Cambridge: Cambridge University Press.

2009. *Collective Behaviour and Public Opinion: Rapid Shifts in Opinion and Communication*. London and New York: Routledge.

Vehlken, S. 2019. 'Contagious Agents: Epidemics, Networks, Computer Simulations', in C. Borch (ed.), *Imitation, Contagion, Suggestion: On Mimesis and Society*. London and New York: Routledge, pp. 157–76.

Vincent, G. E. 1904. 'The Development of Sociology', *American Journal of Sociology* 10(2): 145–60.

Vaananen, J. 2015. *Dark Pools & High-Frequency Trading for Dummies*. Chichester: John Wiley.

Wagner-Pacifici, R. 2010. 'Theorizing the Restlessness of Events', *American Journal of Sociology* 115(5): 1351–86.

Wald, P. 2008. *Contagious: Cultures, Carriers, and the Outbreak Narrative*. Durham and London: Duke University Press.

Walker, A. 2013. '"What Can a Crowd Do?": Revisiting Tarde after the Demise of the Public', *Distinktion: Scandinavian Journal of Social Theory* 14(2): 227–31.

Wansleben, L. 2015. *Cultures of Expertise in Global Currency Markets*. London and New York: Routledge.

Ward, J. 2001. *Weimar Surfaces: Urban Visual Culture in 1920s Germany*. Berkeley, CA: University of California Press.

Weber, M. 1978. *Economy and Society: An Outline of Interpretive Sociology*. Berkeley, LA: University of California Press.

  1998. 'Preliminary Report on a Proposed Survey for a Sociology of the Press', *History of the Human Sciences* 11(2): 111–20.

  2000. 'Stock and Commodity Exchanges ["Die Börse" (1894)]', *Theory and Society* 29(3): 305–338.

Weingart, B. 2014. 'Contact at a Distance: The Topology of Fascination', in R. Campe and J. Weber (eds.), *Rethinking Emotion: Interiority and Exteriority in Premodern, Modern, and Contemporary Thought*. Berlin: Walter de Gruyter, pp. 72–100.

Williams, R. H. 1982. *Dream Worlds: Mass Consumption in Late Nineteenth-Century France*. Berkeley, CA: University of California Press.

Witte, K. 1977. 'Nachwort', in S. Kracauer, *Das Ornament der Masse: Essays*. Frankfurt am Main: Suhrkamp, pp. 333–47.

Wright, F. L. 2000. 'Broadacre City: A New Community Plan', in R. LeGates and F. Stout (eds.), *The City Reader, second ed.* London and New York: Routledge, pp. 344–9.

Zaloom, C. 2003. 'Ambiguous Numbers: Trading Technologies and Interpretation in Financial Markets', *American Ethnologist* 30(2): 258–72.

  2006. *Out of the Pits: Traders and Technology from Chicago to London*. Chicago, IL: University of Chicago Press.

Zimmerman, D. A. 2006. *Panic! Markets, Crises, and Crowds in American Fiction*. Chapel Hill, NC: The University of North Carolina Press.

Zizek, S. 2015. 'Capitalism Has Broken Free of the Shackles of Democracy', *Financial Times* 1 February.

Zweig, S. 2009. *The World of Yesterday*, trans. A. Bell. London: Pushkin Press.

Index